MW00398503

More advance praise for

A FEW WORDS IN DEFENSE OF OUR COUNTRY

"At last, the biography that Randy Newman has long deserved. The emotional precision, the humor and sweep, the truths and secrets behind his remarkable body of work . . . it's all here in Robert Hilburn's heartfelt and indispensable account of America's finest songwriter. Leave it to Hilburn to pull back the curtain on the incredible life of Newman, a shy genius who clearly trusted him enough to point him in all the right directions. It's more than a great read, it's an invitation to revisit Randy Newman's work with renewed appreciation for the man who uniquely defined the American Experience just when we needed it most."

—Cameron Crowe

"Every time I go to Disneyland and hear Randy Newman's fanfare that announces the thrill-ride of the 'Cars' ride, I marvel at his genius for infiltration.

Robert Hilburn's book makes a very good case for Newman being the composer of two or three songs that might serve as the national anthem of a more curious and a less vainglorious America. Some of those songs are heartbreaking and chilling, others are just flat-out funny."

—Elvis Costello

"With *A Few Words in Defense of Our Country*, Robert Hilburn does an extraordinary feat: he reminds us that it is passion within a songwriter that is always the genesis for music. Hilburn's thoroughly researched and skillfully narrated bio fully brings Newman's passion to life. This book stands as the definitive biography of one of our greatest songwriters."

—Charles R. Cross, author of *Heavier Than Heaven: A Biography of Kurt Cobain* and *Room Full of Mirrors: A Biography of Jimi Hendrix*

A FEW WORDS IN DEFENSE OF OUR COUNTRY

ALSO BY ROBERT HILBURN

PAUL SIMON: The Life

JOHNNY CASH: The Life

CORN FLAKES WITH JOHN LENNON:
And Other Tales from a Rock'n'Roll Life

SPRINGSTEEN

A FEW WORDS IN DEFENSE OF OUR COUNTRY

THE BIOGRAPHY OF
RANDY NEWMAN

ROBERT HILBURN

BOOKS

New York

Copyright © 2024 by Robert Hilburn

Jacket design by Terri Sirma
Jacket photograph by Tony Newman
Jacket copyright © 2024 by Hachette Book Group, Inc.

Hachette Book Group supports the right to free expression and the value of copyright. The purpose of copyright is to encourage writers and artists to produce the creative works that enrich our culture.

The scanning, uploading, and distribution of this book without permission is a theft of the author's intellectual property. If you would like permission to use material from the book (other than for review purposes), please contact permissions@hbgusa.com. Thank you for your support of the author's rights.

Hachette Books
Hachette Book Group
1290 Avenue of the Americas
New York, NY 10104
HachetteBooks.com
Twitter.com/HachetteBooks
Instagram.com/HachetteBooks

First Edition: October 2024

Published by Hachette Books, an imprint of Hachette Book Group, Inc. The Hachette Books name and logo is a trademark of the Hachette Book Group.

The Hachette Speakers Bureau provides a wide range of authors for speaking events. To find out more, go to hachettespeakersbureau.com or email HachetteSpeakers@hbgusa.com.

Books by Hachette Books may be purchased in bulk for business, educational, or promotional use. For information, please contact your local bookseller or Hachette Book Group Special Markets Department at: special.markets@hbgusa.com.

The publisher is not responsible for websites (or their content) that are not owned by the publisher.

Print book interior design by Amnet

Library of Congress Control Number: 2024941638

ISBNs: 9780306834691 (hardcover); 9780306834714 (ebook)

Printed in Canada

MRQ

Printing 1, 2024

To
Randy Newman
for the music and the message
and
Lenny Waronker
for the unending belief

"I heard a record on the radio one day back in the sixties by Julius LaRosa called 'I Think It's Going to Rain Today.' Randy's song was so mysterious—something about kicking a can down the street, like that's how you treat a friend. I never heard a song like that before; it was so cynical. I actually never heard Randy himself sing it till much later. What grabbed me was the sadness in Randy's voice. Sadness and cynicism, it's a strange combination but Randy always manages to pull it off. I like his singing. It's the epitome of laid-back, and I think he's got that covered all by himself. King of the mountain, that's who he is and always was."

BOB DYLAN

CONTENTS

PROLOGUE (1)

I'm interested in this country: geography, the weather, the people, the way people look, what they eat, what they call things . . . maybe American psychology is my big subject.
RANDY NEWMAN

When the national debate over fundamental human values led more than two thousand extremists to storm the United States Capitol in 2021 after President Donald Trump's failed reelection bid, horrified Americans asked themselves how their country could have gotten to this point. Much can be learned from what Randy Newman's most insightful songs had been warning us about for fifty years.

Millions around the world can hum "You've Got a Friend in Me," Newman's disarming composition for *Toy Story*, but most would be astonished to learn that the heart of his legacy is in the dozens of brilliant compositions detailing the injustices, from racism to economic disparity, that have contributed to the United States being as divided as at any time since the Civil War. *Rolling Stone* has declared that a single Newman song, "Sail Away," tells us more about America than "The Star-Spangled Banner."

"I've always gone against the two things that sell 90 percent of the records in America," he says. "It's kinda like I came across a fork in the highway and took another road—away from how the medium had been used for a thousand years. I don't write love songs, and I don't write in the first person. It's not what interests me. The songs are about things that need to be noticed, places like ghettos and slums that should shame everyone. It hurts to see people living like that in this rich country, where the fact that one zip code entitles you to better medical care and the wrong one can be a death sentence."

Newman's boldness and range have established him as one of the most acclaimed songwriters ever in American pop—he combines the craft of the George Gershwin and Cole Porter era and the personal commentary of Bob Dylan and the rock era. That may sound like hyperbole, but only if you're not familiar with his work.

Randy was twenty-eight in 1972 when he wrote a song whose language was so fiercely defiant that it still stands as one of the most explosive slices of social commentary ever released by a major record label in America. Dylan's protest songs had an aggressive, revolutionary edge, but radio stations, for the most part, felt safe playing them because the language was well within the normal limits of sociopolitical debate.

In "Rednecks," a savage attack on racism, North and South, Newman's words shattered those limits:

We're rednecks, rednecks
And we don't know our ass from a hole in the ground
We're rednecks, we're rednecks
And we're keeping the niggers down

Hearing those early lines, it was easy to assume Newman was attacking Southern bigotry, but things changed abruptly in the third verse as he took aim at Northern sanctimoniousness. The young man from Los Angeles was serving notice that he would call out offensive behavior wherever he found it. (We'll discuss the appropriateness of this monstrous slur in detail in chapter 10.)

Now your northern nigger's a Negro
You see he's got his dignity
Down here we're too ignorant to realize
That the North has set the nigger free

Yes, he's free to be put in a cage
In Harlem in New York City
And he's free to be put in a cage in the South Side of
    Chicago
And the West Side

The lines were all the more startling when written because it was just four years after the assassination of Dr. Martin Luther King and the accompanying rage in the Black community that led to street uprisings in more than one hundred US cities—leaving underlying tension that would rise and fall until another massive eruption after police murdered a defenseless Black man, George Floyd, in 2020 in Minneapolis.

To allow himself greater creative freedom in "Rednecks," Newman employed—as he would continue to do—a device he had seen in literature: the unreliable narrator. In the song, he assumed the role of a racist and expressed the racist's views, feeling that the absurdity of the words was more powerful than the common first-person pronouncements that had long been the blueprint for protest music. "There is a bit of the old don't-tread-on-me in the American attitude—even some lawlessness at times," he says. "You can especially see this in parts of the South where some people resent anything they feel has been handed down from on high—meaning the North. They make more of it than they should, and it messes up the country, but no area is guilt-free."

From "Rednecks" to "A Few Words in Defense of Our Country," Newman has written about what he sees as America's shortcomings with such rich storytelling and sharply drawn vignettes that he seemed to be a novelist living in a musician's body; music critics and cultural commentators frequently refer to novelists when describing Newman's approach, and it's significant that they reach as high as Mark Twain and William Faulkner to convey his originality and depth.

A favorite among discriminating, literary-minded music fans who delight in his blend of Jewish intellectualism, political liberalism, and healthy dose of contrarianism, Newman leans heavily on humor, satire, and irony to make his judgments feel less pedantic. In 2012, he mocked the legions of Americans who opposed Barack Obama's presidential candidacy solely because he was Black. In a twist on Irving Berlin's classic "White Christmas," Newman wrote "I'm Dreaming" to reflect the racist's stance. It includes lines that are classic as well:

> *He won't be the brightest, perhaps.*
> *But he'll be the whitest*
> *And I'll vote for that.*

Newman's focus goes beyond race. As the effects of the Ronald Reagan era began to be felt during his governorship of California in the late 1960s, a second target emerged in his compositions—a national worship of money that not only changed people's values but often made them intolerant of anyone in lower economic positions. Over time, that vision contributed to a deepening divide between the rich and poor as well as growing disregard for the needs of the homeless and mentally ill, a gradual decline of the middle class, and deregulation of the financial industry. Springsteen would release a dark condemnation of this social shift in the acclaimed album *Nebraska* in 1982, the second year of Reagan's presidency. "It's Money That I Love" preceded it by three years.

In a dozen studio albums, he has also examined a wide range of social ills. "Half a Man" ridiculed homophobia. "You Can Leave Your Hat On" addressed the objectification of women. "The Great Nations of Europe" recounted evil aspects of colonization. "Yellow Man" called out Asian stereotyping. "Burn On" warned about the damage to the environment—all targets that helped stretch the boundaries of pop.

~

Randy was born into a musical family. His uncles—Alfred, Lionel, and Emil—were royalty in film music circles for decades, a reign that stretched from the early days of the talkies through the 1960s. Alfred, the most successful, received forty-five Academy Award nominations and a record nine Oscars. Randy, who studied music composition at UCLA, was expected to follow his uncles into film music, but he was so intimidated by the prospect that he switched to writing pop songs as a teenager. He was hailed as a pop wunderkind with an LP in 1968 that is widely considered one of the greatest debuts ever.

Thanks in part to his extensive classical music training, Randy brings a sophistication and sweep to his songs that far exceeds the three-chord playbook followed by most pop and rock songwriters; it has been said he plays an orchestra the way Hendrix played a guitar. His own struggles, too, helped him understand bullying and abuse, and his vocals sidestep the pop norm of trying to hook the listener into singing along. Instead, his vocals make you feel the pain and abandonment of society's outcasts. Sadness and cynicism, but also compassion and outrage.

Randy followed the debut with a series of acclaimed albums—notably *Sail Away*, *Good Old Boys*, and *Land of Dreams*—that finally gave him the courage to tackle film music, and he delivered a series of scores, from the tender, evocative Americana feel of *The Natural* to the innocence and warmth of *Toy Story*.

Living up to the standards of his uncles, Randy has received twenty-two Oscar nominations and two statuettes.

~

Randy loved working with orchestras in films, but he felt that the songs in his albums were ultimately more important. They were things he felt needed to be said, and largely weren't said, in pop music, and they remain his most significant work. Refocusing on pop in the late 1990s when he was nearing sixty, an age when most of the best songwriters were in decline, he delivered three albums—*Bad Love, Harps and Angels*, and *Dark Matter*—that reflected the commentary and ambition of his best early work.

As millions of Americans reexamine the country's past to find heroes who stood for principle during troubled times, Newman is a prime candidate for even greater respect and acclaim. His songs will speak to Americans for generations to come about a strange and tragic period in the country's history, a time when ideals of diversity and justice were pitted against some of the nation's darkest impulses.

PROLOGUE (2)

One more thing to know about Randy Newman before we begin his story: he's funny, the master of an art form—humor—that has all but disappeared in pop music. Wry, wise, and winning, Newman's humor comes at you from all sorts of surprising directions—it can make you smile, and it can make you laugh out loud. Sometimes he's just having fun with a song, but mostly he's using humor to help illuminate his views on social oppression.

The humor came naturally. Randy's brother, Alan, says he had a strong sense of jocularity from childhood on, including strange behavior that would often exasperate people. When Randy was about twelve, he took all his presents into the family bathroom on Christmas morning and locked the door behind him. Then he started "oohing" and "aahing" loudly as he opened each one, leaving those outside trying to figure out which ones he liked. In school, Randy once came up with a cock-and-bull story about how he couldn't do a homework paper because his family couldn't afford a typewriter, Alan said, adding, "When my parents went to open house, the teacher said, 'Oh, you poor people. Randy told me about your problems'—or something to that effect. My parents at the time, no doubt, dressed to the nines."

And there was the time that Randy had so much trouble finding a parking spot in UCLA's notoriously overcrowded campus lots that he bought a plastic Jesus, put it on the dashboard, and parked the car in a nearby church lot. It worked fine until someone stole the car. Despite his predilection for laughter, Randy doesn't always go for the humor card. As lovely as anything he has written, "Baltimore" is a late-1970s song without a touch of mirth. The words and melody speak about the widespread decay of many American cities with the grace and grittiness that writer James Agee and photographer Walker Evans brought to *Let Us Now Praise Famous Men*, the landmark 1941 book about the struggles of sharecropper families during the Great Depression.

But Randy does lean toward humor in much of his finest work.

When asked to write a song for Frank Sinatra in the early 1970s, Randy didn't try to flatter the singer's image or style in "Lonely at the Top"; he flat-out mocked them. Sinatra passed.

I've been around the world
Had my pick of any girl
You'd think I'd be happy
But I'm not
Ev'rybody knows my name
But it's just a crazy game
Oh, it's lonely at the top

Listen to the band, they're playing just for me
Listen to the people paying just for me
All the applause— All the parades
And all the money I have made
Oh, it's lonely at the top
And all the money I have made
Oh, it's lonely at the top

A world away from the sophistication and style of "Lonely at the Top," Randy gave us some of his funniest images in his biggest pop hit "Short People," a song so politically incorrect that most record companies might not even release it today. The lyrics in part:

> *They got little baby legs*
> *That stand so low*
> *You got to pick 'em up*
> *Just to say hello*
> *They got little cars*
> *That go beep, beep, beep*
> *They got little voices*
> *Goin' peep, peep, peep*
> *They got grubby little fingers*
> *And dirty little minds*
> *They're gonna get you every time*

In his ambitious 1995 musical *Randy Newman's Faust*, Randy used humor to address religion and morality in America. In his version of the Faust legend, Satan engages the Lord in a wager for a young man's soul. In the rousing opener, "Glory Train," we are introduced to the Lord (sung by James Taylor) celebrating His leadership and promise of salvation with an adoring group of angels—only to have the Devil (Newman himself) break in and angrily reject all the Lord is saying. His tirade includes the lines:

> DEVIL: *If I might intrude*
> *Just for a moment*
> *If only to inject a note of reality*
> *On this festive occasion*
>
> *In all my life*
> *I don't believe I've ever heard such bullshit*

Even from you
A master of bullshit
You know it
I know it
It's bullshit
Bullshit

All of the faith and prayer in the world
All of your dumb show and circuses
You know it's a lie
It'll always be a lie
The invention of an animal
Who knows he's going to die

Humor is rarely heard in pop music because it is so difficult to employ effectively, especially when dealing with significant subject matter. It's such a delicate creative balance that no one has come close to matching Newman in the rock era, and it would be surprising if anyone ever does.

A FEW
WORDS IN
DEFENSE
OF OUR
COUNTRY

PART ONE

You can usually recognize a great songwriter's work the moment you hear it: an Ellington melody, a Hammerstein lyric, a McCartney or a Dylan song. All proclaim their composer's identity readily to the listener's ear. The same can be said of Randy Newman's compositions. His satirical, ironic lyrics set to an Americana harmonic structure often camouflage a melancholy tenderness that is surely a part of his soul. Fans and fellow songwriters know when they hear his music that they are listening to the work of master. Think of "Sail Away," "Davy the Fat Boy," and "Louisiana." Amazing songs. Add to this extraordinary gift his ability to literally make you laugh out loud at some of his observations, and you've met a unique twentieth-century pop song maestro. My generation recognized his immense talent, and future generations will discover and re-discover Randy Newman.

PAUL SIMON

CHAPTER ONE

The Newman Roots
A Friend Named Lenny and
An Eye Problem

— I —

When Randy awoke on his fifth birthday in the family's triplex apartment across from Beverly Hills High School, the surprise present that his father, Irving, had slipped into the room overnight told him a lot about how he would spend the rest of his life: a brown upright piano.

Even at that age, Randy had heard countless tales about the legendary role his uncles played in Hollywood film music. Alfred Newman alone wrote the score for more than 200 movies, including *Wuthering Heights, How Green Was My Valley*, and **All About Eve**, and served as music director at Twentieth Century–Fox Films for two decades. The youngster delighted in the story about how the quick-tempered Alfred got so tired of Charlie Chaplin's nitpicking about the music for one of the actor-director's films that he chased Chaplin around the soundstage until cornering him and hitting him on the head with a baton. In time, however, the idea of a career in film music became increasingly daunting as Randy realized the expectations he'd have to meet.

Movies, however, would play such a strong, recurring role in Randy's career that it's only fitting that his family history is filled with script-ready details, including coming to America as immigrants fleeing an area of Russia now known as Ukraine to avoid the horrors of anti-Semitism, and a mother's steel-will drive to build a future for her ten children; she even sold Alfred's dog to pay for his piano lessons.

~

Luba Koskoff, Randy's paternal grandmother, was eleven when she arrived in America in 1894 with her mother and younger sister. They headed to a Jewish ghetto in New Haven, Connecticut, where Luba's brother and father ran a produce business. Through them, she met Michael Nemorofsky Jr., who had come to the United States four years earlier from Russia and landed a job delivering produce for the Koskoffs. Part of a small social circle, Michael and Luba started seeing a lot of each other and were married in the summer of 1897 when he was twenty-three and she was a month shy of fourteen. He had already changed his name to Newman.

Michael would play only a fleeting role in the family story. While he struggled to pay the bills, Luba, who was barely five feet tall, stayed home with the steadily growing family (there would be seven boys and three girls born between 1900 and 1917), consumed with planning a better life for them. Luba's father was a cantor who passed along his love for music, and she sensed that the couple's first child, Alfred, had a special gift. She started him on piano lessons when he was five and was jubilant when the instructor raved about him.

Word about this New Haven prodigy spread quickly—even to New York, where three years later he began taking lessons (often on scholarship) with top-grade pianists. To watch over Alfred, Luba spent considerable time in New York, leaving her mother to take care of the other children in New Haven—a devotion that would cause deep resentment and hurt among several of her other children.

Alfred's future in music was threatened four years later when the family was in such bad shape financially that he was often reduced to playing piano in restaurants and on fill-in assignments in theaters to help pay the bills. His talent, however, was too strong to deny. Playing piano at thirteen at the Harlem Opera House, he so impressed vaudeville star Grace La Rue that she hired him to accompany her on tour, where he was sometimes allowed to lead the orchestra. The vaudeville troupe likely thought having a teenager on the podium was a crowd-pleasing move, but Alfred did so well that he became at nineteen what is believed to be the youngest conductor ever to front a Broadway musical. During the 1920s, he led orchestras for shows written by such giants as George Gershwin and Jerome Kern.

When his parents' marriage ended, Alfred became the titular head of the family, ruling it as he would eventually rule much of film music. In 1922, he brought Luba and his nine siblings to Elmhurst, New York, a short train ride from Broadway. Though grateful for all he did for them, the siblings' hard feelings deepened over the years as they watched Luba continue to dedicate her time and attention to her prized child.

The family migration west began in 1930 when Newman answered the call of Hollywood. Movie studios, fresh from the silent era, raced to keep up with the demand of enthralled filmgoers to hear as well as see. Broadway looked down at the frenzy, considering the theater to be the true home of the musical, and there is no sign that Newman felt differently.

Even so, Alfred was intrigued when celebrated Hollywood producer Samuel Goldwyn offered him a three-month assignment conducting Irving Berlin's score for a film titled *Reaching for the Moon*. Goldwyn was known for his taste in films and an uncanny ability to spot young talent. At the time, Newman was music director for *Heads Up*, which featured numbers by one of the greatest songwriting teams in Broadway history, Richard

Rodgers and Lorenz Hart, whose compositions included such standards as "My Funny Valentine" and "The Lady Is a Tramp." But the lure of Goldwyn's offer was strong. The clincher was when Berlin personally asked Alfred to work on the film. Alfred told Luba that he would see her in three months and headed to California.

The movie was a disaster. Berlin clashed with director Edmund Goulding, who threw out all but one of the songwriter's numbers from the film—the lively but soon forgotten "When the Folks High Up Do the Mean Low Down," sung by Bing Crosby, who was making his film debut. Despite Berlin's exit, Newman remained on the project. *Reaching*, starring Douglas Fairbanks and Bebe Daniels, was a box-office flop, and that could have been it for the Newman family film presence except that Goldwyn needed someone to head his music department, and the recommendation of Berlin, a gin rummy partner from Goldwyn's days in New York, was enough for him to offer Newman the position.

The money was attractive, and Newman was excited about Goldwyn's upcoming project: *Street Scene*, a Pulitzer Prize–winning drama that was a sensation on Broadway in 1929. To make Hollywood even more alluring, Charlie Chaplin wanted Newman to orchestrate *City Lights*. *Street Scene* was a contemporary look at disillusionment and stress in a lower middle-class neighborhood, set chiefly on the steps of a Manhattan brownstone. Newman's music—which was played over the opening credits—has been widely hailed as a definitive portrait of life in New York City. The haunting melody, influenced by George Gershwin's "Rhapsody in Blue," would be repeated in numerous films over the years, including *Gentleman's Agreement* and *How to Marry a Millionaire*.

There was no turning back. Alfred phoned Luba: Join me in Hollywood—and bring the kids.

Alfred's success led four of his brothers—including future composer-conductors Lionel and Emil—to follow him west from New York and work in the entertainment business. After working as a Broadway producer and being active in Democratic politics in New York, Robert (Bobby) Newman became a successful executive in Hollywood, working in various capacities for Samuel Goldwyn Productions, John Wayne's Batjac production company, and Howard Hughes's Summa Corporation. Marcus Newman was a celebrated theatrical agent who was credited with luring big-name talent to Las Vegas showrooms; his clients included Marlene Dietrich and Peggy Lee.

Randy's father, an aspiring musician, wanted to join the musical brothers, but Alfred told him no. Deeply insecure, Alfred felt that his success was largely a fluke and didn't want to entrust more of the family's future to one profession. He redirected Irving, who was thirteen years younger, to pursue medicine. Though demoralized, Irving, who adored Alfred, signed up for undergraduate studies at New York University before moving on to medical school, which wasn't easy. Most leading medical schools at the time had strict quotas on Jews, and they filled quickly. Irving finally found an opening at the University of Alabama, but his time there soon ended. Though not a religious Jew, he was as quick-tempered as Alfred, and he slugged a dean who used an anti-Semitic slur.

With his options reduced even more with that red flag on his record, Irving turned to his brother Robert for help in landing an opening at Louisiana State University's School of Medicine, which was centered in New Orleans rather than Baton Rouge, home of the main LSU campus. Robert used his Democratic ties in New York to pull strings with someone in Louisiana governor Huey Long's administration, clearing the way for Irving to be in New Orleans for the start of classes in 1935.

~

Irving never had trouble finding girlfriends. He was smart and had movie-star good looks, reminiscent of Robert Donat, a British actor best known for his Oscar-winning role in *Goodbye, Mr. Chips*. But Irving had never seen a woman as lovely as Adele Fox, who he met by chance at a Mardi Gras dance. Born in Brooklyn in 1916, Adele moved with her family to New Orleans to join relatives. Her father was a former barber whose bouts of depression apparently left him unable to work, leaving her mother to support the six children by taking in boarders and renting beach chairs in the summer on Lake Pontchartrain. Irving and Adele, who was nicknamed Dixie, began a relationship almost immediately, and she moved with him to Los Angeles after he finished medical school in 1938.

Knowing Luba's resistance—even outright hostility—toward any woman who wanted to take away one of her boys, Irving kept his marriage to Adele in October of 1939 from Luba for more than a year. To preserve the secret, he lived in the hospital where he conducted his internship and Adele stayed in a nearby apartment. One reason they moved to San Francisco in 1940 for his residency was to be able to live together without having to deal with family tension.

When they were pushed apart in 1943 while Irving served as an Army flight surgeon in the North African and Italian campaigns during World War II, it was hard on Adele. She was pregnant and didn't have many friends in Los Angeles. After giving birth to the couple's son on November 28 at the old Cedars of Lebanon Hospital in Hollywood, she took her boy to live with her family in New Orleans. He wouldn't see his father for two years.

Randall Stuart Newman was so surprised the morning he awoke to have his mother tell him that his father was asleep on the couch that he bit Irving on the arm to get a rise; after all this time, he wanted to make sure he wasn't dreaming—or at least that's how he told the story for years. The truth, Randy said in 2022, is that he was trying to scare his father into going away. He didn't want to have to share his mother with anyone.

Though often celebrated as a sanctuary from the savage reign of white supremacy in the South, New Orleans had a long history of racial injustice, complete with race riots, housing segregation, and Ku Klux Klan chapters. After his parents reunited in Los Angeles following the war, Randy would revisit the Crescent City enough as a youngster to have memories of that injustice, starting with the "white" and "colored" signs at water fountains and on ice cream wagons.

— II —

It was hard to tell who was more excited—Luba or Alfred—when Irving returned to Los Angeles with Adele and Randy in early 1945. Luba's resentment of Adele had given way to affection, and she loved it when Randy came over to her cottage in nearby Westwood and played the piano. Luba, called Nana by the grandkids, raved about the youngster as if he were another prodigy, a point Irving duly noted.

Alfred led the welcome-home party, introducing Irving to friends and various musicians who played on the composer's films, many of whom became Irving's patients in what turned into a celebrity-heavy practice. Irving was excellent at diagnosis and had a friendly, outgoing manner, yet he would remain haunted by his dream of a career in music, and he wrote pop songs for years. But he knew that the odds against ever leaving medicine to pursue a music career were overwhelming. The only real hope for his branch of the family to become part of the Newman musical tradition was for Randy to take the place that had been denied him.

Both Alan and Randy felt their father had ability as a songwriter. "He was a very talented songwriter, but he grew up in the wrong era," Alan said. "I think a lot of his songs could have been jazz standards." As it happened, the only song of Irving's that was recorded was "Who Gave You the Roses," which he wrote for his mother. It was the back side of a 1954 single by Bing Crosby, and it may have gotten there as a favor; the main side of the single was "We Meet Again," a song co-written by Alfred Newman for the film *Desiree*, starring Marlon Brando. In any case, the record didn't make the pop charts.

"There's no doubt that my father wanted me to be a musician more than I did," Randy said. "He thought that what my uncles Al, Lionel, and Emil did was just the greatest job in the world—art, high art, a great thing to do." The goal would eventually contribute to a lingering tension between father and son.

~

Among those at Irving's welcome-home party was Simon "Si" Waronker, an industrious studio orchestra member who had much in common with Alfred. Si was born into a poor family in Los Angeles's Boyle Heights district in 1915. His father gave him a violin at age five, followed immediately by private lessons. Fairly quickly, the word "prodigy" was tossed his way, too. Si's teacher even convinced the local elementary school to create a half-day schedule for the boy so that he could use the rest of the time to practice. Doing as well in his studies as with his violin, Waronker skipped grades regularly, allowing him to graduate high school at thirteen. He soon headed to Philadelphia for violin lessons on scholarship and received additional scholarships to study in Europe. Rising anti-Semitism in the early 1930s, however, caused him to return to California.

To support himself while attending the University of Southern California for two years, he took whatever jobs he could find (from a strip club in LA to a gig with Gus Arnheim's orchestra) before landing in Alfred's studio orchestra. He played in the unit for years before deciding he wasn't world-class enough to have a future as a musician and set his sights on the record business, which was starting to assert itself in Los Angeles after long being centered in New York City.

Waronker started Liberty Records in 1955 with the plan of using his musician friends to record some singles to introduce the company. The first release was Lionel Newman's version of "Conquest," a march written by Alfred for the 1947 film *Captain from Castile* that would become the popular fight song for the USC football team. From that modest start, Waronker built a small but respected company, touching in its first decade on mainstream pop (Julie London's "Cry Me a River"), country (Willie Nelson's "Night Life"), surf-rock (Jan and Dean's "Surf City"), and goofy novelty (the Chipmunks' "The Chipmunk Song"). To expand, Si opened a music publishing company, Metric Music.

None of this would have been important in Randy Newman's story except for a connection that was as unlikely as it was crucial. Si's and Jeanette's son Lenny, who was two years older than Randy, would follow his father into the record business, not as a songwriter or performer, but behind the scenes, finding and nurturing talent. In that role, Lenny would be as essential in Randy's career as Luba had been in Alfred's. "Lenny believed in me before I believed in myself," said Newman. "When I started, I didn't have much confidence or motivation, but I had him and that meant everything."

— III —

Reporting over the years about Randy and Lenny meeting as toddlers, the media often made it seem like they bonded in the delivery room—and the accounts were not that far off. It's possible that Lenny saw baby Randy briefly before Adele headed to New Orleans with him, but chances are the boys met at the party welcoming Irving and the family home from the war. Randy was just past one and Lenny just over three.

What matters is that the pair, both extremely smart and relatively shy, became inseparable soon after the birth of Irving and Adele's second son, Alan, in March of 1947 when the family moved to a house in the 1300 block of D'Este Drive in Pacific Palisades' stylish Riviera neighborhood. The area was home to the world-class Riviera Country Club, whose members included Humphrey Bogart, Gregory Peck, and Mary Pickford, though the Newmans could only see it from the outside. Jews weren't allowed at the time. This elitist nature of upscale Pacific Palisades enabled Randy to see the nation's socioeconomic disparity all the more clearly. The community ranked third among Los Angeles's sixty-five sectors in average income, yet last in percentage of people of color (less than 1 percent Black) during most of Randy's childhood. He wouldn't have a Black classmate until he reached UCLA.

It wasn't long before Randy and Lenny, who lived just two minutes away on Romany Drive, were playing together daily, usually at the Newman house or on periodic vacations in Las Vegas. Gambling was a favorite pastime of Si Waronker and several of the Newman men, prompting one wife to declare, "When I need to find my husband, I know he's either at the casino, Hollywood Park, or Santa Anita."

Despite the age difference between the boys, Randy was as tall as Lenny and stronger, which balanced things, especially when it came to two-man baseball games in the Newman backyard. They would take turns batting and pitching, calling out "single" or "double" or "out" rather than chasing the ball around the yard. As the oldest, Lenny umpired, but Randy was quick to challenge his calls, causing the games to be interrupted for several minutes by arguments; neither boy liked to lose. Randy, who would later pitch on a Little League team coached by his father, got so upset that he would sometimes go to his room, leaving Lenny by himself in the backyard.

Randy's independence also showed on days when he chose to stay in the house, reading or watching television. Though he would later develop an appreciation for world-class fiction and historical studies, he then most often pored over newspaper box scores, looking at batting and pitching stats from every angle. "I would read baseball stats for hours," Randy said in 2022. "I ended up knowing a ton of stuff . . . I was like quiz show level. I'd see those shows and figured I could win if I only had to answer baseball questions."

When Randy was in grade school, Irving introduced him to a series of sports novels by John R. Tunis, a Harvard graduate who wrote for the *New Yorker* and *Esquire* though is best known for the popular juvenile sports books. What Randy loved most was Tunis's eight-book collection about the fictional exploits of the Brooklyn Dodgers, which began with *The Kid from Tomkinsville*, a 1940 novel that has been cited as an influence for Bernard Malamud's *The Natural* and Philip Roth's *American Pastoral*. Tucked between the tales of heroic feats and subsequent setbacks on the diamond, Tunis's books encouraged fair play and good citizenship, including slaps at anti-Semitism and racial injustice, which may have been one of Irving Newman's reasons for choosing the books for his son. Irving had a strong sense of morality, which helped shape Randy's own sense of justice.

Those and other volumes passed along by his dad meant the world to the youngster. "Getting me to read was one of the nicest things my dad ever did for me," Randy said. "From the time I was seven, he would give me a book and write a little message in it, like 'Dear Son, Remember me. I'll always love you.' It would sometimes make me feel sad, like it was something for me to read after he died." In turn, Randy, perhaps playfully, gave his dad a book for a birthday present, along with the inscription, "Dear Dad, Remember me when I'm dead. Your pal, Randy."

~

It was only natural that music and movies eventually challenged sports for the boys' attention. The first exciting step was visiting a soundstage while one of Randy's uncles conducted the massive orchestra as scenes from a film flashed on the screen. "That made a big impression on Randy," Lenny said, in 2022. "If you listen closely to his records, you can see how the musical touches, even three- or four-second accents, speak directly to what is happening in the lyrics. It's like he is making mini-movies."

The boys would gladly postpone a backyard game (which also included basketball and football according to the season) to go to the movies with their parents. One film that had a major impact on Lenny, especially, was *Three Little Words*, a 1950 tale of veteran pop songwriters Bert Kalmar (played by Fred Astaire) and Harry Ruby (Red Skelton), whose array of hits in the 1920s and 1930s included "Who's Sorry Now" and "Nevertheless (I'm in Love with You)."

Ruby was a family friend who lived in the Palisades, but the boys' fascination with the movie went deeper than that. Lenny loved how this pair struggled until they became a team and everything came together. Even at that age, the story taught him the value of collaboration. The boys soon began playing a new game: pretending to be a songwriting team. Lenny wrote the words and Randy composed the music, but the result wasn't satisfying enough for them to continue the effort for long.

They soon came up with a second, more lasting exercise. Lenny, already in awe of Randy's gifts at composing and arranging, thought it would be fun to pick some more old songs and see if Randy could dress them up with contemporary arrangements—something record-makers were doing at the time. Bing Crosby had hits in 1950 alone with "Harbor Lights," a ballad written in 1937, and "Play a Simple Melody," a catchy number written in 1915 by Irving Berlin.

Standing by Randy's piano, Lenny suggested various old songs until Randy started playing one of them, invariably giving it the modern pop edge that Lenny wanted. In time, this game proved as much fun as two-man baseball. One early effort was "The Way You Look Tonight," a ballad written in the 1930s by Jerome Kern and Dorothy Fields, and sung over the years by such top-line figures as Fred Astaire, Billie Holiday, and Peggy Lee. The boys were just playing in a way, but Lenny felt that Randy's piano arrangements sounded extraordinary, and he started believing that Randy might have a future in pop music.

If Lenny ever thought of collaborating on songs, it was short-lived. He was a competitive kid, but he knew he was not in Randy's league. In time, however, he began thinking of a new role—maybe there was a way to help Randy achieve his potential. Years later, Waronker said, "We had no agenda, but we could gradually feel something building."

— IV —

The childhood sounds idyllic, but the good times for Randy were shadowed by some painful struggles, starting with strabismus, a medical condition commonly known as crossed eyes, and it left him open to puzzled stares or cruel taunts in a period in America when much of the country was insensitive to such matters. In the silent film era, manic, cross-eyed comedian Ben Turpin became a star by causing moviegoers to howl with laughter when he simply looked at the camera.

Randy's eye problem prevented both of his eyes from focusing on the same object. Eventually, the brain would settle on the image supplied by the strongest eye, but it wasn't instantaneous, which caused difficulty at numerous tasks. This lack of muscle control can usually be corrected by surgery, but that didn't prove true in Randy's case. He went through several operations starting at age five, but the situation persisted to some degree through much of his life, likely contributing to his empathy for underdogs of various sorts.

"It wasn't easy for him because people would yell at him for not looking at them and stuff like that," said his brother Alan in 2022. "I'm not sure it made him reserved, but I do think he felt a little persecuted because of it."

Randy downplayed the eye issue—and other personal matters—in interviews because he didn't want to present himself as a victim, not wanting personal trials to become the main story instead of his music, which made him, at times, something of an unreliable narrator himself. "My sole goal was having people listen to my music and my ideas," Randy said. "I didn't want anything to distract from that. I actually spend most of my career writing myself out of my songs."

But Randy also wanted to avoid revisiting other unsettling issues in his early life—and it was easy for him to avoid talking about those days in interviews because music writers had so much else to talk to him about, namely those great songs. In a 1972 *Rolling Stone* profile on Newman by David Felton, there wasn't one sentence about his childhood in the lengthy piece. "It's like I have blocked those years from my memory," he said later. "I have felt so uncomfortable going there for so long that I just can't remember them."

Yet the eye issue left enough of a sting for him to write a song about it years later in what would be his most autobiographical album, *Land of Dreams*. The 1988 song "Four Eyes" is about the anxiety many kids feel when their parents drop them off for the first day of kindergarten. The musical track is a spectacular mix of edgy keyboard/percussion-driven punches and peppery orchestral and choral flourishes that replicate a nervous young-ster's racing heartbeat.

The lyrics begin with Newman, as a five-year-old, trying to understand why his father is driving him to this strange, seem-ingly faraway place, overrun with all these other kids, and then abandons him.

We drove, it seemed like forever,
Further than I'd ever been away from home
Then my daddy stopped the car, and he turned to me
He said, "Son it's time to make us proud of you,
It's time to do what's right
Gonna have to learn to work hard"
I said, "Work? What are you talking about?
You're not gonna leave me here, are you?"
He said, "Yes, I am!"
And drove off into the morning light

Things get even worse on the school grounds as some kids delight in making fun of those strange eyes and glasses.

For a while I stood there, on the sidewalk
A Roy Rogers lunch pail in my hand
Then I heard sweet children's voices calling
And I began to understand
They said, "Four eyes! Look like you're still sleeping!"
"Four eyes! Look like you're dead!"
"Four eyes! Where have you been keeping yourself?"
"Look like you been whupped upside the head."

The song is funny in its way, but also heartbreaking, an emo-tional contrast that would help give Newman's songs empathy and power.

"There's no doubt those painful early experiences gave him a closer view what an underdog might feel like," Lenny said. "We used to joke that outside of our favorite teams, we were always rooting for the underdog. I think Randy's empathy is a combination of someone who grew up feeling something of an underdog and his father's sense of fair play."

In a revealing 1979 interview with Timothy White for *Rolling Stone*, Irving Newman described his son's trials with his eyes, suggesting they were partially responsible for what he saw as a lingering sadness in Randy. "It was terrible," Irving said. "He had to have a lot of operations . . . I think it influenced his thinking a whole lot, his sadness. When he says he doesn't know where [that sadness] came from, I think it has a lot to do with his vision. He couldn't stand, as a kid, exploitation of that; being called 'four eyes' or 'cross-eyed.' He cannot stand that kind of humor . . . when guys cross their eyes like Jerry Lewis or drag their legs like Milton Berle. He thinks it is disgraceful, and so do I."

The final operation was the most traumatic. A noted surgeon guaranteed Randy that the procedure would resolve the problem at least cosmetically; his eyes would be centered. But the operation didn't erase the problem and, Irving said, it devastated his son.

∼

Randy's tendency to isolate himself was an early sign of a behavior trait that would remain for years. Randy's oldest sons recall going into their parents' bedroom during childhood and finding Randy in the bed, watching a movie on television, listening to a ball game on a cheap transistor radio, and reading a couple of books—all at the same time. Some of this behavior was attributed to a deep curiosity driven by an active brain (Irving Newman told friends that tests showed Randy had one of the highest IQs in the Los Angeles school district), but there was also the chance that the sensory overload was driven by other factors.

"He has watched so much baseball on TV that he can call pitches before they're thrown," Randy's son Johnny said. "He'll tell you this next one is going to be in the dirt and then one outside, and I don't think it's just the entertainment of it. He never really had a favorite team. He just hopes for a good game, a close one. Ultimately, I think he's rooting to see something new; when you watch 50,000 hours of television, you're rooting for something you haven't seen before. I think there is something about watching television that is closer to an anesthetic, a way to get away from the pressure of his work and tough memories."

CHAPTER TWO

The World Isn't Fair
The Teen Years and
Some Early Songwriting

— I —

As Randy moved through Canyon Elementary and Paul Revere Junior High, classical music continued to be his north star, sometimes playing the piano well into the night with such volume that neighbors knocked on the front door in complaint. Randy's Beethoven was lovely, but enough is enough at two in the morning. And Randy had plenty of time to practice because he rarely had to spend much time on schoolwork. "It was amazing," Alan said. "He couldn't fail in school if he tried, and I'm talking about all the way through UCLA. I had a class with Randy there, and I'd study all the time and he would just look at my notes the night before, and I'd get a B and he'd get an A."

Despite the hours at the piano, Newman doesn't believe he truly applied himself growing up. As he told music writer Gil Podolinsky:

> I never worked the way some kids worked. Playing was fairly easy for me, but there's a point at which if you don't practice, it's just not going to come . . . I remember playing one of the Chopin

etudes—I must have been twelve or thirteen—and . . . I thought I was buzzing along pretty well, but I'd never heard the piece played. It said *presto* or something, and I'd say, "Well, this sounds like presto to me." Then I heard someone else play it. Jesus! These internal lines, movement that wasn't even there when you played it at the tempo I was playing it at. I knew I was never going to be a pianist. I never thought I was going to be a performer at all."

Away from the piano, Randy pursued his own interests, including a pair of passions that, quite accidentally, proved to be valuable case studies in race relations in America in the 1940s and 1950s: baseball and popular music. Watching all the great Black talents finally being liberated in both fields, he, like millions of young Americans, became more sensitive to the evils of segregation—especially at a time when Black or other minority faces were generally cast in embarrassingly subservient roles in movies or television.

"He had this thing about bullies, which is something you can sense in some of his songs," Alan said. "There was a time in junior high when this big, older kid cut in front of him in line, and Randy called him on it. My brother ended up getting punched in the nose for it, but it didn't deter him from trying to correct what he thought was unfair behavior."

Randy was only three in 1947 when Jackie Robinson—who grew up about twenty-five miles from Pacific Palisades in Pasadena and starred in four sports at UCLA—became the first Black to break the color barrier in the major leagues, earning Rookie of the Year honors for his inspired play and causing a race among team owners to sign other Black players. During Randy's years at Canyon, however, the exploits of such future Black Hall of Famers as Hank Aaron, Willie Mays, and Roy Campanella were highlighted in the daily sports pages. This revolution on the diamond ridiculed the racist claim that Blacks were inferior or the fear that true, red-blooded Americans would not buy tickets to integrated games.

Rock and roll was an even more impactful breakthrough for young Americans when it began surfacing in the white teen music world in the early 1950s, thanks chiefly to changes in pop radio. Many white teens in Los Angeles first heard R & B records on *Harlematinee*, a show hosted by Hunter Hancock, a white disc jockey from Texas who featured hits by such artists as Louis Jordan, the Orioles, and Wynonie Harris—records that sounded more exotic and sensual than the AM pop fare of the time. Soon, other local broadcasters on small LA stations adopted R & B formats, and a growing white teen audience tuned in.

Dick "Huggy Boy" Hugg, a white DJ who was younger and more prone to hip teen jargon than Hancock, had a more mysterious edge because his program was broadcast late at night from the front window of Dolphin's of Hollywood, an R & B record shop in Los Angeles's mostly Black South Central neighborhood. Owner John Dolphin had wanted to put the store in Hollywood, hence the name, but he couldn't find anyone who would rent space to a Black man. When Lenny was old enough to drive, he and Randy went to Dolphin's and browsed through rows of records, few of which they had ever heard. Eager to hear new sounds, they would also drive to the top of the foothills in the Trousdale Estates area, near Palisades, late at night, a time when the signals from various powerhouse stations—especially Chicago and New Orleans—carried regional hits across the country.

The teen enthusiasm for R & B hits was so strong by 1954 that a few singles, notably the dreamy, uplifting harmonies of the Crows' "Gee" and the Chords' "Sh-Boom," became bestsellers at record stores in white neighborhoods. The stage was set for Elvis Presley, Chuck Berry, and the rock explosion of 1956, the year Randy turned thirteen.

~

Fats Domino didn't look like a teen idol, but his warm, infectious sound struck Randy with the same life-changing force that millions of teens attributed to Elvis and the Beatles. Though Alan bought lots of 45 rpm singles, Newman only remembers buying four as a youngster—and two were by Domino. (One of the others was the Beatles' "From Me to You.") Domino was only twenty-eight in 1956, but the roly-poly, five-foot-five New Orleans native looked older (Elvis was twenty-one) and did not offer a trace of rebellion in his feel-good mix of Louisiana shuffle, boogie-woogie, R & B, and even occasionally country and Cajun. Where rival rocker Little Richard kicked his piano bench out of the way onstage so he could stand up and pound the keys while screaming the lyrics to "Tutti Frutti" and "Long Tall Sally," Domino sat politely, smiling warmly at the audience as he gently swayed from side to side. He had been turning out R & B hits since 1950 for Imperial Records, but things broke open in 1955 when his recording of "Ain't That a Shame" connected with the larger pop world. The record spent eleven weeks on top of the R & B charts and reached No. 10 on the pop charts.

The single would have gone higher except that most mainstream radio stations in America resisted playing records by Black artists, fearful of offending white parents who didn't want their kids listening to Black music. Dot Records, a small indie label in Tennessee, rushed out a version of "Ain't That a Shame" by Pat Boone, a smooth-singing white teen idol who would soon rival Elvis for record sales in the decade. Boone's record made it to No. 1, and he was soon on his way to Hollywood, where he starred in movies and became yet another celebrity patient of Dr. Irving Newman.

Domino's influence on Randy was multilevel. Early on, Randy played Fats's songs on the piano during breaks from Brahms,

Mozart, and Beethoven. Later, his vocal style would reflect elements of Domino's conversational drawl, and his eventual performance style would reflect Domino's anti-flamboyance. The latter was in keeping with what Randy's uncles told him about always letting the music speak for itself—don't hype in interviews or in performances.

~

The only other fifties artist to touch Randy as deeply as Fats Domino was Ray Charles, who studied classical piano as a boy at the Florida School for the Deaf and Blind in St. Augustine, Florida. Charles showed up on the R & B charts in the early 1950s with records that were covered years later by Elvis Presley, Bobby Darin, and other white artists. With the call-and-response vitality of "I Got a Woman" in the mid-1950s, Charles broke into the white market. Randy's interest in the singer-pianist soared even more in the summer of 1959 when Charles's recording "What'd I Say" was such a hyper-effusive display of sonic power that it pushed him to superstardom in the pop world. But the *Genius of Ray Charles* album sealed the deal for Newman.

The LP was compelling on several levels as Charles offered customized versions of some pop standards, much as Lenny had urged Randy to do after *Three Little Words*. Among them were Johnny Mercer and Harold Arlen's "Come Rain or Come Shine" and Irving Berlin's "Alexander's Ragtime Band," but Charles also covered two numbers associated with Louis Jordan, the Black bandleader who had the talent and vision in the 1930s to mix jazz, swing, blues, and boogie-woogie and then top it off with a comic flair. In Charles's hands, "Let the Good Times Roll" and "Don't Let the Sun Catch You Crying," two of Jordan's signature numbers, felt right at home among the more pop-styled songs. The album was such a hit that Charles went even further three years later by releasing two widely influential collections of country songs by such writers as Hank Williams ("You Win Again") and Don Gibson ("I Can't Stop Loving You").

"I loved Ray Charles, and I still do," Newman said. "I felt he always went to the right place, whatever he was doing with the song, singing, or playing the piano. He made you feel the song, and that's the most important thing in what we do. You've got to make the listener feel what you are saying is authentic."

Newman wasn't interested in updating old songs in his own career, but he learned a lesson that would prove crucial. As a songwriter and record-maker, he wouldn't limit himself to a single music genre. He wanted to be free to draw from any source—classical music, pop standards, R & B, Broadway, jazz, rock, and film. He was particularly fond of such jazz figures as Oscar Peterson and Thelonious Monk and country stars like George Jones and Hank Williams.

~

The Newman boys' exposure to Black culture took another uptick when his parents hired Lucinda Hicks.

Randy's mother suffered from severe migraines in the late 1940s and early 1950s, causing her to spend days at a time in a darkened room. Needing someone to assume the household chores, the Newmans hired Hicks, a large, outgoing Black woman who had moved to Los Angeles a few years earlier from Wharton, Texas, a small town south of Houston. The Newmans were still in the Beverly Hills apartment, but Lucinda stayed with them after the move to Pacific Palisades—a dozen years in all.

Despite the cleaning and cooking, Lucinda always seemed to find time for Randy and Alan, showering them with affection—starting with walks to Roxbury Park in Beverly Hills where she let the boys run around to their hearts' content. "Those were great times," Randy said, displaying some teasing sibling rivalry.

"Lucinda would push my brother in a stroller, and I used to say, 'Leave him, Soozie, leave him. Let's go home.'"

Both boys enjoyed Lucinda's sense of fun and adventure. "We loved being around her," Randy continued. "She taught me how to ride a bike and she had a boyfriend, Aaron, who was a big baseball fan who played catch with me. Lucinda always made fun of him because he was a Yankee fan at a time when the Yankees were the only all-white team in the majors. She'd also dance around the floor to those great records by Fats and Joe Turner, and she sang in a choir. She'd get all dressed up in white and my dad would joke, 'Oh, you look like an angel.'"

Alan credits Lucinda with helping mold their sensibilities toward social issues. "I'm sure she made it a number one issue for Randy," he said. "I used to crawl in bed with her and sleep, so the idea of not being able to drink at the same fountain was ridiculous even as a little kid." Randy added his own memories. When he was around six, he used the N-word, and Lucinda was furious. He recalled, "She told me not to ever use that word, and she whacked me with a switch from a tree."

~

The arrival of rock had an even bigger impact on Lenny, whose love of the new style corresponded with the opening of Liberty Records. Once he started classes at University High School, he spent his free time at the label's offices on North La Brea Avenue in Hollywood. As the owner's son, he could wander from office to office and even sit in on informal staff meetings. Every aspect of the business intrigued him, from the pressing of records to the artwork to, above all, the recording sessions, all of which he would later use in encouraging Randy to write pop songs.

A key moment for Lenny came in early 1958 when he heard Eddie Cochran, a gifted singer-guitarist who had switched from country to rock after seeing Elvis Presley, preview one of his new songs for his father. Lenny couldn't believe what he was hearing as Cochran—just three years older—sang a raucous teen lament, "Summertime Blues," which he wrote with Jerry Capehart. Following the song's soon-to-become famous final lines—"Sometimes I wonder what I'm gonna do / But there ain't no cure for the summertime blues"—Lenny shouted, "That's great! That's a hit!" With a grin, Cochran declared, "Hey, I want him with me every time we go into the studio. I love his enthusiasm."

"Summertime Blues" was not only a Top 10 single for Cochran but also later became a signature concert number for the Who. Liberty staffers were soon seeking Lenny's judgment, and the accompanying boost in confidence made him think more and more about Randy.

Listening to copies of songs that were being sent to Liberty by publishers, Lenny believed Randy could do better. His feelings, to be sure, were based more on faith than evidence; Randy had only experimented with a few isolated tunes at this point. But Lenny was ready to make his move. Soon after Randy's fifteenth birthday, Lenny insisted, "Randy, you've got to start writing songs!"

Not one to show emotion, Newman listened, and then walked into his room to listen to a baseball game. The story may have been an urban myth among Randy's friends, but Alan knew Randy was intrigued and, sure enough, he soon began taking a stab at pop songwriting.

— II —

Randy and Lenny saw less of each other as they progressed in school. Two grade levels meant a world of different friends and activities, and those changes increased in 1959 when Lenny enrolled as a business major at USC, still spending off hours at

Liberty Records. Randy was at University High and bound for rival UCLA. It could have been a turning point in Randy's relationship with Lenny, but the bond remained tight.

"Uni" was one of Los Angeles's most prestigious public high schools, boasting a celebrity alumni list that ranged from Elizabeth Taylor and Judy Garland to more contemporary names Nancy Sinatra and the Doors' John Densmore and Robby Krieger. But Randy didn't hang out with the celebrity crowd. Foster Sherwood, who lived near the Newmans, met Randy at Paul Revere and they spent increasing time together during the Uni days, taking turns driving each other to school. Though Newman would frequently be described as nerdish in high school because of his shyness, Sherwood disputed the description:

> We kinda kept to ourselves. We weren't part of the cool crowd by any means, but we weren't nerds either. The thing that stood out about Randy was [that] he was so smart. You'd notice him in class because he always picked up on things so fast even though he never seemed to work at it. He concentrated on things that interested him. Apart from music, his main interest was history. That's one of the things I later found so compelling about his music, in his lyrics, the way that he draws on a lot of historical lessons. He wasn't particularly political in high school, but he was always quick to point out hypocrisy or unfairness. It was a deep part of him.

Randy found little of interest in the customs of high school. He checked out the usual dances, school plays, and football games, but he invariably felt uninvolved. He remembers going to a football game against a big Uni rival and seeing everyone around him going crazy, but he was so bored that he remembers telling himself, "I don't give a fuck." He did join a male fraternity, but only, he says, in hope of attracting girls.

~

Teen rebellion was a dominant social attitude in the 1950s that was explored memorably in a series of films, including *The Wild One* (even though Marlon Brando was almost thirty at the time), *Blackboard Jungle* (set in an unruly inner-city high school), and, most powerfully, *Rebel Without a Cause* (starring a magnetic James Dean).

Randy went through his own unruly period, but Sherwood describes it as on the lower end of any rebellious scale. His most troubling moments involved a series of auto accidents, several of which were attributed to the eyesight problem and others simply to bad luck—the kind of humorous tales you might expect in some of Newman's eventual songs. The first time his father let Randy back the car out of the garage, the car bumper snagged the garage door spring, causing the door to come down on the car roof. There was also the time he drove over the curb onto someone's lawn.

Some of the accidents, however, were the result of too much alcohol, especially Ripple, a cheap, fortified wine. Newman acknowledged over the years that he couldn't do things in moderation, but he wasn't even driving the night of the most serious accident—he was in the back seat.

"It was the time of a school dance, maybe the prom," said Sherwood, who received a PhD in history from UCLA and taught history at California Institute of the Arts (CalArts) before entering the construction business. "A bunch of us got together at some guy's house while his parents were out of town, and we got all beered up before setting out for the dance. But we didn't make it. On the way, 'What'd I Say' came on the radio, and someone, maybe Randy, yelled 'Turn it up,' and the driver ran into a parked car when he reached for the dial. He was hurt the most, getting most of his teeth knocked out."

Randy knew he was also injured because he was bloody and could stick his tongue through his chin. At the hospital, he learned that he also suffered a slipped disc. Police investigated the incident but released the teens to their parents.

~

Eventually, some of those around Randy started wondering if the misadventures weren't his way of rebelling against the family's high hopes for him. "My father's love for Randy was never in doubt, but there were a lot of expectations that went along with that," said Alan Newman, who became a renowned oncologist in San Francisco.

> Just look at what happened. My father wanted to be a musician, but became a doctor . . . and Randy becomes a musician and I become a doctor. I'm not saying my dad would have bought him a piano and encouraged him to play if Randy didn't have talent. But my father was the kind of dad who would not let you win. There was this competitive thing going on all the time. I felt Randy was in between a rock and a hard place for a long time with his music. When Randy started on his career, my dad was proud of him, there's no question in my mind about that. But he was also a little jealous.

Alan wasn't sure Randy would agree with him, but he felt his brother seemed to do everything he could in high school to fail even though he never did—things like filling a garbage can with trash and dumping it on a classroom floor just to get a laugh. "I think a lot of it was to disappoint my father."

The rebellion didn't include easing up on music. "It's not like Randy really had a choice," Alan continued. "He has been compulsive about music. He writes because he has to, not because somebody made him. It's just innate." Randy assumed he would follow his uncles into film scoring, but the thought continued to unnerve him.

During this period, Lenny was progressing rapidly at Liberty, exhibiting a career discipline that gave him experience that would be useful in helping mold Randy's future. The label had come a long way in five years, including the signing of its biggest hit-maker: a fifteen-year-old, pop-flavored rocker named Bobby Vee. Over the next five years alone, Vee would have eleven Top 40 hits, including "Devil or Angel" and "Take Good Care of My Baby." This didn't mean Liberty was close to the level of Columbia or RCA among record companies, but it was attracting a talented group of studio musicians and budding songwriters that included Glen Campbell, Leon Russell, Jackie DeShannon, and David Gates, each of whom would all go on to major careers.

Lenny found a mentor in Snuff Garrett, a cocky high school dropout from Texas with an unshakable belief in his ability to make hit records. Only three years older than Waronker, Garrett was hired in 1959 as a promotion man and showed such a gift for picking hits that he was soon promoted to staff producer, where he delivered a jukebox full of Top 40 singles with the likes of Vee, Gene McDaniels, and Gary Lewis & the Playboys.

Not much more than a gofer at first, Lenny was awed by Garrett's ability to find the right songs, inspire artists, and schmooze with musicians. As soon as he worked up the nerve, Lenny told Garrett about his friend, "this great songwriter." Garrett listened to some of Newman's songs, but he wasn't impressed. Privately, he told Waronker, "His music is just too weird." Undaunted, Lenny tried to get Garrett's attention in another way. Reverting to reworking the old hits, Lenny talked Randy into playing his contemporary arrangement of "The Way You Look Tonight" for Garrett. But again, the producer didn't think it was worth recording. Waronker wasn't deterred. He kept pitching Newman to others around the building. It was, he felt increasingly, just a matter of time.

While Lenny had a career game plan, Randy didn't approach college seriously. Yes, UCLA was a world-class university with an outstanding music department, but the primary reason he enrolled there was probably its location—just eight miles from his front door. "I didn't think I was ready to go away to school," he said. "I was a mess organizationally. As soon as I started UCLA, I was told to be sure to see your counselor about this or that, but I didn't even know who my counselor was. I ended up taking all these classes that had nothing to do with my degree, and a lot of days I had so much trouble finding a parking place that I often just gave up and went home."

As Lenny kept pushing him toward pop music, Randy studied orchestration and composition with renowned Italian composer, pianist, and writer Mario Castelnuovo-Tedesco, whose other students also included composer John Williams.

However, Randy was increasingly anxious about a life in film music. "When I was still a kid, I'd see my uncle Al working on a picture and see him really moaning and groaning," he said. "And this is what really got me: He'd play something and ask, 'What do you think of this?' Here was this great composer and he was not secure with his writing. He was asking me what I thought, and I was just eight years old. I think it spooked me. How could I ever do anything good if it was this fucking hard?"

As time went by, pop music became an increasingly attractive alternative. It was less frightening territory for Randy than film scoring and, crucially, he knew he'd always have Lenny by his side to reassure him. "When I started pop songs, I would write something and think, 'oh, that's good,' only to get down on it soon after that," Randy said. "But I would talk to Lenny, and I'd get up again because he liked it. He was my ambition and my courage. He was my backbone. It's not so much that (pop songs) seemed easier than doing films, it was just there. When Lenny suggested I try and write some songs, that was the start really."

Randy would phone Lenny as soon as he finished a song. "In the early days, he'd call at eight or nine o'clock in the morning," Lenny said. "That's when you are the most frightened—when you finish a song—and Randy would be wanting to hear what I thought, and I always loved them. It wasn't like I was trying to make him feel good. I really loved them."

A breakthrough came when Lenny found a sympathetic ear at Liberty for Randy's songs. It was Dick Glasser, who was hired in 1960 to run Liberty's publishing arm, Metric. When Randy played Glasser one of his new songs, probably one called "Don't Tell on Me," Glasser complimented him and urged him to keep in touch. The tune was never recorded, but Lenny couldn't have been happier. "That's great," Lenny told Randy. "Keep writing."

CHAPTER THREE

"They Tell Me It's Summer"
"Golden Gridiron Boy" and
Metric Music

— I —

As soon as the phone rang early one spring morning in 1962, Lenny knew that it was Randy with another song. He also knew there would be no small talk; these morning calls were all about the music. Sure enough, Randy announced the title, "They Tell Me It's Summer," and began playing a sweet, heartache ballad. Randy's voice was a bit rough for such a delicate tune, but he wouldn't be singing on the record anyway. The opening lines:

They tell me it's summer
But I know it's a lie
Cause summer's for laughing
So why do I cry?

They tell me it's summer
And the sun shines, it's true
But it just can't be summer
When I'm not with you

This wasn't a song that would stand out once a legion of young writers soon revolutionized rock with lyrics and themes that aimed for a wider audience than lovesick youth. Still, "They Tell Me It's Summer" seemed creditable enough commercially in the waning days of the old pop order. Dylan's first album of his own songs, *The Freewheelin' Bob Dylan*, was only a year away.

Rockers in the 1950s and 1960s didn't just shake up pop music because they were young, sexy, and rebellious—they also overturned the longstanding division of labor in pop where writers generally only wrote and singers mostly just sang. The transition began in force in the early 1950s when pop artists started having major hits by reaching outside the traditional Tin Pan Alley supply of writers to cover country hits, notably Patti Page's recording of "The Tennessee Waltz" (co-written and recorded by country bandleader Pee Wee King), Tony Bennett's "Cold, Cold Heart" (Hank Williams), and Perry Como's "Don't Let the Stars Get in Your Eyes" (co-written and recorded by Slim Willet). When Page's single sold two and a half million copies—huge for the time—other artists recorded the song, resulting in nearly five million combined sales worldwide. With another two million in sheet music sales, "The Tennessee Waltz" was believed to be the most successful non-holiday pop song to that point.

By embracing musical genres long dismissed as unworthy, mainstream labels and radio stations soon cut out the middleman as fans demanded the original country or R & B versions, opening the door for the likes of Chuck Berry, Buddy Holly, and Johnny Cash. Within a decade, folk, R & B, country, and rock singer-songwriters dominated pop music. The best of these writers introduced songs that not only spoke more freely about their own experiences but also challenges in the world around them.

Despite the shift, there were still pop artists who didn't write their own songs and depended on a group of New York publishers to supply them with tunes that would appeal to mainstream teens. The most celebrated of these firms were housed in the Brill Building on Broadway at 49th Street, where teams of songwriters would huddle around a guitar or a piano in small cubicles and try to come up with another golden hit. The teams were highlighted by Leiber & Stoller ("Jailhouse Rock" and "Charlie Brown"), Mann & Weil ("On Broadway" and "You've Lost That Lovin' Feelin'"), Bacharach-David ("I Just Don't Know What to Do with Myself" and "Walk on By") and Goffin-King ("Will You Love Me Tomorrow" and "A Natural Woman"). Of the Brill Building contingent, Randy's favorite was Carole King, whose strength, like his at the time, was composition; her then-husband, Gerry Goffin, was the lyricist. "I thought she was the tops," Randy said, citing "Down Home," "It Might as Well Rain until December" and "Will You Love Me Tomorrow" as some of his favorite Goffin-King tunes. "One thing she had that I also had to some extent was that she knew classic Gershwin and Rodgers tunes and she would use those . . . harmonic changes."

The New York publishing powerhouses had easy access to the leading record producers, which helped them keep tabs on when the top singers were looking for material so that a publisher could quickly assign one or more of its songwriting crews to write a song in the style of that artist. The publishers would then usually hire a singer with a similar vocal style to make a demo of the most promising songs as part of their sales pitch. Being based in Los Angeles, Randy was at a major disadvantage. Without the New York entrée, Metric's best chance of getting a song recorded was to concentrate on artists signed with its affiliated label, Liberty, whose roster leaned toward young, polite mainstream pop idols, including Bobby Vee and Vic Dana.

Randy was in luck with "They Tell Me It's Summer" because the tune was ideal for one of Liberty's hottest acts—the Fleetwoods, a pop trio from Olympia, Washington, that gained national attention in 1959 when its dreamy ballad "Come Softly to Me" spent four weeks at No. 1 on the charts, followed by another silky No. 1 single, "Mr. Blue."

There were whoops and hollers in the new Liberty offices on Sunset Boulevard in the heart of Hollywood when news came back that the Fleetwoods wanted to rush a single out for summer. Hopes went even higher in August when *Billboard,* the major weekly record industry trade, reviewed "They Tell Me It's Summer" in its prestigious "Spotlight" section, alongside reviews of singles by red-hot Gene Pitney, highly regarded newcomer Aretha Franklin, and established hitmakers Dinah Washington and Brook Benton. "Here's another soft, soothing ballad performance by the trio," *Billboard* declared. "Good season material and it has a chance."

Could Randy really have a hit the first time out?

Well, no. The single didn't generate enough response to enter the magazine's Top 100 sales chart until October, which was too late for the summer angle to connect with listeners. It was the single's flip side—"Lovers by Night, Strangers by Day," a lilting but minor romantic number, that lured enough buyers into record shops to justify the initial chart position, No. 83. Still, it was exciting for the Metric staff to be part of a successful record, even if it was the back side, and Newman made the same money because writers of both sides of a single shared sales royalties equally. The single moved up the charts for seven weeks before peaking at No. 36, but Randy wasn't celebrating. He didn't much like the way the Fleetwoods interpreted the song, an early example of what would be a recurring problem for him.

— II —

"They Tell Me It's Summer" was a family affair from the start. Irving peppered Randy with advice, including the value of songs tied to holidays or seasonal activities. "He was really into the old songwriter thing of 'Oh, we're at war, let's write a war song' or 'It's summer, let's write a summer song,'" Randy said. That strategy had a long history of success, from Irving Berlin's "White Christmas" and "Easter Parade" to such 1950s hits as the Four Freshmen's "Graduation Day" and Marty Robbins's ode to high school proms, "A White Sport Coat (and a Pink Carnation)." When Randy started writing "Summer," Irving even offered some lyric suggestions, and Randy used a couple, including this noted change:

> They tell me it's summer
> So I look to the sky
> But I can't see the sun shine
> Cause there's tears in my eyes (changed from 'Cause all I do is cry.)

Once the single was released, Alan rushed to record shops to buy copies and to talk excitedly about the single in hopes of convincing merchants they had a hit on their hands and needed to order more copies. (Alan would also support Randy by singing on some of the demos, but he never considered a music career.) Randy's mom, ever the supporter, joined in by putting a scrapbook together.

As soon as "Summer" took off, Randy began working on another seasonal song, this one suggested by Lenny. A huge football fan, Waronker thought a record about high school football could have a lot of youthful appeal. Randy quickly came up with "Golden Gridiron Boy," the story of a scrawny high school band member whose dream girl only has eyes for the school's football hero.

In another early morning call, Randy sang the song for Lenny, who privately didn't think much of it, but he passed the lightweight song along to the Metric staff; they, too, were underwhelmed. This time, Irving was key to getting the song recorded.

He would regularly tell his patients, especially those in the entertainment business, about what a great songwriter Randy was and, in some cases, give them a tape of Randy's latest tune. As soon as he got demos of "Golden Gridiron Boy" (one of the rare times Randy sang on a demo himself), Irving passed them along to his show-biz patients, including Pat Boone. A couple of days later, Boone called to say he liked the record and wanted to meet Randy.

"Irving Newman was a great diagnostician," Boone said. "He could tell you exactly what was wrong with you and what to do about it. He also had a great sense of humor, and we got to be friendly. One day, he starts telling me about his kid, Randy, who was attending UCLA and wanted to be a writer. He said, 'Give him a desk and a place to hang his hat and you could probably publish his tunes.' That's when he gave me this tape with the football song on it."

Boone still recorded for Dot Records, which had relocated to Los Angeles, and he was so impressed with the tape that he tried to get the publishing wing of the label to sign Randy, but he couldn't convince those in charge. Boone recalled, "They said, 'He's just a kid. Let him write a couple of hits and then we'll sign him,' so we turned Randy Newman down, and I've always regretted that. I so admire him as a songwriter and performer. He's so unique."

After briefly thinking about recording "Gridiron" himself, Boone realized that he—at twenty-eight and married with four daughters—was too old to assume the role of a high school student, but he thought Randy's voice worked well on the demo, and he talked Dot into making a record of the song with Randy. Though uncertain about his voice, Randy was willing to give it a try. He went into one of Hollywood's top studios on October 12 so that Dot would have time to rush the single to radio stations before the end of football season. The session was co-produced by Boone and Jimmie Haskell, one of the nation's fastest rising young arranger-composers, and it featured a rhythm section that included the ever-present Glen Campbell on guitar. For the flip side, Randy wrote an even more forgettable song, "Country Boy," the story of a dyed-in-the-wool country boy trying to woo a big city girl.

The "Summer" and "Gridiron" topics came naturally to Randy. "I was so damned shy around girls," he told *Rolling Stone* in the late 1970s. "I really didn't have many dates. I was strange-looking—and I was a bad driver. I'd be trying to get my arm around a girl who didn't want to know about it while I drove the family car up on some sidewalk. They were mostly girls I liked who didn't like me; it was tough."

Between false starts and full takes, Randy and the musicians recorded the songs around ten times each, and finished off with another ten or so takes of a third Newman song, the bouncy "Everybody Else but You," which was never released. Despite Boone's enthusiasm, the Dot promotion staff was indifferent to the record. In a full-page ad in the November 10 issue of *Billboard*, "Golden Gridiron Boy" was buried near the bottom of a group of fifteen new Dot singles. The publication didn't even bother reviewing it. "Gridiron" was simply listed, without comment, at the bottom of a list of some fifty records released that week. The message to radio program directors and record store owners was, "Don't bother." And they didn't.

Some of the Metric staff were surprised that Randy didn't seem any more disappointed by the record's failure than he had been excited over the Fleetwoods' modest success. But Lenny knew Randy's make-up. "He just didn't show his feelings; it's not in him," Waronker said. "I've seen him excited, but even his excitement is sort of tempered."

Growing up, the Newman offspring often heard their uncles, who worked with many of the big stars in Hollywood, make fun of how celebrities tended to brag about their latest projects—invariably exaggerating the success. This disdain left an impression with Randy. "I got to where I thought when someone bragged that you should beware of everything they said, and I never wanted to be in that position of bragging myself," he said. As many would observe over the years, Newman avoided boasting to the point of leaning toward self-deprecation. "If you put yourself down, there's nothing left for anyone who wants to attack you," he said. "You've already admitted there are problems. I also found it easier to not expect something big so you wouldn't be hurt if something didn't work out."

Coupled with his shyness, Randy tended to operate behind this emotional shield for years, causing casual acquaintances to scratch their heads. But that doesn't mean Randy wasn't nervous in the studio. He wrote the Dot single as "Gridiron Golden Boy" but was so anxious in his first recording session that he scrambled the title the first time through, ending up with "Golden Gridiron Boy."

~

Dick Glasser was so pleased by "They Tell Me It's Summer" that he offered Randy a Metric songwriting contract—a $100 monthly retainer plus whatever songwriting royalties resulted. Glasser, who made records under the name Dick Lory, became such a fan that he recorded another Newman song ("I Got Over You") for Liberty.

At nineteen, Randy Newman was a professional songwriter.

"I think he was amazed when he got his deal because he was actually making money," Waronker said. "Like everyone, he worried while growing up what he's going to do for money, but money wasn't an overriding thing with him. He had this incredible desire to be the best. That was his drive. He also realized that songwriting was separating him from the family. It was tough following in Alfred's footsteps. The power his uncle had affected everyone around him, including Randy. I don't think that Randy started writing songs just to separate himself from Al and Lionel, but once he got going, he realized he could do something they really couldn't do."

By the end of the year, Metric had copyrighted over a dozen Newman songs, but writing felt torturous, especially the lyrics and themes. The company wanted simple pop songs that radio craved at the time, which meant, in Randy's mind, mostly mundane love songs. Even though the bar was low, he faced some of the same psychological issues—insecurity versus perfectionism—that hounded Alfred Newman. Whether nature or nurture, the conflict would plague Randy for years.

Of his other songs that year, two were released by Liberty as singles—"Someone's Waiting," a lonesome soldier's lament recorded by Gene McDaniels, a pop-R & B singer who had a No. 1 single in 1961 with "One Hundred Pounds of Clay," and "Looking for Me," an expression of youthful anxiety recorded by Vic Dana. "Waiting" was the B-side of a record that reached No. 31 on the charts, but the vocal was overwrought and the arrangement disappointing. The single didn't chart. The Dana record also flopped.

Even if he was writing for mainstream radio, Randy injected the music itself with enough nuance to give most of the songs a fresh, independent edge. But the cover versions invariably missed the nuances, partially because the Metric demos leaned toward the homogenized pop middle-of-the-road style. The move made business sense because the demos aimed for the commercial sweet spot at the time and labels, after all, were trying to sell records. They weren't out to please critics or even Randy.

Whatever else you felt about the Brill Building hits, the best of them sounded awfully good, and it was no accident; the demos reflected character and sometimes wit, largely because most of the top songwriters controlled their demo sessions. Randy could have demanded to take over his demo sessions, but it wasn't his nature at the time. "It fit in with my history," Newman said. "I was pushed every step of the way. I wasn't eager to write songs or make records, and it was the same with demos. I wasn't like Bacharach or Paul (Simon) or Carole who took charge. Who was I to tell Leon Russell or Glen Campbell what to do? I don't know if it was laziness or cowardice or something else, but I was very reluctant to speak up."

— III —

Liberty was an attractive entry-level spot for Randy and other talented musicians, many of whom came to Los Angeles in pursuit of their dreams. Among them was Jackie DeShannon, who began singing country songs on a radio show in Kentucky at the age of six under her real name, Sharon Lee Myers, and Jeannie Seely, who knew she wanted to be a country singer ever since singing a song at a third-grade assembly in a small town in Pennsylvania. Besides several of her own hits, DeShannon later co-wrote with Donna Weiss the silky, seductive "Bette Davis Eyes," which won a Grammy in 1982 for song of the year. Seely's recording of Hank Cochran's "Don't Touch Me" in 1966 stands alongside Patsy Cline's "Crazy" as one of the most celebrated ballads ever in country music. At Liberty, however, both young women were just hoping, like Randy, to get a song on the radio.

"There were so many things going on," DeShannon said of the energy and comradery at Liberty. "You could walk through the halls and pop into anyone's office—sales, promotion, whatever. It was like a high school after-party. We were also encouraged to write with each other, which Randy and I did. I could see right away that he was an amazing talent." Their collaborations included "Hold Your Head High," which DeShannon recorded for Liberty, along with one of Newman's solo compositions, "Did He Call Today, Mama?"

A desperate expression of romantic insecurity, "Did He Call" was produced by Jack Nitzsche with the robust R & B flourish that he brought as an arranger to some of Phil Spector's hits. It was the flip side of DeShannon's first hit, "Needles and Pins" in 1963, and the Beatles liked the sexy, energetic tone of "Needles" so much that DeShannon became a support act on their 1964 American tour. The band also played the "Needles and Pins" and "Did He Call" singles for producer George Martin, who made it a point to keep an eye on the young writer in Los Angeles.

Seely took a secretarial job at Liberty, hoping to showcase her songs for some of the writers and producers in the building, and she, too, ended up writing a song with Randy. "I didn't play the guitar very well, so I thought I'd try to figure out some things on a piano at the office," she said. "Randy came down the hall and saw me trying to pick out a song, and he volunteered to help. He showed me how to play what I was hearing in my head. I knew what an incredible musician he was, and I just loved that he would take time with me. Who else would waste time with a secretary?"

Written as a country song, Seely's "Anyone Who Knows What Love Is (Will Understand)"—the one on which Newman helped her with the music—was an attempt to explain why a woman would stay in what appeared to be an unhealthy relationship, a theme showcased a few years later in Tammy Wynette's country standard "Stand by Your Man."

Rather than pitch the song to the country market, Metric pushed it in 1964 as an R & B song to Irma Thomas who recorded for Imperial, which was then owned by Liberty. Thomas, the "Soul Queen of New Orleans," was coming off a Top 20 pop hit when Imperial released her version of "Anyone Who Knows," coupled with Jerry Ragovoy's "Time Is on My Side," which became one of the Rolling Stones' first hits. Thomas's single reached No. 52 on the *Billboard* charts. She later recorded three other Newman songs, including "While the City Sleeps," another strong number. Randy's feel for R & B also resulted in "Love Is Blind," a 1963 torch song recorded by Erma Franklin, the older sister of Aretha, and the episodic "I Don't Want to Hear It Anymore," recorded by Jerry Butler in 1964, but most of his tunes leaned toward the larger pop market.

— IV —

While Randy continued to take classes at UCLA and write songs at Metric, his uncle Lionel gave him a job writing short musical passages (often just a few seconds long) for a series of Twentieth Century–Fox's television properties, including *The Many Loves of Dobie Gillis*, *Lost in Space*, and *Judd for the Defense*. The most significant assignment was *Peyton Place*, a soap opera spin-off from the hugely successful, racy Grace Metalious novel and a subsequent motion picture starring Lana Turner. The TV show was such a runaway success in 1964 that Epic Records released a soundtrack album, featuring music from the show as performed by "The Randy Newman Orchestra," no less. It was a random collection of instrumental music, ranging from the lush show theme by Franz Waxman to a series of rock-tinged exercises written by Randy, featuring occasional surf-rock touches and such titles as "Blue Watusi" and "Randy's Riff." Movie soundtrack albums were common at the time, but a soundtrack for a TV show was a rarity, and it didn't catch on.

Lionel, too, may have been responsible for singer-songwriter-actor Bobby Darin, the most formidable talent that Newman had worked with at this point, asking Randy to co-write "Look at

Me," a Frank Sinatra-esque song, for the 1964 film *The Lively Set*. Darin, who prided himself on spotting upcoming talent, spread the word among New York publishers about this terrific young songwriter in Los Angeles.

The most memorable moment at Fox was when Beatles producer George Martin introduced himself. Eager to meet the young songwriter that Lennon and McCartney had brought to his attention, he was surprised to find Randy stuck in what reminded him of a factory assembly line, a bunch of writers turning out short instrumental pieces on command for films, often without even seeing the footage. While praising Randy for his music, Martin kept asking himself what such a talented young writer was doing in a place like this. Years later, Newman said his duties were even more menial than Martin had thought. Aside from the rare musical assignment, he was mostly just running the copy machine and making copies of music for the orchestra and the conductor. There was no sense in the Fox offices that they had a future star in their midst.

More than money, the experience gave Randy the opportunity to observe the world of film music, including meeting future giants in the field. Though he was working in pop music, he pictured film scoring as a fallback possibility or even his eventual destination.

The most notable of the composers in the Fox group was John (then Johnny) Williams, who would become the premiere film composer of his generation, thanks to such films as *Star Wars* and *Close Encounters of the Third Kind*. In fact, Williams would accomplish what was once considered impossible: passing Alfred Newman in the number of Oscar nominations (fifty-two versus forty-five) though not in Oscar wins (five against nine). Williams said:

> Randy was still a teenager when he used to appear at some of the
> Fox composer lunches. He'd just sit there, very quiet. I think

Lionel was trying to expose Randy to what film scoring was about. I knew Randy's father well, and Irving used to always complain that Randy didn't want to study, that all he wanted to do was watch television, but I eventually realized he was a very serious musician who was very knowledgeable about the film music repertoire. He was just getting started and very much in the shadow of his family. I just saw he was a nice kid and he was dedicated to music despite what Irving said. But the self-deprecating thing was very typical of the Newmans. I think part of it was a sort of defensive armor. Beneath it, though, they believed in themselves, the same as Randy did.

Martin and Williams weren't the only industry figures encouraging Newman, who struck them as humble and serious: a disarming combination. Lou Adler, a record company owner and producer who was in the early stage of a career that would include working with the Mamas and the Papas and Carole King, heard some of Randy's Metric songs and offered a piece of helpful advice. "He told Randy not to double the vocal melody in his piano part, [but to] come up with something on the piano that would add a new dimension to the song," Waronker said. "The only reason to double the melody in a demo or on a record was to help a singer who isn't very good stay on pitch or remember the melody."

This suggestion played directly to Randy's ability as composer and arranger. He could now add harmonic and rhythmic textures that would contrast and complement the vocal melody rather than just mirror it. For the rest of his career, he would employ this approach to help achieve the cinematic touches that had long intrigued him.

CHAPTER FOUR

A Creative Awakening
Roswitha and
A New Publisher

— I —

Wanting experience in the record business, Lenny arranged in 1964 to go to New York and work in Liberty's promotion branch, which put him in contact with the Brill Building and its celebrated writers, an experience that reinforced his belief that Randy could compete with the best of them. When Randy joined Lenny for a few weeks that summer, Lenny took him to meet one of their songwriting heroes, Jerry Leiber.

"Jerry was such a star that Randy and I went to his office with a lot of trepidation and fear," Waronker said of the trip. "But Jerry was unbelievably nice and asked Randy to play some songs, one of which Jerry liked a lot. I think it was 'Friday Night,' which sounded like something Jerry and Mike [Stoller] had done with the Drifters. It was later recorded by the O'Jays. Just before we left, Jerry told Randy, 'These are good.' Randy was so thrilled. In the elevator, he kept saying, 'This is like something from a Judy Garland or Mickey Rooney movie.'"

Randy was excited just being in New York City, which was saluted in such Brill Building hits as "On Broadway," with its seductive opening lines about the glamour of Broadway. He hailed a taxi one day and asked the driver to take him all over the city so he could get a feel for the places and people. He was gone for hours, and Lenny remembered the experience as a turning point. "I think he began thinking of himself as part of the music community that he admired."

By then, Randy had written nearly fifty songs that were copyrighted by Metric, about a third of which were recorded. Though the covers were by such admired vocalists as Jerry Butler, Lou Rawls, and veteran Frankie Laine, few came close to being a hit—or satisfying to Newman. For most of that time, the idea of ever writing great songs likely seemed as distant as writing a successful film score.

Inspired by the New York trip, Randy continued to write the mainstream songs that Metric wanted, but he began experimenting with material that had more of a personal edge, musically and, especially, lyrically—songs that meant something to him. The improvement was so striking that two of the songs from that period would become the first of his own songs he would record since the "Gridiron" novelty. It was the start of a two-year creative explosion that gave us a peek into where Randy was headed.

— II —

Randy's spirits were lifted in another magical way in 1964 when he saw Roswitha Schmale lounging in a bathing suit by an apartment building pool. Born in Germany, she had recently moved to Los Angeles where she worked as a translator for the Bank of America. He was so smitten that he walked right up to the pool and jumped in, fully clothed. He wanted to get her attention, and that was the first way that came to mind. He was never very good at opening lines. The plunge worked.

The pair started talking, and Randy soon asked her out (they saw the second Peter Sellers Pink Panther movie). Roswitha (pronounced "Rose-VEE-tah") was smart, good-hearted, down-to-earth, and cute as a button. She was Randy's first serious relationship, and those close to him were delighted, except, perhaps, his parents, who wondered—as parents tend to do—whether she was good enough for their son. Decades later, Randy would still remember the discomfort of the day he introduced Roswitha to his father. "There was not even a 'how do you do,'" he recalled. "He just started telling her about how awful I was as a pitcher in Little League. He said I was so bad one day that I ran off the mound in tears. The strangest thing is he didn't just tell her that story once, but several times." The embarrassment of that Little League story was so unsettling that Newman would use it, virtually word for word, in a song more than fifty years later.

Because of his shyness, Randy tended to bring someone with him when he visited Roswitha, often Alan or pal Foster Sherwood, to help keep the conversation going. Alan's first sight of her was when he and Randy got together with a friend who lived in the building to serenade Roswitha outside her window at two in the morning. "We were singing things like 'A Bird in a Gilded Cage' and 'Sweet Adeline,' and she told us to go away because we were keeping everybody awake," Sherwood said.

Lenny described Roswitha as a strong, positive force for Randy, speaking about her eventual influence on his personal life in ways reminiscent of Lenny's role in Randy's professional life. She both helped organize things around the house so that he could concentrate on his music, and she was very much a glass-half-full balance to his glass-half-empty outlook. "She took care of him and gave him confidence," Lenny said. "He had little demons, and he could be aloof, but she helped him become more comfortable with himself—a better person. He also continued to reach for more in his writing."

~

The rush of new songs included two that Randy would include on his first album, recordings that reflected much of the deep authenticity that he admired in Ray Charles's music. "Bet No One Ever Hurt This Bad" addressed romantic loss with an aggressive presence, especially in the painful currents of the music itself, that suggested a pop auteur at work. "Living Without You," equally powerful, acknowledged its New York roots in the opening lines:

The milk truck hauls the sun up
And the paper hits the door
The subway shakes my floor
And I think about you
Time to face the dawning gray
Of another lonely day
Baby, it's so hard
Living without you

Randy was moving fast. He might have also recorded a third, worthy song from this period, but "I've Been Wrong Before" was a statement of romantic anxiety meant to be sung by a woman. A fourth song, "Just One Smile," would prove the most important of the early batch, because it caught the ear of a New York publisher who would help expose Randy's music to a higher grade of singers than Metric had been able to reach.

Aaron Schroeder, a veteran New York songwriter who co-wrote several hits for Elvis Presley, including "Stuck on You" and "It's Now or Never," wasn't one of the elite East Coast publishers, but he was aggressive and had a good eye for talent, representing future Rock & Roll Hall of Fame members Gene Pitney and Al Kooper.

Whether Schroeder heard about Randy via Darin or simply through industry buzz in LA, he was so excited about Randy's new songs, especially "Just One Smile," that he offered him a songwriting contract with his January Music publishing firm. He thought the heartache tale with a soaring, torch-like drama would be perfect for Pitney, his biggest act. The contract ($250 a week) was a big increase over Metric, but the real lure was that January was closer to the major leagues of pop. The pairing came at the perfect time for Newman and Schroeder—Randy was gaining New York clout and Aaron was getting a young songwriter at the exact point that he was taking a major step forward artistically. "Aaron just loved 'Just One Smile,'" Randy recalled. "If he had his way, that's the kind of record he would have wanted me to keep writing all the time. He liked songs with a strong hook."

Lenny was equally enthusiastic about "Just One Smile," which Randy played for him before leaving Metric. "I went nuts when I heard the song," he said. "It was fantastic, but then he says he is going to take the song to Aaron Schroeder, and I got really angry. He just listened and said, 'It's business.' He was much more mature about it than me. It made sense for him. Aaron was a real go-getter." One other reason Lenny didn't put up a fight to keep Randy was that he didn't know how much longer he would be at Metric himself. Dick Glasser had gone to Warner Bros. Records, which was fast emerging as a respected new player in the industry. He headed the A&R department, which was responsible for finding and developing artists, and he hoped to someday bring Lenny to the label. Despite the split between the old friends, things were soon back to normal, and Randy continued to call Lenny when he had a new song.

Pitney's version of "Just One Smile" became a Top 10 single in England in 1966, but the song got the most attention when it was included on Blood, Sweat & Tears' debut album in 1968. Al Kooper had brought the song with him when he helped organize the band. "The demo just killed me," Kooper said. "I put that song under my belt and just waited for the time I could use it on a record. We didn't become close personally. The story you always heard about Randy was that he wasn't like the rest of us. He didn't hang out a lot. But I still admired his work."

Kooper's reference to Randy's reputation reflected his reserve, the way he was focused on the music, not the lifestyle—preferring to spend his off time at home working rather than schmoozing with other musicians in clubs all night. "It's not like he was a recluse," said Alan Newman. "Randy had lots of friends in high school and later, but [he has] never been a poser or acted like a 'rock star.' He was only interested in the music."

~

One of Schroeder's strengths as a publisher was a strong presence in London. Knowing about George Martin's interest in Randy, he sent a demo of "I've Been Wrong Before" to the Beatles producer. It was the only time Randy made his own demo and used more than a piano on it. Martin thought the ballad was perfect for Cilla Black, a young singer from Liverpool with a winning blend of every-girl persona and a surprisingly big, smoke-edged voice. By the time Martin took her into the studio in early 1965 to record the song, she already had four Top 10 singles in the UK. Though she never attracted much attention in the United States, Black, who was championed by the Beatles, was part of a respected group of British female singers who were solid-to-superior vocal inter-preters, a group that also included Dusty Springfield, Lulu, and Sandie Shaw.

"I've Been Wrong Before" expressed romantic insecurity with a striking arrangement that mixed a steady, understated piano tenderness with a tense string section accent to serve as a warn-ing of the uncertainty ahead. The single was released in late April, rising to No. 17 on the British charts—the highest of any

Newman song yet. It might have gone even higher, but some listeners were confused by the lyrics. What exactly was going on? Was it supposed to be a hopeful song or a desperate one? Reaction among critics ranged from "best thing she's done" to—again—"weird."

This was Newman at his finest so far, a record that could finally compete with the tracks coming out of New York. Not only would Dusty Springfield cover the song, but Elvis Costello reached back for it thirty years later for his *Kojak Variety* album—and it stood up well. Still, Randy's accomplishments were limited. He realized that he still needed to find his purpose as a writer if he was going to set himself apart from his peers. This was a challenge that Lenny couldn't do for him. In the end, all Randy needed to do was look around him and draw upon the pain of the childhood bullying, his family tensions, and the various forms of injustice that were rampant in the country, but it would take him another seven years to put the pieces together.

— III —

The world had gone through a profound shift culturally and politically from when Randy first heard Fats Domino to when he signed with January Music—from grandfatherly, former World War II general Dwight D. Eisenhower in the White House to the charismatic, forty-four-year-old John F. Kennedy, who promised the nation to put a man in space and enact meaningful civil rights reform. It was an exhilarating time to be young, and Randy felt part of that, but the youthful optimism was shattered by the rifle shots in Dallas in November of 1963; the world suddenly seemed in turmoil at every turn, from escalating war in Vietnam to racial inequality at home.

Twelve years after the milestone US Supreme Court decision *Brown v. Board of Education* had ruled racial segregation in public schools unconstitutional in 1953, little had changed—as a large percentage of white parents, north and south, resisted student busing or redrawing boundary lines.

After reading about racial unrest around the country for years—from Emmitt Till's lynching to the murders of three Freedom Riders in the South—Newman watched as Los Angeles's long-simmering racial problems erupted in the summer of 1965. The city's ruling class had kept Blacks mostly confined, through segregated housing and police targeting. But Black anger over injustice shook Southern California on the evening of August 11 after a Highway Patrol motorcycle officer stopped Marquette Frye, a twenty-one-year-old Black man in a 1955 Buick, on suspicion of reckless driving in the overwhelmingly Black neighborhood of Watts, about twenty miles from the Palisades.

Amid charges of police brutality, the situation escalated into six days of conflict, including thirty-four people killed (nearly two-thirds of them Black), more than 1,000 injured, just under 3,500 arrested, and more than $40 million in property damages. Scenes of the uprising filled Los Angeles television screens. Much of that week's fury was traced to the passage a year earlier, with overwhelming white support, of a state ballot measure that overturned a 1963 state fair housing act aimed at ending decades of tyrannical racial segregation in housing in California. (The proposition was declared unconstitutional in 1966 by the California Supreme Court.)

A state commission, headed by former CIA director John A. McCone, released a report the following December that pointed to reasons behind the rage in Watts and other Black neighborhoods, including high unemployment, inferior schools, and second-class living conditions. Recommendations ranged from improved schools and better police-community communications to more low-cost housing and more adequate health-care facilities. Decades later, millions of Americans would point to the same issues.

"The Watts riots had a profound effect on me," Randy said. "Watching it, you could see the fires up and down Vermont and Western. I don't know why it took me so long to write about the subject. I knew pretty early that race was the big issue in this country." It would take a few years for Newman to figure out how to deal with these issues in his songs, but the seed was planted. Feeling he had taken all the necessary music courses, he would leave UCLA a few courses shy of a degree (he was later awarded a BA degree) to devote even more time to his songwriting. He soon produced his first pop standard.

— IV —

"I Think It's Going to Rain Today" combined a dark but tender melody with sad, despondent images to touch listeners so deeply that it would eventually stand as the most recorded of all his songs, including versions by Judy Collins, Barbra Streisand, Peggy Lee, Bobby Darin, Nina Simone, and Peter Gabriel. It would be the third song from the Schroeder period that Randy would include on his debut album. "Rain" was an advance for him musically and lyrically. In the somber tune, he uses a major key of A to tell the quiet and downbeat story rather than go with the more traditional minor key that is often associated with sadness and drama. He goes on to use a complex series of chord progressions to accompany the characterization that he wants the music to convey. The bridge of the song is so different from the mainstream pop harmonic repertoire that it works to emphasize the enigmatic lyrics.

Part of its appeal are lyrics so elastic that the song can strike listeners as cynical or comforting. In an interview with the BBC, Newman said "Rain" is "a song about empathy; it's a song about the fact that we all have pain, we all have sorrow."

Even so, Randy would speak about the song at various times with misgivings. "I wrote it at my parents' house, and I remember looking out the window," he said. "It was a sunny day, and I started playing something, and the song suddenly went in a different direction. I liked it very much at first. It did what many of my songs don't do—it was a direct feeling. The guy's down. But I went through a time when I was critical of it."

Broken windows and empty hallways
A pale dead moon in the sky streaked with gray
Human kindness is overflowing
And I think it's going to rain today
Scarecrows dressed in the latest styles
With frozen smiles to chase love away
Human kindness is overflowing
And I think it's going to rain today

Lonely, lonely
Tin can at my feet
Think I'll kick it down the street
That's the way to treat a friend

Bright before me the signs implore me
Help the needy and show them the way
Human kindness is overflowing
And I think it's going to rain today

Early on, Newman called the song "sophomoric" and "maudlin" in interviews, even suggesting it was written as a spoof of ever-so-sensitive folk-accented songs that were popular at the time. He singled out Simon and Garfunkel in an interview with England's *Disc and Music Echo* in 1969. "I resent Paul Simon's belief in himself as a poet," he said. "I resent his pretention. I don't like people who never come out of the meadow. Or never make a sound louder than 'Ah.'"

The outburst was surprising for someone whom the publication described as a "shy and unassuming man, definitely modest about his own ability as a writer." Perhaps rattled himself by his harsh comment, Newman continued. "Don't get me wrong, though. I pick on Simon and Garfunkel because they are well known . . . and they make nice records, which I like listening to. It's just that I have to look at things critically. And the person I pick on most anyway is myself." In time, he would become a major Simon admirer.

Newman didn't name a specific record as his target, but the duo's "The Sound of Silence" was dominating pop radio in America in the weeks before he sent "Rain" to Schroeder in the early weeks of 1966. The tone of both songs was wounded, and both were influenced by the ambition and wordplay that Dylan brought to the pop world, though both Simon and Newman soon would move away from Dylan to pursue their own musical concepts.

But there was another, more personal reason for Newman's discomfort. Decades later, he acknowledged in one of our interviews that he let too much of himself slip into the song. "Maybe the whole thing was that it was too close to the way I was," he said.

Parts of the "Rain" lyrics did fit the profile of someone who, as several close to him suggested, had a glass-half-empty nature. Unlike people who wake up on a sunny day and say, "What a lovely day," a longtime Newman observer told me, "Randy is more likely to stare at the same blue sky and say he thinks it's going to rain," the friend said. "He worries about everything."

All of which helps reinforce the nature of someone who often preferred being at home in the comfort of his den, a trait that would surprise those—including journalists—who met him at social occasions or for interviews where he was unfailingly gracious and warm. "Basically, he has always been an outsider; he never felt comfortable being around people, though he does very well in those situations," Waronker said. "He works at being comfortable regardless of his insecurities. He's too well-mannered to just sit down and ignore people. But he's concerned about how he's doing; he's never had real confidence. If he goes to a party, he's usually the first one to arrive and the first to leave."

Asked years later about his homebody nature, he said, "I don't want to go anywhere much, I never have, whether it's shyness or laziness or what. Maybe the best word is 'apathetic.'"

As soon as the January Music staff heard Randy's demo of "Rain," the search began for someone to record it, though there is no sign that Schroeder's team recognized how special the song was. If the company had sensed the song's potential, the smart move would have been to hold out for the most respected singer possible. Instead, the song ended up with Julius La Rosa, a capable but undistinguished pop figure whose biggest hit was an Italian novelty song, "Eh, Cumpari," in 1953. He couldn't have been further from the young, contemporary market that was now the creative and commercial center of pop. La Rosa's version was recorded on May 20 and released by MGM Records as a single, but it flopped. That could have been the end of "Rain" except that tapes of Randy's demo fell into the hands of other industry figures, one of whom was Judy Collins.

Born in Seattle in 1939, Collins grew up around music; her father, a singer and pianist, exposed her to folk music, including trailblazing figures Woody Guthrie and Pete Seeger. Hoping to be a singer, Collins moved in 1961 to New York's Greenwich Village, the heart of the nation's growing folk music movement. After just a few club appearances, she was signed by Elektra Records, a leader in contemporary folk at the time. The *New York Times* pop critic John Rockwell would later describe Collins's appeal this way: "She is the eternal pretty, romantic, idealistic, lonely young girl, full of soft, yearning dreams." By her third album, *Judy Collins 3* in 1964, Collins was moving from traditional folk music to songs by some of the nation's rising young songwriters.

"The Village was crawling with fabulous songwriters," she said. "Because I was the only girl singer in town who didn't write her own material, everyone started coming up to me with their songs. I'd just walk the street and Tom Paxton or someone would come up and give me a tape of his new song or sing it for me."

Collins was preparing to record her sixth album, *In My Life*, in 1966 when a friend (she doesn't remember who) passed along Randy's demo of "Rain." She immediately added it to the album, alongside tunes by Dylan, Leonard Cohen, Kurt Weill, Jacques Brel, and Lennon-McCartney. "I flipped out over the song, which is how I am," she said. "When I hear a song, I know immediately if it's right for me. I don't sit back try to analyze it. I don't even think about the meaning. I just ask myself, 'Is this something I want to sing?'"

The album was her most successful yet, breaking into the Top 50 on the pop charts. Months after visualizing himself as part of the pop elite on the New York visit, Randy had a song on an album alongside some of the most respected artists of the era.

— V —

Just as Randy was wrestling with his future direction in 1966, Lenny asked a big favor. He had finally joined the A&R staff at Warner, and his bosses were desperate for a song for one of their new acts—the son of the label's biggest selling artist and former co-owner. Francis Wayne Sinatra, known professionally as Frank Sinatra Jr., started singing in clubs in his teens and was ready in the mid-1960s to attempt a recording career.

Lenny flashed on a radio-friendly, youth-oriented song with a killer riff that Randy had started working on at Metric, but soon discarded. Lenny was embarrassed to ask him to revive the old song, "Susie," but he needed this. As the newcomer in A&R, Waronker was assigned the tedious and unglamorous task of listening to all the unsolicited tapes the label received regularly from songwriting hopefuls, on the off chance that one of them seemed promising. If he found a suitable song for Sinatra Jr., it could be a big step toward becoming a Warner producer with his own acts.

Randy—who Waronker has lauded as the most loyal person he ever met—understood, and located the sixty-second tape, which was so aimless and silly that you can tell why he lost interest in the song. He tried to pick up where he left off, but after going through a few rhymes—Susie, doozy, bluesy—the phrase "coat to wear" came to him. That, somehow, led to "bear" and was the start of the lilting, upbeat "Simon Smith and the Amazing Dancing Bear."

It was that fast—one of those serendipitous moments that songwriters talk about when a song suddenly presents itself. As always, Randy was soon on the phone to Lenny even though he knew it wasn't the song Waronker needed. Before singing "Simon Smith," he even said, "Sorry, Len." Lenny didn't care. He loved "Simon Smith." The song showcased Randy's ability to weave together social observation, mirth, and musical touches that were as suitable for Broadway musicals, or even vaudeville, as they were for pop. The "Simon" song seemed straightforward on the surface, a fanciful feel-good story of a young man celebrating good times with a lovable dancing bear. The lyrics:

I may go out tomorrow if I can borrow a coat to wear
Oh, I'd step out in style with my sincere smile and my
dancing bear
Outrageous, alarming, courageous, charming
Oh, who would think a boy and bear

Could be well accepted everywhere
It's just amazing how fair people can be

Seen at the nicest places where well-fed faces all stop to stare
Making the grandest entrance is Simon Smith and his
    dancing bear
They'll love us, won't they?
They feed us, don't they?
Oh, who would think a boy and bear
Could be well accepted everywhere
It's just amazing how fair people can be

Who needs money when you're funny?
The big attraction everywhere
Will be Simon Smith and his dancing bear
It's Simon Smith and his amazing dancing bear

As with "Rain," however, Randy's interesting images led some
listeners to wonder about a possible second layer to the tune.

Why did the young man need to borrow a coat?
What was he saying in the line "how fair people can be"?
Did people accept him only because of the cute bear?
Do you need a gimmick, like a dancing bear, to break
    through a layer of social indifference?

Where "Rain" had the feel of a pop classic, "Simon Smith"
was seen as a good-natured novelty, and there wasn't the same
rush by other singers in America to record it. But Alan Price, a
British singer with tastes ranging from rock to English music
hall, zeroed in on the wit and carnival-like sparkle of the song.
A year older than Newman, Price was the original keyboardist
for the Animals, a band whose aggressive mixture of blues and

R & B made it a leading force in the British rock invasion of America, thanks to such hits as "Don't Let Me Be Misunderstood." While lead singer Eric Burdon's growly vocal style made him the band's most identifiable member, Price's organ work was also a winning feature.

Burdon and Price were moving in different career directions in 1966 but shared an interest in Newman's songs. Burdon featured three of them on his *Eric Is Here* album, which he recorded in the fall of 1966. They included "I Think It's Going to Rain Today" and "Mama Told Me Not to Come," the wildly amusing story of the psychedelic-spiked party scenes that would become a symbol of 1960s youth culture. "I was writing about a kind of frightened person at a party," Randy said. "It wasn't me, but I do remember going to a party and thinking about how noisy and dark it was, and everybody asking these questions."

It begins:

Will you have whiskey with your water
Or sugar with your tea?
What are these crazy questions
That they're asking of me?
This is the wildest party that there ever could be
Oh, don't turn on the light 'cause I don't want to see

~

Eric Is Here was only released in the United States, where it went unnoticed, but "Mama" was too infectious to be forgotten; the song would resurface four years later at the top of the US pop charts in a recording by the pop-rock group Three Dog Night.

Price, meanwhile, released a single of "Simon Smith" in Britain in the spring of 1967, and it went to No. 4 on the charts, leading him to record seven more Newman compositions for his next album, *A Price on His Head*. As for "Simon Smith," Price was surprised when critics started reading hidden meanings in it. He told journalists that he simply liked "childlike songs."

Paul McCartney was another fan. As a guest reviewer for the British pop weekly *Melody Maker*, the Beatle predicted the record would be a hit. "It's so much better than the period, vaudeville stuff because it's a bit modern," he wrote, adding playfully: "It's hip. . . . No, I hate to see that word in print. It's good. 'Good' doesn't date like 'hip.' Yes, I like Simon Smith and his high-class dancing bear."

When Newman looked back years later at his songs of that period, he seemed to side with Price. He didn't feel he was making a statement in "Simon Smith," describing it as simply the story of someone finding he could use humor or a loveable bear to get people to accept him. He felt that the song's most distinguishing feature was its whimsy. "There's not a lot of humor in pop music," he said. "And I think that caught a lot of people's attention, especially inside the music industry in England. It helped me stand a bit apart. I picked up on humor early. The first time I played a comedic song was at a friend's house in Santa Monica when he asked me to play something for his mother— and she laughed. It made a big impression on me."

During his teens, Newman relished the humorous bite and commentary of a new wave of strikingly original comedians whose irreverent social observations were as revolutionary (and sometimes sold as many albums) as rock musicians. Among his favorites at the time were Lenny Bruce, Bob Newhart, Jonathan Winters, and the team of Mike Nichols and Elaine May.

Going forward, Randy wouldn't just rely on humor, however; he would also use his songs to make statements.

CHAPTER FIVE

Lenny, Mo, and
Warner Bros. Records

— I —

Lenny Waronker's quiet, understated demeanor sometimes blinded industry competitors to his strong sense of ambition. From the earliest days at Liberty, he longed to hold a key position at a major record company, and he couldn't have landed at a better one than Warner Bros., where he immediately began thinking about how to bring Randy along with him. Apart from his initial resolve to push his friend into pop music, the Warner connection would be his most important contribution to building Randy's career. Formed in 1958 as the recording wing of the Warner Bros. movie studio, the Burbank company wasn't a major label in the 1960s, but it would soon become one thanks largely to the philosophy and steady hand of Mo Ostin, a widely admired executive who believed in concentrating on artists who were as visionary as they were talented.

Born Morris Meyer Ostrofsky in New York in 1927, Ostin was a jazz fan who majored in economics at UCLA and followed his love of music to become comptroller at Norman Granz's Clef Records, a jazz outpost whose roster included Charlie Parker and Count Basie. Granz soon made Clef part of Verve Records, which was such a model operation that Frank Sinatra—disenchanted with his longtime musical home, Capitol Records—tried to buy it with the goal of giving artists more creative freedom.

Outbid by MGM Records, Sinatra teamed up with Warner Bros. in 1960 to start Reprise. In the process, he lured Ostin from Verve to run the new label, where Ostin worked alongside Joe Smith, a former Boston DJ, on the Warner Bros. side. The reserved Ostin, who was named president of the combined labels in 1970, and the personable, outgoing Smith worked together so well that Warner for years was known in the music business as the "Mo and Joe Show."

In his three decades at Warner, Ostin relied heavily on Sinatra's artist-oriented philosophy in building the label into arguably the most powerful and respected record company in America, with a roster that would also include Prince, Madonna, Neil Young, Fleetwood Mac, and R.E.M. "Frank's whole idea was to create an environment [that] both artistically and economically would be more attractive for the artist than [what] anybody else had to offer. That wasn't how it was anywhere else," Ostin said. "You had financial guys, lawyers, marketing guys. Their priorities may not have been the music. One of the great things about Warner, I always felt, was [that] our emphasis and priority was always about the music."

Warner was slow getting into rock, partially because Sinatra insisted on no rock and roll. Sinatra hated rock and roll. But Ostin recognized the importance of joining Columbia, Atlantic, and other rivals in embracing this cultural and commercial revolution. Aside from the Everly Brothers, the Burbank team's only significant rock act at the start of 1966 was England's the Kinks, which was signed by the Reprise division after Ostin convinced Sinatra the label would go broke if it didn't sign rock acts. By the end of the 1960s, Warner-Reprise (simply Warner from now on in this text) would sign such gifted and original artists as Jimi

Hendrix, Joni Mitchell, Neil Young, the Grateful Dead, James Taylor, and Randy Newman.

But first, Joe Smith, who was convinced that San Francisco was going to be the next hotbed of rock, made a signing early in 1966 that would give Lenny's career a major boost. Smith, who would later sign the Dead, purchased the financially troubled Autumn Records, whose chief attraction at the time was the Beau Brummels, a band that had scored a Top 20 single with the hook-filled "Laugh, Laugh." When none of Warner's established A&R producers apparently had interest in the Autumn acts except the Brummels, Smith turned to Lenny, still the new kid on the block, and asked him to comb through the roster on the off chance there was a hidden gem.

Expectations were low, but Lenny took the assignment seriously and saw a glimmer of potential in two acts, the Tikis and the Mojo Men. Assuming the role of producer for both groups, he started searching for material and found a song for the Mojo Men right away—Stephen Stills's "Sit Down, I Think I Love You" from the first Buffalo Springfield album. Rather than follow the model of producers who make all the decisions on a recording, Lenny relied on the lesson he picked up on *Three Little Words*—the value of collaboration. Needing an arranger, he turned to Van Dyke Parks, a young pop visionary with outside-the-box musical interests like Randy's—from ragtime to orchestral.

But how could Waronker convince someone who had worked with Brian Wilson on the Beach Boys' ill-fated but inspired *Smile* concept album to get involved with such a small-time project? He went all out, offering Parks carte blanche. Parks responded with a baroque arrangement that combined Beach Boys sunshine with a wide array of imaginative musical brushstrokes that sounded fresh yet in line with the decade's fascination with psychedelic touches.

While working with the Mojo Men, Lenny was also trying to find a song for the Tikis, a Bay Area outfit that had started as a Beatles cover band. He had become intrigued by the group's high-pitched vocals and wanted a song that could showcase them. He found it on the car radio on the way to work in the final weeks of fall: a delightful, carefree number from an upcoming Simon & Garfunkel album, *Parsley, Sage, Rosemary, and Thyme*. Getting an advance copy, Lenny was surprised to find that the song—"The 59th Street Bridge Song (Feelin' Groovy)"— was only a minute and a half long, too short for a commercial single. Unable to get the song out of his head, he stretched the Simon composition to two and a half minutes, which was ideal for radio formats.

For the arrangement this time, he recalled Leon Russell's impressive work at Metric. Once again, he asked the budding rock star if there was anything he wanted to try in the studio, and it turned out that Russell had been longing to record something using flutes the way people usually use strings. It sounded strange, but Lenny told him to do it. The Tikis didn't like the song or Russell's arrangement. They even changed their name on the "Groovy" record to Harpers Bizarre (a play on the magazine *Harper's Bazaar*) because they didn't want to damage the Tikis name with what they privately feared was going to be an "appalling" record.

In late November, the band went into Western Recorders Studio in Hollywood to record "Bridge" with a session lineup that included Glen Campbell on guitar and Leon on harpsichord. Waronker made the group's Ted Templeman and Dick Scoppettone do their vocals over and over until he felt they were right—as many as thirty takes. The band went home exhausted and discouraged.

Both singles entered the *Billboard* chart in February of 1967, each resting in the Top 40 in March. Where the Mojo Men peaked at No. 36, the Harper's Bizarre single climbed to No. 13. Simon, who was notoriously hard to please, liked the record enough to look up Waronker on his next trip to Los Angeles and congratulate him. The twin hits gave Lenny's confidence a major boost, and he started thinking of ways to involve Randy.

Sensing the potential of the Harpers Bizarre's single, Lenny was already putting together an album for the band. At the time, record companies typically responded to a surprise hit single by rushing out an album as fast as possible, surrounding the single with cover songs, instrumentals, or other blatant filler. The goal was to get fans to spend four dollars on an album containing the hit song rather than shell out under one dollar for the 45 rpm single. Lenny wanted a real album, backing the single with carefully designed versions of appealing new songs or imaginative cover versions. To help him, he began assembling his own repertory group—led by Randy, Van Dyke and, eventually, guitarist Ry Cooder. Lenny would have added Russell, but Leon was signed to Dot Records.

— II —

There wasn't a more fascinating figure in the music business in Los Angeles in the mid-1960s than Van Dyke Parks, a world-class raconteur who could fascinate you with his wise, old-school aura and knack for coming up with tantalizing musical ideas with the ease of someone striking a match.

By the time the Hattiesburg, Mississippi, native moved to LA in the early 1960s, he had worked as a child actor in New York (including appearing as a neighbor on Jackie Gleason's *The Honeymooners* sitcom) and studied piano and composition at Carnegie Tech. Brian Wilson, the most respected young musician in Los Angeles at the time, was so intrigued by Parks's ideas about music that he hired him to write lyrics and arrangements for *Smile,* the follow-up to the Beach Boys' triumphant *Pet Sounds* album. That alone led most record executives to think about signing Parks; the problem was they didn't know if his unique musical vision could sell records. Yet Lenny seized the moment and signed Van Dyke to Warner, where Parks felt an immediate connection with Newman. Van Dyke was twenty-four, and Randy was twenty-three.

Ry Cooder would soon join Lenny's team and he, too, was independent, inspired more by colorful American roots music than by what was on the charts. Born in Los Angeles in 1947, Cooder fell in love with country music—"hillbilly" as he preferred to call it—and later embraced vintage folk and blues sounds. In junior high, he was playing guitar and checking out his heroes at the Ash Grove, a local club whose headliners ranged from Muddy Waters and Howlin' Wolf to Doc Watson and Bill Monroe. During his mid-teens, Cooder's countless hours watching his favorites as part of the Ash Grove's audience evolved into him playing guitar on the club's stage. He later was in a group with contemporary bluesman Taj Mahal and on sessions for Captain Beefheart's cult gem *Safe as Milk*.

Wary of how major labels could corrupt musicians by pushing them in increasingly commercial directions, he felt a kinship with the Warner contingent. He had learned from playing studio sessions elsewhere that quality wasn't the chief goal of most producers.

"It was obvious . . . that if I wanted to keep playing the same rock-and-roll bottleneck guitar licks I could work a lot of sessions and make a lot of money," Cooder said. "But I also knew that I'd eventually be strip-mined. I could feel it beginning to happen, the tendency of people to say, 'Just do the same thing you did on that last record.' You'd try to tell them you could do something better, but they'd say, 'We don't want better. We want the same.' You get to where you don't feel like you are making music, you are just stamping out music." At Warner, Waronker promised Cooder that he could record his own album, and that led to a series of tasteful, influential collections.

For his part, Randy was still a writer and arranger with no concrete thoughts about making his own records, but he enjoyed the adventurous musical atmosphere at Warner. He would even look back on his early years there as a musical graduate school. "Every time you do something when you are starting out, you learn so much," Randy said. "That was especially true of that first album with Harpers Bizarre. You're always asking yourself, 'Is this right?' 'Should I double that? Did I leave room for the guitarist?' I learned the best time I have in the studio is with an orchestra. It helped prepare me to make my own album."

Lenny believed Randy's playful sensibilities would be perfect for Harpers Bizarre and asked him to write and arrange two songs. Templeman, who would later be a Warner producer who worked with such artists as Van Morrison and Van Halen, was skeptical. "Skinny and bespectacled, Randy looked more like an architect than a musician," Templeman thought upon first meeting him. After hearing some of Randy's songs, however, he was sold. "Lenny was right," he wrote in his autobiography. "Randy was a hell of a writer."

The first song Newman played for Templeman was a colorful piece that would have fit nicely in a Cole Porter musical about high society. In "The Debutante's Ball," Randy lets us know quickly that he's speaking of the upper crust by noting that the male party guests needed a number after their name to be invited:

Oh, I think Quentin B. Taylor the Third is here
And I see John Thomas Bailey the Ninth
And I guess every rich girl in the world is here
And they all have the time of their life

He also applied back-to-back Porter-esque rhymes:

Oh, if you're invited
You should be delighted
Not everyone's asked to come
No one gets stoned
It's all chaperoned

Equally inviting was the lively orchestral arrangement that spoke to Newman's goal of making the listener see as well as hear what was taking place. To establish the formal dance feel, he employed a waltz rhythm and a flashy, party-spirited instrumentation— lots of flutes and brass, both of which were uncommon in pop music at the time. A backing chorus and a forty-five-piece orchestra added to the society ball atmosphere.

For Waronker, the song helped define the band's new identity— sweet-sounding voices with an edge to them. A second Newman composition, the equally theatrical "Happyland," recalled how old-fashioned carousels speak to the child in all of us—again with an arrangement that makes you feel you are walking among the carnival rides and games of chance.

Lenny's repertory group contributed four other songs to the album—Randy's "Simon Smith," two selections co-written by Russell, and Parks's "Come to the Sunshine," another Beach Boys–flavored welcome to summer built around a fireworks display of orchestral sounds. To add to the LP's daring range, the lineup included versions of Rodgers & Hammerstein's "Happy Talk" from the musical *South Pacific* and Prokofiev's *Peter and the Wolf.* Thanks to the single's exposure, the album reached No. 108 on the pop charts that summer—ninety places higher than the new Beau Brummel LP.

The album, titled *Feelin' Groovy,* also brought another welcome validation. Soon after it was released in April, Alfred Newman phoned to congratulate Lenny and Randy on its musicality. It was one of the few times Randy heard any approval from his uncles. Alfred would soon be offering Randy more congratulations. After three years of dating, Roswitha and Randy decided in early 1967 to get married.

— III —

Before setting a date, the couple went through the old-country custom of Randy formally asking Roswitha's parents for her hand. The truth, she knew, was that her parents, who still lived in Germany, weren't happy with the idea. She had been gently breaking the news about their relationship for some time, and her parents were protective; they hadn't met Randy, and they were likely hoping for a son-in-law with a secure career, not a songwriter. Eventually, Randy wrote a letter to the Schmales.

> I'm sorry not to have written sooner, but I've been very busy and this letter is very important to Roswitha and me. I wanted to devote some time to it. I'm sure Roswitha has told you something about me, but I think you deserve to hear something from me concerning what I do and what I want for Roswitha and myself.
>
> I'm twenty-four years old [and] was born in Los Angeles where I live with my mother and father. My father's a doctor. Both my mother and my father and my brother Alan, who is nineteen, love Roswitha very much as I guess everyone who has ever known her must love her. I'm a composer of music and though I know this might not seem the most secure job in the world, I do receive a weekly salary from a music publisher and with other outside work I do for motion pictures and television, I manage to do fairly well. Music is very important to me and I want to be as successful in it as I can. I've wanted nothing else as a career since I was a child.

As you know I have asked Roswitha to marry me and she said, "yes." Of course, neither she nor I would do anything without the approval of our parents. I know it must be difficult to think of your daughter living so far away, but I can only ask for your approval of our marriage and reassure you that I will make Roswitha as happy as I can. . . . I do love her very much and I think she loves me. On your approval, we plan to be married on June 17 of this year. I hope to hear from you soon. Deepest respect and love, Randy.

Roswitha's parents granted their approval, along with the hope that he would marry their Catholic daughter "in a church or is that not likely."

~

Randy and Roswitha were married in a June wedding in Las Vegas, still the family's favorite getaway spot. In a ceremony in the couple's room at the Sahara Hotel, a justice of the peace began with a stock joke about gambling. "He said marriage is not a 100 percent proposition—sometimes it's fifty-fifty, sometimes sixty-forty." Alan Newman said, "He was quoting the odds in Vegas—which was perfect. I was praying Randy would not catch my eye or I would have totally cracked up."

"Roswitha was really a take-charge type, which is what Randy needed," Foster Sherwood said. "When they got married, Randy's mom made a big point of handing his checkbook over to Roswitha because she knew Randy wouldn't know what to do with it."

As friends saw it, Roswitha was born for the support role Randy needed. As a child in Düsseldorf, Germany, she went through a series of traumas; the family house was bombed during World War II, and her older brother was killed when stairs collapsed. In addition, her mother suffered from a brain tumor.

From the age of three, Roswitha was the family's acting care-taker. She learned the trade so early that it was second nature when she came to America, if not first nature. Acknowledging his own dependency, Newman himself later told *Rolling Stone*, "I need someone to take care of me. I could have been to a place fifty times and still get lost. When she goes away to visit her family in Germany, the ship begins to sink."

The newlyweds moved into a rented house on Laurel Terrace Drive in Studio City, closer to the Warner headquarters in Burbank where Randy was spending much of his time with Lenny. Randy wasn't signed to the label, but he was at the center of a vision Lenny had at Warner.

— IV —

Lenny next turned to Randy to write two songs for the second Harpers Bizarre album, principally "The Biggest Night of Her Life," another theatrical number whose story seemed to be about a girl looking forward to her sixteenth birthday party, but whose suggestive undercurrents suggested she was hoping to lose her virginity. Released a few months after *Feelin' Groovy*, the second LP, *Anything Goes*, went slightly higher on the charts, but it was the last chart album by the group.

Increasingly confident in Randy's ability to deliver whatever was needed, Lenny then asked him to write a song for Van Dyke's debut album that would prove far from the widescreen exercises he wrote for Harpers Bizarre. "Vine Street" was a wistful reflection of the innocence and struggle of a musician's early days. In keeping with Parks's own bold sonic sensibilities, the track featured an effervescent, string-heavy arrangement that reflected a buoyancy and freedom that felt rooted in his cinematic instincts.

For the most part Parks wrote the other tunes—a celebration of pure musical imagination with little regard for conventional pop boundaries. Parks was fascinated with music of various stripes, leading him to blend American genres, bluegrass to Broadway, to link the country's past and present sensibilities. It was a dazzling album. When it was finished, much of the Warner brass, however, was shocked to learn the eight-month project had cost $87,000, more than any previous Warner LP by far. When Waronker and Parks played the album for Joe Smith, who would later head Elektra/Asylum Records and Capitol Records, he admired the orchestral imagination but didn't hear anything that could appeal to radio programmers. He looked at the album title, *Song Cycle*, and asked, "Where are the songs?"

Smith wasn't alone in that view, but Ostin and Waronker had such respect for Parks that the album was released during the final weeks of 1967. As feared, the majestic work was too far from pop convention to pick up any airplay. A typical program director question was, "How does this fit into rock and roll?" Sales didn't even reach 5,000 copies.

Critics, however, were enthusiastic, including Pete Johnson, who praised Parks in a perceptive piece in the *Los Angeles Times*: "It's not what you would call a rock 'n' roll record. In fact, there is no term for what it is, its only link to recent developments in pop music being its emancipation from traditional musical structures. It is an always serious album, though the solemnity sometimes bursts into humor. Sixty-five people are credited with making musical sounds on the album, but their diverse efforts are unified by a mind which is painfully involved in producing an audible artistic imprint of his joys and sorrows."

Lenny wasn't worried that he was straying too far from the commercial pulse of rock. It was a time of experimentation; the most important artists were taking risks. Dylan angered his early folk following in 1965 when he went electric, and Brian Wilson and Lennon-McCartney were locked in what seemed like a personal struggle to outdo each other by moving creatively into new areas—Wilson responding with the landmark album, *Pet Sounds*, after hearing the Beatles' *Rubber Soul*, and the Beatles, in turn, delivering *Sgt. Pepper's Lonely Hearts Club Band*. And so it went.

Newman and Parks weren't alone in looking beyond the three-chords-and-a-guitar blueprint of rock. Laura Nyro, Jimmy Webb, and Harry Nilsson were also songwriters with emotional ties to the Great American Songbook days. Paul Simon was also headed toward a solo career in which he would constantly evolve, eventually creating a synthesis of the best of earlier decades and contemporary musical textures from around the world.

"I felt during that time that the goal in making records was to grow and to change," Waronker said. "It was almost like an obligation—it's what kept the music exciting."

— V —

Things had been going so well that Lenny was shocked to learn that his relationship with Randy was threatened in the summer of 1967 when A&M Records, another upcoming LA label that would become an industry power, was trying to sign Randy as a recording artist. The company had heard enough good things about Randy to use one of his songs, "Snow," on a Christmas single for singer Claudine Longet in 1966. When Liza Minnelli recorded her first A&M album, her songwriter-husband Peter Allen and producer Larry Marks chose three Newman songs, including "The Debutante's Ball" and "Happyland." Seeing Randy as someone who could record his own songs, A&M offered him a $10,000 recording contract. They weren't worried about Randy's gritty vocals. This was the company that would soon sign Joe Cocker.

Lenny had been wanting to sign Randy but felt he needed to establish himself more at Warner so it wouldn't look like he was just signing Randy because they were friends. Now that A&M had stepped in, Lenny tried to tell himself that Randy would never walk away, but Randy had left him before—for January Music. Randy, in turn, was upset that Warner didn't seem willing to match the A&M offer when Lenny did start talking about a contract. For a moment it appeared Randy might sign with the rival label. When Lenny explained the situation to Ostin, however, the label chief stepped in and matched the $10,000 contract. As of September 15, 1967, Randy Newman was on the Warner roster.

~

As the new year approached, Lenny felt it was time to make Randy's first album, and he asked Van Dyke to co-produce with him. "I think we had an ideal team that really worked well on Randy's album," Parks said. "Randy was determined not to make the same mistakes that I did with being obscure. He had songs that [spoke] about the American experience and told them so beautifully."

It wasn't a total step into the unknown for Lenny, because he had been hearing some of Randy's new songs for some time. One of the reasons he waited was he wanted to give Randy time in the studio to become familiar with the recording process. Even with Lenny's guidance, Randy, however, feared the worst. "I would go to his place in Studio City in the morning to pick Randy up [on the way to the recording studio], and I can remember a siege mentality before a session," Parks said. "He was smart enough to be scared to death."

PART TWO

Around the time of Randy Newman's *12 Songs*, his second album, way back in the late sixties, his producer, Lenny Waronker, liked to call him "The King of Suburban Blues Singers." There was an affinity between Robert Johnson, whose *King of the Delta Blues Singers*, a collection of songs recorded in 1936 and 1937, shared a sense of fate as a joke everyone would get sooner or later.

Me and the devil, was walking side by side
Me and the devil, was walking side by side
You can hold my hand, honey, you know I love to see you
   smile

It wouldn't be long before Randy would play the devil himself in *Sail Away*, and as the slave recruiter tempting Africans on the boat to the USA, enter into a classic role, the Yankee Pedlar, the Slick Willie, the All-American con artist, who can sell swampland in Florida to New Englanders and the Middle Passage as a vacation. "He traded the landlord out of bed and breakfast and left with most of the money in the settlement," Constance Rourke wrote in 1931 in *American Humor* of her match to Randy's slave man—the only difference being that he left with all the people.

As a song title, "A Few Words in Defense of Our Country" is the book Randy Newman has been writing all these many decades down the pike. He's played every role, from the worst to—everyone else, he himself hiding in the same crowd of anyone listening.

GREIL MARCUS, author of *Mystery Train*

I don't remember when Randy Newman burst into my life, but I will never forget the song "Political Science." It was such a funny, smart, original take on the absurdity of nuclear war. I quickly memorized the lyrics and to this day can sing the whole song. I thought about it a lot after 9/11, when one of the big questions that arose was: "Why does everyone hate us?" Whenever I saw or heard that question, I thought of the line in Randy's song: "They all hate us anyhow, so let's drop the big one now!" The cleverness of the lyrics, their ability to capture the mood of the times, and the catchiness of the melody were all pure Randy Newman.

THOMAS FRIEDMAN, three-time Pulitzer-winning columnist,
New York Times

My favorite Randy Newman song is "Living Without You," a cut from his first record, from 1968. It's short, barely two and a half minutes, but it contains everything that made Newman such a singular writer: pathos, belligerence, urgency, ennui, sensitivity, bottomless emotional intelligence. Something wildly and unabashedly human. The instrumentation gets loud and frenzied just as Newman starts repeating "It's so hard, baby, it's SO HARD"— it's as if Newman himself can barely stand the depth and earnestness of his own suffering. He has to make fun of it a little. I can't think of another song that captures the tedium and hopelessness of heartbreak quite so astutely. It took me decades to realize that there's no way to soothe that kind of loss, to make it end when you want it to end. Newman knew this in his early twenties: "Ev'ry one's got something / And they're out tryin' to get some more / They got something to get up for / Well, I ain't about to." It's a declaration of defeat, and it is perfect.

AMANDA PETRUSICH, pop critic for the *New Yorker*

CHAPTER SIX

A Classic Debut Album
"Love Story" and
"Davy the Fat Boy"

— I —

On the afternoon of December 8, 1967, Newman went into the Western Recorders studio in Hollywood to begin work on an album that proved to be one of the most accomplished debuts of the rock era. The eleven songs mixed reflections on American attitudes with cinematic orchestral textures—a blend of an old Newman family musical tradition and a touch of what would become a new one.

Randy was twenty-four when the LP was released the following April—about the same first-album age as three singer-songwriters against whom he would be measured throughout his career: Dylan was two months shy of his twenty-first birthday when his self-titled debut album arrived; Paul Simon was twenty-three as the first Simon and Garfunkel LP reached stores; and Joni Mitchell was twenty-four when she completed her debut. In the end, Newman's collection would stand as the most substantial. Over half a century later, it still has the feel of a masterpiece.

Ellen Willis, whose writings in the *New Yorker* and elsewhere in the late 1960s placed her at the forefront of the nation's first wave of rock critics, hailed the debut in an insightful review that could well apply to every album Newman would make. She declared that the songs "show an intimate familiarity with, and an affection for, all the nuances of American life—the setting and characters, the family relationships, the romantic fantasies, the euphemisms—as well as an unsparing awareness of our oppression of old people, fat people, and other nonmainstream types."

Lenny watched in awe at Randy's capturing of the moment:

He grew up in a great neighborhood, so his story wasn't about survival in the normal sense. As he got older, it was more about survival as an artist and as a composer. He didn't come from an easy family—the Newmans were tough and competitive. Songwriting helped him find himself in a way. Gradually, he would express his anger and pain in his music—and he developed such a strong sense of what's right and what's fair that he wasn't afraid to take on anything. From that first album, however, he wasn't obsessed with being the most popular, he was driven to be the best.

Reflecting on that point years later, Randy told former Warner executive Joe Smith for his book *Off the Record: An Oral History of Popular Music*, "I don't think I was ever hungry for success. I was talking to my mother about that just the other day. She told me I never wanted anything. There was this motor scooter I wanted one time, but I didn't seriously want it because I knew if I got it, I'd die. . . . It wasn't that I was disdainful of success, but it didn't tear me up when I didn't get it."

The songs on the first album gave us such a bold and consistent portrait of American "nuances" that it felt like they were conceived in a single, blinding burst of creative energy. But they were written over three years, yet linked; each was written after the fateful day in 1964 when Newman decided to start writing songs he cared about. The strength of the album was as much sonic as thematic. Uninterested in pursing the three-chord foundation of rock, Newman drew upon his background of classical composition and film music exposure to reinforce and expand what he was saying in the lyrics, much like the way film music enriched what was on the screen. In early interviews, he even laid out his game plan, frequently saying he wanted to pretend the Rolling Stones had never existed. Notably, he didn't say the Beatles because he admired that group's melodic gifts and the classical touches that George Martin helped the quartet explore.

~

One of Waronker's first moves with the album was getting Lee Herschberg, an experienced recording engineer who had worked with Bing Crosby, assigned to the project. Herschberg, who would go on to a Grammy-winning career that included numerous albums with Frank Sinatra, was open to new ideas and so highly regarded around the Warner building that he could help spread the word among the old guard that this kid Newman was special.

"Randy and some of Lenny's other young artists were outside my realm of experience," said the Korean War veteran who was in his late thirties at the time. "For all the [time] I had been working previously to that, the song was the important thing, but they were mostly love songs. These new songs began to have deeper messages, and that was what Randy was about. I was floored by his stuff. It was so unlike anything I had ever heard. Sometimes I even had to ask Lenny what the songs were about."

In the studio, Herschberg, like so many, found Randy to be shy and self-deprecating but unfailingly polite to the musicians. "He was completely comfortable in front of a twenty- or thirty-piece orchestra, but I think he was a bit nervous when he was at the piano by himself. I got the sense he was wondering if people were going to like what he was doing or even understand his music. That's got to be a big thing in the mind of artists, especially daring young ones—thinking 'Here is the record company investing money in me, and am I going to be able to come through with something that's going to reach people, that they're going to buy?' He knew he was doing something different."

— II —

For someone who didn't set out to write love songs, the album's opening track, "Love Story," was a surprise—at least the title. The song was unlike anything you'd have heard on the radio; it felt both classic (orchestral touches that were fresh and alive) and contemporary (attitude and wordplay that felt youthful). The story line carried the wry point of view of one of those engaging single-page sketches in the *New Yorker* that compel readers to tell friends, "You gotta read this."

Newman described "Love Story" as about someone who looked at life with low expectations. "I'm not saying he's a bad guy, I think he's probably a good guy," Randy said. "He's just asking for very little; it's a very impoverished dream. That's what is interesting to me. I liked writing about someone who doesn't have the big *West Side Story* dreams." At the same time, Randy was offering a contrarian view of much of commercial music—a celebration of marriage and the happy-ever-after hopes that were especially popular in the 1950s when he was beginning to pay attention to pop radio. "Love and Marriage," a Frank Sinatra hit from 1955, was typical of the romantic fantasies with its giddy refrain of how love and marriage go together like a horse and carriage.

Against that background, "Love Story" was more powerful in its gentle understatement.

I like your mother
I like your brother
I like you
And you like me, too
We'll get a preacher
I'll buy a ring
We'll hire a band
With an accordion
A violin
And a tenor who can sing

You and me, you and me, baby
You and me, you and me, you and me, baby
You and me, you and me, you and me, baby
You and me, you and me, you and me, baby

We'll have a kid
Or maybe we'll rent one
He's got to be straight
We don't want a bent one

He'll drink his baby brew
From a big brass cup
Someday he may be president
If things loosen up

You and me, you and me, baby
You and me, you and me, you and me, baby
You and me, you and me, you and me, baby
You and me, you and me, you and me, baby

I'll take the train into the city ev'ry mornin'
You may be plain—I think you're pretty in the mornin'

And some nights we'll go out dancin'
If I am not too tired
Some nights we'll sit romancin'
Watching the Late Show *by the fire*

When our kids are grown
With kids of their own
They'll send us away
To a little home in Florida
We'll play checkers all day
Until we pass away

Newman used the orchestra to punch up a singalong chorus that would have been a Grammy contender if there were a category for irresistible pop passages; it made the sting of the final line more striking. "Love Story" was remarkable and daring, and you couldn't wait to hear what was next. Rick Nelson recorded "Love Story" for his own album *Perspective* after hearing a Randy demo of it. Nelson's LP, which also featured songs by such heralded young writers as Paul Simon ("For Emily, Whenever I May Find Her") and Harry Nilsson ("Without Her"), was designed to project a more mature image and sound for the former teen idol, who was now twenty-seven and no longer called himself Ricky.

John Boylan, a young songwriter who produced the album, learned about Newman while listening to a Paul Simon interview on a New York FM rock station. Simon had just returned from England, and the DJ asked him if he had heard anything there that he liked. Simon mentioned a version of Randy's "Happy New Year" by a young singer named Beverley. The DJ played the record, and Boylan was hooked. "It's a short song, just two minutes, but it conveys a whole sad story," Boylan said. He was so eager to hear more Newman songs that he called Aaron Schroeder the day after the broadcast and asked for copies of all of

CHAPTER SIX | 89

Randy's demos. Besides "Love Story," John and Rick put three other Newman songs on the album, including "I Think It's Going to Rain Today" and "So Long Dad."

There was such a growing interest in Randy's songs among A&R staffers at record labels, Boylan recalled, that the demos were treated like collector's items. Boylan later managed Linda Ronstadt, who sang "Bet No One Ever Hurt This Bad" on her 1969 album *Hand Sown . . . Home Grown*, but she found Randy on her own, an indication of the enthusiasm among LA musicians and songwriters for Newman.

Following "Love Story" with "Bet No One Ever Hurt This Bad," "Living Without You," and "Linda," Newman sang each of the heartache tales with a pain that felt deeply ingrained. As the songs built, you had a sense the characters were using these breakup complaints to cover up a deeper emptiness. Nothing felt conventional.

From "No One," the lyrics in part:

Since you went away
I can't face the day
And night brings nothin' but pain
Thought I could go on
I see that I was wrong
Baby, please come home— I just can't stand to be alone

In a change of direction, Newman talks about family matters in "So Long Dad": a young man brings his fiancée to meet his frail, long-neglected father on an obligatory visit. It was one of his personal favorites on the album.

Home again and the streets are not much cleaner
And the quaint old southside scenery
Is quaint no more

Just older than before
Go up the stairs and down the hallway
To my daddy's door
Your son is home, Dad, and he's found a girl
And she's the greatest girl in all the world
I think you'll like her, Dad, I hope you do
But if you don't that's all right, too
What's new? Do you still work at the drugstore?
Is that true? Still polishing the same floor?
I missed my good old Dad
My, but I'm glad to see you

Home again
But we won't be staying here, Dad

Come and see us, Poppa, when you can
There'll always be a place for my old man
Just drop by when it's convenient to
Be sure and call before you do
So long Dad

On casual listening, the song can come across as straightforward, but the son's callousness emerges at the end. "In this case, the narrator isn't unreliable, he's just nasty," Newman said. "It's a big idea . . . being nasty to your father. I know some people thought I was mean and nasty because of that song, but I never accepted that assessment. I was just noticing something and pointing it out. I also liked the way the arrangement was evocative of a neighborhood, maybe in Chicago, that doesn't exist anymore. It just feels like it could be from *Strawberry Blonde*, that Jimmy Cagney movie about Chicago. It was like this unspecified ethnic neighborhood, and that kind of thing interests me."

To Newman, the song didn't seem all that personal, but Van Dyke Parks years later hailed it as an early awareness by Newman of the "collapse between the generations."

Waronker was elated at the album's material. "You could feel this major shift when Randy went from writing songs for others and when he became the artist," he said. "I always felt he had ambition, but it really blossomed on that first album. All of a sudden, he was able to find his true voice, as a lyricist for sure, and it allowed him to expand."

Despite his mixed feelings about "I Think It's Going to Rain Today," Randy included it to make sure his own interpretation of the deceptively complex number was available. "Cowboy" was inspired by the 1962 film *Lonely Are the Brave*, a modern western about the slow but inevitable passing of an era. It mixed minimal but affecting lyrics—"Cold gray buildings where a hill should be"—and a pensive Aaron Copland-ish score.

Two other numbers highlighted the scope of Newman's pop auteurism. In just sixteen lines, "The Beehive State" told about matters as varied as the sociocultural differences within the country to the give-and-take of the spoil system:

"Since you're the delegate from Kansas
Will you kindly take the floor
And tell us what is Kansas thinking
And what is Kansas for?"
"Well, Kansas is for the farmer
We stand behind the little man
And we need a firehouse in Topeka
So help us if you can"

"I see the delegate from Utah
Our friendly Beehive State

How can we help you, Utah?
How can we make you great?"

"Well, we gotta irrigate our deserts
So we can get some things to grow
And we gotta tell this country about Utah
'Cause nobody seems to know"

The song grew out of Randy's fascination with geography and what he felt was the mystery of some states. "I remember thinking of Delaware," he said. "If you're from out west, Delaware's obscure, you don't know what the hell it is or even where it is, you don't know who lives there. And then I looked and tried to find another state and came up with Utah, which is sort of mysterious even if you are from out west."

"I Think He's Hiding" was a response to a social concern of the day. As dramatized by a 1966 *Time* magazine cover headline, "Is God Dead?" there was increasing talk that God was disappearing as a force in American life. In "I Think He's Hiding," Newman assumed the role of a true believer who maintained that God hadn't gone away at all but was hiding and would soon return to judge us. "I don't play it much because of calling God 'the Big Boy' in the song," Newman said in 2023. "It's too casual and colloquial. Religion is too important to people to show that kind of disrespect. 'God's Song' (which he wrote in 1972) doesn't do that, which is why I still do play that."

— III —

The album's closer, "Davy the Fat Boy," was the standout, as striking an advance in Newman's writing over "I Think It's Going to Rain Today" as that song had been over anything before it. "Davy" introduced one of Randy's defining themes, human cruelty, and was a major step in what would become his key writing characteristics, a valuable literary device—the unreliable narrator.

The approach was elastic enough for writers to use it for a variety of purposes, from speaking in the voice of a child who simply didn't understand the situation to a flagrant liar or, in extreme cases, someone delusional or psychopathic. The use of an unreliable narrator also served as a wall between the songwriter and the listener, which was especially attractive for someone a national magazine would later describe as being "notoriously contemptuous of self-revelation."

The term "unreliable narrator" was introduced by American literary critic Wayne C. Booth in *The Rhetoric of Fiction*, an influential 1961 book about the mechanics of fiction, but American authors had been employing unreliable narrators as far back as the 1800s, most notably in two of the century's greatest works: Edgar Allan Poe's *The Tell-Tale Heart* and Mark Twain's *Adventures of Huckleberry Finn*. In the twentieth century, Nobel Prize winner William Faulkner emerged as the modern master of the genre in such works as *The Sound and the Fury* and *As I Lay Dying*, while numerous other works demonstrated the power and flexibility of the approach, including Vladimir Nabokov's *Lolita*, Anthony Burgess's *A Clockwork Orange,* and J. D. Salinger's *The Catcher in the Rye.*

To most listeners, Newman's song "Davy the Fat Boy" was about a despicable young man who vowed to a dying couple to take care of their son, but betrays the parents for his personal gain and damages the boy by turning him into a carnival-like attraction. His actions are reminiscent of Robert Mitchum's portrayal of the unchecked evil of Harry Powell, a murderous religious charlatan, in the 1955 film *The Night of the Hunter.* Newman's song is even more ominous because of its jovial, carnival-inspired musical spirit.

I've been his friend since we were little babies
I was a comfort to his mother and a pal to his dad
Before they passed away they say,
"Take care of our Davy
You may be the only friend he ever will have"
Davy the fat boy, Davy the fat boy
Isn't he round? Isn't he round?
What do he weigh, folks?
Can you guess what he weigh?
It's only a quarter
Win a teddy bear for the girlfriend
Or something for the wife
You've got to let this fat boy in your life

I think we can persuade him to do
The famous fat boy dance for you
Give me half a chance
I just know you'll like my fat boy's dance

Davy the fat boy, Davy the fat boy
Isn't he
Isn't he round?

Because both deal with manipulation in a theatrical way, "Davy" and "Simon Smith" (which was not on the album) are frequently linked in descriptions of Randy's work. But "Davy" is a deeper and darker song. The young man who breaks his vow is heartless, whereas "Simon Smith," by contrast, is charming or even sweet.

After deflecting questions about "Davy" over the years, Newman finally, in late 2023, said that the idea for the song came after reading some novels that dealt with human cruelty in stark, unsettling terms—novels as different as William Lindsay

Gresham's *Nightmare Alley* (1946) and Calder Willingham's *End as a Man*, written the following year. Both were made into movies, Willingham's retitled *The Strange One* in 1957 and Gresham's twice, first starring Tyrone Power in 1947 and then Bradley Cooper and Cate Blanchett in 2021. *End as a Man* depicted dehumanizing hazing practices in a Southern military school, while the truly nightmarish *Alley* was about (spoiler alert) a shrewd, heartless con man who becomes fascinated with the deceit and grotesqueness of carnival sideshow life, including the lowly "geeks," who were so troubled the only thing they had to offer was biting the heads off live chickens. After years of using his trickery to great advantage, the con man comes to a humbling end, back in the circus, himself a geek.

Equally important, the stories apparently touched Newman because of a moment of cruelty in his own life. "I used to have this friend who was a better athlete than I was, and I always thought my dad liked him better, and we had a big blowup when I was around twelve or thirteen," Randy said. "I told my father, 'You like him better than me' [because] that hurt. It was a big idea to me—the idea of a parent favoring another kid who isn't his own."

"Davy" laid the foundation for everything to come.

— IV —

Warner was thrilled with the album, titled simply *Randy Newman*, and critics agreed. Newman received congratulatory messages from celebrated peers like Paul McCartney and Brian Wilson. The label's enthusiasm was spotlighted in a full-page ad in *Billboard* magazine to herald the LP's April release. After all, Randy had given them an album with at least eight songs that could be reasonably described as memorable—because of their originality, craftsmanship, and subject matter. Most record companies were pleased to get an album with even one memorable song.

Beneath a drawing of a serious-looking Newman in glasses, the ad proclaimed:

> He writes, plays, sings . . .
> He does it all,
> And no one today does
> It quite as well.
> Reprise presents
> The initial album
> Offering of
> A true musical
> Prodigy . . .
> Remarkably expressive,
> Legend to be
> RANDY NEWMAN.

Even in an industry known for hyperbole, the boast struck many of the industry pros as over the top. "I'm sure all those adjectives would have bothered him, but I don't know he was even that much aware of it," Waronker said. "He was so focused on his music that he'd shut himself off from things that could get in the way. He's smart that way."

Lenny was uncomfortable with the cover photo of Newman in a casual suit and a bright yellow turtleneck that made him look out of step with young America. When Alan went around to record stores to see if the LP was in stock, he often found the *Randy Newman* album in the adult pop section next to Sinatra or Andy Williams—if he found it at all. But Waronker didn't want to go to war over the cover; he needed the full support of every department of the label when the record was released.

The news from radio, the key to building an audience, was not good. Program directors complained about everything from the tone of the album (it wasn't rock and roll) to the meaning of several songs (what is this story about the Fat Boy even about?) to the down nature of some of the lyrics (particularly the couple's death at the end of "Love Story"). Sales were under 5,000, about the same as *Song Cycle*. Decades later, *Pitchfork*, one of the most influential review sites of the Internet era, would name both in its list of the hundred greatest albums of the 1960s.

Newman retreated to his house in Mandeville Canyon rejecting Waronker's pleas to start writing for a follow-up album. As weeks went by, Lenny kept hoping Randy's shutdown would be temporary, simply reflecting high-level anxiety that would be understandable after the commercial failure. But he gradually realized Randy was in a deep depression, reverting largely to the same activities that had comforted him ever since childhood—reading and watching television, usually alone in his room.

"When I made the album, I thought it could really be big," Newman said. "It was different, and I hoped people wouldn't hate my voice. Maybe they'd listen and pay attention to the songs, but they didn't, and that hurt my feelings. I knew I had to make a second album. But I kept putting it off."

As Waronker kept pressing Newman about why he wasn't working on new music, he finally heard the chilling words, "Lenny, nobody cares."

In retrospect, his reaction shouldn't have been that much of a surprise. In his first extensive exposure to the press, Randy had been surprisingly downbeat in a series of interviews in the late 1960s, though he sometimes tried to soften his frustration with humor. "It's suffering for me," he told Nick Logan of *New Musical Express*. "It's getting to the point where I may think of getting into pool cleaning or something. I meet people who are jolly and love work. But to me, it is still unpleasant." Around the same time, he said to Royston Eldridge of *Melody Maker*, "I don't like what I do in retrospect. I can't retain my pride in anything no matter how many people pat me on the back and say how great one of my songs is. It doesn't do anything for me."

Years later, Newman regretted the bleak language. He even made a point to stop giving interviews that were so negative because he knew how irritating it must sound—complaining about something most people would think was a dream life. However, he didn't deny the accuracy of the comments. He said, "I meant what I said 100 percent."

∼

As the year wound down, Randy's reputation in the industry got an unexpected boost when three revered music figures—the songwriting duo Jerry Leiber and Mike Stoller, and pop-jazz singer Peggy Lee—asked him, an industry novice, to write an arrangement for a new song they hoped would revive their stagnant recording careers. Leiber and Stoller hadn't written a Top 40 hit since 1963, and Lee, who had been one of America's most popular singers since the 1940s, hadn't had much pop presence since the early 1960s recording of Leiber and Stoller's bluesy feminist anthem "I'm a Woman."

When their paths crossed again in the fall of 1968, Leiber and Stoller felt their new song was perfect for Lee. "Is That All There Is" was inspired by "Disillusionment," a short story by German Nobel Prize–winning author Thomas Mann. After reading it, Leiber, the team's lyricist, began writing a song about a woman who looks back at what she feels was an unfulfilled life. Stoller set the words to music.

The pair reached out to a several singers, including Marlene Dietrich and Barbra Streisand, before settling on Lee. They hadn't approached her earlier because she, for reasons never fully explained, had severed ties with them after "I'm a Woman,"

CHAPTER SIX | 99

returning demos of their new songs unopened. Rather than mail the demo of "Is That All There Is" to her, Leiber personally handed it to her at a post-performance party following one of her shows in September of 1968 at the Copacabana nightclub in New York. When she called them a week later, Leiber and Stoller were overjoyed to hear her say, "I will kill you if you give this song to anyone but me. This is my song. This is the story of my life."

The three got together a few weeks later at Lee's home in Los Angeles, where the singer, known to be demanding in the studio, started the meeting by playing them a new album that she loved. It was Randy's debut, and she insisted they hire him to do the arrangement on the song.

Randy was on board—until he heard a demo of the song, which he thought was flat-out awful. Not wanting to offend the writers, Randy turned to Lenny for advice. "I just remember it being a bad show song," Lenny said. "The demo was no more than piano and voice, maybe even Jerry singing. I'm not sure, but it was bad." Listening to the demo together, they both realized the problem wasn't the song, but the arrangement, something Randy could fix.

After writing the arrangement, Newman conducted the orchestra when Lee recorded "Is That All There Is" in January of 1969 at Capitol Studios in Hollywood. By numerous accounts, the arrangement, with its strong sense of world-weary German cabaret atmosphere, saved the project. In Leiber and Stoller's autobiography, *Hound Dog*, Stoller wrote, "Randy's contributions were beyond the scope of what arrangers and orchestrators normally do. I'll be forever grateful to him."

Despite all that, Capitol refused to release the single. The promotion staff couldn't imagine radio stations playing such an offbeat, existential single, and many at the label had privately lost faith in Lee's marketability. When the stalemate dragged on for months, it looked like the whole project had been in vain. But Lee didn't give up. She went on the offensive by singing the unreleased song on Joey Bishop's late-night network TV show, hoping a strong viewer response would force Capitol to release the single— and that's what happened. Rushed out, "Is That All There Is" climbed to No. 11—and every copy of the record carried the words "Arranged and conducted by Randy Newman."

Music buyers probably didn't notice the credit, but the Grammy voters picked up on it, giving the record three nominations, including one for Randy's arrangement—the only win, however, went to Lee for contemporary female vocal. She was so pleased with Randy's contributions that she included two of his songs—"Love Story" and "Linda" (which she retitled "Johnny")— on her next album.

While Randy was working on the Lee record, Warner made the bold decision to re-release his debut album with a new cover (a moody, thoughtful headshot of Newman). Surprisingly, *Billboard* treated it as a new release, giving it a prominent review in its December 21 issue. As if the LP hadn't been on store shelves for months, the review read, "Randy Newman, a bright new writing talent, makes his album debut with this collection of topnotch original material, including 'Love Story,' which has drawn . . . recording interest from other artists. 'Bet No One Ever Felt This Bad,' 'Linda,' and "I Think It's Going to Rain Today' are among the other fine cuts." The result, however, was the same. The album was ignored in the year-end rush of releases. Fortunately, Randy had other things to keep him busy.

～

There was speculation that Newman's involvement with "Is That All There Is" lifted his spirits enough for him to resume writing, but he had already rallied shortly before Leiber and Stoller approached him. A song he wrote for the next album, "Let's Burn Down the Cornfield," showed that he hadn't lost his fondness for unusual themes. "Burn" was likely a first for pop music: a pyromaniac's idea of a love song. But Newman's confidence was shaken enough that he decided to do without the orchestra this time on the new album and leave arrangements to others. He wasn't comfortable, however, with the results of the "Cornfield" session in August of 1968 and returned to the isolation of his home. He wouldn't return to a recording studio for another eight months.

CHAPTER SEVEN

12 Songs
Harry Nilsson and
The Troubadour

— I —

Desperate to get something on tape before another writing stop-
page, Lenny booked two three-hour sessions on April 3, 1969, at
Western Recorders as soon as he learned that Randy had some
songs. The morning session went well enough to keep working
through the afternoon one, but things were tense. It had been just
over a year since he and Randy had come up with a single usable
track.

Despite being rattled by the reception of the first album, he
could have stuck to the goal he outlined in that album, but he
backed away from what he was calling a serious mistake in that
LP: the rich orchestral shading. "Truthfully, it was a strategy,"
Newman said of the changes he made in the second album. "It
was me thinking, 'They don't like what I did, so I'll do something
else. . . . It was that simple and that crass. I was just trying to be
more commercial, and I've never been able to do it."

Even so, it was a remarkable album—more conventional without the blazing, personal orchestral mix that Randy brought to
the first album, even radio-friendly—but still lively and fun with

a remarkable series of offbeat themes. Despite the LP's high-spirited tone, Randy reduced his role. He just wanted to write the songs—thus the title *12 Songs*—and sing them, which made Lenny nervous. For all the attention Randy's writing was getting, Lenny also prized his ability as an arranger who placed the songs in exquisite musical frames—and now Randy wanted to leave the frames up to others. The move ended up frustrating Randy, because arranging was one of the things he enjoyed most about the music-making process.

"The sessions were difficult for him because he didn't have the control that he had on the first album," Waronker explained. "When we went in with an orchestra on that first album, the song was done in an hour and a half later, and that's the way it went 70 percent of the time. In hindsight, I think there were times when he felt he wasn't involved enough with *12 Songs*, and that bothered him."

Waronker was encouraged, however, by several of the new songs themselves, one of which stands as Newman's most overt venture yet into social commentary: "Yellow Man," which touched on various Asian stereotypes. Newman got the idea for it watching *Footlight Parade*, a 1933 movie musical featuring a specialty number, "Shanghai Lil," that was praised at the time for its flashy staging but viewed as embarrassing decades later for its racist overtones. Even in the early 1970s, there was such little focus on Asian bias in the United States that most listeners, even liberal ones, probably thought Newman's song was a harmless novelty, even a witty joke.

"Yellow Man" satirized the nation's limited understanding of Asian culture:

Very far away in a foreign land
Live the yellow woman and the yellow man
He's been around for many-a-year
They say they were there before we were here

Eatin' rice all day
While the children play
You see he believes
In the family
Just like you and me

Oh, yellow man, oh, yellow man
We understand, you know we understand

He keeps his money tight in his hand
With his yellow woman he's a yellow man

Got to have a yellow woman
When you're a yellow man

Randy was so fond of the song that he strayed from his own game plan and wrote the arrangement for the intro, giving Waronker hope that he might do the arrangements for the rest of the album, but that didn't happen. Newman wasn't joking with "Yellow Man," as he made clear on the LP by placing the song between two tracks with racist undercurrents. The grouping began with "Underneath the Harlem Moon," a 1932 composition by Mack Gordon and Harry Revel that was demeaning to Blacks. The history lesson continued by following "Yellow Man" with Randy's own "Old Kentucky Home," which pointed out how racial and class stereotyping had always been an accepted part of American pop music. The words move from demeaning hillbilly stereotypes to a snippet of a Stephen Foster minstrel song that employed Black caricatures from Civil War days.

Turpentine and dandelion wine
I've turned the corner and I'm doin' fine
Shootin' at the birds on the telephone line

Pickin' 'em off with this gun of mine
I got a fire in my belly
And a fire in my head
Goin' higher and higher
Until I'm dead
Sister Sue, she's short and stout
She didn't grow up—she grew out
Mama says she's plain but she's just bein' kind
Papa thinks she's pretty but he's almost blind
Don't let her out much 'cept at night
But I don't care 'cause I'm all right

Oh, the sun shines bright on
My Old Kentucky Home
And the young folks roll on the floor
Oh, the sun shines bright on
My Old Kentucky Home
Keep them hard times away from my door

Brother Gene, he's big and mean
And he don't have much to say
He had a little woman who he whupped each day
But now she's gone away
He got drunk last night
Kicked mama down the stair
But I'm all right so I don't care

About "Kentucky Home," Newman told *Rolling Stone*, "the funniest part of the song is taken from Stephen Foster—the 'sun shines bright.' Now it was probably about 'pickaninnies' or 'darkies' at some point. It's about mountain people's ignorance or making fun of people who think that's funny. It's a good song because Stephen Foster wrote the hook."

Randy was back in the studio in early May for his second try at capturing the psychological shading of "Let's Burn Down the Cornfield," and this time Lenny brought in Jack Nitzsche as co-producer and arranger. His "Cornfield" chart called for a tension that was supplied by Ry Cooder's slashing bottleneck guitar. Cooder was so adept at emotionally charged guitar accents that the Rolling Stones considered asking him to join the band after guitarist Brian Jones's death in 1969, but the Stones decided on Mick Taylor, in part to keep the group's British identity intact.

Recording the tune, Newman flirted with Stones textures in what would stand as one of his most satisfying ventures into rock. It was an interesting turnaround for someone who had said he wanted to make music as if the Rolling Stones (and most rock) had never existed. Here, he showed how well he could flourish in rock-and-roll territory. Nitzsche was so impressed that he enlisted Newman as a jack-of-all-trades a few months later when he produced the soundtrack for *Performance*, a morbid, sexually charged film starring Mick Jagger.

In the album's sequence, "Cornfield"—with its smoldering sexual implications—was placed in the middle of another three-song grouping. The pairing began with the scorching "Have You Seen My Baby?" Another step in Randy's expanding pop vision, his vocal was a tip of the hat to his longtime favorite Fats Domino, whose influence was almost nonexistent on the first album. On the track, Randy's vocal phrasing was reminiscent of Fats's style, which Greil Marcus memorably described in *Mystery Train*, his landmark 1975 look at rock's impact on American culture. He pointed out that Newman's "somnambulant personality determined his choice of a lazy, blurred sound, where words slide into each other, where syllables are not bitten off, but just wear out and dissolve." In addition, Randy's New Orleans–based, shuffle-driven piano work fit perfectly with the story of a man who has lost all reason in his pursuit of a troubled, free-spirited girlfriend.

Listening to Fats's cover of "Have You Seen My Baby?" produced by Richard Perry the same year as *12 Songs*, it's easy to think Domino is echoing Newman's phrasing. In fact, Newman, who did the horn arrangement on the Domino recording, told *Rolling Stone*: "When we did it, it was like him imitating me imitating him." (Trivia note: After Newman's album was released in early 1970, Peggy Lee also released a sensational, feverish version of the song, changing "milkman" to "some woman.")

Have you seen my baby
On the avenue?
You know she's driving me crazy
With the funny things she do
I seen her with the milkman
Ridin' down the street
When you're through with my baby, milkman
Send her home to me
Hold on, hold on, hold on
Hold on, hold on, hold on
You know it's been so long
Since she have been gone
Hold on, hold on, hold on

I seen her with the gypsies
Dancin' in the wood
She's always been unfaithful to me
She ain't never been no good
I say, "Please don't talk to strangers, baby"
But she always do
She say, "I'll talk to strangers if I want to
'Cause I'm a stranger, too"

Hold on, hold on, hold on
Hold on, hold on, hold on

You know it's been so long
Since she have been gone
Hold on, hold on, hold on

By following those two songs with "Mama Told Me Not to Come," the album was off to a robust start. Despite Newman's uneasiness during the sessions, the recordings made you feel you were at a happening psychedelic party. As recording proceeded, Randy continued to come up with songs so funny—sometimes sly, sometimes zany—that some critics wrote about him as if he were a stand-up comic.

"Suzanne" again found Randy mocking the sensitive sixties strain of commercial folk music, only this time the target was the whispered reverence of Leonard Cohen's composition of the same name. "That was making a little gentle fun of Leonard Cohen's song in a way," Randy said. "His 'Suzanne' is really kind of a great song, but loving 'someone's perfect body with your mind' is a little abstract for my taste. My 'Suzanne' was something that just felt good. I wasn't trying for a piece of art or anything. I was still feeling my way in terms of what I wanted to write about."

Even so, Randy's "Suzanne" was another step in spotlighting unhealthy attitudes. As some fans and critics began examining his lyrics more intensely, some would see this as a reflection of female vulnerability in a society where the power rested with men. In the menacing tune, Randy assumed the role of a would-be stalker, lying in wait for Suzanne, whose name and number he found scrawled in a telephone booth.

The lyrics begin:

I saw your name, baby
In a telephone booth
And it told all about you, mama
Boy, I hope it was the truth

I took down your number
Looked up your address, Sue
And I was hopin' that maybe
You could love me, too
I'm gonna wait in the shadows
For you to come by
I'm gonna wait in the shadows, baby
For you to come by
And then I'll jump from the shadows
And try and catch your eye
Gonna run my fingers through your hair
And love you everywhere

Now I don't want to get too romantic
That's just not my way
But when I get my arms around you
I'm gonna rock you all the night
Gonna rock you all the day

Suzanne, you won't know it but I'll be behind you
Don't try and run away from me, little girl
Wherever you go I'll find you
And when you go to the pictures
And I know you do
Don't take no one with you
'Cause I'll be there, too
Suzanne

"Lucinda" was a fantasy that toyed with three prominent strains of American teen pop of the period. For someone who grew up near the beach, it's only natural Randy would do a variation of the California-based beach song craze. Even Tennessee-bred Pat Boone joined in with "Beach Girl" in 1964. But Randy didn't stop with the locale. "Lucinda" (named after the former Newman family housekeeper) also served to mock the teen-tragedy theme of such songs as "Leader of the Pack" and "Teen Angel" as well as all the pop odes about the wonders of high school graduation.

The narrator comes across a girl lying on the beach in her graduation gown just as a huge garbage truck heads her way, scooping up all the debris left by partygoers. He tries to warn Lucinda, who may have passed out from alcohol, but the truck rolls over her, burying her in the sand. The smoldering arrangement also benefits from Randy's shuffle highlights and more blistering bottleneck guitar. "I went to the beach every day for a few years, and you'd hear all kinds of strange stories, but that really happened, I believe—a girl involved with a beach cleaning truck, though I don't think it killed her," Randy said. "I just made up this story. The idea of lying on the beach in her graduation gown was a very sort of California thing and I was just, as I often am, trying to make people laugh."

The remaining songs also moved in surprising directions. "If You Need Oil" was no doubt the first pickup song starring a gas station attendant and "Lover's Prayer" told of a selfish guy's idea of a perfect sexual partner. The latter song began:

> *Don't send me no young girl to love me*
> *With their eyes shinin' bright*
> *All the young girls are afraid of me*
> *Send me a woman tonight*
> *Don't send me no hand-holdin' baby*
> *'Cause I been with babies before*
> *Don't send me nobody that's crazy*
> *Don't send me no young girls no more*
>
> *I was entertaining a little girl up in my rooms, Lord*
> *With California wines and French perfumes, Lord*

She started to talk to me about the War, Lord
I said, "I don't want to talk about the War."

Don't send me nobody with glasses
Don't want no one above me
Don't send nobody takin' night classes
Send me somebody to love me

Where the first album confused some of the old guard at Warner, there was enough enthusiasm throughout the label to build hopes of a big seller this time, hopes that were pushed even higher by the attention Randy continued to get in the industry, including the raves of Harry Nilsson. Harry was the talk of the music world after his recording of Fred Neil's "Everybody's Talkin'" was featured in the film *Midnight Cowboy*.

— II —

Released in May of 1969 while *12 Songs* was still being worked on, *Midnight Cowboy* was an X-rated account of two social outcasts struggling to survive on the gritty streets of New York. It won the Oscar for best picture and created enough interest in the Nilsson single for it to be a radio staple for months. Numerous industry observers predicted superstardom for the singer who had a commanding three-octave voice and an imaginative writing style that was elastic enough for both mainstream and underground radio.

Like Randy, Nilsson had fans in the Beatles; John Lennon would eventually produce one of his albums. In turn, Nilsson was a fan of Newman—calling him "brilliant" in a 1969 interview. When they met, Nilsson told Newman that he was going to include "Simon Smith" in his next album, *Harry*, which was due in August. Despite the exposure of "Everybody's Talkin'," the album fell far short of RCA's expectations. The problem was the LP didn't include "Everybody's Talkin';" the song had appeared on Nilsson's previous album, *Aerial Ballet.* Rather than search for the old album for the hit, fans picked up the movie soundtrack, which contained Nilsson's version of the song.

However, Nilsson proceeded with plans for an album featuring only Newman songs. Titled *Nilsson Sings Newman,* it included ten songs, from "Vine Street" to "Yellow Man." Randy was touched, but, in his worrisome way, warned Nilsson that the album was a terrible idea. "Randy's reaction sounds like his typically funny way, but he wasn't trying to be funny," Lenny said. "He told Harry, 'You've had a big hit. What are you doing these songs for? This stuff has proven not to be successful. It's a big mistake.' Randy absolutely believed that."

But Nilsson persisted. The arrangements were minimalist, focusing chiefly on Randy at piano and Harry's vocals. Once the pair was finished, however, Nilsson, who served as his own producer, spent hours adding vocal overdubbing and occasional instrumental punctuation. Nilsson's wife, Diane, sat in on the sessions and was alarmed by her husband's behavior. Harry, she said in Alyn Shipton's 2013 biography *Nilsson,* "would try to add everything except the kitchen sink to a track. He would have so many layers that in the end, he would get confused and not know which sounded best." The reason, she suspected, was heavy cocaine use, the first time she had seen him with the substance. Afterward, Randy was respectful when talking about the album, though he still viewed it as a mistake.

Nilsson Sings Newman received generally positive reviews, but sales were again disappointing. Nilsson would eventually make the Top 10 with two albums in the early 1970s before personal problems gradually wore him down. He died in 1994 at the age of fifty-two.

— III —

Leading up to the release of *12 Songs*, Warner's inner circle focused on how to sell more albums, and the consensus was that Randy needed to tour. Before the age of MTV music videos and the social network's ability to anoint stars hourly, touring was a powerful weapon. It could not only build a strong grass-roots following but also could persuade radio who was hot, thus who to play.

Peter J. Philbin, who worked at Columbia Records during the slow but eventual rocket-like rise of Bruce Springsteen in the 1970s, knew the importance of touring. "In rock in those days, someone could succeed based on his talent and work," said Philbin, who dealt with Springsteen in publicity and then in A&R.

> You didn't have to wait for the right manager or the right label or the right marketing plan to get ahead. In fact, if you did wait, it felt phony, it felt fabricated. The organic way to do it—which is what Bruce did—was to perform a hundred or 150 shows a year. Maybe to just twenty-five people a show the first time around, but if you were good, you'd find fifty people at the club the next time and then a hundred. They might bring with them somebody from the press or somebody from radio or somebody who worked in a record store. It was basically building your own train. You got the train rolling down the tracks and you said, "Welcome aboard."

Ideally, the thinking at Warner went, Randy would play the Troubadour in Los Angeles when the album was released in February of 1970. The 400-seat club was the leading showcase in the nation for rising singer-songwriters. Each Tuesday night, industry tastemakers—radio programmers, talent bookers, agency reps, the press—would gather to pass judgment on the latest record company offering. It was at the Troubadour where Elton John would become a star overnight in August of 1970.

But was Randy, who had never done a live show, ready for such scrutiny?

The Warner strategists wanted to test him with a warm-up date in some club outside the industry or media spotlight, and Erik Jacobsen, a record producer and manager in the Bay Area, came up with the ideal spot—the Lion's Share in San Anselmo, north of San Francisco. As soon as Jacobsen mentioned Randy's name to the club owner, the booking was made. The owner had lost another club in nearby Sausalito when, he believed, neighbors burned it down to protest the noisy crowd it attracted. The experience left the club owner wary of name acts who might draw another loud crowd. Since he had never heard of Newman, he doubted anyone else in the area had either. The booking was set for October 16 to 18, when Randy would be joined by Ry Cooder.

Alan Newman, who was attending medical school in San Francisco, rounded up some classmates to help make sure the audience response was strong. More than a traditional music club, the Lion's Share had the feel of a restaurant, with long tables, tablecloths, a low ceiling, and the piano facing a wall. "The setup was very awkward, and I felt bad for [Randy]," Cooder said. "It was a dinner place, people sat there chomping away on their salads. But what could you do? We had to make the best of it, and it turned out fine. In fact, the crowd went crazy. They just loved him." Alan, whose pals supplied much of that love, said that Randy felt pleased with the experience. "He seemed good, he really enjoyed it. I think seeing people respond to his music helped his confidence."

The set ranged from cover versions of old favorites—including Fats Domino's "Blue Monday"—to two key songs from the new album, "Underneath the Harlem Moon" and "Yellow Man," suggesting Newman's growing interest in social commentary. After the show, he told *Rolling Stone*'s Bruce Grimes, "I was afraid I might be misunderstood, and someone would jump on stage and beat the hell out of me."

Randy also said to Grimes, in what is believed to have been Randy's first national interview, "I came up to see what it's like in front of an audience. . . . There's a possibility that I will play the Troubadour in the spring, but I'll have to wait and see."

Grimes was circulation manager of the magazine, helping take it from a Bay Area publication to a national one. He went to the Lion's Share concert as a fan of the first album, not on assignment, but he was so enthusiastic afterward that he asked if he could write about it and, thanks to *Stone* record review editor Greil Marcus's support, the publication ran a glowing review-feature when *12 Songs* was released. Grimes kept in touch with Newman for a few years, visiting him both in the studio and at home in the Palisades.

Newman didn't strike Grimes as particularly ambitious beyond wanting to write good songs:

> I always thought Randy's priority was writing songs, and his performing them was almost a means of getting them out there. I think another goal was to get the respect of his peers. That may be even more important to him than audience acceptance. When we later spoke about his writing and LP sales, I sensed . . . a disappointment and frustration rather than insecurity. I think to Randy, at least back in the late sixties and early seventies, it was more a matter of him wondering why people didn't get him rather than thinking he wasn't good. I think the battle between openness and privacy was also at the core of Randy's procrastination. Randy may have been conflicted about how much he wanted to reveal about himself through his writing.

After the three nights at the Lion's Share, Randy headed back to Los Angeles to await word on the Troubadour and work on the soundtrack for *Performance.*

~

The Stones were scheduled to perform the music on the album, but problems within the band prevented it, and the project was handed over to Nitzsche, who shared much of the Stones' musical DNA. The band's sole contribution was "Memo from Turner," a Jagger-Richards song that Jagger sang.

Randy was only scheduled to conduct the orchestra, but his role grew. He played Hammond B3 organ on "Memo from Turner" (whose basic track was cut in Los Angeles with Titelman on guitar and Cooder supplying the bottleneck licks, and later mixed with Jagger's vocal from London). Randy also handled the vocal on "Gone Dead Train," a song that Nitzsche and Titelman wrote with him in mind. A revised—mostly speeded-up—version of the "Gone" album track was released as a single in England, and it was so well received that hard-core Stone fans debated whether "Memo" or "Train" was the stronger record. Newman's vocal showed a blues swagger that felt at home alongside the Stones.

Titelman and Newman had known each other since the Liberty days, but they bonded during the *Performance* sessions. Titelman had grown up in the music business, showing such passion and instincts that virtually every key figure he met in Los Angeles studios—from Spector to Nitzsche to Waronker—became a mentor of sorts. Lenny, who had long admired Titelman's taste and way of gaining the confidence of artists in the studio, eventually hired Russ as a producer at Warner.

— IV —

As Randy sat at the piano and sang in his deep-dish Southern drawl at the start of his six-night Troubadour engagement on February 24, 1970, it was easy for industry insiders to mistake this new arrival for some sort of contemporary bluesman. The music included substantial blues elements, and the vocals had an inescapable Delta flavor. But unlike so many of his peers, Randy wasn't trying to echo the old blues masters.

Thanks to the intimacy of the club, Newman's originality and ambition were even more apparent than on a record. This was only his second club stint, yet he was in command during a forty-minute set that ranged from "Love Story" to "Mama Told Me Not to Come." The conversation in the room afterward was enthusiastic.

Watching the show, it was easy to imagine Newman reworking the blues tradition the same way Dylan had reworked the folk tradition in Greenwich Village clubs a decade earlier. Randy, industry insiders largely agreed, was on his way to stardom, though some observers were a bit puzzled: "Where is the guitar?" and "when's he going to get a band?"

Reviews of the album were ecstatic, from the *Los Angeles Times* to *Rolling Stone* (by Bruce Grimes, who included parts of his Lion's Share interview in the piece). Setting the pace was Robert Christgau, the widely influential "Dean of American Rock Critics."

Declaring *12 Songs* the album of the year, he wrote this rave:

> As a rule, American songwriting is banal, prolix, and virtually solipsistic when it wants to be honest, merely banal when it doesn't. Newman's truisms—always concise, never confessional— are his own. Speaking through recognizable American grotesques, he comments here on the generation gap (doomed), incendiary violence (fucked up but sexy), male and female (he identifies with the males, most of whom are losers and weirdos), racism (he's against it, but he knows its seductive power), and alienation (he's for it).
>
> Newman's music counterposes his indolent drawl—the voice of a Jewish kid from LA who grew up on Fats Domino—against an array of instrumental settings that on this record range from

rock to bottleneck to various shades of jazz. And because his lyrics abjure metaphor and his music recalls commonplaces without repeating them, he can get away with the kind of calculated effects that destroy more straightforward meaning-mongers. A perfect album. A+

To the dismay of Warner, *12 Songs* did not sell substantially more than the debut. Newman was even more downcast than after the first album. He seemed to draw from Alfred Newman when he spoke in an interview about how draining and agonizing writing could be—and there was little payoff for him. The joy of writing a good song would only last a few days or even a few hours because he knew he had to go through the whole process again.

Lenny also knew of Alfred's struggles early on. "Al had it all, this great house and stuff, but it wasn't really about that," Waronker said. "For him, too, it was about being the best. He would go crazy when he was writing a score. My father would get phone calls at seven or eight o'clock at night when we were having dinner, and we'd all be quiet because my father was trying to comfort Al. Often, he had to go over to Al's house and sit with him to reassure him that what he was working on was great. I think Randy grew up around that and he got totally immersed in it."

Alfred Newman's daughter, Maria, a composer-violinist who Randy describes as the finest musician in the family, also sees a family connection. "The Newmans are a combination of gifted and insecure, and that can lead to a lot of things," she said. "It can make you work harder, but also make you constantly question yourself. Sometimes I wonder if that insecurity didn't contribute to the music. If Randy wasn't so insecure, I wonder if his music would be so profound."

On the personal front, Roswitha gave birth to the couple's first child, Amos, on July 18, 1968, and they shared their joy with an insert photo inside the new album jacket. It showed the couple walking out of a neighborhood food market during the holiday season—Amos in Roswitha's arms, a shopping bag in Randy's.

~

One positive effect of the delay between albums is that it created a certain mystique about Randy. This was a time in pop when artists tended to release albums rapidly, often an album a year or more (more than thirty total albums in the 1960s alone for the Rolling Stones, Beatles, and Beach Boys).

"People in the creative community were wanting to know what was going on, when Randy was going to have another album," Lenny Waronker said. "His first two albums had made that much impact among other artists. There was a story that went around about one of the writers in the Laurel Canyon group were writing a song, and everyone else was going, 'What a great song.' Finally, Jackson Browne said, 'Yeah, it's good,' but why don't we go to Sunset Sound, where Randy was working on a new album, and see how it stands up to his stuff.' That was the kind of respect he enjoyed."

CHAPTER EIGHT

The Bitter End
Bob Dylan and
A Novel Movie Idea

— I —

After the Troubadour, Warner wanted to put Randy on the road as soon as possible, but Mo and Lenny knew there was no way to get him to crisscross the country doing dozens of shows. It was hard enough to get him into the studio to make a record. The impasse was broken when Bob Krasnow, a Warner executive known for his off-the-wall ideas, came up with a novel plan: have Randy record a live album.

Though rare for new artists, especially those without any hits or touring history, a live album would showcase Randy's Troubadour strengths and help keep his name alive in the industry for the two years (fingers crossed) it'd take him to write and record his next studio LP. This led Warner to book him into the Bitter End, a New York City equivalent of the Troubadour, for three nights that fall.

Krasnow's plan also, crucially, included a teasing bit of subterfuge. Warner would package and promote the live album as a bootleg to make it appear that music had been leaked by someone who had gained secret access to the tapes. Bootlegs had become an underground sensation a few months earlier after *Great White Wonder,* a collection of unreleased Bob Dylan material, suddenly appeared at swap meets and in small indie record shops without the knowledge or permission of his record label. The lure was new songs or alternative versions of songs not commercially available. Even though the Newman LP would list Reprise Records on the cover, the rushed, no-frills design would give the illusion of something outside the normal music business machinery.

Before the Bitter End shows, Warner had one more promotion request for Randy: sing "Love Story" and "So Long Dad" on a Liza Minnelli TV special in June. Randy was fine with performing the songs, but he wasn't comfortable with a skit on the variety show and drew a line. The idea, he said, was for Liza to sing "Tradition" (from *Fiddler on the Roof*) and have everyone in the cast join hands and dance around exuberantly, but he and Jimmy Webb wanted no part of it. Randy didn't want to be anyone's dancing bear.

~

The Bitter End engagement, September 17 to 19, was a success on several levels. The shows, focused on material from the first two albums, were warmly received, and Alan Newman was again on hand to lead the cheering. Several of Randy's peers took advantage of his first New York performance to check him out, including Dylan. He and Randy went next door to the Tin Angel, a café frequented by musicians, with some friends, including Titelman, who co-produced the album with Waronker.

Randy wasn't in the Dylan camp musically, but he admired Dylan's impact on pop culture and his way with words. "He writes with such power that his words feel like they belong on a monument or on the side of a building," Randy said. "He's the best lyricist this music has produced." But Randy's poor eyesight betrayed him at the café. He was going on and on about how much he liked Dylan's songs when suddenly he felt Titelman kicking him under the table. It turned out Randy wasn't talking to Dylan at all, but blues-folk musician John Hammond Jr., who resembled Dylan in the dim light. So, Randy just turned to Dylan and started telling him all the same stuff. "At one point, he told me he was thinking of moving to Los Angeles, and he asked if I thought he could write a song like 'Lucinda' if he did move out there," Randy said years later. "I was so caught up talking to him, I replied, 'Oh yeah.' When I thought about that later, I wondered if he was just being facetious about writing a song like 'Lucinda.' I mean it was just three chords. I should have said, 'Why would you want to?'"

Mike Jahn's *New York Times* review of the opening show was short, but enthusiastic: "Randy Newman is a young songwriter from Los Angeles, and rather special . . . a rare gift for words poignant and haunting, combined with a mildly Gershwin-esque sense of melody. . . . He creates fascinating vignettes about commonplace places and people, understated magnificently . . . . There is an air of some kind of majesty to what he does."

While on the East Coast, Randy guested on David Frost's national TV show and played the Main Point, a popular coffee house in the Philadelphia suburb of Bryn Mawr. He then flew to London to perform a few songs as a promotional event with other artists at the popular Revolution Club.

Richard Williams, one of England's premiere pop critics, was a fan who planned to take advantage of the showcase to spread the word about Newman in a review. But Randy had problems with the microphone cord and was displeased with the room's noisy environment—as Williams put it, the "ringing of cash registers and the conversation of the allegedly hip audience." Randy was at the piano for less than five minutes before saying "bye-bye" to the rude audience and left the stage. Williams defended him in his review. "All I can say," he wrote, "is that his performance had the same effect on me as those of Van Morrison and Nico. He's a true original, and we can all use some of that."

Despite the London experience, Randy realized on the flight back to Los Angeles that the Troubadour was no fluke. He enjoyed performing; the interaction with fans and the applause felt awfully good. He was ready to promote his next album with a full-blown club tour. "I knew that writing was the most important thing I do, but I really enjoyed performing." There was more good news. On New Year's Eve of 1970, Roswitha gave birth to the couple's second son, Eric.

— II —

Krasnow's plan worked fabulously. The response was overwhelming when promo copies of the live album, titled *Randy Newman Live*, were sent to radio and critics in the spring of 1971. *Rolling Stone* was so impressed that the magazine reviewed the promo LP and urged Warner to formally put it out. "The insights of the songs are so devastating that I can't think of a single American who wouldn't be better off for having heard it," Tim Crouse raved. "Now that Dan Ellsberg is done with the Pentagon papers, he might think about getting *Randy Newman/Live* into mass circulation."

Warner released the LP in June. Besides ten songs from the first two albums, including "I Think It's Going to Rain Today" and "Davy the Fat Boy," the package contained four new songs, most importantly a left-field tale of sexual insecurity ("Maybe I'm Doing it Wrong") and a show-biz song that would draw laughter and applause at Newman's concerts for decades: "Lonely at the Top," the song Randy had written for Sinatra.

"There was a massive drive at Warner to get Frank a hit," Newman told *Rolling Stone*. "I thought—maybe stupidly—that he would be ready to make fun of that leaning-against-the-lamppost shit: 'Oh, I'm so lonely and miserable, and the biggest singer in the world.' I never bought that part of him. I thought he'd appreciate that. I played it for him at his office . . . and he just said, 'Next.' I also played 'I Think It's Going to Rain Today.' He said, 'I like that one.' But he couldn't hide his bitterness at young people's music." Before realizing that no pop star was going to take a chance on "Lonely at the Top," he also played it for Barbra Streisand—again to no avail. She got the humor, Randy said, but "she worried that people would believe she was being serious if she sang it, and she was probably right."

By the end of the year, estimated sales on *Live* were approaching 50,000—five times the combined sales of the first two albums. Titelman was not surprised. "If you weren't familiar with Randy Newman, you could put this record on for these thirty-six or whatever minutes and it told you everything you needed to know about him," he said. "Those great songs, including beautiful ballads that could make you cry and songs that you had to sit and think about. You also could hear these great vocal performances; you could hear what a genius piano player he is and crucially, you had audience reaction. You hear people cracking up and laughing at some of the songs and the next moment you could hear a pin drop. It told you that Randy was a serious artist, and he was also hysterically funny."

Randy responded with a short tour that included a return to the Troubadour and his biggest venue yet, the 1,800-capacity Royce Hall on the campus of his alma mater. The needle was finally starting to move for him—including within the film world.

— III —

Movie producers had been approaching Randy about film scores since his debut album, but the longstanding intimidation caused him to turn down everything or at least sabotage exploratory meetings. A producer, who was apparently attracted chiefly by the Newman family name, asked Randy to play him a sample song. Randy responded with "Davy the Fat Boy," only to realize midway through that it wasn't the most appropriate choice. "The absurdity of my singing this song about a fat kid for this overweight [three-hundred-pound] producer finally hit me," Randy told *Rolling Stone*. "When I finished, he said, 'That's wonderful; do you have any songs about blind people or bald men?'"

In the weeks between the Troubadour and the Bitter End in 1970, Randy took a deep breath and finally agreed to write a film score, chiefly because he felt comfortable with producer-director Norman Lear. If he was going to be nervous on his first film project, Randy wanted at least to be working with someone he felt good about. Lear was a television comedy writer who would soon create such hit TV sitcoms as *All in the Family* and become one of Hollywood's most prominent liberal activists.

This was Lear's first film, *Cold Turkey*—a satirical comedy that poked fun at corporate greed, media frenzy, religion, and, briefly, President Richard M. Nixon. The plot involved a giant tobacco company plan, as part of a public relations campaign, to give any US city $25,000 tax-free if all its residents could give up smoking for a month. Randy didn't even read the script; he was sold on Lear.

During the sessions, Randy relied heavily on Arthur Morton, a veteran orchestrator who had assisted on *From Here to Eternity* and *Chinatown*, to turn his musical ideas into workable pieces for the orchestra, a common practice in film scoring. "Eventually in my career, I would write down everything for the orchestrator and indicate exactly what to do for a scene," he told me in 2021. "But Arthur was so good, and I was hesitant so I didn't tell him much of anything. I'd just make a suggestion now and then, and Arthur finally said, 'Your ideas are good, why don't you tell me more ideas, what you'd like to see in the movie. That helped a lot, but confidence is something that comes and goes in film scoring."

Likely picking up on Randy's anxiety, Lear showed up regularly at Newman's house to check up on him. "It was a strange time," Randy said in the film's DVD liner notes. "I probably didn't inspire confidence in him, but he was nervous about doing the film himself."

When Randy asked Lear what feel he wanted in the film, he was told small-town Americana, which is what Newman delivered, including an outwardly upbeat song, "He Gives Us All His Love," that reflected the community's strong religious sensibilities. The song was warm and embracing. Backed by tender orchestral strains, Randy sang it in the movie against a backdrop of a lonely little dog wandering through mounds of trash, looking for someone to give some love until, finally, a lonely hand does reach out. The opening verses:

He gives us all his love
He gives us all his love
He's smiling down on us
From up above
And he's giving us all his love
He knows how hard we're trying
He hears the babies crying
He sees the old folks dying
And he gives us all his love

United Artists had concerns about the film's box-office potential but released *Cold Turkey*, which starred Dick Van Dyke and Bob Newhart, in early 1971, and the film grossed a respectable $11 million. Though things seemed to go well in the project, Randy wasn't over his nervousness about film scoring. He wouldn't accept another assignment for a decade. But he did respond to one offbeat cinematic idea.

— IV —

Michael Laughlin, a producer in early stages of developing *Two-Lane Blacktop*, a youth-oriented road film starring James Taylor and Dennis Wilson, was so enthralled with all the gifted young singer-songwriters on the scene that he came up with a novel idea for a film—and he wanted Randy involved.

"The plan was to let each songwriter do what was later called a 'music video' of a new song, and then we'd put them together in a film," Laughlin said. "They were free to do whatever they wanted in terms of script or story. I was thinking something that would run around ten minutes each. It was all very casual, just seeing if there was interest." Laughlin mentioned the idea to numerous young songwriters, including Van Morrison, Kris Kristofferson, and Elton John, but Randy was apparently the only one who took it seriously. "I was excited," Laughlin said, "because I loved Randy's first album, the way he drew upon the history of American music."

In a *Rolling Stone* piece by David Felton, Randy described his original vision for his short film. "My part opened up on this ship with these sailors running around yelling sailor stuff, you know, 'lubber the mainmast' and that type of shit. I was a recruiter for the slave trade—you know, white suit, dark glasses, sort of a Warren Beatty, brooding type of part . . . . Eventually it cuts to the jungle and there's thousands of natives. And the band plays, you know, 'Take Me Out to the Ball Game,' just to get the natives interested. And then I come out and have the band play 'Camptown Races,' and the natives go 'doo-dah, doo-dah' and get all excited. And then I'd have a tenor sing 'Did your Mother Come from Ireland,' and the natives would keep goin' 'doo-dah, doo-dah, doo-dah,' getting out of control until the band plays some real scary shit to shut 'em up. And then I'd sing a song about America."

Laughlin didn't expect to hear from Randy for weeks, but Newman was back in two days, playing "Sail Away" on an upright piano in the producer's Studio City office. The song was a scathing look at America's slave trading days—at once wildly offensive and inarguably true. "Randy saw the whole thing visually, and this was years, of course, before the music business had videos," the producer said. "He even had a bit of a sailors' jig just before the song. You could sense he was into film in quite a sophisticated way. But above all was the song."

> *In America you'll get food to eat*
> *Won't have to run through the jungle*
> *And scuff up your feet*
> *You'll just sing about Jesus and drink wine all day*
> *It's great to be an American*
> *Ain't no lions or tigers*
> *Ain't no mamba snake*
> *Just the sweet watermelon and the buckwheat cake*
> *Ev'rybody is as happy as a man can be*
> *Climb aboard, little wog*
> *Sail away with me*
>
> *Sail away*
> *Sail away*
> *We will cross the mighty ocean into Charleston Bay*
> *Sail away*
> *Sail away*
> *We will cross the mighty ocean into Charleston Bay*
>
> *In America every man is free*
> *To take care of his home and his family*

You'll be as happy as a monkey in a monkey tree
You're all gonna be an American

Sail away
Sail away
We will cross the mighty ocean into Charleston Bay
Sail away
Sail away
We will cross the mighty ocean into Charleston Bay

In a masterstroke to end the film, Newman proposed handing each young man an arrival gift in Charleston: a basketball.

The film fell through, but Newman had a head start on his next album. "Sail Away" would be one of his half dozen most prized songs—one that helped define his future in music. Meanwhile, *Rolling Stone* was so optimistic about Randy's potential after hearing some early tracks from the new album that the magazine went out on an attention-grabbing limb in February of 1972. It named him the *Rolling Stone* Rock Star of the Year.

CHAPTER NINE

Another Classic Album:
Sail Away

— I —

By the time recording began on the third album in late 1971, Randy had been living with "Sail Away" for over a year, looking forward to working again with an orchestra to provide an essential component. Uncle Emil even agreed to step in and conduct the fifty or so musicians. The song was the perfect storm—a composition that combined Randy's gift for seductive melodies and exemplary storytelling with a growing desire to move deeper into social commentary without succumbing to protest-pop.

Waronker and Titelman, who would again co-produce the LP, were so excited by the finished track that you could imagine them playing it for the musicians at the start of every session as if to say "We're doing something special here." It remains one of the great works in American pop. After opening with the smoothly moving chords of a Sunday church procession, Randy eventually injects chromatic elements that help the listener recognize that something underhanded is going on. The open fifths that repeat through the verse help portray the outward calmness of the slave trader's pitch as well as the calmness of the ocean that will take the slaves all the way to Charleston Bay.

The new album, also titled *Sail Away*, didn't reunite Randy and classical music on every track, but in welcome, revealing moments. As much as he was correctly identified as a pop artiste, Randy, at heart, was still a child of classical music. When asked to draft a list of his favorite recordings for the BBC Radio 4 program *Desert Island Discs*, his first choice was Beethoven's String Quartet No. 16 in F major, Op. 135—the version by the Hollywood String Quartet, which was composed of top players from film studio orchestras.

Though artists invariably cite different favorites over time when asked to name their favorite tracks, the telling thing about Randy's choices was the ratio of classical orchestral music to pop recordings. His other selections included Alfred Newman's "Goodbyes" for the film *How Green Was My Valley*, Stravinsky's *The Rite of Spring*, the first movement of Shostakovich's Symphony No. 15 in A major, and the fourth movement of Mahler's Symphony No. 9 in D major. The pop side was represented only by jazz composer-arranger Fletcher Henderson's "The Stampede," country star George Jones's "The Door," and Ray Charles's "Come Rain or Come Shine," from the *Genius of Ray Charles* album.

~

Lenny sensed a difference in Randy in the weeks leading up to the *Sail Away* sessions. "As great as he was on *12 Songs*, he had such a difficult time that he was so worn down by the end that he just left the studio. He wasn't there for the mixing of the album, which made it rough. He was in a much better place when we started *Sail Away*."

The atmosphere in the studio was also brightened by the response to the live album: the feeling that an audience was building. It also helped that Randy only had to write six of the dozen songs, since the remaining numbers were already in hand: "Sail Away," "Lonely at the Top," "Simon Smith," "He Gives Us All

His Love," "Dayton, Ohio – 1903," and "Last Night I Had a Dream." In the end, the new and old songs fit together beautifully, as measured by the number of respected artists who covered, live or on record, one or more of them: Ray Charles, Etta James, Linda Ronstadt, Bobby Darin, Dave Matthews, Gladys Knight, Don Henley, Wilco, Sonny Terry and Brownie McGhee, Tom Jones, Joe Cocker, and Jerry Garcia.

Once again, Waronker and Titelman brought together a group of Los Angeles's most admired players for the sessions, including guitarists Cooder (bottleneck) and Clarence White, drummers Jim Keltner, Earl Palmer, and Gene Parsons, and bassists Chris Ethridge, Wilton Felder, and Jimmy Bond. The musicians' combined résumés included sessions and tours with John Lennon, Nina Simone, and the Byrds. Randy was at the piano.

Said Keltner:

> What I loved about Randy was you didn't know what was coming next in the studio. He would sing the song for you before the session, but then he would sing it differently once you started playing. The goal was to create magic, and that happens by musicians bouncing off each other, one guy rushing here a little bit, then pulling back. You want everyone to feel comfortable in the studio. In one of the first sessions I worked with Randy, the lyrics were so funny I couldn't control my laughter, so I blew a take. It made me really mad at myself because the take was going so well. After that, I had to purposely not pay attention to the lyrics to make sure that didn't happen again.

Just as the tracks on *12 Songs* were appealing live, many of the new songs would also become instant concert favorites, starting with "Political Science," a Dr. Strangelove-like sendup of military hawks and conservative isolationism that drew more laughs with each outlandish verse:

No one likes us—I don't know why
We may not be perfect, but heaven knows we try
But all around, even our old friends put us down
Let's drop the big one and see what happens
We give them money—but are they grateful?
No, they're spiteful and they're hateful
They don't respect us—so let's surprise them
We'll drop the big one and pulverize them

Asia's crowded and Europe's too old
Africa is far too hot
And Canada's too cold
And South America stole our name
Let's drop the big one
There'll be no one left to blame us

We'll save Australia
Don't wanna hurt no kangaroo
We'll build an All-American amusement park there
They got surfin', too

Boom goes London and boom Paree
More room for you and more room for me
And every city the whole world round
Will just be another American town
Oh, how peaceful it will be
We'll set everybody free
You'll wear a Japanese kimono
And there'll be Italian shoes for me

They all hate us anyhow
So let's drop the big one now
Let's drop the big one now

Though the laughs felt great in clubs, Randy worried that the song could lead people to think of him as a contemporary Tom Lehrer, who was popular in the 1950s and 1960s for such winning pop parodies as "The Vatican Rag." Randy was a fan of Lehrer's humor, but he didn't want to be known primarily as a humorist, rather than a serious songwriter, and he felt that could be a danger with more songs like "Political Science." War was too easy a target, at least for the young pop audience.

"God's Song (That's Why I Love Mankind)" was more in line with his core vision: humorous, but with more accompanying, thought-provoking touches. Millions of Americans had to balance the humor of the song with the fact that it just might be making fun of their faith. After all the times he was disappointed by cover versions, Randy called Etta James's version of "God's Song" as one of his favorites. "It took some courage because the song is pretty rough for the community she comes from," he said. "And her version really takes God on more than mine does. I didn't hit him hard at all."

Cain slew Abel, Seth knew not why
For if the children of Israel were to multiply
Why must any of the children die?
So he asked the Lord
And the Lord said:
Man means nothing, he means less to me
Than the lowliest cactus flower
Or the humblest yucca tree
He chases round this desert
'Cause he thinks that's where I'll be
That's why I love mankind

I recoil in horror from the foulness of thee
From the squalor and the filth and the misery

How we laugh up here in heaven at the prayers you offer me
That's why I love mankind

The Christians and the Jews were having a jamboree
The Buddhists and the Hindus joined on satellite TV
They picked their four greatest priests
And they began to speak
They said, "Lord, a plague is on the world
Lord, no man is free
The temples that we built to you
Have tumbled into the sea
Lord, if you won't take care of us
Won't you please, please let us be?"
And the Lord said
And the Lord said

I burn down your cities—how blind you must be
I take from you your children and you say how blessed are we
You all must be crazy to put your faith in me
That's why I love mankind
You really need me
That's why I love mankind

"God's Song," which would become another audience favorite, was written within months of "He Gives Us All His Love," and the pair address Randy's ability to write a song based on his own ideas and something to reflect a filmmaker's needs. He never felt he needed to wave an atheist's flag. Besides, if you looked at the song hard enough, you would see "He Gives Us All His Love" had a sharp edge. If God was truly merciful, why wouldn't He do more to protect His flock than merely smile down on us?

When asked over the years what he does believe in, Randy's frequent answer is: "I believe in not hurting anybody."

~

"You Can Leave Your Hat On" and "Burn On" would keep the laughs coming in clubs—"Hat," an erotic tale of women as sex objects, and the pollution-minded "Burn On," an outlandish ode to Cleveland's Cuyahoga River, where oil slicks occasionally caused the river to catch fire. Randy makes the situation in "Burn On" all the more outrageous by having the narrator view the burning with an unbending civic pride. Emil again conducted the orchestra.

Sample lyrics:

Cleveland, city of light, city of magic
Cleveland, city of light, you're calling me
Cleveland, even now I can remember
'Cause the Cuyahoga River
Goes smokin' through my dreams

Burn on, big river, burn on
Burn on, big river, burn on

"Old Man," one of the few times Randy didn't play the humor card, stood alongside "Sail Away" and "God's Song" as a premiere moment in the album. Randy called it one of his favorite compositions at the time.

Everyone has gone away
Can you hear me? Can you hear me?
No one cared enough to stay
Can you hear me? Can you hear me?
You must remember me old man
I know that you can if you try
So just open up your eyes, old man

Look who's come to say goodbye
The sun has left the sky, old man
The birds have flown away
And no one came to cry, old man
Goodbye, old man, goodbye

You want to stay, I know you do
But it ain't no use to try
'Cause I'll be here and I'm just like you
Goodbye, old man, goodbye

Won't be no God to comfort you
You taught me not to believe that lie
You don't need anybody
Nobody needs you
Don't cry, old man, don't cry
Everybody dies

Randy didn't see the song as all that personal at first. It was inspired by the cold isolation of a scene from Stanley Kubrick's *2001: A Space Odyssey*—a moment when parents on earth sing "Happy Birthday" to their astronaut-son in space. But the distance from home only made the astronaut feel lonelier. Randy wanted to write about a son who was raised with little connection to his father.

Watching Randy sing the song in the studio, Waronker and Titelman sensed the family connection. "That was such a desperate narrative, the guy saying goodbye to his father," Russ said. "And then there was the subconscious part of it, which is why the music itself is so achingly beautiful, the strings and the harmonics on the piano. I even heard that Irving, after first hearing it, asked Randy, 'Why are you always killing me off in your songs?'"

About the song years later, Randy said, "It sounds like something my father would say. If he listened to 'So Long Dad' or this one, I'm sure he thought it was about himself—like Warren Beatty hearing Carly Simon's 'You're So Vain.' I wonder if there are people that heard that song and will never like me after that. It's the risk of being a really unpleasant fellow. Maybe my father deserved it, maybe he didn't, but I think the kid should have had more respect for his father."

The album's final number, "Memo to My Son," also had a personal edge: a message to his son Amos about the days ahead.

> *Maybe you don't know how to walk, baby*
> *Maybe you can't talk none either*
> *Maybe you never will, baby*
> *But I'll always love you*
> *I'll always love you*

In a CD reissue package of the album in 2002, Randy said, in part, "The big idea of the song—if there is a big idea—was about fathers who weren't interested in kids until they could laugh at their jokes. In fact, my father was kind of like that. They weren't interested in the 'coo coo coo' stuff and the physicality of picking up a baby, all of which I love. Some people don't know how to deal with little human beings."

Sail Away brought together the highlights of the first two albums—the orchestral sweep of the debut with the more raucous urgency of *12 Songs*. Stephen Holden's review in *Rolling Stone* delivered that message.

"[The album] is further confirmation—as if any more were needed—of the fact that Newman is our most sophisticated artsong composer and also the most self-consciously American. His first album . . . was a brilliant but overly ornate presentation that magnified the bizarre pathos at the surface of the songs while obscuring their deeper intentions. The second studio album . . .

was a stunningly executed change-of-pace, showcasing the bitter ironist in a new guise—that of the consummate rock-and-roller. *Sail Away* is Newman's most mature album, a work of genius." Holden placed the LP in the company of recent releases by John Lennon and Paul Simon as a milestone within the "evolving rock-as-art-song form."

Sail Away also picked up a glowing review by Lester Bangs, in the hip, upstart rock journal *Creem.* Calling the album "positively devastating," Bangs, a critical auteur and author who was highly influential in underground circles, wrote: "A moralist disguised as a sarcastic misanthrope, Newman allowed us to wallow in our need to relegate anybody to the status of baboon, to feel the repugnance, the naturalness, and a kind of curious kind of objectivity all at the same time. It was masterful. It was profound, and damn little is these days."

Newman was hailed in similar terms in England, where he did a few live shows in early 1972 to warm up for his most extensive US tour. Reviewing Randy's March 6 concert at Royal Festival Hall in London, Keith Altham of the *New Musical Express* ranked Randy as "the most original of all current contemporary songwriters, for he never seems to borrow a note or a chord change from anywhere," asserting that "his ideas are certainly his own."

Critiquing the same concert for a rival music weekly, Michael Watts wrote, "What makes Randy more than just a clever comedian is a thick streak of humanity that runs through his work. While many of his situations are awful and the characters are immoral, he has a tender side that contrasts strongly with his ironic compositions."

— II —

Sail Away quickly entered the US Top 200 album charts that summer, where it stayed for more than four months, driven by Randy's active touring. Thanks to urging by Ostin after the success of the live album, Newman had a manager in place. Rather than a hard-core rock firm that might try to bend Randy into a more conventional and commercial mode, the Warner chief recommended BNB Management, which represented a broad range of entertainment figures, including Andy Williams, the Carpenters, and Bill Withers.

Mace Neufeld, the "N" in BNB, was a Yale graduate who flirted briefly with songwriting before turning to management and eventually enjoyed his greatest success as a film producer, amassing such credits as *The Hunt for Red October* and *The Equalizer*. He jumped at the chance to represent Newman. "Those early albums were unlike anything I had heard," Neufeld said. "I was even more impressed after I spent some time with him. He was a voracious reader who could talk to you about any subject."

To promote the new album, BNB lined up some fifty dates, starting with preview stops in Europe followed by a series of US shows that would run to early December of 1972. Neufeld accompanied Randy to the European shows where he marveled at the fans' enthusiasm. "Randy was already on his way to becoming a superstar among his peers in the music world," Neufeld said. "The challenge was to translate that excitement to the pop audience without a lot of help from radio. I was thrilled by the concert in Amsterdam where about 90 percent of the audience showed up with mimeographed lyrics to his songs. They were that much into him." That same excitement was mirrored in the US dates, as measured by an album sales spurt in cities on the tour.

Because he had other clients, Neufeld sent a bright young newcomer at the firm with an interest in contemporary pop on the road to be Randy's day-to-day contact. Elliot Abbott, who was born in Brooklyn in 1946, had a 24/7 sense of humor, and they soon bonded. He would play a key role in Newman's early career.

"Randy had a reputation for hating to work, so my goal was to try to make him enjoy going on the road," Abbott said. "As it turned out, he told me once, 'When I'm writing alone at home, there's no one applauding. It's just me and I'm banging away. It feels good to have that applause.'" Abbott sensed in the beginning that Randy was very, very shy and used humor as his entrée. "He was always looking for practical jokes," he said. "Whenever we checked into a hotel, he would go into my room first and pick up the pillows and sit on them and then say, 'Enjoy your sleep,' as he headed for his room. Every time we headed for a rental car on the road, he'd offer to drive, knowing I had heard so much about his driving problems that I would never let him get behind the wheel."

Abbott also spoke about occasional trips with Randy to one of Los Angeles's racetracks and a memorable night in a Las Vegas casino. "We were at the blackjack table, just the two of us, and I noticed that the dealer tended to keep his head down," he said. "But every once in a while, he would take a peek at us, and we won. Then, when we were about ready to take the money up, he basically said to leave it and we did and we kept winning, maybe six or seven hands in a row, so it was a good stack by this point. But finally it was time for the dealer to take his break and he looks at the stack and looks at Randy and says, 'I like your stuff.'"

~

The touring twosome became a threesome in June as Jim Croce was brought in to open some shows. Croce, a young singer-songwriter from Philadelphia, signed with BNB just before his career took off with a series of mostly playful, everyman folk-pop hits including "You Don't Mess Around with Jim" and "Big Bad Leroy Brown." In fact, "Mess Around" entered the national sales chart less than a month after he started opening for Randy, and it rose to No. 8 while the tour was still in progress. This could have caused ego problems, but Randy delighted in Croce's success, and Croce was in such awe of Randy's writing that he couldn't imagine closing the shows.

"They had a lot in common," Abbott said. "They were both married with little kids, and they led very normal lives, outside of the fact they were on the road playing music. They really enjoyed each other's company. Randy never treated Jim like he was the opening act, and he was crushed when he was killed in the 1973 plane crash."

The tour's most memorable stop was on October 26, when Randy played New York's prestigious 2,700-seat Philharmonic Hall (now David Geffen Hall), complete with a fifty-piece orchestra conducted by his uncle Emil. Abbott came up with the idea to play the Philharmonic as album sales mounted. "But it turned out we were talking almost $50,000 for the orchestra, so I had to go to Warner Bros. where Bob Regehr, who was head of artist development, said, 'Fine.' That was it." The backing was typical of Warner's support of Newman.

True to form, the only person who didn't like the concert idea was Randy. Abbott recalled: "When I told Randy what we were going to do at the Philharmonic with an orchestra, he said, 'Why do you want me to do that? It's going to be horrible. I don't think we could ever sell it out.'" In the weeks leading to the show, Newman continued to express doubts. "He was saying it was going to be the biggest embarrassment of his career," Abbott said. "But when we got to New York, the atmosphere was incredible. The hall was packed, and I got more requests for tickets than for any other show in my life."

Abbott was backstage as Randy walked on stage and saw the audience—which included Dylan, Paul Simon, and Barbra Streisand—welcome him with a standing ovation. "He looked back at me, as if to say, 'What's going on?' He still had no sense that people loved his music that much. Then it happened all over again after intermission. Randy got another standing ovation. I'll never forget the big smile on his face at the end of the show."

Writing in the *New York Times*, Don Heckman continued to spread the word about the range of Newman's ambitions. "His gifts have been compared by some reviewers (including this one) to those of Cole Porter, but I suspect that George Gershwin might provide a more accurate parallel. Like Gershwin, Mr. Newman has a mastery of the entire sweep of musical invention and architecture that is rare, almost to the point of nonexistence, in today's pop music world. And, taking it one step past Gershwin, Mr. Newman is also a brilliant lyricist."

— III —

By the end of the year, sales of *Sail Away* were approaching 300,000, but Randy didn't think of it as much of a victory. As much as he would say over the years that he mainly cared about the reaction of his peers to his music, he did care about sales. "Even though *Sail Away* was a big increase, I still considered myself a commercial failure," he said. "I would follow what other young songwriters were doing at Warner. I could see that *Sail Away* was selling around 50,000 or 100,000 at one point, but I knew that Neil Young and James Taylor had sold 500,000 or a million at same time (eventually three million for both *Harvest* and *Sweet Baby James*). Then other Warner artists came along and they, too, sold a million or more. I believed in my albums, but I still felt kinda ignored."

That discrepancy led to a series of newspaper and magazine articles, asking the same question: Why isn't this brilliant songwriter selling more records? Some writers felt that Randy's music was too sophisticated; others wondered if the themes weren't too eccentric; still others felt that Randy simply didn't fit one of mainstream pop's major commercial streams. He wasn't a rock-and-roll hero (à la Dylan and Young) or a confessional singer-songwriter (Taylor or Mitchell), and certainly wasn't an accessible hitmaker (Elton John). Bottom line, his rich creative vision left him on the fringes of commercial pop. Why would you even expect massive sales?

Rolling Stone took advantage of the sales upswing in 1972 to have Dave Felton write the magazine's first lengthy profile of Newman, and one of the things Felton wanted to explore was how Randy spent his time during his "retreat . . . into the indolent privacy" rather than working on new albums.

What he learned was Randy wasn't in bed with the covers over his head, but he did devote whole days to television—a range of programs that found room for *The Adventures of Rocky and Bullwinkle and Friends, The New Zoo Revue,* hours of news, and Japanese variety shows—and reading books including *Winesburg, Ohio* and John Toland's *Rising Sun: The Decline and Fall of the Japanese Empire,* as well as lighter fare by Agatha Christie and Herman Wouk. In 1972, he was still doing a lot of reading, but much of it dealt with the subject of his next album.

— IV —

Despite all the hours together on tour, one thing that Abbott didn't know was that Randy was becoming obsessed with a song idea that had been brewing in him for over a year, one that helped finally define his subject matter.

This was a time when pop was increasingly focusing on race and urban ills, a fragment of the mainstream output, to be sure, but with some significant works, especially by Black artists. After the hymn-like grace of Sam Cooke's "A Change Is Gonna Come" in 1964, Curtis Mayfield, the following year, delivered gospel-coated declaration in "People Get Ready" (which Martin Luther King Jr.

adopted as the unofficial anthem of his movement) the following year. They were joined by James Brown's explosive "Say It Loud—I'm Black and I'm Proud" (co-written by Pee Wee Ellis) in 1968, Gil Scott-Heron's "The Revolution Will Not Be Televised" in 1971, and Stevie Wonder's "Living for the City" in 1973.

The issue was on Randy's mind on the *Sail Away* tour. Despite the acclaim the song received for its censure of racism in this country, Randy wanted a more illuminating expression of the anger and rage that the subject deserved. He didn't share his father's combative instincts but inherited some of his anger, all of which he funneled into "Rednecks."

The path to the song began back in December of 1970 when Newman tuned in ABC-TV to see talk show host Dick Cavett interview Lester Maddox, the segregationist governor of Georgia. Many of the race-baiting Southern figures in the United States Senate—notably Strom Thurmond of South Carolina and Theodore Bilbo of Mississippi—had faded from the national scene, but the outspoken Maddox, a former restaurant owner in Atlanta, was part of a proud new wave of Southern stalwarts. Maddox came to national attention when he responded to the federal Civil Rights Act of 1964 by vowing to close his restaurant rather than serve Blacks. He threatened African Americans with an axe handle if they dared walk into his establishment and so relished the public attention that he began selling souvenir axe handles for two dollars each.

Newman detested Maddox's views and looked forward to seeing him make a fool of himself on Cavett's show, but the program was a major disappointment, an ambush in which Cavett and his guests ganged up on the governor, causing him to eventually walk off the show. Upset by what he saw as grandstanding, Newman wanted to write a song about the incident, one that would express Maddox's bigotry and, at the same time, condemn the hypocrisy of the North about its own segregationist practices.

By the end of 1972, the song was beginning to take shape. It would be the foundation of a concept album that would put the song into a wider context. At a time when slipping a few love songs into his repertoire would have been a winning commercial strategy, Newman doubled down on his underlying instincts: songs that mattered to him. "I sort of knew that I wasn't going to change things in the country, but I felt I had a duty to try and make people like me a little better," he said. "It isn't like I was pandering politically or anything. I said what I meant. That was always in my mind."

— **V** —

Without taking his eye off Randy, Lenny had shown enough promise at Warner by then for him to be named a vice president and head of A&R, and he assembled a strong team of producers, including Titelman, Templeman, and Tommy LiPuma. Besides overseeing the talent roster, he produced or co-produced eight Gordon Lightfoot albums and six Arlo Guthrie albums, as well as four for Ry Cooder, two each for James Taylor, Maria Muldaur, and Rickie Lee Jones, and one each for Paul Simon and Michael McDonald. In addition, he served as executive producer for Eric Clapton and Brian Wilson collections, among others.

Though the Randy and Van Dyke albums brought massive critical support, Waronker's first album with Lightfoot was significant because it proved he could sell records in big numbers. The 1970 LP, *Sit Down Young Stranger*, sold more than a million copies and contained a Top 10 single, "If You Could Read My Mind."

Lightfoot had begun his recording career in his native Canada in the 1960s, attracting enough attention as a singer-songwriter to be signed by Albert Grossman, who also managed Dylan. After four albums for United Artists Records, however, Lightfoot was still largely unknown in the United States at the end of the decade and began looking for a new label in 1969. He was soon attracted to Warner, which was widely seen as the home of promising singer-songwriters, including fellow Canadians Joni Mitchell and Neil Young.

Lenny was surprised one day when Mo asked him if he'd like to work with Lightfoot. An admirer of such Lightfoot songs as "Early Morning Rain," "Ribbon of Darkness," and "Did She Mention My Name," Lenny responded with excitement: "Is he available?" Years later he said, "Besides Gordon's vocals and lyrics, I loved his melodic instincts and the way he performed the songs with his band, always live in the studio, which made him unique."

Lightfoot's uniqueness also included his ability to write lengthy historical narratives, starting in 1966 with "Canadian Railroad Trilogy," a detailed, six-minute account of the building of the cross-country Canadian Pacific Railway in the late 1800s. The song is regarded as a national treasure in Canada. Because of its length and subject matter, however, the song seemed like a one-off affair until Lightfoot presented Waronker years later with another six-minute song, this one chronicling the sinking of the SS *Edmund Fitzgerald* in Lake Superior in 1975. The event, which resulted in the death of twenty-eight crew members, was well known in the Midwest, but it wasn't part of national lore the way "Trilogy" had been in Canada, so its commercial prospects were shaky. But Lightfoot had been performing the song live and was excited about the reaction. Lenny released the single, and it blew up overnight, rising to No. 2 on the *Billboard* chart.

Also in the mid-1970s, James Taylor asked Lenny to produce his *Gorilla* album. While Waronker and co-producer Titelman were working on the collection, they started talking with James about a cover song to supplement his own tunes. Russ pushed for the classic Motown hit "How Sweet It Is (to Be Loved by You)."

Lenny loved the song (written by the team of Holland-Dozier-Holland), but he worried that the song had been such a staple of pop radio for years—with hit versions by Marvin Gaye and Junior Walker & the All-Stars—that the public might not be able to get behind a third version.

Driving home that night, however, Lenny was listening to an oldies station when, of all things, the song came on, and it still sounded so great that Lenny changed his mind. Taylor's version was so stylish that the single went one spot higher on the pop charts (No. 5) than Gaye's had in 1965. To make it even sweeter, Gaye later said good things about it.

But Lenny didn't only work with established figures. One of the most notable chapters in his production history was a newcomer: Rickie Lee Jones, a young Los Angeles singer-songwriter whose self-titled debut album combined the grace and assurance of Joni Mitchell with the gritty street imagery of Tom Waits—music that went from richly theatrical to deeply sentimental. The album (co-produced by Russ Titelman) sold over a million copies and included the Top 5 single "Chuck E.'s in Love."

Through it all, Lenny was waiting for Randy's next album.

CHAPTER TEN

Good Old Boys *and*
The N-word

— I —

"Holy hell, we're gonna die!" Abbott wisecracked (mostly) when
Newman first played "Rednecks" for him in a New York hotel
room during a brief East Coast tour in 1973. "He knew the song
was going to upset people—to put it mildly—but it's how he saw
the world," Abbott said years later. "I loved it. There was no
hesitation on anyone's part at Warner Bros.—certainly not [from]
Lenny, Mo, or Russ when they heard it—and why should there
be? When someone with Randy's artistry puts the truth in front
of you, what are you going to say—'You've gone too far'?"

In the coming weeks, Randy began working on songs to fill out
the concept album. "I felt I needed to explain 'Rednecks,'" Newman said. "I wanted to show why the guy in the song would be so
angry about the hypocrisy surrounding the racial issue in this
country. That's what the song was about. I wasn't trying to forgive
the South for its role in treatment of Blacks, but I wanted to point
out the North couldn't take all this moral high ground. I wanted
to continue the discussion of race. One song wasn't enough."

On hotel stationery and in spiral notebooks, Randy spent
months outlining a series of songs that gave the "Rednecks" lead

character a wider cultural context. Over more than forty-five pages, Randy listed potential song themes and titles, page after page of revised lyrics and even mini-portraits of personalities in various songs. When Lenny saw the notes, he was amazed. Randy had never come close to devoting that much time to an album.

On one sheet, Randy described how he pictured his "Rednecks" narrator: "Not unsympathetic character despite the 'Jew and Nigger' [slurs]. Married with a two-year old daughter, living in a small apartment in Birmingham, Ala. Possibly works in steel mills and on weekends and free time serves as a counselor/playground supervisor at a park nearby . . . fairly intelligent and intellectually restless and dissatisfied with his life." Newman even gave the narrator a name, Johnny Cutler. The rush of ideas and crossed-out lyrics documented how Randy seemingly questioned every line of a song to weigh its place in the story. Whole songs came ("Birmingham," "Marie") and often went ("If We Didn't Have Jesus," "The Joke," and "My Daddy Loves Dixie Howell"). At times, Newman put words down simply as placeholders in the album: "uninhibited wild bar-type singalong thing," "crazed blues," "song to the father, possibly upon father's death." He also proposed various noises between tracks to link the songs—phone calls, TV shows, traffic, children playing.

Aside from brief trips for live shows, Randy spent the rest of the year on the project. Of particular interest in the Johnny Cutler notes was "Birmingham," because it was the song, after "Rednecks," that told us the most about Cutler. The lyrics went through several revisions, which provide a look at Randy's writing process. Where he began one version with the line "Let me tell you something," he eventually dropped it and went directly to Cutler's background. He later rearranged some verses and threw out others altogether (including a peek into Cutler's self-destructive side with a tale of building a summer home in

Huntsville that he burned down for fun). Ultimately, "Birmingham" exhibited a compactness and detail that was characteristic of the finest short stories.

Got a wife, got a family
Earn my livin' with my hand
I'm a roller in a steel mill
In downtown Birmingham
My daddy was a barber
And a most unsightly man
He was born in Tuscaloosa
But he died right here in Birmingham

Birmingham, Birmingham
The greatest city in Alabam'
You can travel 'cross this entire land
But there ain't no place like Birmingham

My wife's named Mary
But she's called Marie
We live in a three room house
With a pepper tree
I work all day in the factory
That's alright with me

Got a big black dog
And his name is Dan
Who lives in my backyard in Birmingham
He is the meanest dog in Alabam'
Get 'em Dan

Birmingham, Birmingham
The greatest city in Alabam'

You can travel 'cross this entire land
But there ain't no place like Birmingham

In less than three minutes on the album, Randy, without any mention of race, showed the narrator and what's important to him, including the regional pride that extended beyond the boundaries of Birmingham to his Southern heritage. By contrast, "Marie" appears to have been written rather quickly; there is little rethinking of its lyrics in the Johnny Cutler papers. Backed by one of Randy's tenderest melodies, the song conveys Cutler's attempt to express his love for his wife. He apologizes for his behavior, which speaks to the lack of self-worth that fuels his racist anger and his resentment of the way his state and region have been treated by Northerners.

You looked like a princess the night we met
With your hair piled up high
I will never forget
I'm drunk right now baby
But I've got to be
Or I never could tell you
What you mean to me
I loved you the first time I saw you
And I always will love you, Marie
I loved you the first time I saw you
And I always will love you, Marie

You're the song that the trees sing when the wind blows
You're a flower, you're a river, you're a rainbow
Sometimes I'm crazy
But I guess you know
And I'm weak and I'm lazy
And I've hurt you so

And I don't listen to a word you say
When you're in trouble I just turn away

But I love you and I loved you the first time I saw you
And I always will love you, Marie
I loved you the first time I saw you
And I always will love you, Marie

Another song that would become a defining number, "Louisiana" (later "Louisiana 1927"), is only mentioned in the notes as a "possible" entry. It grew out of Randy's longtime fascination with the Southern state, thanks in part to his mother, who told him stories about the region, including the Great Mississippi Flood of 1927 and the state's celebrated governor, Huey Long.

— II —

Before writing about the flood's impact, Randy wanted to learn about the events surrounding it, including the politics. Others in pop music were offering valuable looks at social issues by asking questions (Marvin Gaye's "What's Going On"), offering hopeful ideals (John Lennon's "Imagine"), and expressing outrage over misuse of establishment power (Neil Young's "Ohio"). Newman wanted to explore the flood issues more deeply. He wouldn't admit to becoming something of a social crusader, but the music suggested the process had begun. Years later, he would describe these as his "significant" songs, the ones he cared the most about.

Reading about the 1927 disaster, he learned that it was the most destructive river flood in the country's history—covering more than twenty-five thousand square miles with water sometimes reaching thirty feet high and uprooting hundreds of thousands of people. Gradually, Randy began to see how one of the flood's most dramatic chapters could fit the theme he was addressing—the factors that hardened anger and resentment about Northerners and even power brokers in Louisiana itself.

The flood had such shattering impact that it's no wonder some of the nation's most respected musicians have addressed it, from blues figures Charley Patton and Bessie Smith to Dylan. The water's buildup in the upper portions of the river in the summer of 1926 was already so punishing that Smith, heralded as the "Empress of the Blues," recorded "Backwater Blues" in February of 1927. That account of a woman being driven from her home took place two months before what history would mark as the official starting date of the disaster. In June, Barbecue Bob, a popular blues artist of the 1920s, recorded "Mississippi Heavy Water Blues," which speaks about the death of a loved one.

Two years later, Patton wrote "High Water Everywhere," a blues standard that touched briefly on racism and injustice, and the team of Memphis Minnie and Kansas Joe McCoy came up with "When the Levee Breaks," popularized half a century later by rock superstars Led Zeppelin. Dylan stepped aboard the flood train on his 2001 album *Love and Theft* with "High Water (for Charley Patton)," a tribute to the bluesman that focused on the human suffering.

The power of Newman's "Louisiana 1927" is that it side-stepped the concentration on personal struggle in the earlier tunes to confront the factors surrounding the flood, including politics and race. This would give the song a deep relevance as those issues resurfaced decades later. In a single, illuminating line, Randy speaks for all the Louisiana flood victims—and anyone—who felt they had been sacrificed by the federal government and even their local public officials: "They're trying to wash us away."

There's much to justify that anger at local Louisiana office-holders and social elites. In *Rising Tide: The Great Mississippi Flood of 1927 and How It Changed America*, author-historian

John M. Barry provides a portrait of greed, racism, betrayal, and misuse of public power. In his book, Barry devotes four chapters to the manipulation behind the "sacrifice" of New Orleans's St. Bernard and Plaquemines parishes—a devastation scripted by non-elected white power brokers. As the storm rapidly approached southern Louisiana, a group of leading bankers and businessmen—who routinely set policy in the city—held a strategy meeting on April 14, 1927, during which a newspaper publisher, James Thomson, proposed dynamiting a levee south of New Orleans to divert the flood waters from the heart of the city; it was a radical idea, but there's no evidence of any opposition being raised. New Orleans had a history of severe flood damage, and panic was setting in.

The business leaders had no authority to take such action, so they set about ensuring that city, state, and national officials would do so, and everyone fell in line. The word from Washington, DC, was that Calvin Coolidge's administration would respond "sympathetically" to the dynamiting plan if formally requested by Louisiana governor Oramel Simpson and if the federal government was not officially involved. Simpson, too, agreed—as long as the city met certain conditions, including a written promise to compensate all those driven from their homes for their loss.

Less than twenty-four hours after the dynamiting, a levee on the west bank of the Mississippi north of New Orleans broke, greatly reducing the threat. If the explosions had been delayed even one day, there would have been no need for the sacrifice. And the promise of repayment? In a 2005 interview on NPR, Barry said the federal government did not a pay a single penny for the clothing, food, or shelter of any one of those 700,000 people.

Randy condensed those facts into a heartbreaking expression of lower-class helplessness, Black and white; the ultimate, one-sided struggle between the haves and have-nots. He wanted a song that would speak to society's victims of any era, and he did it so well that the song would have a strong second life as nature again imperiled New Orleans in the early 2000s. The lyrics to "Louisiana 1927":

What has happened down here is the winds have changed
Clouds roll in from the north and it started to rain
Rained real hard and it rained for a real long time
Six feet of water in the streets of Evangeline
The river rose all day
The river rose all night
Some people got lost in the flood
Some people got away alright
The river have busted through clear down to Plaquemines
Six feet of water in the streets of Evangeline

Louisiana, Louisiana
They're tryin' to wash us away
They're tryin' to wash us away
Louisiana, Louisiana
They're tryin' to wash us away
They're tryin' to wash us away

President Coolidge came down in a railroad train
With a little fat man with a notepad in his hand
The President say, "Little fat man isn't it a shame what the
  river has done
To this poor cracker's land."

Louisiana, Louisiana
They're tryin' to wash us away
They're tryin' to wash us away
Louisiana, Louisiana

They're tryin' to wash us away
They're tryin' to wash us away
They're tryin' to wash us away
They're tryin' to wash us away

Talking about the song years later, Randy recalled an experience he had while on tour in Mississippi. "There was this older guy driving me around, a liberal volunteer-type fellow," he said. "We talked about this and that, and I asked him why people in the state that don't have health insurance didn't jump on Obamacare and he said, 'Well, we don't like being told what to do.' And that's especially true if something is coming from the north, which is why I said in the song that the clouds rolled in from the north."

— III —

Early in 1973, Randy was ready to move forward on the album that he was calling *Johnny Cutler's Birthday*. He had been playing individual songs for Lenny and Russ for weeks, but neither had heard the songs collectively. Randy, too, wanted the songs on tape to better measure what he had. At Warner's Amigo Studios with Titelman at his side, he recorded thirteen songs (with just voice and piano), introducing each with a few words to explain the song's place in the story.

Prefacing "Rednecks," he said, "This begins with the sound of children playing, presumably some boys playing football . . . and in the distance a park band concert. Johnny Cutler and his daughter are at the park, presumably sitting on a park bench. [There's] some desultory conversation, [Cutler says,] 'Why don't you play with those kids?' and she whines a bit. . . . Ultimately, after he loses his temper, she goes off and he quiets. The kids' voices fade and he [begins singing]: 'Last night I saw Lester Maddox on a TV show.'"

In some of the introductions, Randy seemed to be speaking as much to himself as to Titelman, still trying to find his way through the lyrics and sequencing. For all the talk about the early lack of motivation and direction, Newman was in absolute control. He no longer needed anyone to push him. There was nothing tentative about his voice, and he appeared comfortable admitting he still had questions about the album. Rarely far from humorous asides, Randy introduced a song titled "Birmingham Redux" by saying, "What is to follow is highly tentative, even more tentative than what I've done up to now . . . not crazy about it."

"Doctor, Doctor," which would be heavily revised and retitled "Back on My Feet Again," gives us more biographical information about Cutler. Randy introduces it this way: "The next scene takes place in a doctor's office. His brother's been committed for being mentally ill. The doctor says he has very little information about his brother—Johnny Cutler's brother—and Cutler proceeds to give it to him." Using Cutler's troubled brother as the narrator, the song also offers another glimpse of depression and braggadocio driven by low self-esteem and the constant, obsessive issue of race.

Regarding "Louisiana 1927" in the notes, Newman simply indicated it would be sung by Cutler's brother, David, at the birthday party. On the demo, however, the song asserts a commentary and power that would eventually make it a turning point in the album's framework.

Titelman was enthusiastic. "It was going to be totally unified, something like a Berg opera, where nothing really happens, but everything is revealed," he said in a Warner newsletter at the time. Listening to the tape later, Waronker thought the story had a cohesion and plot discipline that might make for a compelling stage musical.

Before finishing the album, Newman spent the next two months on a tour that was preceded by a warm-up date on March 16 in Lafayette, Louisiana, where he thought it might be time to preview "Rednecks." As good as a song might sound in the studio, there's nothing more informative for an artist than hearing an audience's response. In Lafayette, Elliot Abbott sensed Randy sizing up the audience in the show's early moments to see if people were paying attention to the words and seemed to be understanding the songs. Satisfied they were tuned in, he began "Rednecks."

"I was holding my breath when he got to the N-word," Abbott said. "There was this hush in the club—as if everyone was thinking, 'Whoa, what did I just hear?' I didn't know what to think. But the crowd quickly picked up on what the song was about when he got to the lines about Harlem and the South Side of Chicago. The place went wild. Randy was elated."

But Newman later got a letter from a young Black man who was at the concert and was disturbed being in a room with 1,500 white people who were standing up when Newman sang the slur word. Randy phoned the letter writer and explained why he used it, trying to assure the man of his purpose.

Before Lafayette, Randy had already been testing some of the other Cutler material on audiences, including "Birmingham," "Guilty," and "Marie," according to a setlist history put together by Gary Norris, who was Newman's official archivist from 1994 to 2006. Norris was a fan turned friend who would play a valuable role in preserving demo tapes, notebooks, and other material that would shed light on Newman's career and process—objects that were of no particular interest to Newman. Born in Glendale, California, in 1954, Norris moved to the San Francisco area with his parents in 1968, where he discovered Newman's music in a movie theater in 1971. "The music of *Cold Turkey* was a revelation," Norris said. "I bought Randy's first three albums immediately and eventually got *Sail Away*, which remains my favorite."

The fascination was so deep that decades later Norris didn't just remember the venue where he first saw Newman (Berkeley Community Theater), but the date (November 4, 1972). In his

enthusiasm, he worked his way backstage to meet Randy, a practice he repeated at several future shows. Norris gradually made
enough of an impression for Newman to share his phone number, which Norris called occasionally, asking details about old
songs or what Newman was working on. Visiting Newman's
home, Norris was amazed by the stacks of demo tapes and studio
outtakes (more than three hundred tapes), notebooks, and other
papers and he began organizing them.

~

Randy was encouraged by how well "Rednecks" was received in
the North and South, but he was still uncertain about the Cutler
album. Sensing his frustration, Waronker and Titelman talked
him into returning to Amigo Studios for three days in July of
1973 to make a demo of the songs that Randy felt most strongly
about, including "Rednecks," "Birmingham," and "Louisiana
1927." They hoped it would help him visualize the rest of the
story. In the studio, Randy introduced a new song he wrote in the
everyman spirit of "Louisiana 1927," the feeling of abandonment
that was common among Southerners. The backdrop of "Mr.
President (Have Pity on the Working Man)" was economic hard
times, not raging waters. To brighten the frequently dark tone of
the album, the song offered a lighter and more universal edge.

> *We've taken all you've given*
> *But it's gettin' hard to make a livin'*
> *Mr. President, have pity on the working man*
> *We ain't asking for you to love us*
> *You may place yourself high above us*
> *Mr. President, have pity on the working man*
>
> *I know it may sound funny*
> *But people ev'rywhere are runnin' out of money*

We just can't make it by ourself
It is cold and the wind is blowing
We need something to keep us going
Mr. President, have pity on the working man

Maybe you're cheatin'
Maybe you're lyin'
Maybe you have lost your mind
Maybe you're only thinking 'bout yourself

Too late to run. Too late to cry now
The time has come for us to say good-bye now
Mr. President, have pity on the working man
Mr. President, have pity on the working man

Despite the strong material, Randy still wasn't satisfied; he didn't think the songs came together in a cohesive package. As it turned out, Newman only thought about the Cutler project for a couple of weeks before heading out on another tour that would keep him on the road for most of the rest of the year: some thirty shows from Massachusetts to Colorado.

As Randy juggled the Cutler songs, he began thinking about more songs in the style of "Louisiana 1927" and "Mr. President," which led him to all the outlandish tales he had heard about Huey Long, Louisiana's controversial governor and then US senator. Long's larger-than-life story inspired two Pulitzer Prize–winning books (Robert Penn Warren's 1946 novel *All the King's Men* and T. Harry Williams's 1969 biography *Huey Long*) as well as a 1949 film version of the Warren novel that won an Oscar for best motion picture.

Even in the 1970s, Long—who was allegedly assassinated by the relative of a political opponent in 1935—remained such a polarizing figure in Louisiana that the mention of his name could lead to heated arguments. True believers cheered Long—who proudly bore the nickname "Kingfish"—as a populist who defended the common man against corporate greed and political indifference. He, indeed, is widely considered to be one of the few Southern governors who didn't actively play the race card, a position that won him deep support among Blacks in Louisiana. Long's "Share the Wealth" crusade also advocated positions that would be considered extreme by millions of Americans nearly a century later, including a plan to tax the wealthy to pay for such social programs as free college and vocational training, a month's vacation for all workers, free medical care, and a household grant of $5,000 per family.

After first supporting Franklin D. Roosevelt, Long criticized the president for being too conservative in helping the needy during the Great Depression. Amid widespread speculation he was going to run for president on a third-party ticket in 1936, Long wrote a book, *My First Days in the White House*, which was published shortly after his death. Its foreword carried this mission statement: "This book has been published in good faith, without malice, but with a desire to present to its readers a future America under the guidance of its Author."

Yet Long was reviled by others in his home state as a corrupt demagogue, whose state administration was filled with scandal and abuse of power. In a 2019 essay in *The Atlantic*, he was portrayed as the left-wing equivalent of President Donald Trump.

The Louisiana setting was a break from Cutler's Alabama turf, but the history of the state fit the social resentment and mistreatment that shaped so much of the Southern attitude of "Rednecks." Newman wrote a song about Long ("Kingfish") and became intrigued by reports of the song, "Every Man a King," that was co-written by Long as a campaign rally singalong. "It's a pretty snappy song," Randy said. "I wonder how much of it Long wrote. He did it with [Castro Carazo,] the bandleader at LSU." Newman couldn't find a recording of "Every Man a King," but a Southern cousin remembered the song from childhood. He sang it for Randy, who took the words down and then located the music in a museum in Louisiana. The lyrics—which Newman later backed with a ragtime accompaniment that gives his recording the feel of a turn-of-the-century stump speech at a county fair—portrayed Long as the friend of the working man, the one who promised to "save this land." Newman thought it helped explain the us-against-them anger of the state's lower economic class, the prime "Rednecks" constituency.

— IV —

Early in 1974, Waronker and Titelman tried to jump-start Newman's creative process again. Thinking Newman might look forward to arranging and conducting, they booked a studio to record the orchestral portions of "Marie" and the alcohol-soaked "Rollin'," but things quickly bogged down when Randy refused to do the arrangements. He appeared worn down from the months of working on the album and touring.

Rather than cancel the February 27 session, Waronker came up with a novel solution: offer the assignment to Nick DeCaro, a respected young arranger who was a fan of Randy and understood his music. Privately, Waronker was trying to challenge Randy. "Besides keeping things moving, we thought it might piss him off watching Nick conduct the orchestra instead of him and get him back into action, and that's what happened," he said. "We started moving forward."

Lenny booked another session for March 12 to record "Mr. President," which was not on the Cutler demo or even mentioned in the pages of notes. Randy didn't make a point of abandoning the Cutler outline, but the song choices showed that he was slowly doing just that. "It was just such a good idea, and we had a handful of songs that made sense," Lenny said. "I didn't want to let go, but Johnny Cutler just didn't happen. It was clear that he had moved on."

In his role as archivist, Norris found the Johnny Cutler demo tape and he later lobbied to include it on a 2002 deluxe reissue of *Good Old Boys*. Newman didn't like the idea of releasing the unfinished work, but Waronker and Cathy Kerr, who began managing Randy in the mid-1990s, encouraged him to do so. It allowed Newman fans a chance to see the progression of an album that fulfilled the potential of the debut album and signaled everything to come.

As the sessions continued, the enthusiasm resumed. *Good Old Boys* felt like one piece. The final collection would contain twelve songs, including seven from the Cutler project: "Rednecks," "Birmingham," "Marie," "Louisiana 1927," and "Rollin'," plus in different form "Back on My Feet Again" and "A Wedding in Cherokee County." The new tunes featured three pieces in the wider "Louisiana" style—"Mr. President," "Every Man a King," and "Kingfish"—plus two additional Newman songs, "Naked Man" and "Guilty." The latter, which would be recorded by more than three dozen artists, including Bonnie Raitt, Joe Cocker, and Madeleine Peyroux, was another drunken apology to a wife or girlfriend. It ends with the stark verse:

You know, you know how it is with me, baby
You know, you know I just can't stand myself
And it takes a whole lot of medicine
For me to pretend that I'm somebody else

"Naked Man" and "Cherokee County" didn't feel integral to the album concept, more like colorful stories that could have been on any Newman album. Randy offered reasons why they fit, but they weren't convincing; he apparently just liked the songs. "Naked Man" grew out of a story he heard from an attorney friend in Los Angeles. As Randy told it, one naked man was stopped by police on a street when another naked man suddenly ran by. Newman took it from there. "Cherokee Wedding"—which reflected some of the backwoods social inter- action of such Erskine Caldwell novels as *Tobacco Road*—grew out of a colorful novelty Randy had written about Albania, a country in southeastern Europe with a long, colorful history that fascinated him. Newman had an attachment to both songs.

On balance, *Good Old Boys* was Newman's most inspired album yet. It helped Randy define and toughen his social view, convincing him more than ever of the importance of writing sig- nificant songs. "Ultimately, the album reminded me of a great John Ford black-and-white movie where everything, including the people and surroundings, felt authentic," Waronker said. "To me, the album was a genuine piece of Americana."

For everyone present at the final session on August 9, 1974, there was a surreal moment. Randy, Lenny, and Russ heard that President Nixon was resigning to avoid impeachment and loss of office over the Watergate break-in scandal. They turned on the television in the studio lounge to watch Nixon leave the White House. "It was such an important event," Waronker said.

Afterwards, we still had to do "Every Man a King," so I think Randy started playing piano and we all sang. Randy, Russ, and me. We wanted it to sound like a lot of people singing, so we kept overdubbing. We probably ended up with eighteen tracks of us singing. When I heard it all together, I thought it sounded like a fraternity group, which made sense to me. It was just a minute and something, but it felt fitting . . . singing the song by Huey Long after watching the resignation. It was quite funny, but also sad.

Two days after the album's September 10 release, protests broke out in Boston (one of the cities called out in "Rednecks") over the role of student busing to achieve greater integration in the public schools. Fearing the album might worsen the tension in the city, Boston radio stations agreed to not play *Good Old Boys*. Even without protests, however, AM program directors throughout the country, likely concerned about the album's content, avoided the LP. FM programmers did showcase selected tracks.

As before, critics backed Newman. *Rolling Stone*'s Stephen Davis summarized the LP as a "continuation of Newman's deceptive, mercurial work. It mystifies, it confuses, it entertains, it swings. You don't know whether to laugh or cry, and that is Randy Newman's rare and bizarre skill."

As soon as the album was released, a hot topic among Newman fans was which was the better album: *Sail Away* or *Good Old Boys*.

Preferring *Good Old Boys* to *Sail Away*, Robert Christgau wrote in the *Village Voice*: "Contrary to published report, the white Southerners Newman sings about/from are never objects of contempt. Even Newman's psychotic and exhibitionist and moron show dignity and imagination, and the rednecks of the album's most notorious songs are imbued by the smart-ass New York Jew who created them with ironic distance, a smart-ass's kindest cut of all. There is, natcherly, a darker irony: no matter how smart they are about how dumb they are, they still can't think of anything better to do than keep the n———s down. [Letter grade] A."

To promote the album, Warner scheduled a concert in Atlanta, a move inspired by MGM's lavish premiere of *Gone with the Wind* at Loew's Grand Theatre in 1939. Randy would debut much of the album on October 5, 1974, at the 1,700-seat Atlanta Symphony Hall with an eighty-seven-piece orchestra conducted by Uncle Emil. The Warner publicity department announced that Lester Maddox, who was seeking reelection, had been invited; however, Maddox—who would eventually lose to a moderate candidate endorsed by President Jimmy Carter—said he never received an invitation. He also professed, unconvincingly, that he had never heard "Rednecks."

"The evening was beyond fantastic," Titelman recalled. "Randy played the whole record and probably a few other things and he had so much fun. I remember him introducing Emil who was wearing a black tux and bright orange socks which you could see from the audience. Randy said, 'I'd like to introduce my uncle Emil, who came all the way from California to embarrass me in front of all of you.'"

— V —

Despite the potential furor over the N-word, there was little complaint in the media. The *New York Times* and *Los Angeles Times* used it, although an argument had long been made, by both Blacks and whites, that the word was unacceptable under any circumstances, especially when used by whites. Newman wrestled with the issue, finally deciding it was essential to convey the point of the song.

In his 2002 book *Nigger: The Strange Career of a Troublesome Word*, Harvard Law School professor Randall Kennedy maintained that the N-word is acceptable in certain situations, such as in a song where the intent is justifiable, whether the artist is Black or white. Described by the *New York Times* as one of America's most incisive commentators on race, Kennedy declared, "To condemn whites who use the N-word without regard to context is simply to make a fetish of nigger." Further, he wrote that the writings of such white writers as Mark Twain, Eugene O'Neill, Sinclair Lewis, and E.L. Doctorow (among many) "have unveiled nigger-as-insult in order to dramatize and condemn racism's baleful presence." He stood by his position in a 2022 edition of the volume.

~

For all the focus in "Sail Away" and "Rednecks" on racism, there wasn't much awareness of Newman's music in the Black community because it wasn't played on soul/R & B radio stations any more than on pop stations. However, Nelson George, a prolific Black author, critic, and filmmaker with wide musical tastes, picked up on Newman's uniqueness when he heard *12 Songs* as a teenager.

"I had been a fan of storytellers, singer-songwriters like Paul Simon and Bruce Springsteen, but Randy was something different—the way he became the characters and sang through their voices," he said. "The other thing that struck me is he was a white guy coming from California, but there was something about him that reminded me of Ray Charles. He was definitely coming from a different place. Then, there was the whole New Orleans influence, Fats Domino and such. Then *Sail Away* and *Good Old Boys* came along and took things to a different level."

After decades, George still describes the song "Sail Away" with a term that is rare in pop music: "dangerous." "I thought this was one of the most dangerous performances I'd ever heard—and that's still true," he said. "Why is this guy singing through the voice of a slave trader? I don't think many black people were aware of that record. We had heard protest music, but this was political with a capital P. What was so radical is he took the role of the character he was protesting. Pop fans weren't used to that, so it made it very difficult for people to understand just what he was doing . . . and I don't think some people ever figured it out."

George labeled *Good Old Boys* an even more dangerous album. "That song 'Rednecks' made you look at the world through the eyes of someone whose views are profoundly distasteful," he said. "I can tell you as a young Black person, you had to go, 'wait a minute.' You have to really listen carefully to understand the humor and the message. It really made me think, 'who is this guy?' He skirted the line, which is why I thought it was such dangerous music. That's especially true if 'Rednecks' came out today when people are so quick to rush to judgment. There aren't a lot of people who are going to take the time and try to understand where he's coming from."

~

In the annual *Voice* poll, *Good Old Boys* finished third. Behind only Joni Mitchell's *Court and Spark* and Steely Dan's *Pretzel Logic*, it was ahead of albums by Bob Dylan, Stevie Wonder, Van Morrison, Jackson Browne, and the Rolling Stones. In retrospect, third place was too timid. Time has shown *Good Old Boys* was the most accomplished album of 1974.

Bill Flanagan, an influential music writer, editor, and television producer, was in the audience when Newman's 1974 tour reached Boston's 2,600-capacity Symphony Hall in late November, and he attested to the power of *Good Old Boys*. "That album was devastating at the time, and it has not lost one bit of its power," he said. "It was also one of the best concerts I ever saw. When Randy sang 'He's free to be put in a cage in Roxbury in Boston,' the audience cheered. By this time, it seemed clear that Randy was not just writing conventional pop songs, but exploring the American psyche."

Around this time, Randy was saluted in Greil Marcus's *Mystery Train*, which was published in 1975—a book that was as inspiring a call to follow your dreams to its readers (many of whom surely were potential writers and musicians) as Jack Kerouac's 1957 novel *On the Road* had been for its restless devotees. To illustrate how rock-and-roll music helped shape and define

American culture—its subtitle: *Images of America in Rock'n'Roll Music*—Marcus singled out just four contemporary artists: Elvis Presley, the Band, Sly Stone, and Randy Newman.

With all of these accolades taken together, Randy, at thirty-one, was in the top tier of American songwriters, and Hollywood was calling again.

CHAPTER ELEVEN

Ragtime
Saturday Night Live *and*
Mounting Pressure

— I —

Four years after *Cold Turkey*, Dino De Laurentiis, the Italian producer who was trying to expand his movie empire to America, wanted Randy to write the music for the screen version of E.L. Doctorow's top-selling novel *Ragtime*. This was a move into the upper line of film scoring. It even had an A-team director, Robert Altman, who shared Newman's fascination with multilevel storytelling, satire, and flawed characters.

Newman was charmed when he met De Laurentiis at the producer's mansion in Beverly Hills—Randy in his usual casual attire and the host dressed in a suit so expensive Randy figured it must have cost more than his car. "He came racing in with all these ideas," Randy said. "He handed me the book and wanted me to go to Canada to meet with Altman. I got so caught up in everything that I didn't even think about the old Newman family stuff. I just loved the guy."

Ragtime, too, appealed to Newman—a sweeping, deeply interwoven tale of cultural and legal issues that were circulating in America in the early years of the twentieth century, a time of enormous social change. The concerns in the film ranged from racial injustice and sexual awakening to an increasing resistance to immigrants. Randy enjoyed how Doctorow freely placed real-life figures—such as magician Harry Houdini and Sigmund Freud—into wholly fictional interactions in the book. The assignment was also welcome because Randy was in the midst of another period of writer's block—driven partially by the difficulty of matching the creative heights of *Sail Away* and *Good Old Boys*.

As he waited for Altman to finish another film for De Laurentiis, Newman wrote his first song in two years, "Sigmund Freud's Impersonation of Albert Einstein in America," an imaginative story that fit both the style and viewpoint of the film. In "Freud," Newman mixed characters and time in the spirit of Doctorow's book, filtered through his own take on an immigrant's sense of American life—including racial sensibilities—in the early twentieth century.

The world of science is my game
And Albert Einstein is my name
I was born in Germany
And I'm happy to be
Here in the land of the brave and the free
Yes, I'm happy to be
Here in the land of the brave and the free
In the year of nineteen five
Merely trying to survive
Took my knapsack in my hand
Caught a train for Switzerland
America, America
God shed his grace on Thee
You have whipped the Filipino
Now you rule the Western Sea

Americans dream of gypsies, I have found
Gypsy knives and gypsy thighs
That pound and pound and pound and pound
And African appendages that almost reach the ground
And little boys playing baseball in the rain
America, America
Step out into the light
You're the best dream man has ever dreamed
And may all your Christmases be white

"What interests me about the song is that it says things about America by mixing up all kinds of images," Newman said. "'Knives and thighs that pound and pound, and the African appendages that almost reach the ground.' That's pretty good. 'Little boys playing baseball in the rain,' that's America to me. When you read a book like *Ragtime* or Tom Stoppard's play *Travesties* where they both take historical figures and jumble them all up and do whatever they want with them, that's a great device, particularly when everybody's dead."

Around the same time, Randy wrote "In Germany Before the War," another challenging time piece. Neither comic nor satiric, "Germany" is a skillfully designed short story inspired by *M*, Fritz Lang's disturbing 1931 film about a serial child killer. Roswitha had also told Randy about Peter Kürten, a notorious serial killer from her hometown of Düsseldorf whose first victim was a nine-year-old girl. The recording mixed the menacing storyline with pastoral orchestral touches that made it feel like a new style of symphony hall literature; it is about as far as Newman would ever get from pop mainstream accessibility, but it is hard to forget.

In Germany Before The War
There was a man who owned a store
In nineteen hundred thirty-four

In Düsseldorf
And every night at five-oh-nine
He'd cross the park down to the Rhine
And he'd sit there by the shore
I'm looking at the river
But I'm thinking of the sea
Thinking of the sea
Thinking of the sea
I'm looking at the river
But I'm thinking of the sea
A little girl has lost her way
With hair of gold and eyes of gray
Reflected in his glasses
As he watches her
A little girl has lost her way
With hair of gold and eyes of gray
I'm looking at the river
But I'm thinking of the sea
Thinking of the sea
Thinking of the sea
We lie beneath the autumn sky
My little golden girl and I
And she lies very still

There's a good chance a director with Altman's daring would have found a place for some of "Freud" and possibly "Germany" in *Ragtime*, but Altman had a falling-out with De Laurentiis on another film they were working on—a wildly unconventional revisionist western titled *Buffalo Bill and the Indians, or Sitting Bull's History Lesson.* The producer replaced Altman on *Ragtime* with Miloš Forman, the Oscar-winning director of *One Flew Over the Cuckoo's Nest.* As it turned out, Forman didn't want the songs for the film, which disappointed Randy, but it gave him a head start on his next album.

— II —

While Randy waited to begin work on *Ragtime*, television producer Lorne Michaels contacted him about a weekly comedy and music show that was starting on October 11, 1975, on NBC-TV. *Saturday Night Live* would become an influential fixture in pop culture for generations, and Michaels would prove to be an outstanding judge of talent. He had seen Randy perform at a folk club in Toronto in 1973 and was so impressed he went backstage to meet him. At the time, Michaels co-starred in a Canadian TV variety program and figured Newman would make a good guest. Years later, he described Newman as a "genius . . . and I don't use that word often. It's just so evident."

Michaels's top drawing card in launching the show was his close friend, Paul Simon, who had agreed to host the opener, but Michaels held Simon's participation until the second week. He figured word of mouth from the first show and Simon's stardom would make the ratings go up in that second week, giving the show the feel of a winner, and he was right.

When discussing possible musical guests for the second week, Michaels and Simon both thought of Newman. It didn't matter that Randy wasn't a big star—Simon would fill that role; Randy was just the kind of special talent that the show wanted to be identified with. On the telecast, Simon gave Newman a gracious introduction. After singing "Marie," he said, "That's a Randy Newman song . . . Randy is a songwriter I greatly admire . . . [He's] singing a song I wish I had written, 'Sail Away.'" Together, Simon and Newman helped establish an early standard of excellence that would bond millions of young viewers to *SNL*.

The appearance was also memorable in another way. As early as he could remember, Amos Newman knew that his father did something with music because he was always playing the piano around the house. He had also seen his dad onstage at the Troubadour in 1971, but he was so young he fell asleep. It wasn't until he was six that he really understood his father was special. That's when his mother kept him up to watch Randy perform on *SNL*. Imagine the boy's excitement seeing his father singing "Sail Away" at the piano on TV before a cheering studio audience.

"My dad already had five albums out by 1975, but he didn't make a big deal about his work," Amos said years later. "It wasn't like we would have a release party at home every time an album came out. He treated music as simply his job. The TV show was the moment I realized other people liked my dad, that what he did was important."

~

Given the excitement of *Sail Away* and *Good Old Boys,* Lenny hoped Randy would be inspired to begin writing another album right away, but Randy couldn't come up with anything; the motivation that drove him to write those two albums seemed to have slipped away. When Elliot Abbott stopped by to check on him, he found Randy in a dark mood. "He just kept pacing around the piano room," he said. "Finally, he walked outside on the patio— as if he didn't even want to be in the room. When I asked him about it, he said, 'I don't want to go in there; the piano is the enemy.'"

It was a startling comment from someone whose life had revolved around a piano since that morning of his fifth birthday and who had accomplished so much. This wasn't like the shutdowns after the first two albums—Randy just couldn't find the inspiration. When he sat at the piano, he said, it was grinding. "When I'm not sitting there trying to write a song, I get as far away from it in my head as I can," Newman said. "That's why when people ask me about what I did in those days, I usually don't remember anything."

"Pressure is how I saw it," Abbott said of the period. "The pressure on any songwriter, especially Randy, is to keep getting better. His standard was so high with *Sail Away* and *Good Old Boys* that it left him paralyzed to some extent. I felt it was the combination of fearing he couldn't live up to the past work and guilt over not doing his job."

Alan Newman had a different perspective. "I'm not sure fear of commercial or critical failure was the cause," he said. "Everyone was expecting something from him, and in his depressed state, he didn't feel he had anything to give. That was tough for those of us who lived him and worked with him, but it was toughest on him."

PART THREE

Randy Newman is the foremost satirist of our times, starting from his first album in 1968, which was one of those
collections that was so great you remember where you
were when you first heard it. From then on, he was one of
a kind—a singer-songwriter who accompanies himself on
a sixty-piece orchestra. His musical influences go all the
way back to the Great American songbook. Thematically,
Randy has always been willing to speak about the country's problems, but in human and humorous terms. He
doesn't make you feel like you're being lectured. He often
takes subjects, like racism and greed, that you don't expect
to be engaged in pop music, but he finds a way to lead you
there. Randy is likely to surprise you, and you've got to pay
attention because he may be saying something completely
the opposite of what you think he is. Time after time, he
assails our own assumptions about ourselves and our
country.

JACKSON BROWNE

I always admire it when someone can put themselves in the third person and tell a story, especially a story that needs to be told. It's almost like a lost art in pop music, and Randy Newman is a master at it. It's a play with language, a play with words and music; a beautiful way of expressing yourself and grabbing someone's attention. Songs like "Sail Away," "Rednecks," and "Roll with the Punches" really speak to me. They touch a nerve—the whole North-South dynamics of "Rednecks."

CHUCK D

CHAPTER TWELVE

"Short People" and
Some Bruised Feelings

— I —

Browsing the *Los Angeles Times* entertainment section in April of 1977, Randy was shocked to see his name in the summer concert lineup of the 6,100-seat Universal Amphitheatre, one of the city's most prestigious venues. He hadn't done a show in nearly a year and was savvy enough to know that such a high-profile booking wouldn't be a one-off, but the start of a promotional campaign for a new album and tour. That meant he would have just four months to write and record a new collection for the August 23 show.

What the hell?

He was on the phone immediately to Abbott, who had booked the date without telling Randy. It was a move reminiscent of Waronker's bringing in arranger Nick DeCaro to motivate Randy to return to the studio. "I was hoping to provoke him into writing songs again after some two years, but that morning he kept saying, 'You've got to cancel the show,' and finally I said, 'Okay, we'll cancel.'" After a pause, Randy said, "Well, wait, maybe I can come up with something."

Privately, Randy welcomed the challenge.

"That was one of the times where I did nothing," he said of the previous months. "It wasn't that I was just trying to kick back or any of that 'I needed to rest' bullshit. It wasn't, 'Oh, I love doing nothing. This is great.' I felt guilty. This was my job, and I wasn't working, and there were bills to pay. I didn't know if I would ever write again. A highlight of the day would often be sitting by the pool talking to the pool man. It got to the point where Roswitha asked one day, 'What are you going to do with the rest of your life?'"

In one of his most productive spurts, Newman wrote nine songs by August, one of which would be the song most associated with him for years, often uncomfortably: "Short People."

At the time, Lenny and Russ thought they had the album finished before they heard "Short People." They even toyed with the idea of making a provocative new song called "Hard Hat Blues" the opening track and the first single from the LP called *Little Criminals*. It was a commentary that Randy started writing during the *Sail Away* sessions—his angriest song since "Rednecks," a warning against the growing threat facing peaceful protesters from right-wing groups who felt disenfranchised.

"The character in this song was a jerk telling his cohorts to go to a rally downtown and show the demonstrators who was boss by beating the hell out of them," Titelman said. "The song is fifty years old, and look what happened on January 6 [of 2021]."

In an early version, Newman's narrator declared in part:

Is this the land of the brave and the home of the free
What makes them think they're better than me
Goodbye, you bastards . . . Goodbye you bastards, goodbye.

By the 1977 sessions, the key lines had shifted:

Baby, let's go out tonight
They got it all wrong, but we'll teach 'em what's right
We won't let nobody push us around
Maybe we'll go downtown.
Goodbye, Goodbye, Goodbye
Goodbye, Goodbye, Goodbye

But Randy wasn't satisfied with the song and came back two weeks later with a replacement for the album, a song called "Short People." Lenny still favored "Hard Hat," but he and Russ respected Randy's wishes and made the switch.

There would continue to be a conversation—in some cases a debate—between Randy (around six feet tall), Russ (closer to five-ten) and Lenny (about five-six) over the song, a conversation that has expanded over the years to include critics, radio programmers, and fans. After more than four decades, people still ask if the song was written as an attack on prejudice or if it was simply blatantly insensitive; the only point of agreement was that "Short People" was devilishly funny.

Imagine what the Warner staff hearing these lines for the first time:

Short People got no reason
Short People got no reason
Short People got no reason
To live
They got little hands
Little eyes
They walk around
Tellin' great big lies
They got little noses
And tiny little teeth

They wear platform shoes
On their nasty little feet

Well, I don't want no Short People
Don't want no Short People
Don't want no Short People
'Round here

Short People are just the same
As you and I
(A Fool Such As I)
All men are brothers
Until the day they die
(It's A Wonderful World)

Short People got nobody
Short People got nobody
Short People got nobody
To love

They got little baby legs
That stand so low
You got to pick 'em up
Just to say hello
They got little cars
That go beep, beep, beep
They got little voices
Goin' peep, peep, peep
They got grubby little fingers
And dirty little minds
They're gonna get you every time

Well, I don't want no Short People
Don't want no Short People

Don't want no Short People
'Round here

"Short People" contains some of Newman's funniest lines. Who can resist a verse as inspired as "Little baby legs / stand so low / got to pick 'em up / just to say hello"?

In a 2021 Zoom chat, Randy, Lenny, and Russ recalled their early takes on the song:

> RN: "Lenny didn't like it particularly, I could tell . . . . He hasn't laughed at the song yet."
>
> LW: "I was hoping for an up-tempo song, and we got it, but I feared, because of the subject matter, that it wasn't really the kind of up-tempo song we were really hoping for. That's why I didn't laugh."
>
> RT: "I loved it. I thought it was one of the funniest things I had ever heard. I had to hold my stomach I was laughing so hard."
>
> RN: "Not everybody laughed."
>
> RT: "I didn't even think of it [being politically incorrect]. My reaction was strictly emotional. I was howling with laughter."
>
> LW: "I got a phone call from Russ probably thirty minutes after I first heard it, and Russ said exactly that. I think I said, 'Yeah, it's fun,' but I just worried about what people would think."
>
> RN: "And you were right. It was a problem for a lot of people. Radio stations worried about it."
>
> LW: "I have letters that I have framed—people complaining. Steve Ross got them too. Steve was saying, 'What's going on here?'"
>
> RT: "We got death threats at the label."

So, what was Randy's original intent?

RN: "I would go along with whatever people thought about the song when I was asked about it. For instance, a radio guy said, 'The song's all about prejudice, isn't it?' And I said, 'Yeah.' But it wasn't at the beginning. I just thought it was funny and it was. I wrote it because we needed an up song."

In a separate interview, Waronker questioned Randy's remark about the song just being humorous. "Everything he writes has multilevels, and sometimes Randy doesn't want to appear pretentious or too serious, and he kinda downplays things, like some of the lines in the middle—just as when he said 'Love Story' was about a guy with low expectations," he said. "There was so much more to it than that."

— II —

Newman still needed to do finishing touches on the album, but he was in a playful mood the August night of the Universal Amphitheatre concert. Backstage, he told friends he had enjoyed making *Little Criminals*, suggesting a few tracks might even get on the radio, both rare sentiments from him. The audience treated him like the local hero he was, but there was an exchange when Randy's dad came backstage afterward that some in the room would repeat over the years whenever asked about the relationship between father and son. As well-wishers congratulated Randy, Irving rushed up and asked, "What's the matter with your voice? You have a cold?"

The album got off to a good start, entering the *Billboard* chart at No. 121 in November, but Randy's team knew a hit single was needed to keep the sales building—and the single, they agreed, should be "Short People." The Warner promotion staff resisted, despite the strong response when the record was tested on some radio and record store employees at a label convention in Miami. "The reaction was over the top," Lenny said. "We knew that was the song we needed to release."

Unable to convince the powers that be, Abbott came up with a scheme to convince the promotion team to push "Short People" as the single. He phoned an independent record promotion man in Boston whose job was getting radio programmers to play the singles that he brought to them. "I told him I was going to send him a test pressing of a single," Abbott said. "I wanted to know what he thought. A few days later, he calls me and says, 'This is a hit record! I can get it on the biggest station in Boston.'" Without telling anyone at Warner, Abbott told the promo guy to go ahead and push it.

A week later, a promotion executive at Warner who hadn't believed radio would embrace the song phoned Abbott to say something crazy was going on in Boston. "Elliot, you're not going to believe what is happening . . . they're playing 'Short People' on the radio."

Feigning outrage that the station would dare start playing the record that Warner hadn't officially released, Abbott responded: "Those bastards!"

As airplay spread in the Northeast, Warner rushed the single to stores. The album was No. 33 in *Billboard* the week "Short People" entered the chart in mid-November. Two months later, the single was No. 2, even No. 1 in *Cash Box*, a rival publication. The appeal of the single helped push *Little Criminals* to No. 8. Sales passed 700,000, earning Randy his first gold album (for 500,000 sales). By the time the single was in the Top 10, Randy was on the road—in big cities and small—and fans loved "Short People," as did the TV audience when he performed it during his return to *Saturday Night Live* in January. The *SNL* host this time was comedian Steve Martin, who would later team with Randy and Lorne Michaels on a movie screenplay.

Not everybody was pleased with "Short People." Radio stations in various cities, including New York and Philadelphia, initially refused to play the record. *Entertainment Weekly* reported that "undersized listeners flew into a tizzy. . . . midgets picketed Newman's concerts." The lobbying group Little People of America decried the song's crassness, and the founder of Shorties Are Smarter called it "vicious."

Gusto Records, a minor Tennessee label, released an answer single, "Tall People" by the group Short People. It was witless to the point of being unlistenable. In Maryland, Isaiah Dixon Jr., a respected state legislator who fought strongly for human rights issues including making cross burning a felony in the state, tried to get "Short People" banned from Maryland airwaves. When informed by counsel that the move would be unconstitutional, the five-foot-five Dixon said he was "let down, short-changed, and a little upset."

— III —

Newman had planned to write the songs for *Little Criminals* at home as usual, but the deadline pressure led to a change of plans. After several days at the piano with no new tunes, he thought about getting an office.

Unlike the millions of Americans who get up every morning and go to work, Randy got up every morning and was already at work. Figuring that having to go to an office might motivate him, he rented a room in a building in an industrial district a few miles away. He wasn't looking for a high-rise with a gorgeous view; he wanted something spare where he could work with a piano without disruption. Looking back, he felt that the room's claustrophobic atmosphere—there wasn't even a phone—was reflected in the dark nature of many of the album's songs. "It was good for me," he said. "I felt like I was part of the working community. I drove on the freeway, and I'd look at everyone else driving along-side, and I felt normal."

When he sat at the office piano for the first time, he only had three songs. "I'll Be Home" was a ballad he wrote in 1968 at the request of Paul McCartney for Mary Hopkin, a British singer whose debut single, "Those Were the Days," was produced by McCartney and was an international hit that year. Newman didn't think much of "Home" at the time—the kind of tender, late-night reflection that he seemed to be able to write in his sleep—but he liked the arrangement, and he needed material. Though the senti-mental song had an appealing edge, it was not Newman-esque, and some critics described it as filler when the new album was released. The other two songs would rank with his most admired, both left over from the *Ragtime* period: "Sigmund Freud's Impersonation of Albert Einstein in America" and "In Germany Before the War."

Newman was relieved when new songs started coming, the most notable of which continued to touch on social themes. After "Birmingham," "Dayton, Ohio – 1903," and possibly even "Burn On," it was tempting to take "Baltimore," a new song, as some-thing of an in joke—Randy taking listeners on a tour of American cities. But the storyline this time had deep, tender ramifications—the gradual decay of major cities. The imagery and music were among Newman's most eloquent. It's also another of his favorites, a song he thought might even have a chance to be a hit.

> *Beat-up little seagull*
> *On a marble stair*
> *Tryin' to find the ocean*
> *Lookin' everywhere*
> *Hard times in the city*
> *In a hard town by the sea*
> *Ain't nowhere to run to*
> *There ain't nothin' here for free*

Hooker on the corner
Waitin' for a train
Drunk lyin' on the sidewalk
Sleepin' in the rain
And they hide their faces
And they hide their eyes
'Cause the city's dyin'
And they don't know why
Oh, Baltimore
Man, it's hard just to live
Oh, Baltimore
Man, it's hard just to live, just to live
Get my sister Sandy
And my little brother Ray
Buy a big old wagon
Gonna haul us all away
Livin' in the country
Where the mountain's high
Never comin' back here
'Til the day I die
Oh, Baltimore
Man, it's hard just to live
Oh, Baltimore
Man, it's hard just to live, just to live
Oh, Baltimore
Man, it's hard just to live
Oh, Baltimore
Man, it's hard just to live, just to live

Newman said:

I'm interested in geography, and I remember going through Baltimore on a train. Later, I saw a story in *National Geographic* about Baltimore that had pictures of people talking over back fences and those little portable pools in the back yard. That's what inspired me to write about Baltimore, and there was this history of the city being this difficult environment. When I played Baltimore, Miss Baltimore came out on stage with a barrel of letters that they said was about half pro-Baltimore and half anti-Baltimore. Then some city official read a poem he wrote about why I wouldn't like the city. Actually, I was looking forward to going there. I sometimes think I write songs about places I want to play and maybe couldn't before. So, I wrote 'Baltimore,' and there are enough people for me to do a show there.

"Kathleen (Catholicism Made Easier)" was a one-line joke, but a good one—built around the mystery that millions feel surround the highly ritualized religion. The lyrics describe a young man who has always been crazy about Irish girls, mistaking the Italian lyrics to the 1958 pop hit "Nel Blue Dipinto Di Blu," for part of the Catholic wedding vows. "Old Man on the Farm" and "A Texas Girl at Her Father's Funeral" both examine old age. "I think other countries take better care of their older people," Newman said. "I mean, I'm always surprised how people get put into care facilities. It shouldn't be surprising because people have to live their lives, but it seems like families stay closer in other places, like the mother or father who live upstairs."

"Rider in the Rain," with its slow country pace, revives Newman's humor by mocking the macho cowboy image celebrated in books and films—a cowboy who is headed to Arizona, the land of retirement villages, to settle down. The deceptively witty track is doubly engaging because the glossy support vocals sound like something from *Desperado*, an album in which the Eagles relied heavily on the maverick cowboy image. The winning twist on the recording is that the Eagles co-leaders contributed those vocals. Don Henley and Glenn Frey had been fans of Newman since the

Troubadour days. They must have smiled when the word "desperado" popped up in the lyrics. The opening lines:

> *Got a gun in my holster*
> *Got a horse between my knees*
> *And I'm goin' to Arizona*
> *Pardon me, boys, if you please*
> *I have been a desperado*
> *Raped and pillaged 'cross the plain*
> *Now, I'm goin' to Arizona*
> *Just a Rider In The Rain*

Henley knew Randy was having fun with the Eagles' image. "We were fine with that . . . flattered, as a matter of fact," he said. "Contrary to the judgment of some writers, we have a sense of humor about ourselves. I've never had as much fun in a recording studio as we did on those sessions with Randy. There was so much laughing that it was hard to get through a complete take."

The remaining songs have bright musical strains but don't stand thematically with his most prized tunes. The album's cinematic title song, "Little Criminals," builds upon a favorite Newman theme—society's way of finding someone to look down upon, even if it is someone in your own family. "You Can't Fool the Fat Man" draws from the same world of backstreet hustlers. The high-spirited "Jolly Coppers on Parade" expresses a child's dream of the excitement of a policeman's life without knowing the reality of it.

Little Criminals placed No. 8 in the *Voice's* poll of the year's most prized albums. In the *New York Times*, Janet Maslin called the LP "dazzling," declaring it to be the first Newman album with "a full complement of musical witticisms to match the verbal ones"—singling out "Jolly Coppers on Parade" and "Rider in the Rain." She labeled "Short People" his funniest song ever. But there was also an undertow of feeling among some critics and hard-core Newman fans that the collection lacked the ambition and purposefulness of *Sail Away* and the concept-driven *Good Old Boys.*

But it was becoming clear that Randy's entire body of work fit into the boundaries usually assigned to a "concept" album. The importance of Newman's music rests in the totality of his vision. Besides, the issue of *Little Criminals*' place in the hierarchy of Newman's work would soon be moot. The album would be over-shadowed by the "Short People" frenzy.

— IV —

The demand for Newman's live shows was so strong that he spent much of 1978 on tour, including all of May in Europe. The New-mans would often take advantage of European dates for Ros-witha and the kids to spend time with her family in Germany, then join Randy at one or more of the tour cities. Where Amos had gotten an insight into what his father did from *SNL*, his son Eric Newman points to one of the shows on the 1978 tour as his moment of discovery.

"There was this show in Amsterdam, and I was so excited when the crowd got so into the music that they actually chased after my dad as he left the theater," said Eric, a television pro-ducer and writer who created the hit series *Narcos*. "That made a big impact on me, and I started to pay more attention to the words as I got older. Gradually, I started to see how my dad cre-ated characters and wrote from a third-person perspective. He was a phenomenal storyteller."

Randy attracted followers in Europe early on, especially England, Ireland, the Netherlands, and Belgium.

"Randy Newman's popularity in the Low Countries stems from a number of reasons, one [of which] is based on a common misunderstanding," said Wouter Bulckaert, a Belgian who wrote the Dutch biography *Randy Newman*. "Especially in the early seventies, and mainly because of anti-American sentiments due to the Vietnam war, the Netherlands people assumed that Randy Newman hated America, which is of course a massive mistake," he wrote in an email in 2023. "I sincerely think Randy loves his country, although he does not like what he sees happening in [it]. And that is a major difference. So, the audience [and the critics] cheered when they heard a song like 'Political Science,' but mainly for the wrong reasons."

Bulckaert also believes that Randy's underdog sensibilities forged a strong connection. "Maybe because we live in such tiny countries, the position of the outsider is very recognizable for us," he wrote in the email. "Moreover, especially for Belgians, being the underdog is a kind of second skin. Then it may not surprise we sympathize with Randy Newman's characters." The author, too, recognized that Randy's songs were aligned with an honored American musical tradition—the folk commentary of Woody Guthrie and Leadbelly, who addressed the hardships of the common man in America. "But of course, [their] songs talked about a period past, while . . . Newman's songs [were] about the contemporary life of ordinary people in the USA, which was so enthralling to listeners around here."

"Short People," especially, intrigued young Eric:

I was only seven, but I could understand how ridiculous it was to think my dad was expressing the prejudice the record was talking about. When I first heard it, I thought it was a novelty record, something like you'd expect to hear on Dr. Demento's radio show. At the same time, I was terrified when I first heard "Rednecks" and the N-word. I mean, even at that age, we knew never to say certain things. My father had a real conscience about bigotry. It was a really big issue with him. He wouldn't lecture us about things, but it was clear in what he said and how he acted. As I got older, I see where we learned a lot about the world through his music. I'll tell you what he is, more than anything, is he's a humanist.

~

Hoping to build on the album's success, Warner arranged for Randy to be backed by an all-star seven-piece band for a few West Coast dates in August, including stops with support act Bonnie Raitt at the Universal Amphitheatre. In the opening night concert at Universal, Randy introduced the musicians in his typically wisecracking stage manner. "As you may have noticed there are other people—more or less people—up here with me tonight. . . . They are gathered from some of the top second-rate bands in the country [laughter]. . . . I, of course, need no introduction. I'm . . . Mr. Billy Joel" [laughter].

Newman kept things light on most of his song introductions, including "Short People," and the audience responded with laughter. "This is a song that sounds like I wrote the beginning of it and the ending of it, and someone who uses his talent for good wrote the middle of it—like John Denver." When the band left the stage as he performed some songs with just piano, he taunted them, "They're going back to shoot up so they can do the second half."

Before "God's Song," Randy declared, "This is a song in which God is going to speak to all of you through me. I was surprised, but it was such an honor that I went through with it."

Introducing "A Wedding in Cherokee County," he acknowledged the song had nothing to do with the *Good Old Boys* concept: "This used to be . . . when I first wrote it . . . an Albanian wedding song. So, I changed it to Alabama for the *Good Old Boys* album so it would be sort of a concept album like *Tommy* by the Who. But it was originally an Albanian wedding song about the sexual frustration of this young Albanian bridegroom, and it's really in kind of horrible taste, I hope." After the closing "Mama Told Me Not to Come," Newman dropped his wise-cracking demeanor and thanked the audience warmly.

As it turned out, the band experiment was short-lived; it was expensive keeping the top-level players on the road, and the feeling was that Randy was more effective and comfortable in a solo role. Larry Butler, who Warner sent on the band dates as tour manager, noticed during rehearsals that Randy had trouble adjusting to the added musicians.

"As casual as he might seem, Randy took performing very seriously," Butler said years later. "Everything had to be right—the sound, the lights, the audience sightlines. It's the old concept that if the public wasn't comfortable, they weren't going to enjoy the show."

The "Short People" success made Newman even more concerned with his stage presentation. He knew that he wasn't just playing to a group of die-hard fans anymore. People were now coming to see him because of the hit, and they had an attitude of "Okay, let's see what this guy can do." That pressure can lead musicians to blow up when things go wrong, and Randy wasn't immune.

Butler recalled:

It was years later when I went with him to New York where he performed on some benefit show. He was halfway through his set when the guy running the charity came over to me to say he'd love it if Randy would say something nice about the charity. So, I slipped Randy a note between songs asking if he would do that, and Randy did it. But afterward he came over to me and said, "Don't you ever try to adjust what I'm doing onstage, not you or anybody. It's my show. I know what I'm going to do. I know why you gave me the note, but if anyone ever asks you again to do something like that, just say, 'No.' Five minutes later we were joking around, but I saw how serious Randy was beneath all that fun-loving demeanor.

~

"Short People" was a strange time for Newman—sudden attention for a record that was little more than a joke was like experiencing fame on a weekend visitor's pass. It wasn't like the pop world was suddenly knocking at his door. Numerous record stores even reported lots of buyers wanting to exchange *Little Criminals* for another album after discovering it was not a comedy record. He was especially amused when some fans began worrying that he might be tempted by "Short People" to go after even bigger sales.

"Since people I knew in the record business, like Don Henley and Linda Ronstadt and James Taylor, had so many hits, you'd have thought a hit would have fallen on me by accident just being around them," he said. "But I knew that what I do for the most part just doesn't appeal to the mass pop audience."

When he got home from the *Little Criminals* tour, Randy began to think it would be fun to share his bemusement with his fans on the next album. It was a severe misjudgment.

CHAPTER THIRTEEN

A Bad Joke and
Rough Times

— I —

If "Short People" puzzled Newman followers, picture the reaction to the cover of his follow-up album, 1979's *Born Again*—a color photo of him sitting at a wooden desk in a business suit, his face painted, à la KISS, with garish dollar signs. On his desk were the usual business office accessories, including a calendar, lamp, in/out basket, pen-and-pencil set with a decorative golf ball, a phone, and a photo of his three boys also in KISS makeup.

Whoa mama!

It was clearly a joke.

The problem was that few people got it.

Was he putting down rock-and-roll stars as being soulless businessmen in disguise? Was he was hoping to build on his "Short People" attention with something even more outlandish?

"I wasn't making fun of rock-and-roll business types," he said years later. "I was making fun of myself as if I had turned into one."

What should have made the joke obvious was that "Short People," upon reflection, was not that big a hit. Where *Little Criminals* ended up selling over 750,000 copies worldwide, two other albums alone—Fleetwood Mac's *Rumours* and the Eagles' *Hotel California*—were on their way to selling a collective 36 million copies in the United States.

Born Again would prove to be the darkest point in Newman's recording career. Critics largely abandoned him—for the first time, one of his eligible albums would not make the Top 40 in the *Voice* poll—and mainstream radio went back to ignoring his work. The LP only spent eleven weeks on the *Billboard* charts, down from the twenty-nine weeks of *Little Criminals*. When Randy didn't follow the album with the usual round of interviews or live shows, some observers took it as a sign even he wasn't really behind it. Worldwide, sales were under 150,000. Years later, Newman acknowledged that the cover had been a mistake, the result of his belief that his audience—after six albums and all those rousing concerts—would understand the joke.

"You assume that people—at least your fans—know who the fuck you are," he said. "I thought that somehow people would see that the photo was of some stupid asshole in KISS makeup; it wasn't me. But I wouldn't do it again."

~

As with "Short People" and *Little Criminals*, the sideshow surrounding the album overshadowed three of his finest songs, including one of his most insightful numbers yet. "It's Money That I Love" spoke of the incalculable damage that greed would have in shaping the nation's coming cultural and economic divide. The controversy over the album cover caused some listeners to miss the point of the song.

In a review that read more like it ran in a reactionary journal than a liberal, youth-based music magazine, *Rolling Stone*'s Stephen Holden declared that Randy was touching on the Me Decade in a voice that was "unremittingly snide." The review added that the album's tone was immediately established by "a cover photo in which Newman poses as a prosperous young businessman with dollar signs painted, KISS-style, on his face. 'It's Money That I Love,' the opening cut, suggests that in these cynical times, the only thing most Americans care about is material gratification."

To which Randy could have said, "Well, yes! That's the point!"

Ry Cooder, whose career was expanding with a series of hauntingly beautiful soundtrack albums, saw the visionary aspect of Newman's song. "He was always ahead, not just musically, but also politically," the guitarist said. "Listen to 'It's Money That I Love' and look where we are now. He saw things clearly."

~

For all the distraction of "Short People," Randy was in relatively good spirits when he started writing the songs for *Born Again* in the fall of 1978. As usual, the cheering night after night on the road was uplifting. Rather than tempt him to reach a wider audience, the songs felt bolder and more experimental. Lenny and Russ weren't surprised. "One thing I've found while working with serious artists is they aren't going to be tempted to chase after a hit," Waronker said. "For a producer to even mention we need a hit would be a bad thing. A hit is fun to have, but a real artist doesn't want anything to get in the way of them doing their best work."

Though cloaked in humor, "It's Money That I Love" has lines that are agonizing in their warning about the approaching callousness of the times—the disheartening drift from social responsibility that accelerated during Ronald Reagan's two-term presidency.

Newman had seen the effects of Reagan's belief in small government during the former actor's eight years as governor of California—beliefs that Reagan had outlined even earlier in his speech at the 1964 Republican National Convention that nominated Barry Goldwater as the party's presidential candidate. Newman addressed Reagan's eventual impact on the country—especially economically—in "It's Money That I Love."

I don't love the mountains
And I don't love the sea
And I don't love Jesus
He never done a thing for me
I ain't pretty like my sister
Or smart like my dad
Or good like my mama
It's Money That I Love
It's Money That I Love

They say that money
Can't buy love in this world
But it'll get you a half-pound of cocaine
And a sixteen-year old girl
And a great big long limousine
On a hot September night
Now that may not be love
But it is all right

One, two
It's Money That I Love
Wanna kiss you
Three, four
It's Money That I Love

Used to worry about the poor
But I don't worry anymore
Used to worry about the black man
Now I don't worry about the black man

Used to worry about the starving children of India
You know what I say now about the starving children of
*   India?*
I say, "Oh mama"

It's Money That I Love
It's Money That I Love
It's Money That I Love

"Yeah, I saw it coming," Newman said of the nation's greed lust. "I've written about money quite a few times because it's a big thing. I've written about God a number of times because it's a big thing. Those subjects engage me, and there were so many people who used to worry about the poor, say, but they got older and they were intent on feeding their family and earning a living, and sometimes a big living . . . and they just let the other things go and a lot of people suffered."

"Half a Man," another significant tune, attacked homophobia during a time when the call for equal rights regardless of sexual orientation was still in its infancy. The movement was effectively launched in June of 1969 when a police raid on the Stonewall Inn, a gay club in Greenwich Village, sparked six days of street protests that helped inspire a massive upswing in gay activism. Eight years later, the fight for gay rights received far more national attention when Anita Bryant, a mid-level pop singer, led an ugly but successful campaign in what is now Florida's Miami-Dade County against a new ordinance that banned discrimination based on sexual orientation.

Bryant's "Save the Children" campaign—which described gays as "human garbage" —motivated pro-gay groups to become more active in opposing bigotry. In October of 1979, upwards of 125,000 people joined the National March on Washington for Lesbian and Gay Rights. It would be another twenty-one years

before the United States Supreme Court ruled that sexual orientation was covered by the Civil Rights Act of 1964.

Pop music had made a few tentative steps regarding acceptance of sexual orientation, moving from the teasing bisexual
stances of stars like Mick Jagger and David Bowie to the gay
pride celebration of such disco-era hits as the Village People's
playful "Y.M.C.A." But "Half a Man" had nothing to do with
partying. It was about ignorance, ridiculing the absurd notion
that homosexuality was contagious. The song was the outgrowth
of a story Randy's father told him when he was about to enter his
teens: the tale of a patient who, having never shown any homo-
sexual tendencies, inexplicably felt compelled to "go down" on
someone next to him while taking a shower at the YMCA. It was
an odd story to tell a youngster, but it stuck in Newman's memory until the growing anti-homosexual sentiments led him to
address the subject in a song.

> *This big old queen was standing*
> *On the corner of the street*
> *He waved his hanky at me*
> *As I went rolling by*
> *I pulled the truck up on the sidewalk*
> *And I climbed down from the cab*
> *With my tire-chain and my knife*
> *As I approached him*
> *He was trembling like a bird*
> *I raised the chain above my head*
> *He said, "Please, before you kill me*
> *Might I have one final word?"*
> *And this is what he said:*
> *"I am but Half A Man, Half A Man*
> *I'd like to be a dancer*
> *But I'm much too large*

Half A Man, Half A Man
I'm an object for your pity
Not your rage"

Oh, the strangest feeling's sweeping over me
Both my speech and manner have become much more
* refined*
I said, "Oh, what is this feeling?
What is wrong with me?"
She said, "Girl, it happens all the time
"Now you are Half A Man, Half A Man
Look, you're walking and you're talking
Like a fag."
Half A Man, I am Half A Man
Holy Jesus, what a drag

As with "Rednecks" and the N-word, Newman faced a language problem with the pejorative "fag," and again he decided the word was necessary in the story. "I always worried about one word blowing a song out," he said. "But it is exactly what the guy would say." Randy did get complaints. "I got some letters and calls on it," he told former Warner executive Joe Smith for his book *Off the Record: An Oral History of Popular Music*. "It hurt some people."

"Ghosts" addressed aspects of what would later be called Donald Trump's "Make America Great Again" movement; this time, a lonely war veteran wonders about the changes in his life as he gazes out his window and watches "colored kids" play on streets where his own boy did and where the old man was now afraid to walk. It spoke of a segment of society that was largely invisible to millions of Americans, including the media and pop culture: lower- and middle-class whites who felt so disenfranchised that they would welcome the Trump candidacy. It includes the lines:

Stay with me for a little while
You've nowhere to go
I've nowhere to go
It makes me so happy
When you smile
At me
Work all your life
And you end up with nothing
Live in one room like a bum
Once I flew in a plane
And I fought in a war
We lived in a castle
And slept on the floor
And I don't want to be
All alone anymore
I'm sorry

Out in the street
There's little colored kids playing
Where my own little boy used to play
So I sit in this chair
And I ache with the gout
And I talk to myself
'Cause I'm scared to go out
And I just want to know
What was it all about
I'm sorry

Of the remaining songs, the most noteworthy was "They Just Got Married," which offers a twist to "Love Story," this time the account of a couple living out their life in California until the wife dies and the husband heads to Los Angeles where he marries a "foolish young girl with money." Randy described it as a "jaundiced" love song. Also impressive, "The Girls in My Life (Part 1)" is a series of romantic snapshots that invites you to figure out what is really going on.

Elsewhere in *Born Again*, Newman again overestimated his audience. "The Story of a Rock and Roll Band" was a colorful take on the stately sound of one of the period's most popular groups, England's Electric Light Orchestra. But some saw it as an attempt to parlay the group's radio-friendly sound into another hit, while others felt it was a put-down of the band.

"ELO makes really pleasing records to me, things like 'Mr. Blue Sky' and 'Telephone Line'—that unusual string sound that Jeff Lynne almost always used," Randy said. "I wanted to do something with an American fan telling somebody about the band—saying they were some fine English boys, who knew each other in Birmingham and not saying it correctly, giving it the American pronunciation. Jeff Lynne sent me an application for the fan club. I heard he was pissed off, but I indicated, 'No, I really like the band,' and it got sorted out."

The next four tracks were sharply satirical, but the commentary struck some as too subtle. On casual listening, "Mr. Sheep" seemed like a nasty dramatization of the stereotype that was widely applied in the 1960s and 1970s to the millions of people who lived in suburbs and seemed to follow conventional jobs, asking nothing more of life than a family and a steady paycheck. The lyrics—sung in a taunting, condescending voice—begin:

Golly, Mister, where you going?
You'll be late for work
Careful or you'll drop your briefcase
Jesus, what a jerk
There he goes down to the subway
Off to catch the train
Too bad for him

He forgot his umbrella
Poor Mr. Sheep
You're wet, Mr. Sheep
Walk on, Mr. Sheep
Walk on, Tell me, how's your little family?
How's your little wife?
Are you going to live with those monsters
For the rest of your life?
Maybe you got a little girlfriend
Stashed somewhere in town
Maybe you ain't got a little girlfriend
Ha ha ha ha ha
Poor Mr. Sheep
He's a lonely guy too
Walk on, Mr. Sheep
Walk on

The song was another example of Newman being misunderstood. He said he was making fun of the narrator of that song. "I was attacking this nasty bully and all those from the sixties who were making fun of people who were trying to do their job and take care of their family," he said. "But it wasn't clear enough. I never thought I was being too subtle or trying to confuse my audience. I always thought they were in step with me. I was always surprised when someone would ask what a song meant."

The album's other songs—which ranged from rock star posturing to lingering Cold War paranoia—were stylish musically, but they suffered from cloudy definitions.

— ‖ —

Randy believed *Born Again* would be more successful than *Little Criminals*. He recalled how he and his oldest son, Amos, spent a few days at a vacation house near Yosemite after the album was finished. When they returned home on a private plane, the pilot, who had never flown to Los Angeles before, kept checking for directions from the airport. Clueless, the pilot finally turned to Amos, who was nine, for help. "I didn't like flying in small planes anyway, but I remember being unsettled because I didn't want to crash now," he said. "I was so excited to see what *Born Again* was going to do. It's kind of embarrassing to say it now, but I thought 'this is really going to do something.'"

When Warner tested the songs with radio, the news, once again, was not good. "I kept asking what kind of vibe was coming back from radio, and all I got was the programmers felt there was no 'Short People' on the record," Waronker said. "I thought we were over that hump, but we weren't. I kept thinking, 'Those idiots.'"

Randy picked up on the disappointment when he visited the Warner offices. "After I did *Born Again*, everyone was confident about it, about how well it could do," Randy told Mark Leviton of *BAM* magazine in 1983. "It was like the *Titanic*. They paid me a lot of money like it was going to be big, and it was the first album I thought myself was going to be big."

The sales, however, didn't lure Randy from backing away from his practice of writing about the American character. In Europe, where he did a brief tour in 1978, he reaffirmed his musical direction when Phil Sutcliffe, a leading pop journalist in England, pointed out during an interview for *Sound* magazine that Randy's songs suggest two views of America—love for the country as a "pure idea" and acknowledging its "less than pristine reality."

"I don't think you can change the system in the States," Newman replied. "The songs are about things that need to be noticed. Nobody pays attention to me though, and maybe that's as well. I don't want to get into any simplistic kinda rock-and-roll political thing, but it isn't right."

— III —

Back home, Randy was drained. In one of his few interviews in 1979, he spoke with Timothy White for a *Rolling Stone* profile titled "Randy Newman: Bet No One Hurt This Bad." The subject wasn't Randy's songs, but Randy himself. The piece was subtitled "The Unhappy Songwriter Survives an Unhappy Childhood and Blossoms into a Miserable Adult," which suggested a touch of humor. Newman was playful when asked about those who attacked "Short People": "Why don't they leave me alone! Maybe I was right about the little pukes all along."

But the article soon spiraled into darker and more serious matters, offering a rare reflection on Newman's relationship with his family and his father's flat-out suggestion that he still saw sadness in his son.

"Randy was a good, fine kid—much more than you can tell from his strange, bitter lyrics," Irving Newman told White. "I could never believe some of the stuff Randy was writing. I asked him about it, and he said, 'Well, Dad, I'm an unhappy man.' I said, 'What are you unhappy about?' He said, 'I wish I knew. I'm not unhappy enough to have a shrink, but I know I'm a down sort of guy, and I don't ever know what's gonna come out when I sit down and play.'"

In the White interview, Newman also spoke about his role as a father, in a rare venture into his personal life.

I'm not a bad father, but I'm not a first-rate one either. I try not to let them see me as a hero; I may have gone too far. I don't bring work home in any way. My wife is not interested in my work, and neither are the kids, not really. I never play songs for them or anything—I just play them for Lenny. They're totally out of that, and I like it that way. It isn't something I can share. I spend the front of the day writing and the rest of the day coming down to where I can be okay. It sounds so crazy, but it is crazy writing sometimes.

I don't want to be the bad guy, but if I am a bad guy, I don't want it to show up in my work because my work means too much to me. I finally know that I'm going to be a writer all my life in some way. It's more important to me than my family or anything else. It's bullshit if I say that anything means more to me, 'cause none of it does.

Years later, Newman would sometimes repeat in interviews the claim that he valued his art above all, but in 2023, he insisted that the statement was never his true feeling, but an exercise in artistic bravado, an uncharacteristic attempt to align himself with the grand tradition of artists who have boasted about giving their all to their art.

But he stood by the part of the *Rolling Stone* interview where he expressed support for Roswitha, verging on a public thank-you for assuming responsibility of the care of both the children and Randy.

"I'm glad I married who I married," he said. "Especially when I think how I could have ended up, with the lack of self-control I've had in terms of drugs and everything else. Speed, mainly, that was the one I could control the least. I just have never had any moderation about whatever I was doing. . . . My wife was very sane always and wasn't too horrified. I used to tell her to make sure I was alive before she went to sleep because I used to take so many downers to get to bed. She would say, 'Oh, okay. Sweet dreams.' It's good to have her, I'm telling you. Ask Lenny— I could have married somebody like me."

Years later, Randy said his drug period was short. "I wasn't free of drugs or ending up in places I shouldn't have been at three in the morning, but I did luckily have a solid wife and kids," he told music writer Barney Hoskyns. "I don't look on it as fun, the big drug days. There were more downs than there were ups, I thought." Even his smoking was short lived.

But the tension expressed in the interview was genuine. Randy's personal life was under severe strain.

CHAPTER FOURTEEN

Films and the Stage
Ragtime *and* Faust

— I —

Randy couldn't imagine a time when he wouldn't make more albums, but he was looking forward in the early 1980s to reentering the world of film even though he knew he would be giving up lots of creative control.

"I'm an employee. Your prime job—in fact, your only job—is to help the picture, nothing else," he said. "You could write the best piece of music since Beethoven, and if it doesn't fit, it wouldn't be worth a shit. Sometimes you feel like a farmhand or a cog in the machine, but that's the way it should be. It's not always easy, but you have to accept that."

To illustrate the point, he told a story about how things had changed dramatically since the 1930s and 1940s, when Alfred Newman and other leading composers were so respected that they were part of a director's inner circle. By the 1960s, the pecking order had changed.

A magazine review of film director George Stevens's 1965 Biblical blockbuster *The Greatest Story Ever Told* criticized Alfred's use of Handel's Hallelujah Chorus in the scene where Christ is crucified. What the critic didn't know was that the chorus wasn't Alfred's idea. In fact, he had warned the director that the music would be inappropriate, but Stevens, who won director Oscars for *A Place in the Sun* and *Giant*, insisted. In a just world, the story credits would have read "Music by Alfred Newman, except for George Stevens's choice of Handel's Hallelujah Chorus." In time, Randy would have his own stories to tell—the day he became so frustrated by a director's choices that he walked off the picture and the day a director pulled the plug on him.

Even so, Randy was ready for a change in the early 1980s when De Laurentiis informed Randy that *Ragtime* was finally on track. At a stressful point in his record career, he threw himself into the project. Unlike during his college years, Newman was an eager student in the months leading up to *Ragtime*, starting with reading extensively about the period—singling out American historian Barbara W. Tuchman's *The Proud Tower* for special praise. Published in 1965, the book was a look at the shifting cultural and political attitudes of leading nations—including England, Germany, France, and the United States—from the 1890s to the start of World War I in the summer of 1914.

A two-time Pulitzer Prize winner, Tuchman combined an historian's discipline with a highly readable writing style, which made her one of Newman's favorite writers. He became so fascinated with the *Ragtime* era that he wanted to read more about it, finding much to admire later in German-born historian-journalist Philipp Blom's *The Vertigo Years: Change and Culture in the West, 1900–1914*. "The idea of America in 1906 interested me tremendously," he said in the liner notes for a CD edition of *Ragtime* in 2002. "It was a very different kind of mindset. There was a sense that everything was possible. Immigrants were coming—not welcome, but coming. I don't know what the country would be like if it hadn't let the Germans and Italians and Jews in to the extent they did, and World War I hadn't happened yet, which really ended the nineteenth century in a way."

~

Like jazz and rock and roll, ragtime was developed chiefly by Blacks in the southern United States, in this case St. Louis, the home of composer Scott Joplin, the "King of Ragtime." His "Maple Leaf Rag" was one of the biggest selling songs of the sheet music era in pop, and its success contributed greatly to ragtime's popularity with mainstream audiences.

With its fresh, appealing syncopation, ragtime—also like rock and jazz—was widely attacked for reasons rooted in racial prejudice, social elitism, and flat-out musical snobbery. But the style prevailed. In 1911, Irving Berlin used the term (though not the signature sound) in "Alexander's Ragtime Band," the songwriter's first smash. By the beginning of the 1920s, however, ragtime was giving way to the rise of more improvisational and far-reaching jazz.

While waiting for his film work to begin, Newman also listened to a large stack of recordings, from ragtime to pop hits of the period, as well as lots of classical music. This led from Joplin, Eubie Blake, and Fats Waller to waltz master Johann Strauss, a wide range of classical composers (Stravinsky to Mahler), and Percy Grainger, an Australian composer whose distinctive musical turf bridged classical music and English folk music. In the end, Newman was, if anything, overprepared.

Forman's version of *Ragtime* proved to be more conservative than Altman's original vision, reducing the multidimensional story to a single plot line. The film, released in November of 1981, concentrated on the struggle of Coalhouse Walker Jr., a fictional Black ragtime pianist, to gain respect and justice after being set upon by racist members of a volunteer fire station in New Jersey.

Even in his disappointment at the change, Newman was eager to establish himself in the film world, working as strenuously on *Ragtime* as he did on his albums. With two months to write the score, he was in his rented office from 7 a.m. to 5 p.m. most days. "In some ways, it was easier than writing my own songs because I didn't have to pull something right out of the air," he told David Sheff in a 1983 *Playboy* interview. "But in other respects, it was harder because I was dealing with someone else's ideas. . . . It's a real art to match and enhance what is going on up there. You try to help tell the story. You make the romance mean a little more. If the guy is looking happy driving his car, you try to make happy music." Besides the score, Newman also wrote two original songs and reworked Cass M. Freeborn and Edgar Allan Woolf's "I Could Love a Million Girls," a bouncy music-hall-like number that was featured in a Broadway musical from 1906.

"One More Hour" was a lovely but atypical Newman ballad about the power of music to comfort or refresh. It was sung over the film's closing credits by Jennifer Warnes, a pop singer who would later have No. 1 singles with two songs recorded for films, a duet with Joe Cocker on "Up Here Where We Belong," from *An Officer and a Gentleman*, and a duet with Bill Medley on "(I've Had) The Time of My Life," from *Dirty Dancing*.

Newman's other new song, "Change Your Way," the story of a father advising his young son to keep out of trouble, was more in line with the wry observations you would find on a Newman album, and he sang it himself. The song was scheduled to accompany the opening credits, but was eventually dropped.

Reviews of *Ragtime* were mixed, with Vincent Canby of the *New York Times* scolding Forman for his storytelling decisions. "It is superbly acted by a large cast, and it has been immaculately photographed (by Miroslav Ondricek), designed (by John Graysmark) and scored (by Randy Newman). Yet I'm not at all sure that anyone who has not read the book will have any idea what's going on much of the time, or why."

The film was a commercial disappointment, earning just $21.2 million at the box office. *Variety*'s review was a good example of how little attention film critics paid to scores. Though the remarks were positive—"predictably strong is Randy Newman's ragtime-based score"—it didn't come until the seventeenth paragraph of an eighteen-paragraph review, after mentions of the director, scriptwriter, and various designers (production, costume, art).

At the end of *Ragtime*, Randy would also have a misinformed review of his own to cite. The *New Republic*'s Stanley Kauffmann described a waltz number in the beginning of the film as inappropriate. In this case, Newman had written the waltz for a newsreel segment at the end of the movie. The first Randy knew that Forman had moved it was when he attended a sneak preview.

Ragtime received eight Academy Award nominations, including two for Newman: for original score and for original song for "One More Hour." The Oscars weren't the coolest thing among pop-rock musicians because movie music rarely reflected the daring and commentary of the best music being written at the time. Still, Newman attended the awards ceremony on March 29, 1982, at the Dorothy Chandler Pavilion in Los Angeles, where the award for best original score went to Greek composer Vangelis for *Chariots of Fire*. Newman also lost in the song competition to "Arthur's Theme," written by Burt Bacharach, Carole Bayer Sager, Christopher Cross, and Peter Allen.

Jon Burlingame, a writer-critic who specialized in film music and authored the 2002 book *Sound and Vision: Sixty Years of Motion Picture Soundtracks*, lauded Newman's work in *Ragtime*. "I watched the film again for the first time in twenty years and I don't care for it," he said. "Despite how Forman may have used the music, however, the music itself is superb."

During childhood, Burlingame was so passionate about the music from *Peter Gunn* and other television dramas that he eventually began a personal crusade to fill a void he noticed in reviews about television and movies—no one paid serious attention to the music. Because his strict Baptist mother prohibited him from listening to rock and roll, the movie-TV sounds became his alternative. He'd tape the music off the shows so he could listen to them again. As he got older, he searched in vain to find articles about the composers the way he saw countless articles about actors or rock stars. He even contacted TV columnists asking them to cover the subject.

"What I eventually learned was that none of the film reviewers had any idea about the role of music in television and film," he said. "They didn't realize that half the time what they were feeling was the result of the contribution of the composer."

Writing for *Hollywood Reporter* and the *Los Angeles Times*, Burlingame established himself as a go-to guy in the field where he was a big admirer of Newman.

"Randy understood almost innately what *Ragtime* needed," Burlingame said. "He started with the piano and a small, chamber-sized orchestra not to play 'ragtime' per se, but to utilize those early twentieth century American influences, including jazz. I'm blown over to this day. And that song, 'One More Hour,' is just wonderful. He was a major talent."

Even with the frustrations of *Ragtime*, Newman often told friends that conducting the orchestra was one of the greatest experiences of his life to that point. He later revised the quote to say it wasn't just conducting the *Ragtime* orchestra experience that was so great—it was conducting any orchestra on a soundstage: "It's about the happiest I get."

John Williams understood perfectly. "Alfred loved conducting as well," he said. "It's a realization of what's on the page and the hours you've spent putting notes down on the page, and it's suddenly alive and the spirit of what's in there is suddenly released. There's nothing like a good experience on the podium."

Randy elaborated in the *Ragtime* CD liner notes:

> Scoring looks like, and is, a very difficult job. For show business, it's difficult. Everything I do is easier than that. Performing is easier. Conducting is easier. Writing songs is close. But writing for an orchestra is very difficult, I think. You have a limited amount of time, and you must work all day, every day. If I could delay things, I would, but you can't. . . . For me that's a good thing. I'm going through it now, trying to write songs for an album where I just can't make myself go in there and work. Why? Is a question for a psychiatrist I guess.

— II —

While working on *Ragtime*, Randy was thinking about a project even more ambitious than *Good Old Boys*—a stage musical based on some work he admired; first he considered Wagner's *Ring Cycle* and then future Nobel Prize–winning author V. S. Naipaul's 1959 collection of short stories, *Miguel Street*. Ultimately, he chose Goethe's *Faust,* one of the most celebrated tales in Western literature. The musical would give Newman a wider canvas than *Good Old Boys* to address his social concerns and position him outside the pop album arena so he wouldn't be so dependent on radio to find an audience. It, too, would present a new challenge—stepping into Alfred's musical world of Broadway, reaching even higher than his uncle because he would write the musical, not just conduct it.

Johann Georg Faust lived in Germany in the early part of the sixteenth century—a man portrayed in chapbooks as a somewhat shadowy professor who, in effect, sold his soul to the Devil in exchange for unlimited knowledge and power. In England, Christopher Marlowe planted a flag in Faustian history around

1590 with his play, commonly known as *Doctor Faustus*. Then came Goethe with the most influential interpretation of the story. Since the first half of his *Faust* arrived in 1808, more than a hundred writers and composers have crafted their own works, including Lord Byron, Thomas Mann, Lawrence Durrell, Franz Liszt, and Hector Berlioz.

Lenny had been urging Randy for years to tackle a Broadway-type show. "What's important to know is that he didn't just want to do a musical," he said. "He wanted to do this musical. The theme was perfect for him; a chance to write about God and the Devil, good and evil, cruelty and hope, which are things that run through almost all his songs. And he recognized that. It's what made him stick with *Faust* for so many years."

~

As Randy eyed Broadway, an adventurous wing of the New York theater world was in turn exploring the stage potential of his music. Joan Micklin Silver, a filmmaker whose 1975 screen debut, *Hester Street*, was credited with opening doors for female directors in Hollywood, was a Newman fan who obtained the rights to use his songs in an off-off-Broadway revue.

Named after one of his early songs, *Maybe I'm Doing It Wrong* featured some two dozen Newman numbers—including "Short People" and "Sail Away"—and ran briefly in March of 1981 in a small showcase on West 18th Street with just four musicians, including a pianist and a violinist. In the *New York Times*, pop music-cabaret writer Stephen Holden tried to be encouraging, but he clearly was not impressed. Though he said Newman was generally acknowledged to be one of the two or three finest songwriters of his generation, he felt that the production needed better singers and a better choice of Newman songs. He felt the revue realized much of the fun in Newman's songs, but none of the "beauty" or "tragic awareness."

"Honestly, it was at best okay," said Michael Roth, a classi-cally trained musician and Beatles fan who was the show's music director. Though Randy had no part in the production, he and Roth spoke often on the phone and formed a relationship that would continue for years. Roth, whose work has been called "music one could imagine Charles Ives composing had he encoun-tered rock and roll and beat poetry," is a composer and sound artist whose credits range from chamber music and film scores to experimental music and theater. He has collaborated with such leading figures as Al Pacino, Tom Hanks, and Christopher Plum-mer. The Web Opera (thewebopera.com) is an experimental online opera composed and produced by Roth to raise awareness of cyber-abuse and cyberbullying.

Roth reached out to Newman while working on the music for the New York show and subsequent productions in La Jolla and Los Angeles.

> I needed the music for a couple of the songs because the arrange-ments in the published songbooks weren't very good. I realized he was playing everything differently than I ever did, and it was a hell of a lot better. The published songbooks left out a lot of his wonderful idiosyncratic musicianship. You might see what he was doing with his right hand, but not his left hand, which was crucial to understanding the music. On "It's Money That I Love" and other shuffles, the left hand is like a polyrhythm or cross accent with the right. Also, he rarely plays full chords. More often than not, there'll be a note missing from a triad, which, when combined with his attention to voice leading, results in a great sense of open space in his harmonizing and playing, which is very much unique to him.

The connection between Roth and Newman was so strong that Roth wrote his own, more complete musical transcriptions of Newman's music, editing five official anthologies, one of which centered on motion picture, television, and theater compositions, from "He Gives Us All His Love" and "Sandman's Coming" to a piano adaptation of Randy's suite from his score for *The Natural*. Roth said:

> Randy's undeniably sophisticated music palate made him very different from the other singer-songwriters of the day. While many of them would stick to the same three-chord formulas (I-IV-V) that populated most songs in the pop music world, Randy would explore far more advanced musical harmony and orchestrations. That is not to say he wouldn't use those basic chord patterns when it helped serve his storytelling purposes. But his ability to exploit and vary from these common patterns allowed him to convey more complex emotions and characters—sometimes all within the same song, as in "Davy the Fat Boy."
>
> This harmonic sophistication allowed him to create deeper emotions in his songs and convey to listeners a complexity that paralleled his lyrics and themes, leaving the listener slightly off balance and with something much more interesting to hear without straying too far from tonal harmony as to make his songs inaccessible. . . . Even in a song that seems as free and easy as "I Love L.A., he starts with a harmonically very sophisticated jazz-chord based introduction before shifting to a simple A major for the verse. The song further gives us an instrumental bridge in a new and somewhat foreign key (F Major), only to use it to transition the song into a totally new C Major for its close.

In the time with Newman, Roth saw parallels in their lives.

> As we got to know each other better, we would compare our lives and talk about our parents and all that stuff. Obviously, his life is different than mine, but there are similarities with both of

us dealing with depression. Randy said he would visit his father and tell him about something that he did that was going really well and his father would just sit there and watch *Matlock* on TV and say, "Oh, I never heard of that." I don't care who you are, but that hurts.

The most valuable thing to me about being friends with Randy is when we talk as composer to composer. He genuinely likes musicians; he loves talking about music, and he's very supportive. The first question he'll always ask me is, "So what are you writing?" I music direct for him a lot in theater, and I've orchestrated for him, and I've arranged, but he tells me, "Don't forget that you're a composer." He's an enormous supporter of what I write. The relationship isn't all one way.

Continuing to believe in the *Maybe* revue, Silver moved it to a more commercial off-Broadway venue, the Astor Place, in March of 1982, but it still didn't catch on. The *New York Times*'s theater critic Mel Gussow found the focus on social commentary the least appealing aspect of the revue and found many of the songs to be in questionable taste. This didn't encourage a rush to the ticket office. Privately, Newman wasn't a fan of the show, either. He felt the revue was wrong to use such "stagey people . . . actors and not singers," and he felt the song list leaned too heavily on his "cutesy" material.

— III —

Newman was playing *Faust* songs for friends as early as 1981. "The first one I heard was 'How Great Our Lord,' and it was very moving because Randy displayed such passion," said Gary Norris, who collected *Faust* demos and notebooks with the same drive as he had gathered Johnny Cutler material. "I could see how much it meant to him when he finally returned to the studio to do demos for *Trouble in Paradise*. Here he was starting his first album in three or four years, and what does he do? He records six *Faust* songs before he recorded any of the *Trouble* numbers."

Only three of those six songs would survive the long journey to the stage, but they would be among the show's most memorable— "How Great Our Lord," "Best Little Girl," and "Gainesville." In those numbers, Newman told us a lot about his intentions. Yes, there would be his humor (there was humor in Goethe's play as well), but there would also be his eye for society's cruelty and deceit—the classic Newman mix.

Newman downplayed a large theological point to the musical, saying it was mostly a comedy, comparing it to *A Funny Thing Happened on the Way to the Forum*. Reflecting on Newman's comment, Chris Willman, the author of the *Faust* CD liner notes, pointed out correctly that the musical also contained "moments so ineffably sad and beautiful that they could haunt your dreams."

Alan Newman explained his brother's intent this way: "As always, Randy wants to entertain, but the source of his comedy is clearly his observation of human nature and his satire of prevailing culture. I don't think he was 'summarizing' his views of human behavior—*Faust* is not his apotheosis. His viewpoints are clearly there though. When he says it's a comedy 100 percent, he is right, but the source of that comedy comes from his sardonic worldview." Waronker concurred, "You were sure to get Randy's feelings about the world in there. He always tried to tell the truth about people, and that's what he did in *Faust*."

Excited that Newman was working on a musical, Roth assisted him as orchestrator on the stage production, but he knew from the start that there would be problems. "Broadway is not the be-all and end-all of theater," said Roth, whose interest in the theater was largely inspired by artists like Samuel Beckett.

It's an economic center and centrifuge for a lot of great theatrical energy, but it's not always going to be the aesthetic center of anything because, in the end, it is very expensive and so, out of necessity, very commercial. I'm not going to disparage what Broadway is because obviously it can create excellence, as it did with *Hamilton* and many others. But generally speaking, especially when it comes to musical theater, it's not a pure art experience, and Randy is a subversive. He was interested in doing things more commonly found in experimental theaters. Randy understood the challenges. He was aiming high.

CHAPTER FIFTEEN

Trouble in Paradise:
*Another Epic Album and
The Marriage Ends*

— I —

There was little, if any, talk in the media about Newman needing a comeback after *Born Again*, though it wouldn't have been surprising if someone had raised the issue. No one around Randy, however, noticed a sense of urgency when he began work on a new album in 1982 that would be his most accomplished since *Good Old Boys*.

As was his custom, Randy would play the piano—sometimes for days—until the music suggested a character or subject. On slow days, the process led nowhere; even if Newman settled on a character, the story stalled, giving him far more rejections than finished songs over the years. Other times, the song evolved in surprising ways. Few went through as colorful an evolution as the one that would become as synonymous with him as "Short People": "I Love L.A." The song started out as a composition with the goofy title "A Big Smelly Country Song."

Accompanied by a loping country beat, the lyrics spoke about how perfectly decent people can be blinded by wealth and personal comforts to the social problems in the wider community. But Randy had trouble finishing the song, and he turned to Lenny for feedback. In the demo tape, you can sense Newman wrestling with the tune. Retitled "Something to Sing About," it expressed the smug self-satisfaction of a narrator who assures us that everything in his life is good. It begins:

I've got six children
Four boys, two little girls
I've got a bit of money in the bank, yeah
I've got a house on the ocean
A backyard, got flowers all around it.

I love that street
Got friends up and down it
They all get together
When the sun goes down.

Yes, I've got something to sing about
I've got something to sing about

Newman tipped off his uncertainty about the song when he broke into laughter at the end of the tape as he turned to Waronker for a reaction. For one of the few times in the years of previewing songs for his friend, Randy remembers Lenny hating it.

Years later, Waronker couldn't imagine ever telling Newman that he hated the song. "Randy was so intense when he was playing a new song that he'd study your feelings and he would pick up on the slightest nuance," he said. "There were times when he would sing something over the phone, and I would have a difficult time hearing all the words, so I'd ask him to sing it again or I'd wait just a second too long to react in the studio and he'd go,

'You didn't like that, did you?' It was never casual with him; the songs were everything."

Newman set the song aside until a chance conversation with Don Henley. While talking about all the cities with pop theme songs—New York to Chicago —the Eagles co-founder suggested that Randy would be the perfect person to write a theme for the City of the Angels. Randy wasn't a fan of the swagger and braggadocio of city salutes, especially the Sinatra hit "New York, New York." "You can't write a sort of worshipful song about an American city today," he wisecracked. "If asked to write a song about, say, Sacramento, I could do it, but I'd have to lie."

Still, the idea of a Los Angeles theme song intrigued him. Soon afterward, he returned to "Something to Sing About" and began imagining how the song's bluster might be reimagined. The unlikely result was "I Love L.A.," and this time Waronker was elated. The song's narrator falls so completely for the feel-good imagery of his city (the miles of beach, the near-constant sunshine, and the seemingly endless parade of pretty women) that he is oblivious to the city's problems; he sees the bum on his knees as part of the city's charm. Newman's point about homelessness and poverty in paradises was slipped into the cheerful singalong with such subtlety—just twelve words—that it's easy to miss, but it is a memorable slice of Newman satire.

"I thought it was a regular Randy song, not something that would be controversial and misunderstood like 'Short People,'" Russ Titelman said. "More than simply fun, this was just a great song." The full lyrics:

Hate New York City
It's cold and it's damp
And all the people dressed like monkeys
Let's leave Chicago to the Eskimos

That town's a little too rugged
For you and me, you bad girl
Rollin' down the Imperial Highway
With a big nasty redhead at my side
Santa Ana winds blowin' hot from the north
And we was born to ride

Roll down the window, put down the top
Crank up the Beach Boys, baby
Don't let the music stop
We're gonna ride it till we just can't ride it no more

From the South Bay to the Valley
From the West Side to the East Side
Everybody's very happy
'Cause the sun is shining all the time
Looks like another perfect day

I love L.A. (We love it)
I love L.A. (We love it)

Look at that mountain
Look at those trees
Look at that bum over there, man
He's down on his knees
Look at these women
There ain't nothin' like 'em nowhere

Century Boulevard (We love it)
Victory Boulevard (We love it)
Santa Monica Boulevard (We love it)
Sixth Street (We love it, we love it)
We love L.A.

Infant Randy in 1944. *(Adele Newman—Newman Family Archive)*

Randy's dad, Irving, is welcomed home in 1945 after his service as a doctor in World War II. From left: Emil, Irving, George, Betty Grable, Marcus, Alfred, and Lionel. Actress Grable was there with her husband, bandleader Harry James, who was reportedly there to work on a session in the studio at 20th Century Fox that is now known as the Newman Scoring Stage. *(Robert Newman—Newman Family Archive)*

Randy with his mother, Adele, brother Alan, and father around the time the family moved in the Pacific Palisades home in the late 1940s. *(Bob Fuchs—Newman Family Archive)*

Randy at the piano with his father in 1949. *(Adele Newman—Newman Family Archive)*

Lenny Waronker and Randy (with the football) in the backyard of the Newman family home, circa 1950. *(Adele Newman—Newman Family Archive)*

Randy (mugging for the camera on the right) during an outing in Las Vegas in 1954. From top in left row: Adele Newman, Lenny's mother Jeanette and father Si Waronker, conductor Felix Slatkin, his son (and future conductor) Leonard, Lenny's sister, Rosyln. From top in right row: Irving, Eleanor Slatkin, Randy, Lenny, Slatkin's other son Frederic, and Alan Newman. *(Emil Newman—Newman Family Archive)*

Mo Ostin, who helped build fledgling Warner Bros. Records into the nation's most successful and respected label, had deep faith in Randy's music. Circa 1970. *(Michael Ochs Archives/ Getty Images)*

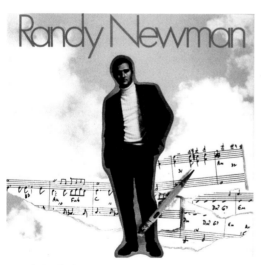

Randy looked so much like part of the old pop male vocal tradition in this cover of his 1968 debut album that many retailers put it in the bins next to Andy Williams. *(Vinyls/ Alamy)*

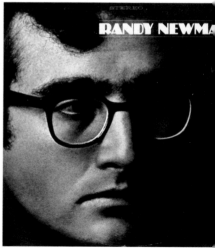

Realizing the error, Warner Bros. ditched first cover and used this more contempora image when it re-released the album later 1968. *(Michael Ochs Archives / Getty Im*

Randy with son Amos and wife Roswitha the day of his 1972 concert at New York's Philharmonic Hall, the first time he was joined on stage by an orchestra. *(Maddy Miller)*

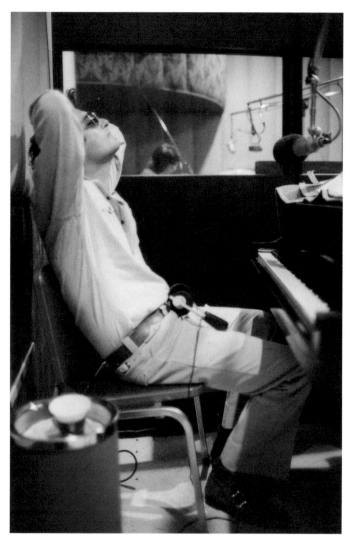

Relaxing during break in a recording session for the landmark, 1974 *Good Old Boys* album. *(copyright Shepard Sherbell/ Corbis/ Getty Images)*

andy meant the cover of his *Born Again* album in 1979 as a joke, but the KISS-like
image (highlighted in this billboard on Los Angeles' Sunset Strip) led to a backlash
among many of his fans. *(Images Press/Getty Images)*

Having fun on the promotional rounds for the *Land of Dreams* album in 1988, Randy and Mark Knopfler yawn and pretend to sleep their way through an interview in London. *(Michael Putland/ Getty Images)*

Randy visits, right to left, Tom Petty, Bob Dylan, and Lou Reed backstage at the first Farm Aid concert in 1985. The event, in Champaign, Illinois, drew more than 85,000 fans and raised over $7 million for family farmers in America. *(Deborah Feingold/ Getty Images)*

dy and Lenny Waronker at a recording industry awards luncheon in 2003.
ve Starr/ Corbis/ Getty Images)

gainst all odds, Randy and his cousins, composers David Newman (left) and Thomas
Newman have matched—or even exceeded—the musical accomplishments of the film
music generation of Newmans. *(E. Charbonneau / WireImage / Getty; Jonathan Leibson /
WireImage / Getty)*

Randy, the composer. *(L. Cohen/ Wirelmage/ Getty Images)*

Randy with director John Lasseter during the making of the film *Cars* in 2006. *(copyright Globe Photos/ Zumapress.com/ Alamy)*

Randy flanked by *Toy Story*'s Buzz Lightyear and Woody, on his Hollywood Walk of Fame star in 2010. *(copyright Paul Smith/ Featureflash/ Alamy)*

Having fun in 2011 on the night of Randy's second Oscar win, this time for the song "We Belong Together" from the film *Toy Story 3. (Dan MacMedan / WireImage / Getty Images)*

ndy and Gretchen on vacation in Africa. *(Patrick Newman)*

he couple on another vacation ride, this time in the Caribbean. *(Alice Newman)*

Randy conducting the orchestra during a session for the movie *Toy Story 3* in 2010. *(WENN Rights Ltd/ Alamy)*

Mitchell Froom produced or co-produced Randy's celebrated trio of albums—*Bad Love* to *Dark Matter*. *(Scott Dudelson/ Getty Images)*

Russ Titelman co-produced six of Ranc albums, including *Sail Away* and *Good Boys*. *(Patrick McMullan/ Getty Image*

Randy with his adult children. From left, Patrick, John, Alice, Amos, and Eric
(*Courtesy of Amy and Stuart Photography*)

Randy plays "Happy Birthday" as Amos' daughter Piper prepares to blow out the candles on the cake Gretchen is holding at Piper's ninth birthday party in 2018. From top at right, Johnny's wife Lindsay is holding Holly and Eric's wife Dana with James. *(Alice Newman)*

I love L.A. (We love it)
I love L.A. (We love it)
I love L.A. (We love it)

Discussing the song in 2021, Newman spoke fondly of his hometown, but he meant the lyrics to be pointed. "The guy in the song is sort of aggressively ignorant," he said. "He thinks the great thing about the city is rolling down Imperial Highway in a convertible with this redhead at his side. To him, everything is so great that he doesn't really see things at all. He doesn't distinguish between 'that mountain . . . those trees and . . . that bum down on his knees.' The truth is, Imperial Highway is kind of a shitty street. In fact, all the streets in the song are kind of shitty, undistinguished. There's nothing taller on Imperial Highway than I am."

Henley applauded the song. "I had no idea what he would write, but I'm sure I figured it probably wouldn't be a paean," he said years later. "But, again, like a lot of Randy's songs, 'I Love L.A.' has been widely misunderstood. It has that duality, that contradictory element. It's a send-up; it's a take-down. It's a satirical song—good-natured mocking disguised as a song of praise and delivered with tongue firmly in cheek. It's a reflection of the classic love-hate relationship that so many of us have with our home cities, and by extension, America itself."

Randy recorded "I Love L.A. on June 21, 1982, the first day of sessions for the new album, and the producers felt he nailed it. Randy, however, felt something was missing and he recorded it again the next day. "I was at first opposed," Waronker said. "I thought there was a lot of life in what we had, but it turned out he was right. He has a great sense of what's right for a song, in this case the tempo. And we reached that same high day after day on the album. Everyone was locked in."

Within a week, Newman had seven recordings that would serve as the center of the album. If the eventual title alone,

Trouble in Paradise, wasn't enough to suggest Newman was again thinking of a loosely connected concept album, his alternative title also pointed you in that direction: *Another Perfect Day*.

— II —

Newman next turned to what would be one of his most inspired mixtures of humor and social observation. "My Life Is Good" combined elements of greed, class snobbery, and privilege. The arrogant tone of the song's character gives the primary verses an extra sting. The lyrics, in part:

> *A couple of weeks ago*
> *My wife and I*
> *Took a little trip down to Mexico*
> *Met this young girl there*
> *We brought her back with us*
> *Now she lives with us*
> *In Our Home*
> *She cleans the hallway*
> *She cleans the stair*
> *She cleans the living room*
> *She wipes the baby's ass*
> *She drives the kids to school*
> *She does the laundry too*
> *She wrote this song for me*
> *Listen*
> *Yeah*
> *The other afternoon*
> *My wife and I*
> *Took a little ride into Beverly Hills*
> *Went to the private school*
> *Our oldest child attends*

Many famous people send their children there
This teacher says to us
"We have a problem here
This child just will not do
A thing I tell him to
And he's such a big old thing
He hurts the other children
All the games they play, he plays so rough
Hold it teacher
Wait a minute
Maybe my ears are clogged or somethin'
Maybe I'm not understanding
The English language
Dear, you don't seem to realize

My Life Is Good
My Life Is Good
My Life Is Good, you old bag
My Life, My Life

In another verse, the narrator is so delusional in his conceit that he imagines an exhausted Bruce Springsteen asking him to take over his place with the E Street Band for a while. "The guy in 'My Life Is Good' doesn't know he's an asshole and that his wife and kids would be climbing the wall," Randy said. "On one hand, he's an unreliable narrator, but he is also reliable. He doesn't know he is hurting people to some degree. I liked that kind of mixture in pop songs; it's something else I had read in books."

"Christmas in Cape Town," which again employed the N-word, was set in South Africa but spoke to racism everywhere. The central figure, one of the most reprehensible of all Newman's characters, is so filled with hate that he tries to convince a disapproving woman from England that bigotry is simply a part of the cultural landscape in Cape Town, a hatred all the more biting because the song is set in the season that celebrates peace on earth. There was no hint of apology, only anger at her for questioning his views. The lyrics in part:

I tell her, Darling, don't talk about things
you don't understand
I tell her, Darling, don't talk about something
you don't know anything about
I tell her, Darling, if you don't like it here
go back to your own miserable country

It's Christmas in Cape Town but it ain't the same
Oh, the boys on the beach are still blowin'
And the summer wind still kicks the clouds around

You know my little brother, babe
Well, he works out at the diamond mine
I drove him out there at five this mornin'
The niggers were waitin' in a big long line
You know those big old lunch pails they carry, man
With a picture of Star Wars painted on the side
They were starin' at us real hard with
their big ugly yellow eyes
You could feel it
You could feel it

It's Christmas in Cape Town but it ain't the same
The stores are open all the time
And little kids on skateboards cut in and out of the crowd
And the Christmas lights still shine
Myself, I don't like to drink the way

I used to, man, you know
It don't seem to get me high
And the beer don't taste the way it
ought to taste somehow
And I don't know why

Don't talk to me about the planes
Man, I've heard it
Just take a look around
What are we gonna do, blow up
the whole damn country?
I don't know

It's Christmas in Cape Town
It's Christmas in Cape Town
It's Christmas in Cape Town

Newman wasn't finished with racism. "Mikey" spotlights Americans who resent the ethnic changes around them. As slow as progress has been for Blacks, Newman's narrator—who could be a drinking buddy of the vet in "Ghosts"—speaks for those who feel the change was moving like a pandemic. Set in a bar, the song again has the economy and character of a short story. In one of its key passages, Newman conveys a time, place, and attitude deftly by simply referring to a lighthearted R & B novelty record from 1961:

You know, Mikey
We've been friends for a long time
You tell me all your troubles
And I've always told you mine
North Beach has changed though
Since we were growin' up

Didn't used to be any spades here, now you got 'em
Didn't used to be any Mexicans here, now you got 'em
Didn't used to be any Chinamen here
Didn't used to be this ugly music playing all the time
Where are we, on the moon?
Whatever happened to the old songs, Mikey?
Like the Duke of Earl

The irony of the bartender longing for "Duke of Earl" is sublime—the song, of course, was recorded and co-written in 1961 by Gene Chandler, the stage name of Eugene Dixon, a Black man.

When later interviewing Randy about the album for *Rolling Stone*, Rob Tannenbaum asked, in a portion of the interview not used in the feature, if Newman held a sentimental attachment to the early days of rock and R & B—if there was a year or decade that seemed more appealing to him. "No," Newman responded.

> In terms of movie music, I might have wished I would have done it at an earlier time . . . 'cause they left you alone more. Pop music? I came along at the right time. I've done as well as you can expect, considering what I did. . . . There's things I wish weren't happening in the world, you know. It's getting more crowded and there's a loss of historicity. You can't make references to Rhode Island and expect that people know there is a Rhode Island necessarily anymore. But basically, I can't think of another time I would have liked to have lived.

~

Inappropriate behavior, which Newman tended to explore in ingenious ways, was targeted in "Real Emotional Girl," a song blessed with a melody so disarming and graceful that many listeners would be surprised to learn the sentiment behind it. Unlike "I Love L.A.," there wasn't even a slight hint to tip you off to its meaning.

She's a real emotional girl
She wears her heart on her sleeve
Every little thing you tell her
She'll believe
She really will
She even cries in her sleep
I've heard her
Many times before
I never had a girl who loved me
Half as much as this girl loves me
She's real emotional
For eighteen years she lived at home
She was Daddy's little girl
And Daddy helped her move out on her own
She met a boy
He broke her heart
And now she lives alone
And she's very, very careful
Yes, she is
She's a real emotional girl
Lives down deep inside herself
She turns on easy
It's like a hurricane
You would not believe it
You gotta hold on tight to her
She's a real emotional girl

Even forewarned about the underlying meaning, it's hard to imagine "Real Emotional Girl" being viewed as anything other than a love song. Timothy White, a perceptive Newman observer, called it the most sensitive song Newman had written to that time. When he asked Newman about it in a *Rolling Stone* interview, he was surprised to hear that it was another portrait of an insensitive male. "I saw the guy as sort of a bad guy," Newman said. "I don't think you should be relating all those confidences— telling anyone that she cries in her sleep. I think it's like the girl's made another mistake."

Newman has heard numerous fans question the meaning of "Real Emotional Girl," along with some of his other songs, but he stands by the way the song was written and recorded.

"Maybe I didn't do it well enough for people to get a song, but when I finish it, I think it's clear," he said. "I never try to make a song obscure. I'm not giving an intelligence test. I'm trying to communicate."

There's also a poignant layer in the song "Same Girl," but this time the references to "nights on the street" and "needle marks in your arm" make it clear that the lavishly orchestrated song is speaking about a junkie.

You're still the same girl you always were
You're still the same girl you always were
A few more nights on the street, that's all
A few more holes in your arm
A few more years with me, that's all

You're still the same girl

With the same sweet smile that you always had
And the same blue eyes like the sun
And the same clear voice that I always knew
You're still the same girl
That I love

"Song for the Dead" was Randy's first anti-war song. He sidesteps overt protest by telling the story through the eyes of a soldier left behind in Southeast Asia to bury comrades killed in battle—and to try to make some sense of the sacrifices in what stands as America's most unpopular war. The lyrics:

Deep in the field
A lone soldier stands
With mud on his boot
And blood on his hands
They left him behind
To bury the dead
And to say a few words on behalf of the leadership
Pardon me, boys
If I slip off my pack
And sit for a while with you
I'd like to explain
Why you fine young men had to be blown apart
To defend this mud hole

Now our country, boys
Though it's quite far away
Found itself jeopardized
Endangered, boys
By these very gooks
Who lie here beside you
Forever near
Forever

We'd like to express
Our deep admiration
For your courage under fire
And your willingness to die
For your country, boys
We won't forget
We won't forget

After the darkness of those songs, Newman returned to the upbeat spirit of "I Love L.A." in "Miami" (another city with stains beneath the palm tree glamour) before switching to the urgency of "Take Me Back," which speaks of the undying hope for second and third chances, and the snarky "The Blues."

Despite Randy's deep admiration for Paul Simon, whose music had moved far from the early folk anguish of Simon and Garfunkel, "The Blues" felt like a bookend to the days when Newman satirized the way folk and blues artists struck him as romanticizing their pain. But Simon himself didn't seem to mind the tease because he joined Randy on the vocals. Years later, he said he was simply pleased to join Randy on a record.

The song begins:

He's gonna tell you 'bout his dear old mother
Burned up in a factory in Springfield, Mass.
He's gonna tell you 'bout his baby brother
Hustlin' down the city streets
And selling his ass for a dollar bag
He's gonna tell you 'bout his uncle Neddy
Locked up in a prison out in Oregon
He's gonna tell you 'bout his best friend Eddie
Killed in a bar fight with a pair of Marines
And a sailor
Oh
He's got the blues, this boy
He's got the blues
You can hear it in his music

In the album, Michael Roth saw the Newman sophistication and daring at work. "While others may have used simple major and minor triads, Randy would stray into seventh, ninth, eleventh, and thirteenth chords, common in jazz but seldom used in pop music. When others might choose a key and stick with it, Randy would often blur the lines of a tonic center by using parallel major and minor keys simultaneously ('Miami') and introduce new keys to the piece for bridges and other sections ('I love L.A.')."

Waronker enjoyed watching Newman and Simon in the studio. "They were both so intense. When Randy got stuck on a word, Paul offered a suggestion, and they are both such perfectionists that they went back and forth until they found the right word—and we're not talking about something anyone would notice; we're talking about an 'and' or 'but.'"

Afterward, Newman expressed misgivings about the song itself. "It made fun of a kid who had trouble, a kid who would rush to his room and play the piano," he told Joe Smith for *Off the Record: An Oral History of Popular Music*. "That was wrong. I can't think of another song of mine I regret in the slightest, but I do regret that one."

— III —

Critics cheered *Trouble in Paradise*. The *Voice* poll welcomed Randy back to its year-end list, voting *Trouble* No. 13—behind Michael Jackson's *Thriller*, which was No. 1, but ahead of such valued works as Prince's *1999* and Simon's *Hearts and Bones*. Chances are that the album would have finished higher except for the likely lingering critical backlash against *Born Again* that caused some critics to dismiss the follow-up outright.

Rolling Stone's Christopher Connelly declared that *Trouble* stood with *Sail Away* as the "apotheosis of Newman's art." The *New York Times*'s John Rockwell, who had begun writing about pop music after years of reviewing classical music, praised the CD: "The arrangements are not original in that they sound unlike anything ever heard before. Instead, their novelty lies in the detail, the subtlety, the texture, the appropriateness of a given touch for the implications of a given song or line or word. They elevate what might be a more familiar sort of Brecht-Weill, cabaret singer-talker into something more musically complex."

While numerous reviewers cited the album's sonic power, some longtime Newman fans complained that the synthesizer emphasis was an attempt to give Newman's records a more polished contemporary feel in hopes of gaining radio airplay. Similarly, some fans pointed to the long list of celebrated guest vocalists (also including Linda Ronstadt, Don Henley, Lindsey Buckingham, Christine McVie, and Bob Seger) as evidence of him seeking mainstream radio support.

Titelman felt that the album's synthesizer underpinnings reflected Newman's evolving musical taste. "The main thing that contributed to the sound on that was Randy's mastery of creating sounds on the synthesizer," the producer said. "There is an orchestra on the album in places, but a lot of the time you are hearing something new. Working with Michael Boddicker, Randy came up with these synthesizer sounds that really transported you to some other place in your listening brain."

Waronker believed the members of the hit band Toto also brought a fresh dynamic to the sessions. "This was a new generation of musicians working with Randy," he said. "They were great record-makers on their own and they were big Randy fans, so they contributed excitement and energy to the studio. When he played 'I Love L.A.' the first time, they got up and applauded. That's the way it pretty much was for the whole album."

In the "20 Questions" feature, *Playboy*'s David Sheff asked if Newman was pessimistic or depressed as some of his songs suggested. Newman, who continued to believe he had been too negative about his life as a songwriter in early interviews, tried to be more upbeat with his answer, but he finally let some rain slip in:

I don't like to write. I feel great when I get something going. I feel terrible when I don't have something going. But my subject matter is not all depressing, and I'm not depressed when I write about it. I'm happier than most people I see. I have every reason to be. I live in a nice place. I have a nice family. I don't have to work nine to five for a bad boss. . . . The big problem with what I do is that I can't guarantee I can do it. If you sell insurance, you sort of know how to sell insurance. But I don't know how I write songs. I can't go out and say, "I'll write you a song" and then just do it.

Even with the critical support, the album, released in January of 1983, only reached No. 64 on the pop charts, most likely another sign of the *Born Again* backlash and radio's continued view of Newman as an outsider. "The Blues" was Randy biggest single since "Short People," but it stalled at No. 51. That left "I Love L.A." as Warner's hope to jumpstart sales; however, radio station program directors around the country told label reps that they liked the record, but "it's an L.A. song, it won't work in our market."

Newman and Warner continued to believe in the song. Randy sang it on his return to *Saturday Night Live* in February, and the label chose it for Randy's promotional video hoping for exposure on MTV, the twenty-four-hour cable music channel that played videos the way radio stations played singles. Amid much skepticism from record companies who had to pay for the making of the videos, the channel was launched in 1981 and soon became such a powerful force that record labels would spend hundreds of thousands of dollars on videos featuring top-selling artists like Michael Jackson, Madonna, and Duran Duran.

The "I Love L.A." video was a modest investment, put together on a $55,000 budget by first-time video director Tim Newman, who was Randy's cousin. But this wasn't a case of nepotism. Tim Newman had an impressive history of directing TV commercials and he felt that "I Love L.A."—with its colorful imagery and a winning, sing-along arrangement—was ideal for a video.

The storyline featured Randy driving a convertible around Los Angeles, a pretty redhead by his side, juxtaposed against scenes of the city, all with a celebratory flair. Patrick Goldstein, the *Los Angeles Times* pop music columnist, named it the video of the year—over Michael Jackson's "Billie Jean"—describing the tongue-in-cheek tour of the city as a mix of David Hockney and Walt Disney. Tim Newman, who went on to direct a series of image-defining, award-winning videos that helped make ZZ Top one of the hottest properties in rock, was one of Alfred Newman's sons, and had palled around with his cousin and Lenny Waronker as youngsters in Pacific Palisades. He remembered Randy as quiet and self-possessed, but always with a wry sensibility.

"Randy's obviously a brilliant musician, but he's also intellectually very curious," Tim said. "He loves to read, which may help explain why every song is like a novel. The video was a labor of love, the chance to work with Randy and show our shared affection for the city. The heart of the video is Randy driving this old Buick around the city, which is another story because Randy's not a great driver and that was kind of fun in a hair-raising way. He didn't have an accident, but we were always on edge."

The video picked up MTV airplay, but its full impact wasn't felt until the following year, when Los Angeles hosted the 1984 Summer Olympics. Nike bought the rights to some scenes for use in a high-profile ad, along with additional scenes of the city and Olympic athletes Carl Lewis and Mary Decker. That visibility made "I Love L.A." known around the world and so popular in Los Angeles that the song was celebrated as an unofficial anthem. Decades later, it would still be played at virtually every professional sporting event in Los Angeles, including Dodgers, Lakers, and Rams games.

~

Even before the high visibility of "I Love L.A.," those who worked with Randy started noticing uncharacteristic behavior in his personal life. Nearing forty, Randy showed symptoms of what is commonly called a midlife crisis. After "Short People," he had been getting a lot of attention, and it was flattering. He no longer needed to stumble into a pool to catch someone's eye.

— **IV** —

There are two types of pop stars when it comes to family and the media: those willing to invite a photographer or a camera crew into the maternity ward if it'll mean lots of exposure, and those who won't even send out a press release about the child's birth— or their own wedding. Newman, of course, was one of the latter, which is only natural for someone who avoided the first person in his writing.

Randy and Roswitha separated in 1983 and divorced two years later, but the first anyone outside of their circle likely heard about it was in 1988 when Randy did a *People* magazine interview to promote his new *Land of Dreams* album. The article's jarring headline also spoke of other trouble: "Randy Newman, Rocked by Illness and a Troubled Marriage, Finds Comfort in *Land of Dreams*."

"I don't know why we broke apart," he told *People* in a rare glimpse of his private life. "Things like that happen. I will always be her friend, and she will always be mine." Roswitha, who by then owned a Pacific Palisades clothing boutique, was equally discreet, though she implied Randy was behind the breakup. "When you get to be forty, things can suddenly change," she said. "I think Randy had to prove to himself that he could make it on his own."

Describing Randy's pain over the breakup, Irving Newman relayed an incident from the couple's separation. "Once we came out of a restaurant, and Roswitha was with us," he said in the *People* article. "Two of the boys got into Randy's car, and the little one, Johnny, looked up and said, 'Daddy, which house do I go to?' It broke Randy's heart."

~

A quarter century later, several people close to Randy spoke more openly about the breakup. Just as Newman had asserted himself in his musical career, he apparently began reexamining his personal life in the early 1980s and found something missing. Several of his friends were alarmed when he began dating a few people. "We started worrying about what might happen to the marriage," Elliot Abbott said. "When it finally became obvious that he was thinking about leaving Roswitha, I told him, 'Oh God, Randy, don't do this.' Others did the same, but the writing was on the wall. At some point, you had to just go, 'It's his life.'"

Finally, Randy met someone who stood out when he was finishing the *Trouble* album in late 1982. Gretchen Preece was a student at California State University, Los Angeles, and worked as a part-time receptionist in an office next door to the writing room Randy rented in West Los Angeles. "Randy didn't have a phone in his office because he didn't want to be interrupted when he was writing, so he'd come over and borrow one of ours," Gretchen said. "I didn't know all of his songs, but my brother had one of his albums and I certainly knew 'Short People.' I remember saying to a girlfriend, 'Oh, God, I am working next door to Randy Newman, and she's says, 'Oh, that sounds like fun.'"

The twenty-one-year-old Preece was a music fan with a warm, outgoing personality, an engaging sense of humor, and a gentle aura of confidence. She had grown up in nearby Sherman Oaks, also around show business. Her father, Michael Preece, was a script supervisor for such films as *The Old Man and the Sea* and *The Getaway*, and who later directed more than 300 TV show episodes—more than sixty episodes of *Dallas* alone.

"I enjoyed it when Randy came to the office because he was always so funny," she said. "Eventually, we'd go to get a bite to eat from time to time because the building was pretty isolated, not much going on. But we were just friends—this was before he was separated." Abbott remembers Randy being concerned around the time of the separation about the children. "He said something that was telling: 'If we could just do 5 percent better with our kids than our parents did with us, we'd be doing great,' his dad was difficult," Abbott said. "I think he always felt that, but the possibility of losing the children in a divorce had made him even more devoted to them."

Newman's anxiety over his relationship with his sons felt as troubling when he was interviewed by Steve Oney for *California* magazine in 1983 as it had four years earlier in Timothy White's *Rolling Stone* profile. "Any time I'm not writing is time not well spent for me," Newman said. "This is a conflict because one of my biggest wishes is to be a better father. . . . You know there are daddies who go on outings and camping trips and that sort of stuff with the whole family. But I don't do it enough."

By that time, the Newmans' oldest son, Amos, was attending the exclusive Steamboat Mountain School, about 150 miles from Denver. The move came after the teenager started having problems in school in Los Angeles. A guidance counselor advised Randy and Roswitha to consider a boarding school, but part of the motivation, Amos felt, may have been to protect him from their mounting problems.

"The breakup was a bombshell," he said. "In hindsight, I could feel the energy in the house changing, but I was away from

Los Angeles for a long time. After three years at Steamboat, I studied photography for two years at Colorado University in Boulder. I wasn't around the way Eric and Johnny were."

Eric, who entered his teens the year his parents separated, also used the word "bombshell" and had more vivid memories of the marital dissolve. "I remember things happening in stages, starting when I was around eleven or twelve when I'd see my mom suddenly break into tears," he said. "She'd sometime stay in her robe all day, which she had never done."

After parting, Randy and Roswitha shared custody of the boys, and Gretchen recalled Randy looking forward to the days when they came to stay with him in the house he rented in Brentwood. "I don't think I've ever seen someone sit down and listen [so attentively] to what his children had to say as Randy at that time," she said. "Even if he was working on a new song, he would make sure they had his complete attention. The boys knew they were loved, and they reached out to me from the start. I felt welcome from the moment I met them."

— V —

The stress on Newman was compounded in the mid-1980s by a severe bout of Epstein-Barr, a virus that causes extreme fatigue and often depression. Some of those close to Newman felt the condition—which was long believed to be stress-related—was triggered by the marriage breakup. "When I'd go over and see Randy, just getting up and walking across the room and back was like climbing a gigantic mountain for him," Lenny Waronker said. "The scary thing was no one seemed to know how long it was going to last."

The syndrome hit suddenly. Newman was playing tennis one day when he collapsed in exhaustion. "It also affects you mentally,"

Newman said. "You can't look forward to anything. Nothing looks good. I was like a candle that suddenly went out."

Even with the family breakup and the two-year Epstein-Barr episode, Randy was unusually productive in the 1980s. Besides *Trouble in Paradise*, he wrote and recorded a second album, co-scripted a wacky western movie with Steve Martin and Lorne Michaels, and composed two film scores, including one based on Bernard Malamud's celebrated novel *The Natural*. It would be one of his most acclaimed.

CHAPTER SIXTEEN

The Natural
La Película Loca and
Peter Asher

— I —

There's a moment near the end of *The Natural* when Robert Redford's character hits a game-winning home run that is one of the
most spectacular scenes in any sports movie. The sequence begins
with Redford, a star outfielder who is seriously injured and can
barely stand at the plate, looking overmatched as the first pitch
streaks by him for a called strike. The camera picks up blood
seeping through Redford's jersey as he wipes perspiration from
his brow. With everything appearing hopeless, the hobbled Redford swings at the next pitch and drives the ball toward a high
bank of stadium lights. As the ball hits one set of lights, an elec-
trical reaction is triggered that causes the other lights to explode
like fireworks as Redford slowly circles the bases.

Of all the elements that contributed to the scene, Newman's
music was the most compelling—not just for the way it conveyed
the triumph of the moment, but how it gently summarized the
Redford character's grand early dreams, his rise, his tragic down-
fall, and then his hard-fought redemption. Decades later, Newman's theme would still be played on TV sports programs and at

stadiums. Sports commentator and baseball superfan Bob Costas called Newman's soundtrack a "great piece of work. The film wouldn't have been half as good without it."

Barry Levinson, who directed the 1984 movie, agreed. "In *The Natural*, you are dealing with a fable, you're not doing a realistic view of baseball," he said. "The sport is filled with all this over-the-top mythology, flamboyant stories like Babe Ruth pointing to where he is going to hit the home run and then hitting it there. The score has to express that mythology, and that's what Randy did. *The Natural* is not *The Natural* without that music."

Yet that scene, shot at the old War Memorial Stadium in Buffalo, New York, was challenged at an early studio screening. After viewing the final edit, an executive leaned over and asked Levinson if he didn't have other music that was maybe more dramatic for the home run sequence. A less secure director might have caved, but Levinson ignored the suggestion. Newman's vision was preserved. It's no wonder he leapt at the chance to work with Levinson again on the film *Avalon* in 1990. This is what he had always hoped working on a film would be like.

~

A former writer for television and movies, Levinson was forty when he made his directorial debut with *Diner*, but it was such an original and assured film that Hollywood thought of him more like a boy wonder. The movie—a semi-autobiographical tale of a group of young men moving into adulthood—was so admired by leading film critics that they took a dramatic step after learning MGM had second thoughts about the movie and might not even release it. The critics warned studio executives that they were going to give the film rave reviews in their publications even if MGM didn't release it. Despite the doubts, the studio sent *Diner* to theaters early in 1982.

It was such a feel-good, underdog story in the industry—Levinson won an Academy Award nomination for best screenplay—that tastemakers were eager to learn what the auteur was going to do next. Among the fans of the film was Redford, one of Hollywood's most bankable actors as well as an Oscar-winning director. They met when Levinson was invited to a weekend of workshops at the Sundance film institute that Redford founded in 1981 in Park City, Utah, to promote the discovery and growth of independent filmmakers. The pair spent time together and sat next to each other on the flight back to Los Angeles.

Before parting at the airport, Redford invited Levinson to contact him with any film ideas. Levinson followed through on the invitation a few weeks later, but Redford didn't think that the idea was for him. During the casual visit, however, the men discovered they were both baseball fans, and they shared stories about their favorite players and memories. During the visit, Redford remembered he had a script about baseball, and he spent several minutes searching through a mound of papers in another room. Finally, he returned and handed Levinson a script, urging him to take a look at it. Levinson read it that night and phoned Redford the following day to say he loved the script, which was based on Bernard Malamud's widely respected 1952 novel of the same name. "Me, too," Redford replied. "Let's see if we can do this."

One of Levinson's first moves was to ask Newman to write the score. "I had been a fan for years," he said years later. "I loved the sense of Americana in his music. The piece that really stuck in my head was this short orchestra passage at the beginning of 'Louisiana 1927,' just a few seconds, but it was just what we needed in our movie."

When TriStar Pictures executives asked Levinson about the music for the film, he said, "We've got to have Randy Newman."

The executives were puzzled.

"Randy Newman? Isn't he the 'Short People' guy?"
Levinson recalled:

It was like a comedy routine. We went back and forth. They kept
bringing up "Short People" and saying stuff like, "Are you kidding me?" and I kept saying we need him. They finally gave in.
Randy understood what I wanted and the whole experience
with him was a joy. In fact, one of my greatest thrills in this
business was when we were racing to finish the picture. We were
editing the film in one room and Randy was in the next room
writing the score on the piano. My chair was right up against
the wall, and I heard what turned out to be the theme at the
moment it was being born. I asked Stu Linder, the editor, to roll
the film footage of the scene where we were going to use it—it
was so thrilling to hear it being born.

Another favorite off-screen moment came late one night when
working on the sound mix. "We were all getting tired and punchy,
and Randy sat down at the piano and he took the melody from
the film and came up with some gag lyrics for an imaginary title
song," Levinson said. "He was just kidding around, writing it off
the top of his head, but it was hysterical."

~

Randy's history with baseball and the Americana sound that Levinson wanted meant he didn't have to repeat the weeks of preparation
he did for *Ragtime,* but he did listen to several old baseball tunes,
starting with "Take Me Out to the Ball Game," some pop recordings from the film's 1939 period (Glenn Miller, Duke Ellington),
and, most importantly, some classical works.

"I also looked at some scores I liked—*Appalachian Spring* by
Copland, *Falstaff* by Verdi," he told Bill Milkowski in a detailed
1984 interview for *Modern Recording & Music* magazine. "What

Verdi did with that is what I really can't do: this unbelievably light, transparent stuff that I have a difficult time with. It's my weakness in terms of orchestration. But I looked at his stuff and it was of some help. You know, real fast, light, amazing stuff."

Because *Modern Recording* was aimed at audiophiles, Newman was free to go into more detail about film scoring than he normally did in interviews:

> I worked with a video of the film and with cue sheets. The music editor will make up sheets with cues and numbers . . . say, it's reel number four and the fifth piece of music on that reel: that'll be logged as M-4-5, which stands for Music Reel 4, Piece 5. Let's say it will be a minute and twenty seconds long . . . your starting point is .00. Redford picks up his bat. At .23, Redford goes to the plate. Some of this is not significant, some of it is very significant in terms of things to catch and play off of. So, you're working from both the video and from the cue sheets. As a matter of fact, you're almost better off working just with the cue sheet rather than looking at the video all the time. You know where you are better with the cue sheet.

With his typical modesty, Newman didn't claim any special achievement for the home run moment. Speaking to Milkowski about things he liked in the score, he cited more subtle elements, such as using saxophones when the "bad" girl was on the screen but clarinets with the "good" girl. He tended to speak about the home run scene mostly in terms of the challenge it posed.

> What scared me the most was the final scene. I don't know if I can talk about it 'cause I don't want to give away the plot, but his final at bat is three and a half minutes of nothing, then the lightning cues; he breaks his bat. Basically, it was difficult to play off of Redford and this final scene is entirely him at bat. You could

start cues off the reactions of the [female actors'] faces, but it was a lot harder with him. You know he's not very demonstrative. The character he played and tends to play is not a musical character, you know what I mean? It's not emotional. And a lot of times there would be a shot of him, and it would feel like the whole thing would stop dead. . . . Redford was all right with the farm scenes, where you pull out the woodwinds and do the Copland Americana stuff. But his more neutral, held-in, manly kind of stuff made it much harder for me to work with.

～

Released in May of 1984, *The Natural* was a critics' favorite though a few reviewers objected to the way the book's ending was rewritten for the screen; Newman shared the majority view that the change was justified. In Malamud's anti-heroic novel, the Redford character, Roy Hobbs, accepts a bribe to throw the game. Hobbs is tormented in the batter's box, but finally swings wildly at a bad pitch. The book ends with Hobbs wiping the "bitter tears" from his face. It was a powerful story, but not the one Redford and Levinson wanted to tell. In the movie, Hobbs succumbs to a bribe before the final game, only to change his mind at the last minute and lead his team to victory. Malamud, according to Philip Davis's 2007 biography *Bernard Malamud: A Writer's Life*, was flattered by Redford making the film and quite enjoyed it.

The film was a success at the box office, earning $48 million in the US to place it as the fourteenth highest take of the year (*Ghostbusters*, with $220 million, finished first). The soundtrack album was widely praised and spent five weeks on the lower rungs of the national sales chart; Newman was nominated for an Academy Award for his score (the trophy went to Maurice Jarre for *A Passage to India*).

For Newman, *The Natural* was a major turning point. "It indicated to me," he said, "that I could do a movie job."

~

There was progress on the theatrical front for Newman early in 1984 when the prestigious La Jolla Playhouse near San Diego announced it would present a revised version of *Maybe I'm Doing It Wrong*, the New York City revue, in a three-week run during its summer season. Susan Cox was to be the new director, and Michael Roth would continue as musical director. Comfortable with Roth and the show's likely new tone, Newman offered input on the production, including attending rehearsals and doing interviews to promote it.

The engagement went well enough for the revue to be picked up for a week at the Roxy on the Sunset Strip in West Hollywood, the celebrated club that had showcased such major pop-rock figures as Bruce Springsteen and David Bowie, as well as occasional theatrical productions like *The Rocky Horror Show*. Again, things went well.

Dan Sullivan, the chief theater critic of the *Los Angeles Times*, acknowledged in his rave review that all he knew about Newman was "Short People" and "I Love L.A.," but that the show made him want to go out and buy all his albums. "The man is . . ." he wrote, "well, let's hold 'genius' until later. [He] writes honest songs—let's put it that way." Showing taste himself, Sullivan singled out "Christmas in Cape Town" and "My Life is Good" for special praise.

Meanwhile, Newman returned to films, but this time in an unusual dual role. He wouldn't just write songs, but also co-write the script.

— II —

When Steve Martin started talking publicly about a comedy western in 1980, there was no sign the project would involve Newman. The movie was first titled *The Three Caballeros*, and

Martin wanted *Saturday Night Live* cohorts John Belushi and Dan Aykroyd in starring roles; the pair was coming off the red-hot film *The Blues Brothers*. But they opted for another film. Martin then asked John Candy to take one of the leading roles, but he also wasn't available.

Not about to give up, Martin asked two writers to come up with a script for *Three Amigos*, but Lorne Michaels, the *SNL* creator who joined Martin in the project, thought they needed a new script, and he suggested they ask Randy to collaborate with them on it. Martin, who started out in the 1960s as a writer on such network TV shows as *The Smothers Brothers Comedy Hour* before a hugely successful career as a stand-up comedian and actor, knew Newman from the days they both played the Troubadour.

"Randy's body of work is staggering," he said. "There's something about it that stands apart from everyone else. It's like going into a room alone with somebody and having them play and sing directly to you. I loved the music, but also the way he threads the needle in his lyrics. In a song like 'Louisiana,' he talks about 'this poor cracker's land'—it could be taken as an insult, but he gets sympathy out of it. The phrase gives you a sense of their lives."

The threesome—Michaels was on hiatus from *SNL*—gathered most days for weeks at Martin's house in Los Angeles where they'd have lunch and spend five or six hours on the script. "Those were some of my favorite memories," the TV producer said. "Randy and Steve both have a sensibility that I love, and we were all just throwing out ideas day after day. It was a true collaboration. Everyone was fully involved."

When the film finally reached theaters in December of 1986, the cast was headed by Martin, Chevy Chase, and Martin Short, and directed by John Landis. The screenplay had some hilarious underpinnings. A Mexican village in 1916 was being terrorized by a bandit, the notorious El Guapo, and his murderous gang.

Desperate, Carmen, the daughter of a village elder, happens to see a movie about three gunslinging cowboys who do heroic deeds. Believing they are real crusaders, rather than the budget-level actors they are, she sends them a telegram, pleading for help. Though she has no funds, she offers to pay them handsomely, believing that, as in the film, the trio would give the reward back to the needy villagers.

In one of the funniest moments, Carmen doesn't have enough money to pay for a full telegram, so she sends a greatly abbreviated one. The result leads the actors, who were frantically looking for work after being fired by their studio, to believe she is a fan who wants them to come to Santo Poco to do a celebrity appearance. Thinking it'll be an easy payday, the Amigos head for Mexico where they strut around the village, waiting for a "showdown" with El Guapo, who they believe is just another actor. It's only then they learn that the bullets in the gang's guns are real and that their lives are in danger. The realization sets off a comedy of errors, lampooning western movie clichés at every turn.

Besides working on the script, Newman contributed a winning cameo (of sorts)—he was the shrieking voice of a singing prairie bush in a scene that plays a key part in the plot. He also wrote three songs (Oscar-winner Elmer Bernstein wrote the score), each of which captured nicely the intended inanity of the hapless characters. The most colorful of the songs was "Blue Shadows on the Trail," a facsimile of the campfire sensibility of such classic cowpoke serenades as "Home on the Range" and "Cool Water." To make the song even more disarming, the title comes from an old Roy Rogers film. Newman's composition includes this verse:

Blue shadows on the trail
Little cowboy
Close your eyes and dream

All of the doggies are in the corral
All of your work is done
Just close your eyes and dream, little pal
Dream of someone

The staging of the song was as delightful as the tune. The Amigos sing it, lonesome cowboy style, around a prairie campfire, accompanied by—Randy's idea—three horses who provide some *da-bum, da-bum, da-bum* punctuation for the chorus.

~

Despite all the talent involved, *Three Amigos* was largely panned by critics. Janet Maslin complained in the *New York Times* that the film was "likable, but it never really finds a distinctive style. Not quite parody and not quite serious, it's more like a lengthy costume party, with [Short, Martin, and Chase] decked out in black, white, and red spangled outfits that contrast brilliantly against the village's dirt-brown grime." Roger Ebert praised Newman's songs but gave the film itself just one of four stars. *Amigos* generated $23 million in theaters, which placed it No. 43 on the list of 1987's top grossing releases (*Top Gun* led the list with $179 million).

In time, however, the likeability factor that Maslin mentioned helped endear *Three Amigos* to enough fans, especially in the *SNL* audience, that it became something of a cult classic. Whatever its limitations, the cast seemed to be having so much fun that it was hard not to be charmed.

Martin has always enjoyed the film but was surprised by the cult attention. When *Empire* magazine, a leading British film publication, requested the trio to pose for a cover photo in 2011, he asked with genuine puzzlement, "Why?"

Informed it was the twenty-fifth anniversary of *Three Amigos*, he responded, "So?"

Michaels wasn't surprised. "I thought it was a hit from the beginning," he said. "Of all the things I get compliments on, *Three Amigos* has always ranked right up there."

— III —

The roots of Newman's next album go back to 1985. On vacation in Hawaii, Lenny read A. Scott Berg's *Max Perkins: Editor of Genius*, a National Book Award–winning biography of the Scribner editor whose roster of writers included Ernest Hemingway, F. Scott Fitzgerald, and Thomas Wolfe. One chapter stood out for Waronker—Perkins's efforts to motivate Ring Lardner, a celebrated newspaper columnist who was known to take a long time between book projects. "Lardner seemed to have the same kind of attitude that Randy had," Lenny said. "When Perkins suggested that Lardner write about his own life, the author replied something like, 'Who in the hell would be interested in that?' I immediately called Randy and told him about the story, hoping it would lead him to write a song or an album about his life."

Waronker doesn't remember Newman taking special note of what he said, but a few months later, Randy played a couple of new songs for him that did touch on his childhood, notably "Four Eyes." They even went into the recording studio in December of 1985, but that was as far as they got because of his Epstein-Barr virus.

By early 1987, Randy resumed writing, still trying to work in the autobiographical style of "Four Eyes." He was so pleased with the songs that he spoke about them at length with Charles Shaar Murray, one of England's premiere music writers, during a four-city European tour in May of 1987. Randy even played Murray some of the songs he had written for the album.

"I got six which are autobiographical for the first time," he said of the album that he wouldn't start recording for another eight months. "They lie, they equivocate, but they do it on purpose. They jerk around time. I got my father comin' to New Orleans in 1948 and tellin' 'em World War II is over because it's the kind of town that wouldn't know. I don't know if anyone'll get the joke. . . . I have another civil rights song, a good one."

That song, "Roll with the Punches," led to Newman addressing civil rights again in the interview, a continuation in some ways of the conversation he had a decade earlier in England with Phil Sutcliffe. When away from the United States, he seemed especially driven to explain his anguish over the country's actions.

As Newman played several of the songs on a piano in the hotel room, Murray reported that the "emotional effect is almost overpowering, this big, unassuming, sleepy-eyed man seemingly almost possessed as he strums at the keyboard and these voices from elsewhere spill from him almost at random. All of America is inside him: the white, the black, the rich, the poor, the generous and the flint-hearted, the passionate and the numb. He teeters on the high wire of his own irony, but he never misses a step."

Later, as Murray was leaving the room, Newman couldn't resist turning his irony and wit on himself. Standing at the door, he sighed, "I've got to stay here in this luxurious hotel suite and worry about the poor."

— IV —

Back in Los Angeles, Newman learned that Elliot Abbott was leaving the management business to work in films with Penny Marshall, who had gone from co-starring in the hit television sitcom *Laverne and Shirley* to directing films, including the comedy *Big*. The search for a new manager was a short one. When Newman mentioned the need for a manager, Mo Ostin and music attorney Donald S. Passman both recommended Peter Asher.

Asher's mother was a professor whose students at one of the leading performing arts schools in England included future Beatles producer George Martin. When Asher and a pal formed a duo, Peter and Gordon, with hopes of a record career, they were generously handed a song by his sister Jane's boyfriend, Paul McCartney. The pair's version of "A World Without Love" was an international hit in 1964. With McCartney's encouragement, the Beatles' Apple Records signed Asher to head its A&R department.

At Apple, he discovered singer-songwriter James Taylor, a young American who was living briefly in London. When Taylor's debut album for Apple didn't catch fire, Asher had such faith in the young man that he quit Apple and followed Taylor to America as manager and producer. The next collection, *Sweet Baby James*, was released by Warner and became one of the most influential albums of the 1970s.

As manager and producer again, Asher then signed Linda Ronstadt and helped lift her to superstardom, thanks to such multiplatinum albums as *Heart Like a Wheel* and *Simple Dreams*. Asher also produced scores of other albums, including artists as varied as Neil Diamond, Diana Ross, and 10,000 Maniacs. In the process, he gained wide respect within the recording business for his ear for excellence and for a low-key, supportive manner that helped bring the most out of his artists.

When Newman and Asher met, they felt so ideally suited that there was no need for a second meeting before deciding to work together.

"There are usually several things you want to know before agreeing to manage someone, but with Randy the talent was so unique that there was no need to think twice," said Asher, who had known about Newman since the days of Alan Price and Simon Smith in England. "Here was one of the finest songwriters in the world. He tends to pretend he doesn't know how good he is, but deep down I think he knows very well that he's a musical genius.

"Everything about him—his arranging, singing, writing, piano playing—is extraordinary, the way he structures harmonies and chord progressions. Early on, he mentioned this long-range project *Faust*, and it sounded so remarkable. I couldn't wait to get started on that. I didn't know if that would finally be the album to bring Randy's sales up to what they should be, but I knew it would be great."

Asher would produce *Faust*, but it would be nearly a decade away.

PART FOUR

I can only speak of Randy in the most glowing of terms. . . .
He was a Newman, so it was only a matter of time before he
would start doing scores, but I was thrilled when he also
started writing pop songs. He turned out to be something of
a philosopher—songs with wit and gorgeous melodies, but
also the ability to understand human foibles. He reminds me
of a kind of musical Will Rogers or Mark Twain, someone
who understands the country very well. Whatever he writes,
he's one of a kind.

JOHN WILLIAMS

Randy's ability to meld his love of classical, popular, and R & B/New Orleans music into songs of such soul, humor, beauty, and bite—make him as unique as he is genius. No one can skewer hypocrisy, delusion, and sheer human fallibility like Randy. On the other hand, with his ballads and film scores, he's created some of the most soulful and gorgeous music I've ever heard. He's also one of my all-time favorite live performers—as a singer, piano player and a hilarious raconteur. He's one of the funniest people I've ever known. For me, there's just no one else with his depth and range.

BONNIE RAITT

My first exposure to Randy Newman's music was actually his second studio album, *12 Songs*. It was and still is as excellent a collection of songs as was ever written and recorded by any singer-songwriter. I envy him on every level: as a lyricist, as a composer, as an arranger with unparalleled skills, as a humorist-satirist and, yes, as a vocalist. One of my few real regrets is that I was persuaded to turn him down when he offered me the opportunity to sing with him the title track of *Toy Story*. When I came to my senses and realized my mistake, I promised him that, should he ever consider working with me again, I'd be there. And he did indeed give me two more chances: in the part of an affable, slightly clueless God singing the song "Northern Boy" in his musical, *Faust*, and then singing his fabulous "Our Town" for the animated film *Cars*. We also performed together on tour for a stretch in the eighties. I admire him above anyone I've ever had the pleasure to work with. Randy Newman is an American master.

JAMES TAYLOR

CHAPTER SEVENTEEN

Land of Dreams

— I —

Land of Dreams was widely seen as Newman's second concept album when released in September of 1988, largely because reviews and his own comments in interviews led fans to view it as such, yet only the first three songs fully lived up to that description.

"I was really pleased with those songs, but they only took my story to the first grade," Newman said. "I didn't see where else to go. There had already been a million songs about teenagers. Lenny was really pushing for more of a unified theme, but it just didn't happen. There were also other things I wanted to address." Even so, the autobiographical elements in the three songs resonated with admiring critics. *Rolling Stone*'s Steve Pond declared of *Land of Dreams*: "Newman has spent much of his career animating and hiding behind disagreeable characters. But the heart of the record is a series of songs that seem to speak directly and frankly about Randy Newman."

"Dixie Flyer" begins things with a warm, rollicking invitation to join little Randy and his mom on the train from Los Angeles to New Orleans, though Randy's storytelling instincts freed him from sticking to actual events. Yes, Dixie Flyer was the name of a train line in the 1940s, but it ran from the Midwest to Florida, not Los Angeles to New Orleans. The trip, however, did begin at Union Station, his dad was an Army doctor, and the attempts at assimilation in an overwhelming Christian land were true. The lyrics, in part:

> *I was born right here, November '43*
> *My dad was a captain in the army*
> *Fighting the Germans in Sicily.*
> *My poor little momma*
> *Didn't know a soul in LA*
> *So we went down to the Union Station and made our*
>   *getaway.*
> *Got on the Dixie Flyer bound for New Orleans*
> *Across the state of Texas to the land of dreams.*
> *On the Dixie Flyer bound for New Orleans*
> *Back to her friends and her family in the land of dreams.*
>
> *Her own mother came to meet us at the station,*
> *Her dress as black as a crow in a coal mine*
> *She cried when her little girl got off the train.*
> *Her brothers and her sisters drove down from Jackson,*
>   *Mississippi*
> *In a great green Hudson driven by a Gentile they knew.*
> *Drinkin' rye whiskey from a flask in the back seat*
> *Tryin' to do like the Gentiles do*
> *Christ, they wanted to be Gentiles, too.*
> *Who wouldn't down there, wouldn't you?*
> *An American Christian, God damn!*

Referring to the assimilation reference during an interview for *Musician* magazine, Newman told Dave Zimmer at the time, "That's never been done. There have been thousands of Jewish songwriters, and they have never done it. To be Jewish in America is different. No one wants to be an American more than a Jew. Irving Berlin was more American than John Wayne. But there's a lack of comfort here for Jews, somehow. Is this really our country? And I think sometimes, maybe not. I don't know how comfortable Jews in Clarksdale, Mississippi, would be. I liked making that joke about the Jews drinking—trying to be like the Gentiles by getting drunk—even if it pisses people off."

"New Orleans Wins the War" was another strong piece of storytelling, largely written through the eyes of a confused five-year-old. Its grandest conceit is the suggestion that the New Orleans townspeople didn't know World War II had ended until Randy's father arrived to inform them three years later—which playfully explains why his daddy took his family to a more enlightened locale without delay.

Don't remember much about my baby days,
But I been told
We used to live on Willow near the Garden District
Next to the Sugar Bowl
Momma used to wheel me past an ice cream wagon
One side for White and one side for Colored
I remember trash cans floatin' down Canal Street
It rained every day one summer
Momma used to take me to Audubon Park
Show me the ways of the world
She said, "here comes a white boy, there goes a black one,
that one's an octoroon
This little cookie here's a macaroon, that big round thing's a
*   red balloon*
And the paper down here's called the Picayune
And here's a New Orleans tune"
In 1948 my Daddy came to the city

Told the people that they'd won the war
Maybe they'd heard it, maybe not
Probably they'd heard it and just forgot
'Cause they built him a platform there in Jackson Square
And the people came to hear him from everywhere
They started to party and they partied some more
'Cause New Orleans had won the war
(We knew we'd do it, we done whipped the Yankees)
Daddy said, "I'm gonna get this boy out of this place
Bound to sap his strength
People have fun here, and I think that they should
But nobody from here ever come to no good
They're gonna pickle him in brandy and tell him he's saved
Then throw fireworks all 'round his grave"
So he took us down to the airport, and flew us back to LA.
That was the end of my baby days
Blue blue morning, blue blue day
All your bad dreams drift away
It's a blue blue morning of a blue blue day
Lose those bad dreams
Those gray clouds above you, what you want them around
with you for?
You got someone to love you
Who could ask for more?
It's a blue blue morning, of a blue blue day
All your bad dreams drift away

"Four Eyes," the song about kids being cruel in school, followed, and that was pretty much it in terms of pure concept, but
not the end of the album's rewards. Two of nine remaining songs
grew out of autobiographical threads, although Newman eventually took them in different directions. "I wasn't able to [pick up]
my story again until 'It's Money That Matters,' which was

something I was seeing all around me, and 'I Want You to Hurt Like I Do,'" which grew out of the domestic issues."

"It's Money That Matters" again dealt with wealth and greed. "The song feels like my neighborhood," he said. "The kid in the song looks around and tries to figure things out, and the answer is that it's money that matters. I didn't exactly pursue that feeling, but I do believe that money counts too much, which is why I've written about the subject as much as I have." The lyrics, in part:

When I was a young boy, maybe thirteen
I took a hard look around me and asked, what does it
*   mean?*
So I talked to my father, and he didn't know
And I talked to my friend, and he didn't know
And I talked to my brother, and he didn't know
And I talked to everybody that I knew
It's money that matters
Now you know that it's true
It's money that matters
Whatever you do
Then I talked to a man lived up on the county line
I was washing his car with a friend of mine
He was a little fat guy in a red jumpsuit
I said, "You look kind of funny"
He said, "I know that I do"
"But I got a great big house on the hill here
And a great big blonde wife inside it
And a great big pool in my backyard and another great big
*   pool beside it*
Sonny it's money that matters, hear what I say
It's money that matters in the USA"
It's money that matters

Now you know that it's true
It's money that matters whatever you do

The opening lines of "Hurt" are drawn from Newman's divorce, but the song then seeks lighter ground by calling for a sort of "We Are the World" anthem for the downtrodden and depressed. The lyrics, in part:

I ran out on my children
And I ran out on my wife
Gonna run out on you too, baby
I've done it all my life
Everybody cried the night I left
Well, almost everybody did
My little boy just hung his head
And I put my arm, put my arm around his little shoulder
And this is what I said:
"Sonny, I just want you to hurt like I do
I just want you to hurt like I do
I just want you to hurt like I do
Honest I do, honest I do, honest I do"
If I had one wish
One dream I knew would come true
I'd want to speak to all the people of the world
I'd get up there, I'd get up there on that platform
First I'd sing a song or two—you know I would
Then I'll tell you what I'd do
I'd talk to the people and I'd say
"It's a rough rough world, it's a tough tough world
Well, you know
And things don't always, things don't always go the way
*   we plan*
But there's one thing, one thing we all have in common

And it's something everyone can understand
All over the world sing along
I just want you to hurt like I do
I just want you to hurt like I do
I just want you to hurt like I do
Honest I do, honest I do, honest I do

In a 1988 interview with Stephen Holden in the *New York Times,* Newman's comments about the song reflected his discouragement over the country's future. "For the first time I agree with people who are depressed about the future," he said. "It's amazing how the imperialist nations have paid for their imperialism. . . . To me, there is a lot of truth in the idea that misery loves company. I'd enjoy seeing 'I Want You to Hurt' done as an anthem with a big choir."

— ‖ —

Uncertain about what else he wanted to share of his life in the album, Newman turned to other themes, including—again—racism. "Roll with the Punches" would stand with Newman's most essential songs, written from the viewpoint of someone who tells the minorities to just wait their turn, like the Irish, Italians, and Jews had to do. The lyrics, in part:

They say that people are livin' in the street
No food in their belly, no shoes on their feet
Six black children livin' in a burned-up room
One bare light bulb swinging
Little black kid come home from school
Put his key in the door
Mr. Rat's on the stairway, Mr. Junkie's lyin' in his own
    vomit on the floor

You gotta roll with the punches, little black boy
That's what you got to do
You got to roll with the punches
Tap it, baby
There's all these boring people, you see 'em on the TV
And they're making up all these boring stories
About how bad things have come to be
They say "You got to, got to, got to feed the hungry"
"You got to, got to, got to heal the sick"
I say we ain't gotta do nothin' for nobody
'Cause they won't work a lick, you know
They just gonna have to roll with the punches, yes they will
Gonna have to roll with them
They gonna have to roll with the punches, yes they will
It don't matter whether you're white, black, or brown
You won't get nowhere putting down
The old Red, White, and Blue
Tap it, baby. Alright.
Look at those little shorts he's got on, ladies and gentlemen
You can see all the way to Argentina
Get it
So pretty
Let 'em go to Belgium, let 'em go to France
Let 'em go to Russia
Well at least they ought to have the chance to go there
We have talked about the red, we have talked about the blue
Now we gonna talk about the white
That's what we're gonna have to do
Now we had to roll with the punches, yes we did
We had to roll with 'em
We had to roll with the punches
Yes, we did
We had to roll with 'em

I don't care what you say
You're livin' in the greatest country in the world
When you're livin' in the USA

"Punches" was another song that was widely misunderstood—so much so that Newman eventually stopped performing it live. "I disagree completely with everything the guy says in the song," he told the *Los Angeles Times*. "I was doing it on a few dates recently, and I've given up because I think a lot of people believe what the guy is saying, which is that sort of Clarence Thomas philosophy that people should do everything on their own, and government should just let people sink or swim. They believe it. And I thought it was clear that this guy singing was so hard-assed, talking about little kids living alone in a dark room with a junkie on the stairway."

In the Holden interview, Newman disagreed strongly with the narrator's declaration that everyone should be strong enough to make it on their own. "I know that given my personality, had I been born disadvantaged in any way, I wouldn't have stood a chance," he said. "I have no self-protection or self-discipline. I would probably have died."

The album's "Masterman and Baby J" and "Red Bandana" take different routes, but add to the racism portfolio, looking at the consequences of generations of injustice. Trapped in a social system that has long denied him an equal opportunity, the Black narrator in "Masterman" finds hope by rapping about his troubled surroundings in a raw, funk-driven way that, unlike early rock, didn't lend itself to white takeover. The Latino commentator in "Bandana" joins a street gang that offered a form of support and pride despite the violence the gang imposed upon its members and outsiders.

Newman was a big admirer of the passion and artful instincts of the leading rappers who found a means of expression in a street-level genre that was more urgent than major labels allowed R & B and soul artists. Chuck D., the leader of the rap group Public Enemy and one of the genre's most visionary early figures, said, "We have to let others know how a Black person feels about his situation in this country and the Western world. . . . Rap is the CNN of young Black America." To the music industry's surprise, young whites began to buy records, ultimately in the millions.

The rappers in "Masterman" aren't as smart or as talented as Chuck D., but they dream of being the biggest act in the world and headlining the Los Angeles Memorial Coliseum. As such, the song speaks of the way hip-hop was an inspiring force in the Black community and eventually became the creative center of American pop, thanks to the imagination of such figures as Ice Cube, Dr. Dre, Tupac Shakur, Lauryn Hill, Kanye West, Pulitzer Prize winner Kendrick Lamar, and Eminem, the field's primary white contributor.

"I liked rap, and I wanted to take a look at it," Newman said. "It was about this kid who lived in a much different LA than I do, and he gets into music and it takes him all the way to the Coliseum where he performs before 100,000 people—at least in his imagination. It's not a story I fully understand by any means, but I think it was kind of nice."

The album's lineup also included two love ballads that felt like "assignment" numbers and, indeed, both were featured in films, though only "Something Special" was written for a movie, a 1987 romantic comedy, *Overboard*, starring Goldie Hawn and Kurt Russell. The more graceful "Falling in Love" was written for the album and later used over the credits of a 1989 romantic comedy, *Her Alibi*. About "Falling," Newman said, "It's about how you just don't know what's happening when you fall in love, it's so overpowering. I was really drawn to that song. I think it was one of the only times I was trying to write a hit." A third ballad, "Bad News from Home," told a different story: a step into film noir shadows, tragic, scary, and unyieldingly mysterious.

The final song, "Follow the Flag," dealt with patriotism at a time when the flag was becoming an increasingly divisive part of the American cultural debate; a symbol of the "love it or leave it" sentiments, which made it seem unworthy for some of being saluted until the nation lived up to its ideals. Newman's narrator appeared to believe in every red and white stripe. But this was another case of Newman overestimating his audience. Many listeners were simply confused. Partial lyrics:

> *They say it's all a lie*
> *But it's not a lie*
> *I'm going to follow the flag 'til I die*
> *Into every life a little rain must fall*
> *But it's not gonna rain forever*
> *You can rise above—you can rise above it all*
> *We will follow the flag together*
> *We will follow the flag forever*

During an interview with Mike Boehm of the *Los Angeles Times*, Newman acknowledged that the song might be too vague. "There's almost no hint that I think the guy is dumb. Yet I don't believe much of what he's saying. I thought of putting a coda on the song [to make its irony more evident], but I didn't." After living with "Follow the Flag" for nearly forty years, Newman still felt strongly about it. "I would hope that people would stop having to give up their life for the flag," he said. "It's hard to say that all the people who have died for the flag have died in vain, so I won't say that. But you see all these little wars where people die, and you wonder what the hell for."

Ten years later, Newman fans would learn that he wrote what seemed like a personal song during the *Land of Dreams* period, but chose not to include it on the CD. The song, "Days of Heaven," appeared on the four-CD retrospective, "Guilty: 30 Years of Randy Newman." It was apparently written while both parents were in failing health, but Randy denied it was a personal reflection.

Randy's mother died at age seventy-two on October 4, 1988, two weeks after the release of *Land of Dreams*. Though he had often spoken about his father, Randy said little about his mother during her lifetime. In 2023, however, he spoke about her tenderly, wishing he had reached out to her more over the years. He also said his father's death, on February 1, 1990, made "Old Man" suddenly take on a far more personal feel.

— III —

With the material for the album selected, Newman went into the recording studio in late 1987 for the first time to make an album without Waronker or Titelman. Lenny had been promoted to president of Warner in late 1985 by Ostin, who had been named chairman of the board. Waronker's appointment was cheered in the industry because it was the first time in years that a "music man" rather than an agent, attorney, or some other business figure was named head of a major label.

Lenny continued to encourage Newman, but he couldn't take months away from his office to produce the album. Titelman had moved to New York, where he worked with Steve Winwood and Eric Clapton, making him unavailable. In their place, four producers shared the responsibility, two of whom renewed fears among some fans that Randy might be trying to be more radio friendly.

Mark Knopfler and Jeff Lynne were the chief creative forces behind two of the biggest selling and most radio-friendly rock groups of the 1970s and 1980s, Dire Straits and Electric Light

Orchestra. Together, the bands had delivered thirteen gold albums in the United States, topped by the Straits' *Brothers in Arms*, which sold more than nine million alone. The 1985 package featured some of the glossiest yet catchiest tunes of the decade, notably the playful "Money for Nothing" single, which spent three weeks at No. 1 in the United States and was a huge success on MTV. Knopfler's guitar work on the track was spectacularly seductive in back of a story about two appliance installers watching MTV and grumbling about the easy rock star life, summarized with the catch line about the musicians getting "money for nothing and chicks for free."

The informal parade of producers on *Land of Dreams* began when Waronker, as label president, dined with Jeff Lynne at George Harrison's mansion in Henley-on-Thames in England. Lynne had co-produced Harrison's *Cloud Nine* album, which was distributed by Warner. Despite the fans' concerns about Lynne being too commercially minded for someone with Randy's character-driven tales, Waronker knew the musician-producer had solid credits and felt the pair would get along well in the studio. Lynne jumped at Lenny's invitation to produce some tracks on the album. Modest and unassuming, he went to Newman's house just before Christmas in 1987 where Randy played him a ballad on the piano. Casually, Lynne—who was in town co-producing what would be Tom Petty's biggest-selling album *Full Moon Fever*—picked up his acoustic guitar and joined on "Falling in Love." Randy was pleased with the added touches, and the pair went over to the garage studio of Petty's guitarist Mike Campbell, where *Fever* was being recorded, to cut the basic track. Hearing about the session, Petty stopped by to play guitar and join on background vocals.

There was so much excitement around the Warner lot that the label produced a promotional video of the song in hopes of picking up traction when *Her Alibi* was released in early 1989.

After a teasing scene from the film, the video shows Randy sitting at a piano, struggling to write a song when the sassy redhead from "I Love L.A." walks in and asks what's going on. Appearing frazzled, Newman looks up and replies matter-of-factly, "It's a new picture, they want me to write a love song for it." The redhead responds sarcastically, "You? A love song. . . . Phil Collins busy?"

In early January, Lenny put Randy together with the team of James Newton Howard, who co-produced Rickie Lee Jones's *The Magazine* album for Warner—and veteran producer Tommy LiPuma, who admired Randy since the Metric days and had worked with Barbra Streisand and Miles Davis. The song was "Something Special," and things went well, leading the pair to also produce three other album tunes, "Four Eyes," "Red Bandana," and "I Want You to Hurt Like I Do."

"It was so inspiring just being in the studio with Randy each day and see how he influences everything," said Howard, who would write the score for dozens of films, including *The Prince of Tides* and [with Hans Zimmer] *The Dark Knight.* They became so close that Howard turned to Randy six years later when he needed someone to cover for him in the studio on the day his wife was due to give birth to their son. "Randy agreed to go into the booth and just keep an eye on things in case some question came up," Howard said. "When I got back, people said he spent the whole day telling jokes, including one about me: 'James has been married so many times that there ought to be a bumper sticker: "Honk if you've been married to James Newton Howard."'"

The final piece of the production puzzle was Knopfler, an English Literature graduate from the University of Leeds who injected Dire Straits with touches that were both sensual and cerebral. During the group's first US tour in 1979, the music was labeled "The Thinking Man's Rock," thanks to such multilevel tracks as the Dylan-esque single "Sultans of Swing," a richly crafted song that reflected subtly on the public's fickleness in art. As with Lynne, Lenny had enormous respect for Knopfler.

Impressed, Dylan checked out the band at the Roxy in LA on that tour, and he not only convinced Knopfler to play guitar on his next album, the gospel-driven *Slow Train Coming*, but also brought him back four years later to produce his secular *Infidels* album. Knopfler, too, was responsible for some highly praised film scores, notably *Local Hero*, in which the music accented the lovely, peaceful village charm of the Scottish comedy-drama.

First attracted to Newman by Three Dog Night's version of "Mama Told Me Not to Come," Knopfler became such a "Newman addict" with the *Sail Away* and *Good Old Boys* albums that he attended a Newman concert in London in 1978 and yelled for "Louisiana 1927" during a request spot in the show—a choice that prompted Newman to shout back, "Ah, there must be an American in the audience tonight."

Knopfler, who brought in a new group of musicians, including keyboardist Guy Fletcher from Dire Straits, ended up producing the remainder of the album. "Mark and I always have fun in the studio, but our time with Randy was filled with often uncontrollable laughter," Fletcher said. "When we left the studio at night, our sides were physically hurting. It's when I really understood the term 'side-splitting.' Randy's dry, often quite dark wit was relentless, and we would often have to stop mid-take as we recorded. I recall Randy doing a vocal, and he wasn't quite nailing it, so he took his trousers off. It worked."

Once again, the label was optimistic. "There was this feeling that we have Randy and all his intelligence and an artist in Mark who knows how to make hits," said Frank Wolf, an engineer who had worked with Peter Asher on 10,000 Maniacs' breakthrough album, *In My Tribe*. "The thinking was this could be great!" Wolf was especially impressed by Randy's vocals. "Whatever the song, he was this great storyteller," he continued. "Some people say he's not a classic singer, but he makes you believe the song, which is what a great singer does."

Despite the label's commercial hopes for the pairing, Knopfler said he didn't feel pressure to boost Newman's sales. He just wanted to make the best record possible. In fact, "It's Money That Matters," the first single from the album, was not one of his personal favorites on the album. The decision to release it first was, he said, "a commercial decision by the record company."

"It's Money That Matters" was seen by some at Warner as a chance to tap into the mainstream affection generated by "Short People" and "I Love LA," and by others as the opportunity to appeal to the larger "Money for Nothing" and Dire Straits audience. After the success of "I Love LA," Tim Newman was the natural choice to direct the video. "For me, 'Money' expresses his disillusionment, or sadness, over the way that money is (what matters)," he said. "I believe much of his feeling for the underdog is in keeping with the tradition of an immigrant Jewish family that came to this country and did well, but never forgot where they came from."

In designing the video, the director featured Randy again driving around town in the Buick, opening it with a short documentary-type scene to present him as a cynical character, complete with an entourage, featuring the redhead from "I Love LA" and a security guy. Randy and Red then speed off in a vulgar display of celebrity egotism. The video didn't have the feel-good punch of "I Love LA," but it was an equally striking visualization of the new song.

The CD finished No. 10 in the annual *Voice* poll. *Rolling Stone*'s Steve Pond described "Rolling with the Punches" as "a brutal dramatic monologue whose narrator, a smug flag-waving white supremacist, spews a survival-of-the-fittest philosophy," and saluted "I Want You to Hurt Like I Do," as the album's "chilling, coldblooded moment, maybe the most unsettling thing Randy Newman has ever recorded—but at the same time it's nakedly honest, certainly callous but maybe caring as well."

Despite his own busy schedule, Knopfler believed so much in the album that he helped promote it, performing "It's Money That Matters" with Randy on a series of television shows, including *Saturday Night Live* and Lorne Michael's other national music program, *Sunday Night*, in the United States, as well as on a BBC concert in England.

Even with the heavy promotion, *Dreams* ran into strong headwinds, not totally unexpected after *Billboard*, the trade publication whose reviews focused on commercial potential rather than on artistic merit, sent an early warning signal. Its review lauded the songs, but warned that the album doesn't appear to have another "Short People" or "I Love LA." The single reached No. 60 on the sales chart, and the album stalled at No. 80, Newman's lowest album chart position since the early 1970s. Looking back, there was some second-guessing at Warner over the choice of "It's Money That Matters" as the single, feeling that the "Money for Nothing" echo was ultimately a negative element. *Rolling Stone*'s review reflected what may have been a wider backlash against the song, declaring it was a "virtual rewrite" of "Money That I Love" and sounded "just like" "Money for Nothing."

Yet it was even more obvious that the great moments on the record—from the New Orleans memories to "Roll with the Punches" to "I Want You to Hurt Like I Do" and beyond—were simply too challenging for radio formats.

~

By the time he finished *Land of Dreams*, Randy had a new day-to-day manager at Peter Asher Management. Cathy Kerr, whose parents both worked in the entertainment business in Los Angeles, grew up loving music and got a job as a receptionist at the company soon after graduating from high school in 1984.

She met Randy when he was the opening act for James Taylor's summer tour that year. "I was familiar with some of his music and seeing him live was memorable," she said. "His stage presence, the music, and of course his sense of humor made a big impression on me. And the audience loved him." Kerr progressed rapidly in the company, eventually becoming vice president. She said:

> Peter was very generous, as were the other managers. They encouraged me to read everything and included me in meetings and were always happy to answer questions. I had never been in this environment before, and I thrived. My responsibilities increased along with a promotion, and Peter put me in charge of a new client, the Williams Brothers. I was thrilled.
>
> As it happened in 1988, most of the clients were on the road for spring and summer tours. Randy was in Los Angeles finishing his album, and I was in the office, so I was able to interact with him regularly. From the start we worked well together. By the end of summer, Peter felt I was a natural fit to be Randy's manager. And, again, I was thrilled. . . . I quickly became a true fan. Listening to his catalog was inspiring and enlightening. "God's Song," "Living Without You," and "In Germany Before the War" stood out immediately—I have a long list of favorite songs. I have seen immense respect and love for Randy throughout the years, from musicians to songwriters to journalists and industry executives and beyond. He is talented, generous, curious, and observant.

Though no one knew it at the time, *Land of Dreams* would be Newman's last hurrah of sorts at the label. The reign of Ostin and Waronker was headed for a shattering, abrupt end. Newman would also redirect his energy to films. When *Land of Dreams* was released, he had only written three film scores in twenty years. Over the next twenty, he would write eighteen and the musical. His world shifted.

CHAPTER EIGHTEEN

Parenthood
Avalon *and*
A Backyard Wedding

— I —

Newman's need for a film agent led to Michael Gorfaine, a Los Angeles native who sang briefly in a rock group before deciding he'd be better off representing musicians than being one. While working at ASCAP, the performance rights organization for songwriters, Gorfaine developed an affinity for movie composers. With ASCAP colleague Samuel Schwartz, he founded the Gorfaine/Schwartz Agency in 1982 and built a star-studded roster that included John Williams, Hans Zimmer, James Horner, Ennio Morricone, and, ultimately, Newman.

"I had been a fan of Randy for years, the albums and the films, so I was excited when his lawyer Don Passman asked if we'd be interested in representing him," Gorfaine said. "We knew all about the Newman family in film music, of course, but that didn't play a part in our wanting to work with him. This was just after *The Natural*. Randy had already proven himself." Gorfaine served Randy as counselor and champion in the film world, routinely sending him score offers, along with reconnaissance about the directors and producers he'd be working with, especially heads-up warnings about those known to be difficult.

The parade of films started with *Parenthood*, the first of three movies over fifteen months. Directed by former child star Ron Howard, *Parenthood* was a good-natured comedy-drama about a subject that interested Randy: the challenges of family life. He also welcomed the chance to work with Howard, who had directed such classy box-office hits as *Splash* and *Cocoon*. "I heard he was a good guy, and he was," Randy said. "I had a good time on the film, one of the best pictures I ever did. I'd put it up in the top five."

Newman quickly came up with a song that Howard showcased in a key early scene in the film. The sparkling, hummable "I Love to See You Smile" conveyed the unbending love that Steve Martin, the film's star, has for his screen wife, Mary Steenburgen—a devotion that held them together despite the strains of family life, not just with their three children but in their interactions with their relatives. The song would later be used in a commercial for Colgate toothpaste.

The lyrics include this verse:

Like a sink without a faucet,
Like a watch without a dial.
What would I do
If I didn't have you?
I love to see you smile.

The lines were "greeting card" in a way that Newman's album songs weren't. What makes it work is the deep affection in Newman's vocal and the schoolboy innocence of the music itself. The film received an approval rating of 91 percent from *Rotten Tomatoes*, and Newman's song received an Oscar nomination, though the award went to Alan Menken and Howard Ashman's "Under the Sea" from *The Little Mermaid.*

"What I loved about *Parenthood* was how 'Smile' makes its point without hitting you over the head and is slightly to the left of center, not what you'd expect," Gorfaine said. "Writing a song for an album and writing a song for a film are separate disciplines. In a film, your aim is to accent what you're seeing on the film, and Randy has a gift for doing that. If you think about it, 'Smile' is the whole film right there." The movie was an important step for Newman, his first sizable moneymaker ($126 million)—and nothing was more appealing to studio executives than a winner. As with actors and directors, composers were often judged by the box-office receipts of their last venture.

— II —

By the time the film opened in the summer of 1989, Levinson was back in touch. He had directed four movies since *The Natural—Young Sherlock Holmes, Tin Men, Good Morning, Vietnam,* and *Rain Man,* the latter a critical and commercial sensation that received four Academy Awards, including best picture, director, and actor (Dustin Hoffman). As much as Levinson wanted to work with Newman again, he didn't feel any of those pictures were right for him. The new venture was ideal.

Avalon traces decades of a Jewish family's assimilation in America. Written, directed, and produced by Levinson, it's an intimate story with autobiographical overtones rooted in his native Baltimore. This wasn't going to be another commercial powerhouse like *Rain Man,* which grossed $354 million worldwide. It was in the art-minded tradition of *Diner,* which brought in a mere $14 million. But Randy was drawn to Levinson and the challenge.

"I pictured him bringing a mix of classical and American music strains that would help define what I wanted to say,"

Levinson said. "I'd just talk about the scenes, how this one was humorous or that one was poignant. I learned the first time we worked together that he has a natural understanding of what is needed. I don't remember ever saying, 'gee, this doesn't work' or 'we've got a problem here.' It all just seemed to fall into place. I like it when there is a little humor even in the drama, and Randy is a master at blending [emotions], that sleight of hand."

The two again bonded. "It was nice," Newman said. "Barry was a very good guy, very smart, and he knew my music enough to feel I'd give him what the picture needed. I tried to help the relationship between the two brothers, and I loved the park scene, which was fairly long; a big city park with all the birds asleep at night outside. I love that kind of thing . . . the lost sounds and words of America."

Avalon received an 85 percent rating from *Rotten Tomatoes* and Newman picked up another Oscar nomination for his score; the award went to John Barry's score for *Dances with Wolves*. Despite the film's failure to meet its $20 million budget in ticket sales, Newman showed he could contribute to a blockbuster and still exhibit the creative independence to work on an arthouse film.

~

While finishing *Avalon*, Newman received a script from his friend Elliot Abbott, who had been asked by Penny Marshall to find someone to write the music for her next film. *Awakenings* was based on Dr. Oliver Sacks's 1973 book of the same title, a nonfiction account of his experiences helping patients who suffered from a type of encephalitis, also known as "sleeping sickness." More than a million people were affected by the disease during an epidemic earlier in the century, many of whom died or were left in a "statue-like" condition, motionless and speechless. In the film, Robin Williams and Robert De Niro co-starred as fictional characters based on Sacks and a patient, respectively.

Newman surprised Abbott by offering to do the music himself. He was interested in the story and thought he could help the picture. "One goal was to use the music to make the doctor seem more intelligent than what you saw on the screen and to [underscore] the deep feeling in the encounters in the ward," he said. "It's not that [the doctor] didn't appear smart, but there was a vague absent-minded-professor thing about him, and I wanted to make him appear to be more like the substantial figure he was."

Randy was bothered by movies in which an actor didn't seem authentic in a role, whether it was the country singers in Altman's *Nashville* or Sharon Stone in *Basic Instinct*. "She gave a great performance in *Casino*, and she didn't need help to show that, but she wasn't presented in a way in *Basic Instinct* that made her seem like she was a successful mystery writer," he added. "Jerry Goldsmith's score is what made her seem sophisticated, and it kicked her up a notch in terms of being someone with a capacity for evil plans. When writing scores, I always looked for ways to make the characters and situations more believable."

Awakenings was nominated for three Academy Awards, including best picture and best actor (De Niro), but not for its score. Around the same time, Randy contributed several songs to a daring if ultimately unsuccessful television series co-designed by Steven Bochco, co-creator of *Hill Street Blues*. The idea behind *Cop Rock* was to surround a crime drama with stylish, evocative music, and Bochco turned to Newman for that. Newman wrote five songs for the pilot, which aired in the September of 1990. Two of them—"Sandman's Coming" and "She Chose Me"—were ballads that would be standouts on his own later albums. The ABC-TV show was dropped after eleven episodes, but Newman was honored with an Emmy for "Under the Gun." He later won two more Emmys for music he wrote for the series *Monk*, a comedy-drama chronicling the investigations of a likeable, obsessive-compulsive police consultant played by Tony Shalhoub. He won in 2004 for "It's a Jungle Out There," a lilting, whimsical tune that was the show's theme, and in 2010 for the song "When I'm Gone."

— III —

On October 6, 1990, Randy married Gretchen Preece in the backyard of his five-bedroom home on Banyan Drive in Mandeville Canyon. Still anxious about the effect of the divorce on his sons, Randy took the unusual step of asking Gretchen to have lunch with his first wife, hoping they would work together in making the boys feel welcome in both homes. They ended up going to a Santa Monica restaurant—just the two of them—and they talked for almost three hours.

"I was terrified because she might have hated me," Gretchen said. "But I just wanted her to know that I wasn't a bad person, that I didn't intend any harm, it's just the way things worked out. We became quite good friends. She was a wonderful person. She welcomed me into her children's arms and became a big part of my kids' lives. This meant a lot to Randy. His eyes always light up being around all his kids and now his grandkids."

Roswitha also gave Gretchen valuable advice about living with Randy.

"She told me, 'You know he tends to want to be isolated by himself, but don't let him do that. If he asks for dinner by himself, don't let him,' and I never have," Gretchen said. "I got the sense Roswitha was very accommodating to Randy, and she kind of regretted that."

Randy was overjoyed when his extended family got along so well, the first three boys and the son (Patrick) and daughter (Alice) that he and Gretchen would have. In the process, he encouraged the children to express themselves and speak honestly—traits that allowed them years later to speak about family relationships with insight and candor.

"I did see my dad was much more present in the lives of Patrick and Alice than in ours, and I think a lot of that was because of Gretchen," Eric said. "I love my mother, but Gretchen was not going to let Dad be a passive participant in the family's life the way my mom had. My mom used to take the kids on vacation alone so that Dad could work on his music, but Gretchen would be like, 'You're going, too.' I think those challenges helped make him better."

Over time, Waronker noticed changes in Newman; he felt Randy started being more relaxed, more open. "Gretchen has been a real positive in his life," he said. "She pushes him more. For the most part, Randy was never really that comfortable around people, he always felt like an outsider. Gretchen helped him feel more like he was part of something." But the softening didn't dull his edge.

Randy was so pleased with his progress on *Faust* that he spoke about it in some interviews with the *Los Angeles Times* in the early 1990s. He would eventually title the work *Randy Newman's Faust*. Given the confusion over some of his past songs, Newman seemed to be preparing his listeners for what was to come.

"I don't want people to think I don't mean anything I sing about," he told Jim Washburn in one of the interviews. "One of the worst things that has happened to me with the nature of the work I've done is [that sometimes people] think that everything is sort of coming out of the side of my mouth. 'Ooooh, does he mean it? What does he mean?' I think it's clear what I'm doing, but maybe it isn't. . . . Things get ambiguous."

Newman, too, took advantage of the interviews to express his disappointment in the nation's direction. "In this country, the Supreme Court for me is a sad thing," he said. "For the rest of my lifetime I know I'll disagree with everything they do. For all the heat that was generated for the Gulf War, where there was such unanimity and passion and everyone was 'ready to go,' I wish that kind of passion could be generated about helping the poor in this pretty rich nation." He was so angry about US policies that he wrote and recorded a song, "Lines in the Sand," which is believed to have been the first song by a prominent artist questioning the Persian Gulf War. Warner released the song to radio in January of 1991, but stations mostly avoided it, and "Sand" never found an audience.

Two years later at Orange County's Irvine Barclay Theater, Newman played four songs from *Faust*, including the gospel-driven "Glory Train," which introduced the confrontation between the Lord and Devil, and "Sandman's Coming," the ballad from *Cop Rock*.

Behind the scenes, Newman and Peter Asher were working on plans for an album and a stage play, including launching them concurrently, which was not the Broadway practice; normally, albums were delayed until after a play had gained enough success to create an audience for them. Rather than a cast album, the idea for *Faust* was to enlist guest stars to sing one or more songs—singers Asher and Newman knew and admired: Don Henley, Elton John, Bonnie Raitt, Linda Ronstadt, and James Taylor.

"It's difficult getting top artists to commit to singing on someone else's record, even if it's a benefit they all care about, because of the logistics involved," Asher said. "But everyone I spoke to agreed instantly. It was like, 'If it's Randy, I don't even need to hear the song. I'll do it.'"

Newman continued to be in artistic control. "There were moments when we kind of went, 'Are we ever going to get all this sorted out?' because it was quite complicated, and he would occasionally change his mind about something because it wasn't working," Asher said. "We were making a record and constructing a play at the same time. But Randy didn't need a lot of hand-holding.

He knew what he wanted. He's one of those artists where the producer's job, in many cases, is just to make sure everything comes out the way he intended."

Frank Wolf, who was back to record and mix most of the album, said there was a lot of confidence in the air. "I wouldn't say that I was working on something that was going to be the number one hit on pop radio," he said. "But I was confident that it would get to Broadway and that the album was going to be one of those things that lived forever. It was so smart and so funny—Randy at his best."

Except for a few dozen live shows in 1990 and 1993, Newman immersed himself even more deeply in *Faust* than he had during the *Good Old Boys* experience. He built upon the early spiral notebooks that were so filled with storylines and scenes that no space on the pages went unused, creating a total of four drafts of the musical. The first was a ninety-five-page treatment dated March 19, 1991, and titled *FAUST: A Comedy with Music by Randy Newman*. The final 124-page version, with "comedy" no longer in the title, was completed in April of 1992.

As the songwriting continued, the world of Warner Bros. Records was in turmoil.

~

For years, Mo Ostin was viewed as a guardian angel who protected Warner artists and employees against interference from bottom-line-driven corporate officials. In turn, Ostin had his own guardian angel in Steve Ross, a flamboyant entrepreneur who was successful in funeral parlor and parking lot businesses but always had his eye on the glamour of the entertainment world. He followed that dream in 1969 when, as head of Kinney Service Company, he purchased the Warner-Seven Arts film and record business for $400 million, soon adopting the name Warner Communications.

Ross was known for a colorful lifestyle and strong appetite for expansion, but he was also widely admired for his ability to find talented executives and give them the freedom to run their operations. He also paid them (and himself) well. Ostin benefited from that freedom. In 1989, Ross created the world's largest entertainment company by merging Warner Communications with Time Inc. to form Time Warner. The deal, valued at $14 billion, brought together Time properties, including *Time*, *People*, and *Sports Illustrated*, and Warner film and recording operations, the *Home Box Office* television network, and several leading cable television systems. It was a rocky period, but Ostin still had his angel at his back—until December 20, 1992, when Ross, sixty-five, died of prostate cancer.

Despite assurances that nothing would change, Ostin felt increasing corporate pressure as a threat to his artist-oriented approach. The sixty-six-year-old titan finally announced in August of 1994 that he was leaving Warner at the end of the year. At the time, the label led the record industry in domestic market share with 22.05 percent. "I hear about guys at record companies meddling with the music of artists who have made them millions of dollars, but Mo wouldn't dream of telling me or Neil Young or R.E.M. what to do," Randy said at the time. "He's someone who can go from talking about Jimi Hendrix to discussing my *Faust* to bragging about how great Green Day was on *Saturday Night Live*. Where are you going to find somebody like that in the record business? They just don't exist."

Waronker soon followed Ostin out of the company. They would reunite (along with Ostin's son, Michael) the following year as the management team at the recording wing of DreamWorks, the entertainment firm launched with considerable fanfare in 1994 by Steven Spielberg, Jeffrey Katzenberg, and David Geffen. Randy would eventually join them at the label. But first: *Faust*.

CHAPTER NINETEEN

Faust
The Album and
The Stage

— I —

Newman went to New York in late 1994 for a workshop production of *Faust* that Lorne Michaels helped arrange with James
Lapine, a director who collaborated with Stephen Sondheim and
has won Tony and Pulitzer awards. The goal was to put together
the team to take the musical to Broadway, hopefully as soon as
the following year. But it didn't work out. Instead, Randy took
Faust to the La Jolla Playhouse, where Michael Greif, the artistic
director, was receptive and where Ostin pledged $375,000 of
Warner funds toward the show's $1.1 million budget.

When Michael Roth joined the production as orchestrator in
June of 1995, work was proceeding on two fronts. The heavy
lifting was in La Jolla where Greif acknowledged the challenge
involved: "The play is extremely ironic," he told the *Los Angeles
Times*. "On the other hand, I think we're all on the lookout for
where we're not too clever for our own good, when in fact the
audience can identify and root for these characters in a way in
which we find they must in musical comedies."

The easier task was the album of *Faust* songs. Newman had
finished writing more than two dozen numbers, of which seventeen

were picked for the CD. Because Asher had left management earlier in the year to become senior vice president of Sony Music Entertainment, he and Newman were joined in the song selection process by Cathy Kerr. She would prove ideal for him, devoted to his musical goals yet sensitive to his discomfort with the record industry machinery.

To help listeners follow the musical's story—and to offer a few more laughs, Randy wrote a playful outline of the story, which he included in the CD package. It reflected a joy of creation that made it easy to see why he spent so much time on *Faust*.

~

RANDY NEWMAN'S FAUST

— I —

It is 4000 BC and the Lord has just created the Universe. He and His Original Angels celebrate the Lord's great achievement ("Glory Train"). Lucifer, the Lord's favorite, and the best-looking Angel by far, makes a little mistake, as will happen at parties, and is banished from Heaven forthwith and forever.

The centuries fly by. Lucifer, the Devil, now reigns in Hell, where to the surprise of many, he has power to be an effective administrator—harsh to be sure, vicious. Even sadistic. Ruthless when necessary but always fair. His life has not been an easy one however, and he longs to return to Heaven where they now have golf, roller coasters, and Hawaiian music. He promises revenge ("Can't Keep a Good Man Down").

The Devil visits the Lord in Heaven. He notices the Lord seems bored and even for Him, a little irritable (note unfortunate reference to Buddhists and lack of modesty in "How Great Our Lord"). He senses that the Lord may have lost a step or two, and decides to take advantage of it. The Devil contends that the

Lord made a mistake when he created Mankind. The Lord says He doesn't make mistakes. Knowing Him and His little, not weaknesses exactly, idiosyncrasies perhaps, better than anyone. The Devil goads the Lord into making a bet—a representative specimen of human life on earth is to be selected, the Devil will try to corrupt the selectee. After negotiating a bit, even at one point considering a Canadian ("Northern Boy"), they agree on Henry Faust, a schizophrenic student from Notre Dame University in South Bend, Indiana ("Bless the Children"). Should the Devil win, he would be permitted to move back up to Heaven. If the Lord wins, He would get Faust's soul, which proves to be so tiny as to be almost invisible, but is important to the Lord, as are we all. The two old adversaries part amicably and get on with the rest of the show.

The Devil makes himself known to the boy and proffers a contract which Henry signs without reading. The Devil is astonished. Henry explains he doesn't like to read on his own time. The Devil dislikes Henry at sight. He's a bad boy alright, but in such an unimaginative, ill-mannered uncultured way ("The Man") that the Devil, though sure of victory, is disheartened by the company he must keep. In any case, the Devil is certain that Henry will come through for him, and that he will once again abide with the Lord in Heaven. Right next door if possible. In addition, the Devil happens to know an important member of the Lord's staff, an English Angel, is angry about the Lord's inexplicably cavalier treatment of his country, which did, after all, win those two Big Wars thereby saving the world ("Little Island").

After spending some hard time with Henry, the Devil zips up to heaven to pass a few quiet hours in the place he knows best. He unexpectedly encounters the Lord and some Angel Children. The Devil complains about having to deal with a barbarian like Henry. The Lord sympathizes, not liking the kid any better than the Devil does, and incidentally, genuinely worried about the viability of his bet—the Devil in Heaven would be intolerable. He'd ruin everything and probably would want to come over all the time and "do things" together like they did as boys. The Lord loads up and with the help of the children, fires off an inspirational song at the Devil ("Relax, Enjoy Yourself").

— II —

Faust has never been in love except with himself. The Lord decides to send down Cupid to shoot Faust to get a love thing going for the boy. The Lord's personnel resources are staggeringly comprehensive. Cupid shoots Faust at a big St. Patrick's Day Easter Bunny Festival in South Bend on Easter Sunday. Henry falls in love with Margaret, the poorest, nicest, and most beautiful girl in South Bend ("Gainesville"). The Devil, raging inwardly at the Lord's perfidy (Cupid is, after all, a mythological figure from a pagan culture), notices Martha, the most sophisticated girl in Indiana ("Life Has Been Good") and one who has been seen not only at Arlington Park, but at Belmont, Aqueduct, and Bay Meadows. The Devil falls for Martha hard as only a middle-aged man can fall for a beautiful but heartless young girl. Believe me. It's the truth. He's headed for trouble ("I Gotta Be Your Man"). Martha seems to reciprocate his feelings for her ("Feels Like Home"). It's a trick. Be Careful. Too late. Martha dumps the Devil ("Bleeding All Over the Place"). Meanwhile, Margaret, against her better judgment, falls in love with Faust ("My Hero"). Faust poisons Margaret's mother so he can be alone with her, sleeps with Margaret, impregnates her, and with the Devil's help kills Margaret's brother, Valentine, who sees Faust leave his sister's humble little sleep chamber. Henry and the Devil are forced to skip town. They head for a cabin the Devil keeps on Lake Superior near Duluth. They bring their own water and stay a year.

In South Bend, Margaret has Henry's child and, crazed with grief and shame, drowns her in a creek. This is the comic high point of Goethe's original play, and one of the most delightfully urbane moments in all of German literature. In a hilarious courtroom sequence, Margaret is convicted of murder and sentenced to die at the Indiana State Prison in Michigan City. She sings a lullaby ("Sandman's Coming") though her baby is, of course, dead. She sings the song to a blanket.

Henry attempts to rescue Margaret who is already in the spirit world in spirit but because she was so good in life, the Angels come down and take her off to Heaven even before she is dead. Henry is impressed. He asks the Lord for forgiveness and takes some of the poison he gave Margret's mother. The Devil laughs, his own move to Heaven seems imminent: He says he's going home to pack. Henry, expiring noisily, with neither dignity nor courage (he tries to induce vomiting to rid himself of the poison) asks again for forgiveness. The Devil laughs but Lo! The Angels descend. The Lord's voice booms down, "He is saved." Henry ascends to Heaven, favoring the Devil with a little wave as he goes. At this point, the impartial observer, if one such could be found, might agree that the Devil has been denied the victory for which he was entitled. Predictably, he is angry, very angry. Then, after rage, depression, deep depression, he stands alone in the cell. Head down, beaten. Even the Lord, watching from above, feels sorry for him.

A wind begins to blow, a warm, dry wind. The Devil's hair is ruffled as the breeze freshens. His cape billows to the East. He wags his tail. He thinks of something that makes him very, very happy. ("Happy Ending").

Written by Randy Newman

~

— II —

Of the song choices for the album, a dozen would stand as cornerstones of the musical, including five that would define the relationship between the Lord and the Devil. Four of them contained some of the show's richest humor and would be placed back to back at the start of the album. In the rousing opener "Glory Train," the Devil continued to ridicule the Lord.

> *Some fools in the desert*
> *With nothing else to do*
> *So scared of the dark*
> *They didn't know if they were coming or going*
> *So they invented me*
> *And they invented you*
> *And other fools will keep it all going*
> *And growing*
>
> *Everybody!*
> [urging, in the proud show-biz tradition, the audience to join
>   in, even though in his enthusiasm he doesn't remember
>   that no one in the audience had heard it before]
>
> *We're a figment of their imagination*
> *A beautiful dream, it is true*
> *A figment of their imagination*
> *Me and you*
> *And you know it*
> *Me and you*

With the protagonists in place, the Devil takes his boastful turn in the spotlight with the bouncy "Can't Keep a Good Man Down." But God soon regains the stage with "How Great Our

Lord," a song in which Newman presents a Supreme Being so human that He teases his subjects just for fun. At one point, the Lord suggests He really doesn't understand all that is happening on earth. When a startled young angel, seeking reassurance, asks the Lord if He really doesn't know the answers, the Lord declares, "Of course I do"—and skips off laughing.

Then the Devil reveals his duplicity in a song that starts out gently, but soon turns evil, moving the musical into darker territory. Identified as "Devil's 1st song" on the 1982 demo tape, it now carried the title "Best Little Girl."

> DEVIL: *I once knew a girl*
> *Her name was Barbara*
> *The cutest little muffin you have ever seen*
> *I was livin' in St. Louis*
> *At the Chase Hotel*
> *And she lived there*
> *With her mommy and her daddy*
> *And her little brother Skipper*
> *Who was just thirteen*
>
> *She went to church every morning*
> *Said her prayers real loud every night*
> *She was the best little girl*
> *In the whole damn town*
> LORD: *Watch it, Devil*
> DEVIL: *But you know I'm right*
> *You know I'm right*
>
> *One morning in the lobby*
> *I whispered in her ear*
> *"Honey, it's too hot today to go to school*

Whyn't you call up
That cute little lifeguard?
He's out by the hotel pool"
They drank all her daddy's whiskey
They took all her mama's pills
They were found the next day
Drowned in their own vomit
Poor little fool
Poor little fool

Four songs later, the confrontation continues after the Devil is dispirited from meeting Henry Faust, whose soul is the subject of a wager with the Lord that the Devil hopes to win to regain entrance to Heaven. In "Relax, Enjoy Yourself," Faust turns out to be such a self-absorbed, hedonistic young man that the Devil wonders if he even has a soul. In a sharp, funny spoken exchange in the musical (but not on the album), Newman points out Faust's empty-headedness in a scene in which the Devil tries to convince Faust to sell his soul.

DEVIL: I am here to offer you the world. Anything you want in exchange for your soul.
FAUST: So, you give me anything I want...?
DEVIL: Correct.
FAUST: And I give you what?
DEVIL: Your immortal soul.
FAUST: So, what's the catch?

Sensing the Devil's torment, the Lord tries to calm him down, but the Devil resorts once more to his vileness. In a song that could truly haunt your dreams, the Devil mercilessly tells a young angel, who had been murdered, about how the Lord will eventually let her killer enter Heaven, pointing to it as a sign of the Lord's lack of moral purpose. Asked to explain his actions, the Lord responds that He works in mysterious ways.

— III —

The musical's second tier of songs survey the human condition in modern times, which in turn raises the question of just what has the Lord achieved over all these years in a world ravaged by the conditions that Newman has addressed throughout his career. The most striking of these songs are ballads, one of which ("Feels Like Home" sung by Bonnie Raitt) demonstrates how the shrewd, sophisticated Martha can make even the personification of evil mistakenly believe someone cares about him, and two ballads for the sweet Margaret (both sung by Linda Ronstadt): the gentle "Gainesville" and the darkly-framed "Sandman's Coming," from *Cop Rock*. Transferred to *Faust*, "Sandman's Coming" is the tragic culmination of Faust's falling in love with Margaret, a young woman so beautiful and innocent that he thinks she must be an angel from heaven. After becoming pregnant, Margaret realizes Faust's true nature and drowns her baby girl to protect her from the evils of the world. Sentenced to death for the crime, she sits in a prison cell, trying to comfort herself and her lost child by singing "Sandman's Coming." As she does, she cradles an empty blanket in her arms. The song begins:

> *Margaret* (in prison): *Close your eyes now, little girl*
> *They don't want to hear you cryin'*
> *You never had a chance,*
> *You never had a chance*
>
> *It's a great big dirty world*
> *If they say it's not, they're lyin'*

Sandman's comin' soon
You know he's comin' soon

These songs are followed by numbers that sound reasonable individually but posed a major hurdle when it came to integrating them into the stage production. By contrast, the sweeping "Happy Ending," the album's closer, is a knockout. Aside from being full of energy and fun, it slyly invites the listener to examine their own beliefs about what constitutes an honorable life.

In the play, Henry Faust sees the Lord's compassion for the distraught Margaret by taking her into Heaven and declares himself so moved that he asks for forgiveness, too. The Devil laughs at the audacity of Faust's request. But the Lord accepts the young man's plea and welcomes him into Heaven. The Devil is outraged and accuses God of accepting this good-for-nothing only to win the bet. The Devil's subsequent depression again causes the Lord to show sympathy. He tries to revive the Devil by ordering a warm wind to pass over him. The gesture works. The Devil might not be able to ever return to Heaven, but there is a place right on earth that fits him just nicely, a city that offers everything he craves.

DEVIL: *I got Las Vegas in my mind*
Seem like it's stuck up in there
Like it's been there for all times
You can take your desert
Goddamn it, give me mine
'Cause I got Las Vegas in my mind

Through these portals
Pass the rich and the famous
Through these portals
Pass the very best at what they do

Man, they're the greatest
It's the land of giant women
But the little man is king
Here in Las Vegas
Man, they got ev'rything
Run with it

They got English girls
With legs so long
You gotta use a stepladder
To lick their love thing
It's a family place too now
So bring the kids along
They're gonna have a real good time here

They got wild women from Borneo
Playin' the piano
In your bungalow
They got monkey women from the Amazon
Or something really funky
From the lands beyond
They're here in Las Vegas
They're here in Las Vegas
Las Vegas
Man, I'm speaking in tongues!

Listening to the track, you can picture theatergoers dancing in the aisles. The album was complete—a spectacular array of ideas and sounds that are intelligent and gloriously entertaining. It was now La Jolla's turn.

Newman was active with his theater team, frequently attending rehearsals, conferring with Greif and Roth, and enjoying the process of building a show. He especially enjoyed working with actors. Those around him saw his spirits soar—the harder he worked, the more he seemed to shed the tension that had long shadowed him.

"Randy had never before worked so closely with actors who treated his songs so thoroughly, especially when analyzing lyrics and subtext, and you could see his respect for them and their process grow as rehearsals went on," Roth said. "He wasn't just 'watching,' he was enormously cooperative and collaborative, and endlessly patient."

In the final weeks before the opening, the production team reviewed the song list, tossing out some and bringing in others, hoping to tell the most cohesive and effective story. The biggest surprise was that "Happy Ending" wasn't chosen as the closer; instead, a reprise of "Glory Train" and "Can't Keep a Good Man Down" was used to say good night.

In the *Voice,* Robert Christgau rated the album an A, declaring in part: "The songs themselves are rich, mocking rock, religion, musical comedy, the Classix, and American culture all at once. . . . If the project reeks of concept album, well, pardon me for reading—the songs do get even better once you take in the plot summary. And if it reeks of burlesque, well, how better to bum-rush Western civ and 'America's greatest art form' simultaneously?"

Not everyone agreed. The theater/compilation concept confused many pop critics, some enough that they didn't even bother to review the album, leaving it with only enough support to reach No. 87 on the *Voice* poll. The album, too, fared poorly on the radio where even the inclusion of the guest stars wasn't enough for program directors to give the tracks much of a spin. Asher, who was used to the heavy airplay and big sales, was still puzzled decades later over the collection's failure to find a large audience. "I love the *Faust* album," he said. "The songs are brilliant, but somehow it wasn't a hit even with Don Henley, James Taylor,

Linda Ronstadt, Elton John, and Bonnie Raitt on it—all at their peak. I don't get it. Some people might say Randy is too smart for them. I don't know. If I heard one of his songs, I'd want to know, 'Who is this guy, what's he doing next?'"

— IV —

Randy Newman's Faust held its La Jolla preview on September 19, 1995. The audience was warmly responsive, and Waronker was thrilled for Randy. He went looking for Randy afterward. "I found him outside the theater," he said. "He was standing by himself, as if he needed a moment to let everything sink in. When he finally saw me, he said something like, 'I just love this,' but the words didn't matter. His face said everything. Randy was just filled with joy. I don't think I had ever seen him that enthusiastic about one of his works. It was like a spiritual moment, like he was in a different place."

Cathy Kerr, too, was in high spirits. "There was a special excitement in the crowd and certainly with the cast and crew," she said. "When Randy was invited onstage at curtain call, there was thunderous applause. The audience loved the show. We could all sense this was something special and were optimistic that *Faust* would go to Broadway."

Critics didn't share the enthusiasm.

The opening lines of Laurie Winer's *Los Angeles Times* critique made you think the musical was an instant classic. "The musical theater got a shot in the arm Sunday night when [*Faust*] had its long-awaited premiere. . . . Here is a score, thrilling and stage-worthy, that turns its back on the overblown, joyless posturing of Andrew Lloyd Webber, a score that brings idiosyncratic, smart humor back into the American musical."

Then, the bad news: "Newman is a great pop writer who can tell complete stories in song, who can write character as sharply and efficiently as, say, Hammerstein or Sondheim," Winer continued. "That does not mean he is necessarily capable of finessing those songs into a show in a way that builds a story or makes sense in a dramatic arc." Yet she ended up rooting for Newman and the musical: "The songs are good enough to drive the show, whether they are integrated or not. It's easy to forgive this musical its sins, even if they are frequent. So, *Faust* is not perfect. Thank God it exists at all."

Newman shook off the disappointment and began thinking about what he hoped would be the next, hopefully improved version of the play. That second stop was a year later at the Goodman Theater in Chicago where heavyweight playwright David Mamet was brought in to help make the musical more stage-ready. But Newman didn't find Mamet's suggestions helpful, and there was little sign of a Mamet stamp in the final product.

In an interview before the September 30, 1996, opening, Greif told the *Chicago Tribune*, "I'm very proud of the fact that we haven't abandoned a lot of the zaniness for something that might be more straightforward." But the paper's critic was not impressed, and hopes of Broadway vanished. Even when *Time* magazine later named *Faust* one of the year's ten most impressive stage productions, it wasn't enough to jump-start things again.

Newman didn't express regrets in an interview with the *Tribune*. One favorite moment of the engagement, Kerr recalled years later, was a matinee performance for public school kids who loved it. "It was a thrill for Randy," she said.

Newman's resilience after two setbacks showed how much he had grown emotionally since he shut down for months after the album disappointments.

Randy had, in fact, already resumed film scoring. During the latter stages of the *Faust* experience, he wrote the score for three high-profile features. The first, again directed by Ron Howard, was *The Paper*, a comedy-drama about a frantic twenty-four hours in the life of an American newspaper. It attracted strong reviews, and Newman received an Oscar nomination for the original song "Make Up Your Mind." (The award went to Elton John and Tim Rice for "Can You Feel the Love Tonight" from *The Lion King*.) The second score was for *Maverick*, based on the popular, fun-minded Western TV series. Newman called it a bad scoring experience because the filmmakers kept wanting something "hokey." Reviews were mixed, but theater owners were pleased; the film earned more than $183 million worldwide.

The third film was simply titled *Toy Story*.

CHAPTER TWENTY

Toy Story
"You've Got a Friend in Me" and
John Lasseter

— I —

Seconds into *Toy Story*, the opening notes of "You've Got a Friend in Me" introduce a song so comforting and warm that it is hard not to fall instantly in love with it and the movie, which is exactly what happened to millions of filmgoers, young and old. *Toy Story* launched a four-film franchise in 1995 that would bring in more than $3 billion worldwide, and it established a bond between Newman and animated film visionary John Lasseter.

Twelve years after Randy started playing the birthday piano in Beverly Hills, Lasseter began his own creative journey in Whittier, a more economically and ethnically diverse city across Los Angeles County. Rather than on a piano bench, this five-year-old would take his place in front of the television and watch cartoons, especially ones with the name Chuck Jones in the credits.

Described by actor-comedian Robin Williams as the "Orson Welles of animation," Jones—as writer, director and/or producer—was a major force behind such iconic Warner Bros. cartoon figures as Bugs Bunny, Daffy Duck, and Porky Pig, most of whom had a teasingly mischievous edge. None reflected that quality as sharply as two of Jones's favorites: arch-enemies Wile E. Coyote and Road Runner, whose explosive "beep-beep" chase scenes may be unrivaled in cartoon history for sheer skullduggery.

Cartooning remained a hobby until Lasseter's freshman year of high school when he saw an animated Disney film, *The Sword in the Stone,* in a neighborhood theater. When his mom picked him up after the showing, the first thing he said after stepping into the car was, "I want to be an animator and work for Walt Disney Studios one day." She told him that was a great goal. Soon after, he sent a letter, complete with drawings and his dream of being an animator, to Disney Studios and was elated to get a warm response to that and subsequent letters.

To prove his dedication to Disney upon graduation from high school, he took the advice of a studio executive and enrolled in a four-year animation program at the California Institute of the Arts (CalArts). He also worked summers at Disneyland where he fell further under the Disney spell: "Just walking through the park after it closed at night, with all the music playing and the lights on, was something I'll never forget."

There was nothing casual about Lasseter's Disney quest. As he progressed from sweeping the Tomorrowland grounds to guiding tours on the popular Jungle Cruise river ride, Lasseter was preparing for the day he would make his own cartoons at Disney Studios. The Cruise was a virtual classroom in comic timing. "As tour guide, you're telling the riders all these jokes, which weren't very good, but you soon learned that you could make people laugh anyway by the way you told the jokes," he said. The experience also intensified his desire to entertain people.

After CalArts, Lasseter was hired by Disney, where he regarded traditional, hand-drawn animation as obsolete; the future, he felt, belonged to 3D computer graphics, an approach that was more efficient and gave animators far greater creative freedom. It was like going from typewriters to word processors.

Computer graphics even enabled filmmakers to move beyond two dimensions in cartoons to three dimensions by adding depth to the images without the need for special glasses.

Lasseter became such a proponent of 3D computer graphics that he was seen as a loose cannon and was abruptly fired in 1983. But Lucasfilm, which was experimenting with the new animation process, hired him for its graphics division, which was renamed Pixar a few years later and where he met Apple co-founder Steve Jobs. As computer technology advanced, Lasseter pushed for longer, more ambitious films, but Pixar was struggling financially and needed a partner to proceed. That led back to Disney Studios, where Jeffrey Katzenberg, head of the studio's animated division, liked Lasseter's plans for a full-length film. A deal was struck even though both sides knew there would be friction between the old-school Disney way of doing things and the upstart Pixar's ambitions.

~

The struggle began almost immediately as the studios disagreed over matters ranging from the storyline of the *Toy Story* project to the use of music. In working on *Toy Story*, Lasseter wanted to break away from what he saw as a weakness in recent Disney animated films—a tendency to play it safe, as in *Aladdin*, by surrounding a single main character with more interesting comic sidekicks and villains. For his film, Lasseter relied on two sets of main characters—a child (Andy) and his favorite toy (cowboy Woody), and the interwoven story of Woody and another toy, a space ranger (Buzz Lightyear) with whom Woody bonds after initially fearing the ranger was out to steal Andy's affection.

With the story in place, Lasseter ran into more resistance. Disney wanted *Toy Story* to be filled with songs in the studio tradition that dated back to *Snow White and the Seven Dwarfs* in the 1930s. This meant a film with six or seven songs in it, and Lasseter balked.

316 | A FEW WORDS IN DEFENSE OF OUR COUNTRY

"He didn't want any songs, and everyone kind of freaked out," said Chris Montan, a former songwriter who headed Disney's film music department from 1987 to 2016. Montan broke the impasse by suggesting that Pixar use two or three self-contained songs, the way Mike Nichols had done with Simon and Garfunkel tunes in *The Graduate* and Hal Ashby had done with Cat Stevens songs for *Harold and Maude*. Described by Montan as "pop-tone poems," the songs would push the story forward without interrupting the action or requiring the characters to sing them.

With Lasseter on board, Montan came up with a short list of composers, and Lasseter's eye went right to one name: Randy Newman. Lasseter admired Randy's albums, but he was particularly enamored with his film work, especially the scores for *The Natural* and *Avalon*. "I saw that Randy could write 'Short People' and 'I Love LA' with a lot of humor, but his music could also be emotional, smart, and subversive at times, and that's what we wanted," Lasseter said. "We were aiming for everybody as our audience, not just kids."

Newman wasn't sure about stepping into the world of movie cartoons, but he agreed to meet with Lasseter. "I was with Randy when John showed us some of the storyboards for *Toy Story*," said Gorfaine, the agent. "After a few minutes, Randy suddenly turned to me and whispered, 'This is great.' As fast as that, we were on board." Once again, Newman was driven in large part by his comfort level with the director. "My first thought was, 'I don't know if I can do this," he said. "But John has this inspirational quality. He could convince you that you were seven feet tall. The more I listened to him, the more I thought, 'I can do this. Yeah, let's do this.'"

As soon as he returned home, Randy phoned Lenny to say he had just seen something that was going to be an absolute smash. "It was unlike him," Waronker said years later. "But he was serious."

— II —

When Newman, as was his practice, asked Lasseter for one word to describe the emotion he wanted the music to convey in a song, the director replied: "Friendship." On March 23, 1993, Newman first played "You've Got a Friend in Me" for Lasseter and Montan, and the lure of the piano keys and Newman's vocal were as disarming as the lyrics.

You've got a friend in me
You've got a friend in me
When the road looks rough ahead
And you're miles and miles
From your nice warm bed
You just remember what your old pal said
Boy, you've got a friend in me
Yeah, you've got a friend in me

You've got a friend in me
You've got a friend in me
If you've got troubles, I've got 'em too
There isn't anything I wouldn't do for you
We stick together and can see it through
Cause you've got a friend in me
You've got a friend in me

Some other folks might be
A little bit smarter than I am
Bigger and stronger too
Maybe
But none of them will ever love you
The way I do, it's me and you

Boy, and as the years go by
Our friendship will never die
You're gonna see it's our destiny
You've got a friend in me
You've got a friend in me

The song captured the spirit of the movie so well that it expressed both of the film's storylines—over the opening credits when sung by Randy to express Woody's devotion to Andy, and again at the end, in a duet between Randy and Lyle Lovett, to reflect the ties between Woody and Buzz. "From that moment on, John had full trust in Randy's storytelling and intelligence," said Montan, who was at the director's side for every meeting and recording session with Newman. "Randy's ideas were always welcome; he was a full collaborator. That kind of trust from a director is something I rarely saw in the 300 films I've worked on."

One of the things Randy most enjoyed, of course, was conducting the studio orchestra. "When he was at the podium," said Frank Wolf, his recording engineer, "it was like he was basking in the sunshine despite the fact he had worked his ass off to get there."

That fun was in full force, the engineer noted, on the first day of recording when Randy spoke to the musicians who understood Disney film music had been the target of critical potshots in recent years. "Good morning, ladies and gentlemen, thank you so much for being here. Now remember this is a Disney film, so we've got to lower our standards." It was all the funnier because of the cadre of Disney executives in the room.

Montan also enjoyed Newman's playfulness in the studio. "Right before starting a cue, he'd begin talking to the musicians, and he knew that made me nervous because we've got like ninety-five or a hundred musicians and every minute costs us," he said. "Randy would go through these jokes and sometimes look my way and make fun of all the money he was wasting . . . 'fifteen thousand, one-hundred, fifteen thousand, two-hundred,' and the musicians loved it."

These good-natured antics set the tone for the sessions. "By doing those little monologues and stuff, he entertained the musicians and helped them relax," Lasseter said. "The music was demanding. Randy didn't do any lazy scores. These were the best players in the world, and they knew he always wanted to use them instead of going to London or someplace to record, and they appreciated that. Randy also took them to his favorite soundstage, the old one at MGM in Culver City [now Sony]. When you walked into the room, you couldn't help but think of its history . . . *Singin' in the Rain* and *The Wizard of Oz*."

That informal approach didn't extend to Newman's work ethic. "I would often go over to Randy's house and be the first one to hear his new stuff and I knew I had to bring my A game," Montan said. "I wanted to make sure I was always honest with him about what I felt because Randy was the most honest person I've ever met. So, when you are with him and his music, you can't be lazy. You have to tell him exactly what you think and be able to back it up."

When Lasseter showed him finished scenes for the first time, Randy took out a wallet from his windbreaker, slowly placed it on a table in front of him, and jokingly patted it. In a whisper just loud enough for Lasseter and Montan to hear, he said to the wallet, "This movie is going to be very nice to you."

~

Released in late 1995, *Toy Story*, which cost $30 million to make, roared out of the gate, grossing some $375 million worldwide and picking up a 100 percent rating from *Rotten Tomatoes*. Newman collected Oscar nominations for best original score and song ("Friend"), though again no statuette. Writing in the *Los Angeles Times*, film critic Kenneth Turan declared that *Toy Story* "creates the kind of gee-whiz enchantment that must have surrounded *Snow White* on its initial release." In 2005, the United States Library of Congress would add *Toy Story* to the National Film Registry for being "culturally, historically, or aesthetically significant."

Despite the music's key role, there was scant reference to it in reviews, as Newman expected. The Disney and Pixar staffs, however, were effusive. "The gift of Randy is the warmth and simplicity in his music," said Tom MacDougall, who was music production coordinator on *Toy Story* and eventually named president of Disney Music. "Everyone else would probably have started the film with something razzle-dazzle, but Randy came in with something totally different, and it was perfect." Then he praised the score in the same spirit others had praised Randy's score for *The Natural*. "If you take 'You've Got a Friend in Me' out of the picture and put something else in, it wouldn't have been the same film," MacDougall said. "You can trace the whole *Toy Story* [franchise] back to that moment."

The victory guaranteed Randy's involvement in more Pixar films, which in turn put Newman among the highest paid composers in Hollywood, making as much as $1 million a movie. Working on assignment was also less draining than his studio albums, and he could write a score in around two months rather than the year or more that it took to write and record an album. That meant more time to spend with family and relax.

"I think it was inevitable that he would score films," Gretchen said. "Because he was rewarded for being so good at it with success and money, I also think he liked being good at something that the previous generation thought was so important. He was special and he had proved it, even if they weren't around anymore to witness it."

He got a chance to celebrate the success in a brief series of concerts with symphony orchestras in 1996 that combined songs from the albums, *Faust*, and the films. In the first of them in Jacksonville, Florida, he hit the first of several high points early with an inspired back-to-back placement of two songs that don't seem on paper to be remotely compatible: the sunny "I Love to See You Smile" and the storm clouds of "Real Emotional Girl." Later, Newman, accompanying himself on piano, wove album songs around a bright array of film, television, and stage work: "You've Got a Friend in Me," "Sandman's Coming," and "Feels Like Home." He even got to conduct the orchestra on the themes to a few of the films, including *Avalon, The Natural,* and *Ragtime.*

Not everything worked later when Newman performed with the ninety-five piece National Symphony Orchestra at Wolf Trap near Washington, DC. Critic Geoffrey Himes noted in the *Washington Post* that "the under-rehearsed NSO faltered in the more challenging sections of the movie music [and] the up-tempo songs were a disaster, for the orchestra had no feel for the New Orleans syncopation Newman favors." Still, he declared:

> The evening was redeemed . . . by the slow songs and the more dreamlike sections of the film music. Newman's 1968 debut album was completely orchestrated, and "Davy the Fat Boy," "Cowboy," and "Love Story" achieved a moody fullness they never had before on a local stage. A clever example of theme and counterpoint from "Avalon" evoked that brass-band optimism of turn-of-the-century Baltimore immigrants. "Louisiana 1927" doesn't sound complete without the signature string introduction it got Thursday night. Best of all was "Marie," a 1974 ballad about deeply flawed but true love that reached new poignancy as the strings built aching chords beneath Newman's deadpan vocal.

The songs on Newman's studio albums would remain his most important work, but the music for films would add substantially to his creative legacy. The success—especially of "You've

Got a Friend in Me"—also gave Newman the massive acceptance that had largely eluded him, especially with a new generation of young people. He was no longer just loved by critics and peers, and the fluke "Short People" was no longer his main calling card. Fans of all ages now thought of "You've Got a Friend in Me" when they heard Newman's name—a song so popular that it felt like a No. 1 record around the world even though it was never released as a single.

"*Toy Story* really spoke to my generation," his daughter Alice said years later. "It followed kids my age through the years. Even when Andy's going to college, it's when we were going to college." One of her fondest memories was the day Randy played "You've Got a Friend in Me" in person for her kindergarten class.

As a child in the 1990s, Patrick remembers Randy being available a lot. "When he would work, especially on a movie, he would be absent, but it wouldn't be for long periods," he said. "When he wasn't doing that, he was accessible round the house, more than any of my other friends' dads, because he was home. We also traveled a lot together. I think my mom was the one who wanted to share these experiences while we were young, and Dad enjoyed traveling."

Finally, Randy's life was good.

CHAPTER TWENTY-ONE

More Movies
"When She Loved Me" and
All Those Oscar Nominations

— I —

Even with the blockbuster results, there was no guarantee that Disney would follow *Toy Story* with a sequel aimed at theaters. In fact, the studio, the dominant partner in the Pixar relationship, first imagined the sequel as a less ambitious direct-to-video venture, similar to the studio's handling of *The Lion King II: Simba's Pride* and *The Little Mermaid II: Return to the Sea*. Lasseter moved on to another animated project, one of four films Randy would score while the fate of *Toy Story 2* was being weighed.

The next two Newman scores were *James and the Giant Peach* and *Michael*. Based on a popular 1961 children's book by British novelist Roald Dahl, *James* was an enterprising mix of live action and stop-motion animation, a fantasy about a British boy who flees to America to escape his abusive aunts. In his new land, James encounters a giant peach that is filled with various human-sized insects who become his new family. Far from the bright, cheerful tone of *Toy Story*, *James* struck many viewers in the spring of 1996 as often dark and claustrophobic. It was a disappointment at the box office, and reviews were mixed—it had more of an art film feel in some respects than the main-stream buoyancy of Disney/Pixar. The *New York Times*'s Janet Maslin called the movie "a technological marvel, arch and inno-vative with a daringly offbeat visual conception" but added that it was also a "strenuously artful film with a macabre edge that may scare small children. And beyond that, it lacks a clear idea of who its audience might be." Newman's music was a standout, and he came away with another Oscar nomination for top score of a musical or comedy (the award went to Rachel Portman for *Emma*), and he has fond memories of the production. Years later he placed it among his most rewarding scores. He had little good to say about his next film.

Director Nora Ephron's *Michael* was the tale of an edgy, atyp-ical angel (played by John Travolta) who comes to earth, alas, to do what angels do. Distributed by New Line Cinema, the film, released in December of 1996, only received a 34 percent score on *Rotten Tomatoes*, and there was no Oscar nomination for Newman. In an interview for the DVD for the film *Pleasantville*, Newman spoke about the *Michael* experience: "I didn't even rec-ognize what the hell I did (for the film) because everything had been moved around so much." All of this made him feel glad to return to Disney, Pixar, and Lasseter on *A Bug's Life*.

~

For the millions of *Toy Story* fans who had waited three years for more of the sweeping accessibility and tender charm of that film, *A Bug's Life* delivered nicely in the fall of 1998—even though filmgoers had to wait until the final credits to hear Newman sing his new song, "The Time of Your Life." It was a sweet, buoyant number that reflected the movie's theme of courage and commu-nity, which led some observers to joke that the film was *Toy Story* with bugs. But *A Bug's Life* was more ambitious than that wisecrack.

Surprisingly, Lasseter didn't automatically turn to Randy for *Bug's Life* because the new film was a departure from *Toy Story*: an action-adventure film in which an industrious ant leads the battle against a giant grasshopper—deliciously named Hopper—who has been exploiting his colony. Lasseter wanted the music to focus on the frantic movements in the cartoon rather than the emotional state of the main characters. Eventually, however, he put his faith again in Newman.

"There was some talk around Hollywood that Randy couldn't do action," the director said. "But I kept thinking about this one scene in *Toy Story* where Buzz had this rocket on his back and he's on the back of a car with Woody. Suddenly, Woody lights the fuse and it takes off. The music was so full of energy and emotion and life; it was fantastic. I remember turning to Chris [Montan] and saying, 'He can't do action, eh?' The score for *A Bug's Life* turned out to be big and glorious, maybe my favorite from any of the Pixar films."

The score was also a Newman favorite. "Think about it—a bug chasing a bug," he told the *Los Angeles Times*. "For a composer, that's tough, just in terms of the amount of notes you need for the music. I mean, what John Williams did on *Hook* was even harder, in terms of technical facility, but I did my best. I remember writing a lot of non-specific songs, because let's face it, a song about a bug isn't going to travel well. You aren't gonna see that on *Barbra Streisand's Greatest Hits from the Movies*, right?"

Film music critic Jon Burlingame also prizes the score. "At the beginning of the movie, Randy starts out with this pastoral piece, again this sort of Americana," he said. "As the camera moves in, we see a bunch of insects all marching along, and Randy launches into this march, a kind of tongue-in-cheek waltz, and it's just completely delightful. Later, the key bug, Flick, goes into the big city, and Randy launches into this Gershwin-esque thing, which is appropriate and hilarious."

The film scored 92 percent with *Rotten Tomatoes* and almost matched *Toy Story's* box-office wallop ($363 million). Newman received another Oscar nomination for score of a musical or comedy (award to Stephen Warbeck's *Shakespeare in Love*), one of three strong entries for him in that year's competition. The other nominations were for song, "That'll Do" from *Babe: Pig in the City* (award to Stephen Schwartz for "When You Believe" from *The Prince of Egypt*), and the score from a drama for *Pleasantville* (award to Nicola Piovani for *Life Is Beautiful*). The nominations brought Newman's total to twelve—which led to something of an industry amusement, getting that many nominations without a win, but the nominations alone signified the growing respect for Newman in film circles. Still, it must have been a difficult Oscar night for Randy.

"That'll Do," sung in the movie by Peter Gabriel in his usual deeply impassioned manner, ranks as one of Randy's most stirring film songs. Maybe it was too difficult to see the beauty of the warm, majestic piece of music when it was applied to a barnyard animal.

Pleasantville, whose themes about the role of television in American life and the dangers of despotism, was another rewarding experience. Growing up, Randy and Alan spent most evenings with their parents watching television just like the family in the movie. Those countless hours were inspiration for "My Country," a song he'd later write that addressed those times.

Feelings might go unexpressed
I think that's probably for the best
Dig too deep, who knows what you will find

Written and directed by Gary Ross, who wrote the script for the Tom Hanks comedy *Big*, the film begins with David, a high schooler in the 1990s who is obsessed with a 1950s TV series about the idyllic adventures of a Midwest suburban family, the

Parkers. Played by Tobey Maguire, the teenager watched each episode so many times that he could recite the lines with the actors. When the TV remote broke, David phoned a mysterious repairman who gave him a special remote that transported him and his sister to the fictional Parkers' house, where conformity reigned. The movie then followed the conflict between David's modern cultural values against the townsfolk's time-warp thinking, gradually leading to social liberation. The music accompanied the various twists and turns in the film stylishly.

It was quite a year, but the upcoming *Toy Story 2* would give Randy his most likely shot yet for an Oscar.

— II —

By late 1997, Disney and Pixar executives were impressed enough by the progress of *Toy Story 2* to think about upgrading the film to theaters. As part of the move, Lasseter was brought back as co-director the following fall. His first challenge was the script, which posed a major problem. In the completed film, we learn that long before meeting Andy, Woody was the star of *Woody's Roundup*, a children's TV animated series that was so popular toys were made of the leading characters, including Woody and a cowgirl named Jessie.

When a ruthless toy dealer learns that a museum in Japan is offering big bucks for a complete set of the *Roundup* figures, he realizes he already has every figure except Woody. After kidnapping Andy's toy, he discovers that his plan may be thwarted because Woody refuses to go to Japan like the other figures, all of whom had been abandoned by their owners and were eager to be housed in a place of honor. Jessie then sets out to convince Woody to change his mind and join them.

The problem, Lasseter felt, was that the filmmakers had done such a good job in the first *Toy Story* of making everyone believe that Woody was devoted to Andy and the other toys, that they didn't know if they could now get viewers to think Woody would leave his gang. "In the story room, we always said that the greatest fear for a toy is anything that will keep them from being played with by the child they love," the director said. "If you were lost, you could be found. If you were broken, you could be fixed, but if you're outgrown, there's no returning, and that's the foundation of what we needed to say, but we tried again and again to communicate that with dialogue, and it just didn't work."

Lasseter turned to Newman.

"What we needed was as far as you could get from 'You've Got a Friend,' but I thought Randy could do it. I remember this lovely, emotional song that Randy wrote for *Faust*, the one Bonnie Raitt sang on the album, 'Feels Like Home,'" he said. "I remember sitting around a table in Los Angeles, telling him we needed a song this time without a happy ending. We needed to break everybody's heart."

Newman's answer was "When She Loved Me":

When somebody loved me,
Everything was beautiful
Every hour we spent together lives within my heart
And when she was sad,
I was there to dry her tears
And when she was happy,
So was I
When she loved me
Through the summer and the fall
We had each other, that was all
Just she and I together,
Like it was meant to be

And when she was lonely,
I was there to comfort her
And I knew that she loved me

So the years went by
I stayed the same
But she began to drift away
I was left alone
Still I waited for the day
When she'd say I will always love you

Lonely and forgotten,
I'd never thought she'd look my way
And she smiled at me and held me just like she used to do
Like she loved me
When she loved me

When somebody loved me
Everything was beautiful
Every hour we spent together lives within my heart

When she loved me

Montan was at his desk in Burbank when he received a tape of the song. He was moved, but he wondered if kids would respond to something so sophisticated and so sad. "It was a pretty heavy idea," he said. "Would you rather be immortal but unloved in a toy museum, or be loved in the present and eventually thrown away? That's a pretty complicated point to get across in one song." Montan realized the song worked moments later when he walked out of his office and saw that his assistant, who had been listening through the door, had tears streaming down her face.

The next decision was to decide who would sing "When She Loved Me" in the film. Because the song expressed a woman's feelings, Lasseter and Montan chose Sarah McLachlan, the award-winning Canadian singer whose *Surfacing* album had just sold eight million copies. McLachlan, who had a gentle, reassuring singing style, recorded five takes of the song in a Vancouver studio, accompanied by Newman on piano. Normally, Montan had a singer do that many or more takes of a song and would then piece together the most effective lines from the various takes into the final version. But he didn't have to change anything in McLachlan's vocal. He asked her to pick the version she preferred because he thought they were all perfect.

Decades later, Lasseter called the "When She Loved Me" experience the "single greatest moment" in his lengthy association with Montan. It is also widely hailed among Hollywood composers as Newman's premiere film song.

"In the movie, Jessie is talking to Woody about her history, and we flash back to her and her owner, and how her owner virtually throws her away," critic Jon Burlingame said. "It's heartbreaking to a large degree because of what Randy is telling us in that song. It makes the whole movie. It's immensely moving and powerful. Randy should have won an Oscar for it."

Toy Story 2 was another smash when it opened in late 1999, earning nearly $500 million at the box office and another perfect score from *Rotten Tomatoes*. Roger Ebert's review spoke of the film's emotional heart. "I forgot something about toys a long time ago and *Toy Story 2* reminded me," he wrote. "It involves the love, pity, and guilt that a child feels for a favorite toy. A doll or action figure . . . is yours the same way a pet is. It depends on you. It misses you. It can't do anything by itself. It needs you and is troubled when you're not there."

Newman picked up another Oscar nomination for the song, but he was denied again; the award went to Phil Collins for

"You'll Be in My Heart" from another animated Disney film, *Tarzan*.

As the film scores mounted, hard-core fans wondered if Randy would ever make another album. Eleven years after *Land of Dreams*, they got their answer. His dedication remained to his own albums. "If I had to quit something back then," Newman said, "I'd quit the pictures."

CHAPTER TWENTY-TWO

Bad Love *and*
Finally, an Oscar

— I —

Randy began work on his debut album for DreamWorks in 1998, a time when the music landscape had changed so fast that three generational figures had risen to the top of the charts and then died since his last CD: Kurt Cobain, Tupac Shakur, and Notorious B.I.G. At twenty-seven, Cobain was the oldest. Randy was now fifty-four, which was seventy-five in classic Pete Townshend terms. To add to the uncertainty, there was the undeniable fact that most artists his age had lost their edge.

There were exceptions. Besides Dylan's dazzling run that started with *Time Out of Mind* when he was fifty-six, Paul Simon released one of his most finely crafted albums, *So Beautiful or So What*, the year he turned seventy—and the equally commanding *Stranger to Stranger* five years later. Following a long uneven period, Neil Young, too, was back in top form at age seventy-six with *Barn*. But those examples were few.

Newman took advantage of the situation to poke fun at himself in one song by assuming the role of a burned-out musician in one of the album's songs. The opening lines to "I'm Dead (But I Don't Know It)":

I have nothing left to say
But I'm gonna say it anyway
Thirty years upon a stage
And I hear the people say
Why won't he go away?

. . . Everything I write all sounds the same
Each record that I'm making
Is like a record that I've made
Just not as good

This was a joke reminiscent of the mock confession of the *Born Again* cover, but this time everyone understood it. Randy was at another high point in his career, coming off the Pixar films and the renewed acclaim accompanying *Trouble in Paradise* and *Land of Dreams*. The new album, however, would signal a shift in Newman's themes. He had written about old folks and the passing of time, but the new material was based more consistently on aging, family, and relationships—warnings and regrets. There was even a second song with the word "dead" in the title. During the pause in writing albums, Randy's work on *Faust* and the film scores had sharpened his skills, especially musically. The new arrangements sparkled in fresh and confident ways.

"I got better doing pictures," he said. "One of the things that scared me about the movies for so long was I didn't think I could come up with music every day, which you pretty much needed to do because of the timetable. I couldn't take days off or get into writing blocks. I had to keep pushing myself, and I found myself writing things I didn't know I could do, especially harmonically. Then other things changed. Around 1994, I think my whole life opened up, I was feeling pretty good—for me. I wasn't always feeling down. My life was broadening."

When Randy had enough songs for the new album that summer, Waronker turned to a producer whose work and approach he had long admired. Mitchell Froom—a decade younger than Newman—was respected in the music world for working with tasteful artists, whatever their sales history. The list ranged from Paul McCartney and Sheryl Crow to Los Lobos and Ron Sexsmith. "I was so sad when I heard about Lenny and Mo leaving Warner Bros. because I knew the label was going to stand for something quite different," he said. "I wouldn't have been surprised at the time if Warner dropped Randy—just as they would have dropped anybody who's not young or didn't fit into what they were looking for at the moment."

The producer's respect for Newman began with "Sail Away."

I was about twenty, trying to get started in a band, and I was first struck by the feeling the song itself gave you—the emotional power of the arrangement and the understated way Randy was singing. It took a while before I understood what the song was about. It seemed at first to be about a positive experience, particularly on the chorus, but listening more closely, you began to understand that it's actually a dark-humored take on a very intense subject, sung from the narrator's perspective. I'd never heard anything quite like it before or to this day.

It's the same with the music. The piano voicings on the song had an influence on popular music for generations. Randy starts the song with a simple, repetitive figure of no more than two notes at a time with his right hand, and moves through different single notes with his left hand to imply different chords. The sound is very simple, but in this case, it gave the song great depth and originality.

Froom and Newman were introduced in Waronker's office where Randy sang several of the new songs, including "The Great Nations of Europe," a lengthy historical narrative in the style of

"Sigmund Freud's Impersonation." Even without the grandeur that the orchestration would add, the commentary made it clear that Newman was still drawn to significant subjects. "Nations" addressed European imperialism's destructive impact on countries around the world, a subject that would become an increasing part of the national sociopolitical dialogue in the 2000s. Again, this was a subject that interested Randy, leading him to a pair of books, Alfred W. Crosby's *Ecological Imperialism: The Biological Expansion of Europe, 900–1900* and Jared Diamond's *Guns, Germs and Steel.*

> *The Great Nations of Europe*
> *Had gathered on the shore*
> *They'd conquered what was behind them*
> *And now they wanted more*
> *So they looked to the mighty ocean*
> *And took to the western sea*
> *The great nations of Europe in the sixteenth century*
> *Hide your wives and daughters*
> *Hide the groceries too*
> *Great nations of Europe coming through*
>
> *The Grand Canary Islands*
> *First land to which they came*
> *They slaughtered all the canaries*
> *Which gave the land its name*
> *There were natives there called Guanches*
> *Guanches by the score*
>
> *Bullets, disease, the Portuguese, and they weren't there*
> *   anymore*
> *Now they're gone, they're gone, they're really gone*
> *You've never seen anyone so gone*
> *They're a picture in a museum*

Some lines written in a book
But you won't find a live one no matter where you look

Hide your wives and daughters
Hide the groceries too
Great nations of Europe coming through

Columbus sailed for India
Found Salvador instead
He shook hands with some Indians and soon they all were
    dead
They got TB and typhoid and athlete's foot
Diphtheria and the flu
Excuse me—Great nations coming through

Balboa found the Pacific
And on the trail one day
He met some friendly Indians
Whom he was told were gay
So he had them torn apart by dogs on religious grounds,
    they say
The great nations of Europe were quite holy in their way

Now they're gone, they're gone, they're really gone
You've never seen anyone so gone
Some bones hidden in the canyon
Some paintings in a cave
There's no use trying to save them
There's nothing left to save

Hide your wives and daughters
Hide your sons as well
With the great nations of Europe you never can tell

From where you and I are standing
At the end of a century
Europes have sprung up everywhere as even I can see
But there on the horizon as a possibility
Some bug from out of Africa might come for you and me
Destroying everything in its path
From sea to shining sea
Like the great nations of Europe
In the sixteenth century

Froom recalled their first meeting:

We talked about the songs a bit, and I remember Randy playing "The Great Nations" on a little spinet piano. But the feeling was very casual; more like we were just hanging out. Most of my questions were concerning what Randy was looking for aesthetically . . . but I did get an early glimpse of his humor. At that point, I had established a working partnership with [co-producer and engineer] Tchad Blake that involved some pretty radical recording techniques which could often alter the sound of instruments to the point of them being unfamiliar. At one point, Randy asked me, "Tchad's not going to make the orchestra sound like it's coming out of my ass, is he?"

That was very funny, but he was also sending a clear message. Randy puts a lot of stock in his arrangements. Every detail has a specific purpose and is meant to be heard. While distorting or otherwise altering the sound of an orchestra might create a cool effect, too much would be lost in the process, and he wasn't slightly interested in pursuing it.

With his film work on hold, Newman began recording the album in late October in Hollywood with musicians chosen by Froom, including drummer Pete Thomas (Elvis Costello), guitarist

Steve Donnelly (Suzanne Vega, John Wesley Harding), bassist Gregory Cohen (Woody Allen, Tom Waits), and pedal steel guitarist Gregory Leisz (Beck, Bill Frisell). The choices represented a shift from the elements—including synthesizer-driven instrumentation and other sonic techniques—that had caused some Newman admirers to complain that the eighties sound left the music cold.

Froom, who was a keyboardist before he became a producer, said:

> Rock and roll has gone through, like, ten-year cycles. There was a sixties sound, a seventies sound, and so forth. If you listen to Bob Dylan or Joni Mitchell or any of them, you hear the sound change with the decade. They're not selling out; they are simply experimenting. He didn't abandon the orchestra completely in those albums, but he definitely got involved with the sound of popular music in the seventies and eighties, perhaps leaning more on the rhythm section and often to great effect. Sometimes I wonder if Randy's extensive use of the orchestra in scoring films and his opening up of song structure in *Faust* led him naturally back to some of his earlier instincts. He had such command of the orchestra at this point.

Froom saw Randy's new orchestral arrangements as a welcome return to the approach of the debut album. "In fact, I think Randy mentioned it once, wondering what his albums would have been like if he had been interested in pursuing the direction of songs like 'Davy the Fat Boy.'" As was typical, Newman recorded the basic tracks with the band and added the orchestrations in much the way he scored a film, flourishes that underscored the sentiments in the song. "The biggest revelation to me," Froom said, "was that after he put his arrangements on the album, I often had a completely different view of what was going on."

— ‖ —

"The World Isn't Fair" was another tune that mixed grand entertainment and savage commentary. Reflecting the historical sweep of "Nations," it imagines someone telling Karl Marx what America was like in the final years of the twentieth century. Randy found a way to inject humor when he pointed out how excessive wealth and sexism collided in the trophy wife syndrome. The *New York Times*'s Stephen Holden would describe "Isn't Fair" as the "most searching song about the state of the union in the age of the millennium."

When Karl Marx was a boy
He took a hard look around
He saw people were starving all over the place
While others were painting the town (buh, buh, buh)
The public-spirited boy
Became a public-spirited man
So he worked very hard, and he read everything
Until he came up with a plan

There'll be no exploitation
Of the worker or his kin
No discrimination 'cause of the color of your skin
No more private property
It would not be allowed
No one could rise too high
No one could sink too low
Or go under completely like some we all know

If Marx were living today
He'd be rolling around in his grave

And if I had him here in my mansion on the hill
I'd tell him a story t'would give his old heart a chill
It's something that happened to me

I'd say, Karl, I recently stumbled
Into a new family
With two little children in school
Where all little children should be
I went to the orientation
All the young mommies were there
Karl, you never have seen such a glorious sight
As these beautiful women arrayed for the night
Just like countesses, empresses, movie stars, and queens
And they'd come there with men much like me
Froggish men, unpleasant to see
Were you to kiss one, Karl
Nary a prince would there be

Oh Karl, the world isn't fair
It isn't and never will be
They tried out your plan
It brought misery instead
If you'd seen how they worked it
You'd be glad you were dead
Just like I'm glad I'm living in the land of the free
Where the rich just get richer
And the poor you don't ever have to see
It would depress us, Karl
Because we care
That the world still isn't fair

The album, titled *Bad Love*, was also bolstered by some of
Newman's most personal songs, a possible offshoot of aging.

Alan Newman had long said he could see pieces of his brother in most of his songs, but it was easier than ever to see those pieces in some of the songs on the CD. As before, personal references were usually just a demarcation point, but their presence was now more likely to spread to other parts of the songs, as in the album's opening track, "My Country."

The song's initial scene came straight from nights in the Irving Newman household. After dinner, everyone would take their places in front of the television set; his mom in a chair, his father on a sofa, Randy on the floor, and Alan in a chair behind him. From there, the lyrics proceed across the years to a time when things wouldn't be so orderly and restrained.

Let's go back to yesterday
When a phone call cost a dime
In New Orleans, just a nickel
Turn back the hands of time
Turn back the hands of time

Picture a room
With a window
A sofa and some chairs
A television turned on for the night
Picture a woman, two children seated
A man lying there
Their faces softly glowing in the light

This is my country
These are my people
This is the world I understand
This is my country
These are my people
And I know 'em like the back of my own hand

If we had something to say
We'd bounce it off the screen
We were watching and we couldn't look away
We all know what we look like
You know what I mean
We wouldn't have had it any other way

We got comedy, tragedy
Everything from A to B
Watching other people living
Seeing other people play
Having other people's voices fill our minds
Thank you, Jesus

Feelings might go unexpressed
I think that's probably for the best
Dig too deep who knows what you will find

This is my country
Those were my people
Theirs was a world I understand

Picture a room, no window
A door that leads outside
A man lying on a carpet on the floor
Picture his three grown boys behind him
Bouncing words off of a screen
Of a television big as all outdoors

Now your children are your children
Even when they're grown
When they speak to you

You got to listen to what they have to say
But they all live alone now
They have TVs of their own
But they keep on coming over anyway
And much as I love them
I'm always kind of glad when they go away

This is my country
These are my people
This is the world I understand
This is my country
These are my people
And I know 'em like the back of my own hand
I know 'em like the back of my own hand

"I see it as an addiction, for me. I can't shake it," Newman told music writer Paul Freeman about television.

And I believe most of the time I've spent watching it I've wasted. But it was also not a bad way to . . . I mean, that's the way I grew up, me and my brother and my mother, my father, we would sit there and watch television. At least we were in the same room, you know? And at least we talked. It may have been about *Jackie Gleason*, but at last my father would talk about this and that. . . . It may not be the Nelson family, but it's true. It's the way I grew up . . . and I assume some others did, too. . . . When I'm watching television now, I can somehow sucker my seven-year-old or five-year-old into watching the same show that I watch. We'll all watch *The Simpsons* together. On some level, we all like it. And I get that feeling of, 'Oh, this is the way things should be.' It's like, no matter how shitty your childhood was, you try to replicate something about it. And that's what I feel. 'Oh, this was good. You know.'"

At the same session, Newman recorded "I Want Everyone to Like Me," a song with an equally vulnerable edge that would be the album's closing track. The childlike innocence feels more like the songs he wrote for films, but there's an edge of fearless confession that makes it serve as the flip side of "I Want You to Hurt Like I Do."

Among the key lines:

I want everyone to like me
I want everyone to like me real bad
I want everyone to approve of me
'Cause when they disapprove of me it makes me feel so sad

I want to earn the respect of my peers
If it takes a hundred years
I'd like to find out where they are, by the way,
For I would run to embrace them
I'm only kidding
I'm really very modest once you get to know me

A house, a little land
Maybe someone to lend a helping hand
A little money set aside
Ah, then I would be satisfied

I want someone to tell me one time
"Honey, you don't look well.
Why don't you lie down for a couple of years
I'll look after things." Yeah.
A grown-up woman would be nice
I'd like to flip her over once or twice
Find out what makes her tick

Some friends to call my own, God knows,
A family and a home
A couple kiddies at my side
To keep me fat and satisfied

I want everyone to like me
That's one thing
I know for sure
I want everyone to like me
'Cause I'm a little insecure

"Randy's incredibly complex," Waronker said. "He needs admiration, and he doesn't want it; he needs to be told, especially with his work, that it's special, and yet he pushes you away; he doesn't really push you away, but he doesn't want to be that person needing to be told. It's what makes him really interesting." Froom, too, was touched by the song: "Don't you think it's true? Most every artist I've ever worked with feels like they've been over-complimented on one hand, and on the other hand they feel like they're undervalued in some way."

In the DreamWorks press kit, Newman was as revealing as in the lyrics. "I do want everyone to like me," he said. "That's why people get into show business. There have been times in my life where I wondered whether I was saying things I really thought or felt or meant, or whether I was saying things to make people like me. I first started worrying about it when I was in the sixth grade, and I still don't know the answer."

However much he departed from his own story in the song, it speaks to something in us in a way that resonates. A characteristic of great songwriters is they dig deep to find something valuable to share—and it's demanding, which is the main reason so many writers eventually lose their creative spark. They no longer dig deep. In returning to the part of his work that he most treasured, Newman was, digging deeper inside himself, especially on "I Miss You."

The ballad is an open letter to Roswitha, a topic that can easily fall into excessive sentimentality as thousands of songs with similar themes demonstrate. But Newman's "I Miss You" succeeds because of the slow, tender way he reserves his "I love you" to the last possible moment—the final line. It is not only one of Randy's most atypical songs; it is one of his most moving. He sings it with an authenticity that even Ray Charles would have admired.

"The song is genuine," he explained in 2023. "I love my ex-wife. We were married eighteen years and I have never written a song about her in all that time."

Waronker was nervous hearing the song the first time, worried that it might be tough on Gretchen. "It's such a difficult thing and it might make people around you uncomfortable," he said, "But Randy is fearless in expressing himself."

Still in my heart
After all these years
Separated by time
And now by distance
I couldn't allow myself to feel
The loss that I feel right now
As I put this song down

You're far away
And happy I know
And it's a little bit late
Twenty years or so
And it's a little bit cold
For all those concerned

But I'd sell my soul and your souls for a song
So I'll pour my heart out

I miss you
I miss you
I miss you
I'm sorry, but I do
I miss you
I miss you
I miss you
I'm sorry, but it's true

I want to thank you for the good years
And apologize for the rough ones
You must be laughing yourself sick
Up there in Idaho
But I wanted to write you one
Before I quit
And this one's it

I miss you
I miss you
And I wanted you to know
I miss you
I miss you
I miss you
And I still love you so

Four of the album's songs fit a broad definition of the album title, *Bad Love*. "The One You Love" is a cautionary tale about the dangers of choosing the wrong partner, while "Shame" is a full-scale siren blast—a song about an old guy so obsessed by a pretty, young woman that he loses all self-respect. The unraveling in "Shame" is Newman's witty, theatrical side, a story filled with compact delights of a one-act play. In it, the narrator begins trying to tempt someone with pretty flowers and keeps at it until he's bragging about his new Lexus—all the while battling with the taunting "shame" voices he hears in his head. He's as much speaking as he is singing, and as the character's tension ebbs and flows. All of it is enhanced by an arrangement that punctuates the drama of the story through the addition and subtraction of instruments from what is otherwise a standard New Orleans jazz combo. The lyrics in part:

> *Pretty little baby*
> *How come you never come around?*
> *Pretty little baby*
> *How come you never come around?*
> *I sent you all them pretty flowers*
> *Now you're nowhere to be found*
> *I call you up at midnight sometimes, I must admit*
> *And when I find you're not at home*
> *My head heats up like a furnace*
> *My heart grows colder than a stone*
> *So what's the good of all this money I got*
> *If every night I'm left here all alone?*
> *It's a gun that I need*

"That's from the point of view of some old spider in New Orleans who throws all dignity to the wind in pursuit of some nineteen-year-old girl with nineteen-year-old skin," Newman said. "I love the idea of the power that young, beautiful people have, the power to crush and maim and destroy. People with all the money in the world, all the power in the world—and some nineteen-year-old can rip 'em up. We can be made helpless. It amuses me enormously and yet, there's a nervous, painful quality to this song."

The remaining songs in the tainted or faded love category are more delicate. "Every Time It Rains" was offered to Michael Jackson, but he passed on it. It's a straightforward expression of loss, while "I Miss You" is more about disrupted love than bad love. The album's final two songs were less essential. "Big Hat, No Cattle" was a slap at the braggadocio and conceit that Newman learned to distrust as a youngster; it was widely interpreted later as being about George W. Bush, who had gone from a high-profile term as governor of Texas to president. "Going Home," written as a World War I ballad, has the feel of an assignment song. When the album was finished, Newman openly declared that it was "the best I can do."

Critics welcomed him back, placing the CD at No. 14 on the *Voice* poll, an impressive showing in a music scene where classic rock-era songwriters had long ago given way to hip-hop and teen-pop stars. The *New York Times*'s Neil Strauss wrote, in part, "that a songwriter as dark and cynical as Mr. Newman has found success as a Disney composer is explained in brilliant bits of pop reductionism like 'The World Isn't Fair' and 'Great Nations of Europe.' Full of choruses catchy enough to be national anthems and verses dark enough to give children nightmares (as well as a few sincere moments of self-pity), *Bad Love* has the consistency and surprise of Mr. Newman's best work."

With high hopes, Newman scheduled a two-month tour of Europe early in 2000 and followed in the fall with a shorter series of concerts in the United States. Crowds were jubilant, but sales of the album were minimal. Released in June of 1999, *Bad Love* barely registered on the charts, dropping off after one week at No. 194, Newman's poorest showing in twenty-eight years. He was angry. He blamed DreamWorks for not promoting the album, an accusation that was all the more stinging because of Waronker's place in the leadership team. The atmosphere was charged. Newman decided to leave the label. But again, the Randy and Lenny friendship would survive the professional break.

— III —

Before reteaming with Lasseter and Pixar, Newman picked up another Academy Award nomination for a song in *Meet the Parents*, a contrived 2000 comedy based on the awkwardness of a young man—a Jewish male nurse—meeting his fiancée's straight-laced, WASP parents. Newman's witty "A Fool in Love" was the nomination (losing to Dylan's "Things Have Changed") and was accompanied in the film by Randy's delightful renditions of the Fats Domino hit "Poor Me" and Muddy Waters's signature number, "Got My Mojo Working."

Applauded by critics, the Universal release tallied more than $300 million, assuring a sequel four years later with an all-star cast (Ben Stiller, Robert De Niro, Barbra Streisand, and Dustin Hoffman) and music again by Newman. *Meet the Fockers* did even better at the box office, but reviewers weren't impressed, and Newman wasn't nominated. In between, he was headed back to Lasseter and Pixar.

Lasseter and his team had a firm game plan for developing Pixar scripts—base the story on universal childhood experiences—and it worked nicely in the case of *Monsters, Inc.*

"Every kid knows growing up that you've got to shut the closet door at night because there's probably monsters in there or under your bed," said Lasseter in 2021. "That's why the monsters in the film look the way they do—we wanted them to be colored and shaped like a kid's drawing of a monster. When you look at Sulley and Mike, we wanted you to go, 'Oh, they're from

Monsters, Inc.' They're not from any other movie. It's not the monsters from *Dracula* or *Frankenstein* or *Star Wars*."

Pete Docter, who co-wrote the story for the first two *Toy Story* films and *Monsters, Inc.*, directed the movie, while Lasseter, who oversaw all Pixar films, was executive producer. Newman again wrote the score and a song ("If I Didn't Have You") that was used in the credits—another expression of friendship that was sung by John Goodman and Billy Crystal, who also voiced the two lead characters.

Filled with inventive touches, the film attracted more than a half billion dollars worldwide. In the *New York Times*, Elvis Mitchell wrote, "Pixar has created a genre that others merely imitate, and while they may do a creditable job—*Shrek* from DreamWorks, for example—they don't get all the small touches right, like the thunderous and jazzy score of *Monsters*. The composer Randy Newman shows touches of Carl Stalling, whose brass construction kept Bugs Bunny and his clique moving."

The comedy received four nominations, including one in the newly established animated film category (losing to *Shrek*) and two for Newman: his fifteenth and sixteenth. Howard Shore won the score Oscar for *The Lord of the Rings: The Fellowship of the Ring*, and Newman faced big-name competition in the song category, including Paul McCartney and Sting. But the years of waiting ended at the Oscar ceremony on March 24, 2002, when Jennifer Lopez announced, "And the award goes to . . . Randy Newman."

As Newman, in dark suit and silver tie, ambled anxiously to the stage, a voice offstage informed the audience of the backstory: "Randy Newman has sixteen Academy Award nominations and now, the Oscar."

At the microphone, he responded with a spontaneous line that would brighten any Oscar night highlight reel: "I don't want your pity."

After the laughter, he continued, "I want to thank first of all the music branch to give me so many chances to be humiliated over the years."

And he kept at it.

When the orchestra started playing the soft exit music, Newman looked into the pit and humorously chided them for doing it so soon.

Then, he got serious—or as serious as he could be in such circumstances.

"I'm very grateful. I want to thank John Lasseter, Pete Docter, all these musicians, many of whom have worked with me a number of times . . . and may not again. Thanks very much, I'm thrilled."

Ten nights later, Randy was in New York having dinner with the head of his new record label.

PART FIVE

We don't know what to do with humorists who sing. Do they mean it? If they sing with some measure of ache, is the pain a put-on? Randy Newman operates in the gap between memoir and mockery. For half a century, he's kept this country in his crosshairs, and himself, by extension, his southern whiteness and, discreetly, his Jewish whiteness. Newman was the first white musician I'd ever heard be funny about being whiteness, who understood it as a kind of paradoxical condition. He works in a kind of Tin Pan Alley style of Americana that stretches right into blackface minstrelsy, instead of kaleidoscopically transmogrifying all that history the way the boys in Steely Dan did. Harnessing the past for the present—with a wink, with a shiv—is part of the Newman thrill.

Bad Love is where I first found him. It came out 1999, in his mid-fifties. It's more of a rock record—a nineties rock record—than anything he'd already done. But the characteristic melancholies persist. The performance is that he's old here (although has Newman ever seemed young?). But the delight is that his sense of satire (of America and himself) has achieved this deepened wisdom. It's got him at his most mordantly funny ("Shame") and his most ardently sad. Which is to say: at some new withering peak.

WESLEY MORRIS, a two-time Pulitzer winner for criticism
(*Boston Globe* and the *New York Times*)

I was living at the beach in Santa Monica when Randy's first album came out in 1968, and the songs were so moving that they made me cry.

To best appreciate his music, it's important to listen to the whole albums, not just one cut. They set a mood and tell a story. He's like a short-story writer who talks about various aspects of life—and his melodies reinforce and color what he's saying, whether it's the warmth of "Feels Like Home" or the tragedy of "Sandman's Coming."

Through the years, his music has remained at such a high level. When I listen to songs like "Lost Without You," about dementia, and "Wandering Boy," about a troubled, lost child, from his recent *Dark Matter* album, he still makes me cry.

LINDA RONSTADT

CHAPTER TWENTY-THREE

Nonesuch Records
Rock & Roll Hall of Fame, Part One
Katrina

— I —

Robert Hurwitz, president of the boutique Nonesuch Records, had Randy Newman high on his signing wish list as the new century neared. Since 1984, Hurwitz had put together a roster of outstanding artists from various genres, jazz to world music and pop. Among them were Laurie Anderson, Philip Glass, Steve Reich, Bill Frisell, Caetano Veloso, Emmylou Harris, and the Buena Vista Social Club (produced by Ry Cooder). The *Boston Globe*'s Ed Siegel declared, "When one picks up a Nonesuch CD, there is a sense of occasion, the feeling that the artists in question have been assembled not as an exercise in star power, but as an exercise in artistic exploration."

The Nonesuch executive viewed Randy in the top tier of American songwriters ever. "If he had been born forty years earlier," Hurwitz said, "Randy might have worked at MGM instead of Pixar and probably would have written Broadway shows instead of albums. Who else could have delivered an album like *Sail Away* and the score for a movie like *Avalon*?" Hurwitz, however, was guarded in his hopes of landing Newman. Despite the problems at DreamWorks, he couldn't imagine Randy leaving Mo and Lenny.

That changed in April of 2000 when Randy's agent Michael Gorfaine met with Hurwitz at Nonesuch's headquarters in New York. "Within the first minute, Mike says, 'Would you like to sign Randy Newman?' and I said, 'I'll sign him on the spot.'"

Months went by before Hurwitz heard more, leading him to suspect that Newman had decided to stay with DreamWorks after all. Randy did soon patch up his relationship with Lenny, but he still wanted a new label. Cathy Kerr phoned Hurwitz in November to say that Randy would like to talk to him in Seattle where he was playing a concert. Hurwitz caught a plane the next day and met with Newman and Kerr at the W hotel before the show. Within twenty minutes, he knew that his wish had come true. The contract was finalized in two weeks.

Another wait followed. Newman wasn't ready to make a new album; he wanted to work on more movies. Over the next several months, Hurwitz checked in regularly, hoping for good news. The pair had engaging conversations, talking casually about a wide range of interests, from politics to classical music, Stephen Sondheim to Beethoven, John Adams to Richard Goode. But Randy simply wasn't ready.

The breakthrough came when Newman went to New York in March of 2002 to perform several of his songs—just him and the piano—for a Bravo cable channel series, *Musicians*. Watching the taping, Hurwitz flashed on his love of pop "songbooks"—albums that saluted the works of the top songwriters of the past, such as Berlin, Porter, and the Gershwins. "I began to picture Randy doing an album like that, his songs alone at the piano just as he was on that stage," he said. "There are some times when you want to hear his brilliant arrangements on record, but there was so much power hearing just him and piano. It made you focus even more on the words."

When Hurwitz mentioned the idea at dinner, Newman's response was predictable; he didn't like it. "As strange as it sounds, Randy sometimes sees himself as a failure," Hurwitz said. "He told me that he wasn't that important." But Hurwitz pressed the point, telling Newman that he, more than anyone else of his generation, was the bridge between the great writers of the first half of the century and those of the second half. Finally, Newman said, he'd think about it."

Three days later, he agreed.

~

In June of 2002, while Hurwitz was waiting for the green light on the album, Newman was inducted into the Songwriters' Hall of Fame—along with Sting, Michael Jackson, Barry Manilow, and the team of Ashford & Simpson. Founded in 1969 by Johnny Mercer, among others, the organization pledged to salute writers from every genre and era, and it wisely reached back to include such landmark figures as Stephen Foster, Woody Guthrie, W. C. Handy, and Jimmie Rodgers as well as honoring rock-era writers, including Bob Dylan, Lennon and McCartney, Paul Simon, Stevie Wonder, and King-Goffin. Next in line for Newman was the Rock & Roll Hall of Fame.

Randy knew that most awards were unreliable barometers, but it was still nice to be honored. He had been eligible for the Rock & Roll Hall of Fame since 1987—under Hall rules, artists can't be nominated until twenty-five years after the release of their first record, which for him was "Golden Gridiron Boy"—but he wasn't nominated until 2004, because many of the voters didn't consider him part of rock's central core. By the 2000s, however, the Hall had expanded its definition of inductees to include top artists from various pop-related fields, opening a door for the likes of ABBA, Madonna, Bob Marley, and Leonard Cohen. But Randy was up against strong competition, including Prince, Jackson Browne, George Harrison, and Bob Seger. Newman was disappointed but not surprised when he didn't make the

360 | A FEW WORDS IN DEFENSE OF OUR COUNTRY

final cut. It would be a decade before his name appeared on the ballot again.

Future Rock Legends, a website started by Neil Walls in 2006, reports in detail on the Rock Hall voting process but is not affiliated with the organization and is often critical of it. One website feature is reader comments about individual artists, and the Newman section had a spirited series of pro and con emails.

Among the positive fan remarks:

"This man is a bona-fide legend, one-of-a-kind, and
    unanimously considered one of the greatest songwriters
    of his generation." (2007)
"Does he deserve to get in? Absolutely. Will he get in? Not
    so sure. He's influential, but he's just a little too
    unknown. The majority of his fans probably started
    listening to him after hearing him sing 'You've Got a
    Friend in Me' from *Toy Story*; hell, that's how I know
    him!" (2012)
"The Rock & Roll Hall of Fame inductees who will vote for
    Randy Newman: Bob Dylan, Elton John, Rod Stewart,
    Neil Young, Crosby, Stills and Nash, Joni Mitchell, the
    Eagles, Fleetwood Mac, Billy Joel, Bruce Springsteen,
    Bonnie Raitt, James Taylor, Paul Simon, Elvis Costello,
    Jackson Browne, John Mellencamp, Leonard Cohen, Neil
    Diamond, Dr. John, Leon Russell, Alice Cooper,
    Donovan." (2012)
"Wouldn't it be wonderful." (2012)

But then:

"If you read some of his interviews, you'll know he comes
    across as difficult and sarcastic. I imagine a lot of people
    at the Rock Hall of Fame just don't like him." (2011)

"Nobody thinks some 4-foot-tall LA jew (SIC) plinking
   away on a piano while s---talking white(s) and the South
   is rock. The Hall shames itself by forcing the issue."
   (2012)

— II —

Mitchell Froom was as wary of the songbook concept as Newman had been, but he wanted to keep working with Randy, so he
agreed to produce the album in January of 2003. With input
from Froom, Hurwitz, and Kerr, Newman put together a list of
songs and drew from it as the sessions proceeded.

In *The Randy Newman Songbook Vol. 1*, the sixteen songs
offer sidelights into Newman's approach. The opening "Lonely at
the Top" makes it clear that he has rethought some of the tunes;
his version is not a casual exercise. He begins "Lonely" with some
stark, deliberate piano notes and then shifts to a playful passage
that introduces one of his greatest jokes, the send-up of show-biz
egotism; only this time less Sinatra-ish and more cartoonish.

The song, from Newman's third album, also tells us that he
isn't going to revisit his songs chronologically in what promised
to be a series of songbook collections, hence the *Vol. 1*. Over the
course of the album (which also has traces of film music including an instrumental reprise of "When She Loved Me"), Newman
takes us back to the mid-sixties for "I Think It's Going to Rain
Today" and far enough forward to include three of his historical
narratives, including "The Great Nations of Europe" and "The
World Isn't Fair." He still uses the N-word in "Rednecks" but, as
the father of a daughter, he tones down the jailbait imagery of
"It's Money That I Love," replacing the closing words, "They say
that money / Can't buy love in this world / But it'll get you a half-
pound of cocaine / And a sixteen-year-old girl" with "a nineteen-
year-old girl."

Some tracks in the series—especially "Sail Away" and "Louisiana 1927"—suffer from the missing orchestration, but the intimate approach puts greater attention on the words, which makes "You Can Leave Your Hat On" all the creepier and "Marie" more aching.

The CD didn't generate enough press attention or radio airplay to spark much curiosity when released in September. If *Bad Love*, an excellent new collection of new songs, could only make it to No. 194 on the national charts, an album redoing old songs stood little chance. Still, Hurwitz was pleased, and proceeded with plans for two additional volumes. They, too, were filled with fresh interpretations and daring juxtapositions—in particular "Dixie Flyer"/"Yellow Man" and "Sandman's Coming"/"My Life Is Good," in *Vol. 2* (2011) and "Old Man"/"Real Emotional Girl" in Vol. 3 (2016).

Even after three volumes, there was so much A-level material left that a possible fourth volume—which could have included such songs as "Roll with the Punches," "So Long Dad," "Christmas in Cape Town," and "Half a Man"—would have been justified.

~

In his film world, Newman looked forward to writing the score for *Seabiscuit*; he was reunited with *Pleasantville* director Gary Ross, and it was another sports movie, the story of one of the most revered racehorses ever. Seabiscuit, whose grandsire was the legendary Man o'War, was a smallish horse who lost his first seventeen races in the mid-1930s, causing him to be sold for $8,000. Slowly, however, he caught fire with his new owner and trainer, winning races against some of the leading competition in the country, most notably winning a match race in 1938 against the larger and more heralded War Admiral.

This rags-to-riches tale made Seabiscuit a symbol of hope during the dark economic depression—a time when horse racing rivaled baseball as the nation's most popular pro sport. The story was still so appealing a half century later that Laura Hillenbrand's 1999 book, *Seabiscuit: An American Legend,* sold more than 2.5 million copies, and that led to a race in Hollywood for the film rights. Ross's film was also warmly received, earning some $150 million and six Oscar nominations, including for best picture (losing to *The Lord of the Rings: The Return of the King*), but nothing for the music. Behind the scenes, Newman and Ross clashed so strongly that Randy walked away during the production's final stages.

"This was the biggest distance I'd ever been from a director in terms of how the music should be used," he said. "He wanted to go really slow to allow David McCullough's narration to sanctify the whole thing, and I didn't want to do that. There was this one scene—one of the races—and Gary asked why I made the music so tense; he wanted something big and beautiful. I said races are tense and we want Seabiscuit to win. Gary said something like, 'forget the race,' he wanted the story to be about the Depression, which he was entitled to do, of course, but I just disagreed."

— III —

Eager to find out when Newman was going to finally make his first album of new songs for the label, Hurwitz flew to Los Angeles in February of 2005, but he was again discouraged when Randy spoke mostly about his film work at dinner. Afterward, Hurwitz, who had once considered a career in journalism, wrote this entry in his daily journal: "We've been talking for six years since we first met in Seattle, and maybe he'll never make a record of new songs; all he wants to do is score movies. Outside of his *Songbook* album (which is wonderful of course), he has not done anything new."

But the conversation, as usual, was so pleasing that Hurwitz added, "But why am I carping? It is a great evening, the food is fantastic, and we talk a ton about the music we both love: Stravinsky, Beethoven, Bach, Mozart, Ravel."

Everything changed the next day when he went to Newman's house. He wrote in his journal:

> Randy has a room off the side of his house where he does all of his composing. "Scattered about are all of the big bound scores of the films he's made in Hollywood; this is the man's main job, and I can see how much it means to him. I don't know what to expect after last night, but after a while, he sits down and plays a half dozen brand-new songs for me—singing in good voice, playing well. They are all terrific, and all I can do is encourage him to finally start his new record. I can't imagine he's playing them for me in order to get my approval, but he seems surprised and grateful for my tremendous enthusiasm.
>
> I try out his Steinway D—it's a wonderful piano with a warm sound and well-worn keys. We had talked about the Mozart F Major Sonata, and in the middle of the second movement, where it sounds modern (and quite chromatic), Randy says, "Mozart must have written that for himself."

Hurwitz returned to New York to await word on the next album.

— IV —

Newman's ties to New Orleans and its music were so strong that he tended to refer to the region with the same deprecating humor that he aimed at himself. "There's a carefree quality to it, a careless quality to it," he told NPR. "I mean, New Orleans is not a place to get your car fixed, you know? It's famous for being

CHAPTER TWENTY-THREE | 365

inefficient and lovable because of it. . . . It's not like other places in the country."

This interest in the city led Newman to pick up early on news reports in late August of 2005 that a major hurricane had formed in the Bahamas and was headed toward the United States, expected to hit Florida and then move across the Gulf of Mexico to the always vulnerable Louisiana city.

Fears were realized as Katrina raged across the Gulf of Mexico, reaching Louisiana on August 29. Floodwaters of twenty feet were reported in New Orleans, causing the evacuation of an estimated one million people from the city and surrounding areas. In addition, an estimated 25,000 people headed to the Superdome for shelter and food, and thousands more sought safety in attics and on rooftops. Among the hardest hit were residents in the mostly Black Lower Ninth Ward, including Fats Domino, who was presumed dead for two days before he was airlifted by Coast Guard helicopter from the third floor of his home.

Katrina's toll was over 1,800 deaths, mostly in Louisiana, and more than $80 billion in property damage, the third largest hurricane ever to hit the nation to that point. Writing in 64 Parishes, a magazine devoted to Louisiana's complex history and funded by the Louisiana Endowment for the Humanities, columnist Jim Bradshaw drew a link between the 1927 flood and Katrina: "Both caused disruptions of life in southern Louisiana for thousands of people that arguably could be outranked only by the destruction caused during the Civil War."

The disaster dominated the national news, with sadness and fear turning to outrage that mirrored the resentment and accusations surrounding Louisiana's 1927 flood, including lack of federal response, an inadequate levee system, and poor local preparedness. Substitute President George W. Bush for Calvin Coolidge in Newman's "Mr. President" and you're up to date. What was particularly damaging in Bush's case was that he remained at his vacation ranch in Texas; the closest he came to Katrina was when he later flew over New Orleans on Air Force One as he headed back to the White House.

A flashpoint for anger came on September 2 during a national fundraising telethon when rapper Kanye West declared, "George Bush doesn't care about Black people." The bitterness in the Black community was compounded when NBC deleted West's remarks about the president from the show's West Coast feed. Looking back on the disaster a decade later, then-President Barack Obama sided with West. "What started out as a natural disaster became a man-made disaster—a failure of government to look out for its own citizens."

In the aftermath, "Louisiana 1927" was embraced so strongly that it became known in some quarters as the state's unofficial anthem, a statement of solidarity, protest, and hope. That fall, Newman joined various New Orleans artists, including Dr. John, Allen Toussaint, Irma Thomas, and the Preservation Hall Jazz Band in contributing tracks to an album, *Our New Orleans,* to raise money to help hurricane victims. Newman's offering was an orchestral version of "Louisiana 1927."

The state's bond with the song became even stronger over time as numerous Louisiana artists recorded "Louisiana 1927" or played it live. Among them was blues singer Marcia Ball, who told the *New York Times*'s Geoffrey Himes, in a report on the song's emotional hold on the state, "There just wasn't a dry eye in the house when I did that song. (It has) one of those simple, irresistible Randy Newman melodies and lyrics that were so real. In truth, so many people did get washed away."

Aaron Neville, the Grammy-winning singer whose high, heavenly, vibrato-style voice makes him one of the most distinctive stylists in pop, is the New Orleans–based singer most identified with the song. He was singing "Louisiana 1927" long before Katrina, but watching television coverage of the disaster—even seeing people he knew on rooftops—gave him an even deeper feeling for it. "When I used to sing the song, it was about something that happened a long time ago," he told Himes. "Now, it's about something that happened to me and my family."

Newman had sung "Louisiana 1927" in his 1994 and 2005 performances at the Jazz and Heritage Festival, and it was memorable both times, especially the first time when the overcast skies added to the drama. Cathy Kerr said:

> This is a hometown crowd for him; they are enthusiastic and hang on to every word and note. The first time he played in 1994, we had no idea what to expect. I looked out from the stage and couldn't see where the people ended. It was a massive crowd. I don't recall the exact setlist, but Randy often will play "I Think It's Going to Rain Today" near the end, and this being New Orleans, I'm guessing "Louisiana 1927" as well.
>
> The weather decided something else, and he couldn't ignore it. About halfway through the set, dark clouds were rolling in and it was going to rain. He started to play "I Think It's Going to Rain Today" just as a solid downpour began. Umbrellas went up and no one moved. And then he played "Louisiana 1927"—it was absolutely perfect. People were swaying together and singing at the top of their lungs.

Both of those performances were before Katrina. When he returned to the annual spring festival in 2008, "Louisiana 1927" would take on even greater import.

Before then, however, Randy joined Lasseter again on *Cars*, the sentimental story of a brash young speedway racer who rethinks his values after finding himself stuck in one of the many once-booming towns along historic Route 66 whose life had been sucked from it when travelers switched to the new, streamlined I-40. Critics were divided; still, the film took in nearly half a billion dollars worldwide. (*Cars 2* in 2011 would fare even worse with critics; Lasseter again directed, but Newman wasn't involved.)

In the end, Lasseter delivered on a promise to Newman about *Cars*. "We really aimed high because we were going to tie into the longstanding connection between music and automobiles, music and the open road," the director said. "It had gone back for decades, and I remember that someone had told me Randy had never been awarded a platinum album for one million sales, so I went to him and promised I was going to get him one with the soundtrack."

To reflect the wide radio listening experience, Lasseter and Montan wanted great driving songs from various genres and eras, some vintage tracks (including Chuck Berry's "Route 66" and Hank Williams's "My Heart Would Know") and some new recordings (Rascal Flatts' "Life Is a Highway" and Brad Paisley's "Behind the Clouds"). Besides the score for the 2006 film, Randy wrote another tender assignment song, "Our Town," which was sung in the film by James Taylor and won a Grammy for best song written for a motion picture. It also brought Newman another Oscar nomination (his seventeenth) although the award went to Melissa Ethridge's "I Need to Wake Up" from the documentary *An Inconvenient Truth*.

But Lasseter delivered on his promise: the soundtrack was the first Pixar soundtrack to top the one million sales mark. Randy had his first platinum album.

CHAPTER TWENTY-FOUR

"A Few Words in Defense of Our Country"
President George W. Bush and
The New York Times *editorial pages*

— I —

Randy had a let's-get-down-to-business air when he walked onstage at Carnegie Hall on the night of October 13, 2006, Nate Chinen noted in his review in the *New York Times*. Wearing a dark pinstripe suit, he was "sharklike and unsmiling." The setlist, too, suggested a serious tone; it included some of his sharpest slices of social commentary, including "My Life Is Good" and "The World Isn't Fair." The highlight was a provocative new song, initially titled "A Few Words on Behalf of Our Country," which Randy had been trying out in Europe. Renamed "A Few Words in Defense of Our Country," it was an assault on the George W. Bush administration, fueled by the handling of Katrina and hawkish steps in the Middle East. At the concert, the lyrics began as a teasing defense of sorts:

I'd like to say
A few words
In defense of our country
Whose people aren't bad

Nor are they mean
Now, the leaders we have
While they're the worst that we've had
Are hardly the worst
This poor world has seen

After reminders of the evils of Caesar, Hitler, and other his-torical villains, Newman addressed what he felt were disgraceful aspects of Bush's actions and offered a raw verse about some "tight-ass" US Supreme Court members.

Robert Hurwitz was in the audience, and he couldn't have been happier. At sixty-two, Randy was still attacking injustice. This song was something Hurwitz thought everyone should hear. As it turned out, an editor at the *Times* had the same idea. Days before Bush's State of the Union address the following January, the paper reached out to Newman and asked permission to use the lyrics to "A Few Words" on its editorial page under the headline "State of the Nation: An Alternative." At least, use most of the lyrics.

"After attending Randy's show at Carnegie Hall and hearing 'A Few Words in Defense of Our Country,' the editor suggested that the song lyrics would be a brilliant Op-Ed piece on their own," Cathy Kerr said. "Randy thought so, too. It turned out that the *Times* edited some of the lyrics. It was disappointing, but we weighed our options and decided to agree to the edits, includ-ing the 'tight-ass' line. To make the full song available, Newman recorded a version with just Randy and the piano, and Nonesuch sent it to iTunes.

The *Times*'s version:

I'd like to say a few words
In defense of our country
Whose people aren't bad nor are they mean
Now the leaders we have

While they're the worst that we've had
Are hardly the worst this poor world has seen
Let's turn history's pages, shall we?
Take the Caesars for example
Why, with the first few of them
They had split Gaul into three parts
Fed the Christians to the lions
And burned down the city
And one of 'em
Appointed his own horse Consul of the Empire
That's like vice president or something
That's not a very good example right now, is it?
But wait, here's one, the Spanish Inquisition
They put people in a terrible position
I don't even like to think about it
Well, sometimes I like to think about it
Just a few words in defense of our country
Whose time at the top
Could be coming to an end
Now we don't want their love
And respect at this point's pretty much out of the question
But in times like these
We sure could use a friend
Hitler. Stalin.
Men who need no introduction
King Leopold of Belgium. That's right.
Everyone thinks he's so great
Well he owned the Congo
He tore it up too
He took the diamonds, he took the gold
He took the silver
Know what he left them with?
Malaria

A president once said,
"The only thing we have to fear is fear itself"
Now it seems like we're supposed to be afraid
It's patriotic in fact and color-coded
And what are we supposed to be afraid of?
Why, of being afraid
That's what terror means, doesn't it?
That's what it used to mean
The end of an empire is messy at best
And this empire is ending
Like all the rest
Like the Spanish Armada adrift on the sea
We're adrift in the land of the brave
And the home of the free
Goodbye. Goodbye. Goodbye.

~

The album featuring "A Few Words" was a year away, but the song caused more media attention for Newman than anything since "Short People." About its fury, Newman told the *Winnipeg Free Press*, "I don't like to write songs about what's happening now. Almost by definition, they become obsolete when what's happening now is over. But this administration is so bad, and they are so clumsy, you find out what they did. You have to notice." In an interview with the *Houston Press*, he went even further: "Nixon broke all the political rules, God knows everyone used to . . . Hoover and the CIA, everybody. But with these guys, it's like they don't even know the rules."

In 2017, Newman spoke about the lingering impact of "Defense" to *Rolling Stone*. "I wrote it because I thought the [second] Bush administration would be one of the worst of my lifetime, maybe the worst we'd ever have. Little did I know [Donald Trump] would make him look like Winston Churchill. The comparisons in the song are ridiculous, saying Bush is not as bad as the Caesars. He's not as bad as [the Roman emperor] Tiberius, because he didn't kill little boys. He's not Hitler or Stalin. But I do that song now, and it gets a bigger reaction. Who could have prepared for this?"

Excluding *Faust*, Newman had released only one studio album in more than a decade, leading many fans to think he had turned himself over to films. On the heels of *Bad Love*, however, this new song caused Newman followers to believe that something might be happening. Expectations for an album were heightened further when word got out in the fall of 2007 that Waronker was returning to the studio to co-produce the CD with Froom. "This was going to be our first album for Nonesuch, and Bob Hurwitz, who has ultimate respect for Lenny, asked what I thought about bringing him back into the studio," Froom said. "Randy and I both loved the idea."

Waronker was so impressed as the songs kept coming that he asked himself a question: Was he overreacting because he was excited to be back in the studio with Randy, or was it just possible that the new songs rivaled Randy's best ever? He and Froom guarded against getting caught up with the idea that Newman was on another spectacular roll.

"You never go into a record thinking this is going to be historic or you're going to blow it," Froom said. "You just try to do your best every day without thinking about some big picture. That's your whole attention. That's why the nicest time is probably at the end, when you can listen to the finished album. That's when you can go, 'Wow, this is really something.'"

They didn't have to wait long. The only other project in Newman's schedule was *Leatherheads*, a witless comedy about the early days of pro football. The recording sessions for what was eventually titled *Harps and Angels* began in October. By January, the celebration could begin.

CHAPTER TWENTY-FIVE

Harps and Angels
*A Song for President Obama and
Rock & Roll Hall of Fame, Part Two*

— I —

Despite the nine years in between them, *Bad Love* and Newman's new album, *Harps and Angels,* felt like companion pieces, with songs of aging, vulnerability, and loss accompanied by the ever-present social observation. Waronker and Froom employed the same four musicians to cut the basic tracks before assembling seventy or so orchestra members on the Twentieth Century–Fox soundstage named for Alfred Newman.

Though one of the last songs written, the title track, with its mortality underpinnings, served as the emotional center. In "Harps," Newman assumes the role of an old man (apparently once again in New Orleans) to reflect on how spiritual values are rooted so deeply in America that even those who have moved toward a more secular stance reach back in times of crisis for comforting faith. Newman often joked about how he is an atheist until he gets desperately sick.

The story begins when the narrator suddenly feels deathly ill and falls to the ground where he immediately says a prayer. He soon hears the sound of harps and angels welcoming him to

Heaven—only to have a voice from above tell him to relax: the harps and angels were a clerical error. The narrator didn't die, but the heavenly figure warns that he had better get his act together because someday he's going to want those harps and angels to take him on his final journey.

Hasn't anybody seen me lately
I'll tell you why
Hasn't anybody seen me lately
I'll tell you why
I caught something made me so sick
That I thought that I would die
And I almost did too
First my knees begin to tremble
My heart begin to pound
First my knees begin to tremble
My heart begin to pound
It was arrhythmic and out of tune
I lost my equilibrium
And fell face down upon the ground
As I lay there on that cold pavement
A tear ran down my face
'Cause I thought I was dying
You boys know I'm not a religious man
But I sent a prayer out just in case
You never know
Lo and behold, almost immediately
I had reason to believe my prayer had been heard in a very
    special place
'Cause I heard this sound
Ooooh
Yes
Ooooh

Yes, it was harps and angels
Harps and angels coming near
I was too sick to roll over and see them
But I could hear them singing ever so beautifully in my ear
Then the sound began to subside
And they sounded like background singers
And a voice come down from the heavens above
It was a voice full of anger from the Old Testament
And a voice full of love from the New one
And the street lit up like it was the middle of the day
And I lay there quiet and listened to what that voice had
*   to say*
He said, "You ain't been a good man
You ain't been a bad man
But you've been pretty bad
Lucky for you this ain't your time
Someone very dear to me has made another clerical error
And we're here on a bit of a wild goose chase
But I want to tell you a few things
That'll hold you in good stead when it is your time
So you better listen close
I'm only going to say this once
When they lay you on the table
Better keep your business clean
'Fore they lay you on the table
Better keep your business clean
Don't want no backstabbing, ass grabbing
You know exactly what I mean
Alright girls—we're outta here"
Ooooh
"Encore. Encore."
Ooooh
(He spoke French)

"Très bien
Encore"
And off they went into the night
Almost immediately I felt better
And I come round to see you boys
'Cause you know we ain't living right
And while it was fresh
I wanted to tell you what he told me
He said, "When they lay you on the table
Better keep your business clean
When they lay you on the table
Better keep your business clean
Else there won't be no harps and angels coming for you
It'll be trombones, kettle drums, pitchforks, and tambourines"
Sing it like they did for me one time
Ooooh—yes
Ooooh—beautiful
Wish I spoke French
So actually the main thing about this story is for me
There really is an afterlife
And I hope to see all of you there
Let's go get a drink

"Harps and Angels" was followed by "Losing You," which touches on personal anguish. It is one of Newman's most straightforward tunes, but also one of his most poignant. He got the idea from his doctor-brother Alan, who told him about a young patient who developed a terminal cancer of the chest lining. The boy's parents were Holocaust survivors who found over the decades that time had enabled them to block out some of the horrors of that time in their lives, but they knew that they wouldn't have time at their advanced age for the pain of their son's death to recede. Alan never forgot what the patient's mother told him:

"I watched my entire family shot and fall into a mass grave and I got over it—I will never get over this."

When he relayed the story, Randy wrote "Losing You," which Froom calls one of his favorites from the Nonesuch albums, citing the mix of stylish orchestral touches, the near blues feeling of the words, and the understated singing.

Was a fool with my money
And I lost every dime
And the sun stopped shining
And it rained all the time
It did set me back some
But I made it through
But I'll never get over losing you
Do you know how much you mean to me?
Should've told you 'cause it's true
I'd get over losing anything
But I'll never get over losing you

When you're young
And there's time
To forget the past
You don't think that you will
But you do
But I know that I don't have time enough
And I'll never get over losing you

I've been cold
I've been hungry
But not for awhile
I guess most of my dreams have come true
With it all here around me
No peace do I find

'Cause I'll never get over losing you
No, I'll never get over losing you

Two songs later, the official version of "A Few Words in Defense of Our Country" restored the words deleted by the *Times*.

I'd like to say a few words
In defense of our country
Whose people aren't bad
Nor are they mean
Now the leaders we have
While they're the worst that we've had
Are hardly the worst
This poor world has seen
Take the Caesars for example
Within the first few of them
They were sleeping with their sister,
Stashing little boys in swimming pools
And burning down the city
And one of 'em, one of 'em
Appointed his own horse to be Consul of the Empire
That's like vice president or something
Wait a minute, that's not a very good example, is it?
But wait, here's one,
The Spanish Inquisition
It put people in a terrible position
I don't even like to think about it
Well, sometimes I like to think about it

Just a few words in defense of our country
Whose time at the top
Could be coming to an end
We don't want your love

And respect at this point is pretty much out of the question
But times like these
We sure could use a friend

Hitler
Stalin
Men who need no introduction
King Leopold of Belgium, that's right
Everyone thinks he's so great
Well, he owned The Congo, and he tore it up too
He took the diamonds
He took the silver
He took the gold
You know what he left them with?
Malaria
A President once said,
"The only thing we have to fear is fear itself"
Now, we're supposed to be afraid
It's patriotic in fact and color-coded
And what are we supposed to be afraid of?
Why, of being afraid
That's what terror means, doesn't it?
That's what it used to mean

You know, it kind of pisses me off
That this Supreme Court is going to outlive me
A couple of young Italian fellas and a brother on the Court
    now, too
But I defy you, anywhere in the world,
To find me two Italians as tight-assed as the two Italians
    we got
And as for the brother, well
Pluto's not a planet anymore either

The end of an empire is messy at best
And this empire is ending
Like all the rest
Like the Spanish Armada adrift on the sea
We're adrift in the land of the brave and the home of the free

Goodbye
Goodbye
Goodbye

The "tight-ass" reference wasn't in the song when Newman began trying it out in Europe, but the audience laughed so hard when he used it one night that it became a permanent—and crucial—part of the song; the audacity of the line conveyed the depth of Newman's anger.

"Potholes" was a mix of lingering wounds and welcome discovery, pointing out that a memory loss can have its advantages. Once again with Newman, it's nothing you'd expect from pop music, not a song that would make you want to sing along. It's the story of his Little League experience of leaving the mound in tears after walking fourteen straight batters—an incident Randy wishes his father's memory would erase. Just as Irving told Roswitha the story, he told Gretchen the story the first time they met and then, awkwardly enough, the second time Randy introduced her.

I love women
Have all my life
I love my dear mother
And I love my wife—God bless her
I even love my teenage daughter
There's no accounting for it
Apparently I don't care how I'm treated
My love is unconditional or something

I've been hurt a time or two
I ain't gonna lie
I have my doubts sometimes
About the ethics of the so-called fairer sex
Fair about what?
But I find time goes by
And one forgives as one forgets
And one does forget
God bless the potholes
Down on memory lane
God bless the potholes
Down on memory lane
Everything that happens to me now
Is consigned to oblivion by my brain

I remember my father
My brother of course
I remember my mother
I spoke of her earlier and I remember that
I remember the smell of cut grass
And going off to play ball in the morning
Funny story about that
Now I used to pitch
I could get the ball over the plate
But anyway, this one time
I must've thrown a football around or something the day
  before
I walked about fourteen kids in a row
Cried
Walked off the mound
Handed the ball to the third baseman
And just left the field

Anyway, many years later
I brought the woman who was to become my second wife
  (God bless her)
To meet my father for the first time
They exchanged pleasantries
I left the room for a moment
It was the first time he had met her, you understand
When I came back
He was telling her the story
Right off the bat
About how I had walked fourteen kids
Cried and left the mound
Next time he met her he told her the same goddamn story!

God bless the potholes
Down on memory lane
God bless the potholes
Down on memory lane
I hope some real big ones open up
And take some of the memories that do remain

Elsewhere, Newman turned to commentary with one of seven songs he wrote for Warner Bros.' *Cats Don't Dance* film, a 1997 animated musical comedy that was a thinly veiled allegory about discrimination against Blacks in the movie industry. The story centered on a cat's dreams of an acting career—and Newman's "Laugh and Be Happy" was designed as a pep talk when the anxious cat was worried about ever getting past the studio's imposing front gate guard. The song wasn't used in the film because of the word "bastards" in the lyrics, and Newman redesigned it subtly to address immigrants coming into the United States. It was a winning salute to underdog/underclass aspiration; a mix between the charm of most of his Pixar songs and his social commentaries. The key lines:

> *That's right!*
> *It's never been about keeping you out*
> *It's about inviting you in and letting you play . . .*

> *You've got to laugh and be happy*
> *Smile right in their face*
> *'Cause pretty soon*
> *You're gonna take their place*

After two songs about economic divisions in the country ("A Piece of the Pie," which raises the blunt question "Living in the richest country in the world, wouldn't you think you'd have a better life?", and "Easy Street"), Newman wrote in "Korean Parents" about what was an obsession in many upscale neighborhoods near the end of the twentieth century—the idea of Asian parents pushing their children to achieve in school so effectively that they outperformed other pupils in the process. Randy then revisited the subject of a wealthy old man's eye for beautiful young women ("Only a Girl"). The album ended with "Feels Like Home," the ballad from *Faust*. It was a rich, inspired collection, with not a false step in it.

～

When recording wrapped up in January of 2008, Waronker and Froom could finally express their excitement. Newman tended to agree with their assessment, repeating the same phrase he stated after *Bad Love*—"the best I can do." In his journal, Hurwitz wrote, "Randy is now sixty-five, and I am hard-pressed to think of a modern songwriter at that age who has the craft and artistry to create a series of songs as deeply moving as the ones on this album. Sondheim wrote *Passion* around that age; it is a very good show, but nothing close to the work that happened earlier."

Critics applauded. The CD finished No. 12 in the *Voice*'s year-end poll, a showing that was especially impressive in a pop world whose audience and critics had veered significantly younger in the new century; Newman was the only leading American songwriter from the 1960s or 1970s who made the Top 25 with a collection of new material. *Rolling Stone*'s Will Hermes declared that the album's best moments "echo [1970s] classics like 'Sail Away' and 'Louisiana 1927,' songs that mixed pathos and bruised patriotism with brutal wit." "Randy Newman is still chronicling the death and potential resurrection of the United States," Patrick Freyne wrote in Ireland's influential magazine, *Hot Press*. "And here Newman is still sharp, incisive, funny, and at times even heart-rending."

The album did far better than *Bad Love* on the charts, reaching No. 20, but those around Newman were mainly looking ahead. Could he keep the creative streak going? They'd have to wait another nine years for the answer.

Randy's personal life was progressing as rewardingly as his professional life, reflecting the changes that friends had seen in him in the early 1990s. A reassuring sign of his opening up was family travels, which by now had ranged from Australia to Vietnam. Randy enjoyed seeing new places, and he took an active part in the adventures. The family would return home with a bundle of souvenir photos, including one of Randy and Gretchen sitting a dozen or so feet in the air on an elephant in Africa.

"He seemed to be more at peace with himself on many levels," Waronker said. "I think he became aware of what he had done and the impact it had. He was easier to be with. He had always been a generous, warm person, but I think it became more evident. He had finally come to terms with himself, and he realized that being Randy Newman wasn't a bad thing—it was a pretty good thing."

— II —

Newman headed to New Orleans to join Dr. John, Allen Toussaint, and other local artists in celebrating Fats Domino's eightieth birthday on February 23, 2008. In a concert at Tipitina's, the city's popular music venue, Randy sang Fats's "Blue Monday" and his own "Dixie Flyer" and "Louisiana 1927." In May, he was back in Louisiana for New Orleans musical hero Dr. John's recording of a song Newman wrote for an upcoming Disney movie and to make his first post-Katrina appearance at the Jazz and Heritage Festival.

The Princess and the Frog was another project attached to Lasseter, who was named chief creative officer of Disney and Pixar animated films when Disney bought its animation rival-partner in 2006. The story could be traced to a Brothers Grimm fairy tale about (among other things) a princess finding the love of her life when she kissed a frog that was transformed into a handsome prince. For the movie, directed by Ron Clements and John Musker, the story was set in the New Orleans of the 1920s jazz age and featured a Black heroine in the lead. "When we mentioned the idea to Randy, his eyes lit up," Lasseter said.

Newman wrote nine songs, employing blues, gospel, and jazz strains that evoked the resilience of the city and the determination of the lead character to work her way up from her job of a maid to running her own restaurant. Two of the songs—the party-minded "Down in New Orleans" and the soul shouter "Almost There"—were nominated for best song in the Academy Awards, but the Oscar went to Ryan Bingham and T Bone Burnett's "The Weary Kind" from *Crazy Heart*. *Princess* was another of Randy's favorite film experiences.

On May 1, Newman sang "Down in New Orleans" at the Jazz and Heritage Festival, and the crowd erupted. "You've got to remember that no one in the audience had heard the song, and it took them a while to understand what it was about," Lasseter said. "But all of a sudden, you could sense people realizing the song was about them and their city and the place went crazy. It gave us all goosebumps."

The day was highlighted once again by "Louisiana 1927." Rarely did the cultural impact of Randy's music feel more pointed and poignant than when he sang this three-decades-old number in this battered, historic city. Introducing the number, Newman spoke about the sadness of seeing parts of the city still in ruins. "It's an awful, awful thing that they would let this . . . awful thing that they would let those blocks and blocks of houses and lives. . . ." By the time he got to the chorus, the audience was singing along.

Because of his concentration on films, Newman hadn't toured extensively in years, but the new album and the festival performance made him eager to face audiences. He did some US dates before heading to London to record a live concert album at St. Luke's, an eighteenth-century Anglican church, with the BBC Concert Orchestra. The twenty-two-song program was broadcast by the BBC and released by Nonesuch in 2011 as a CD and DVD titled *Live in London*. The set began, topically enough, with "The Great Nations of Europe" and ended with "I Think It's Going to Rain Today," an acknowledgment of the song's continuing popularity.

Then it was time for *Toy Story 3*.

— III —

Hollywood began turning out movie sequels in the days of Rudolph Valentino and Sherlock Holmes in the silent era, but the practice caught fire in the 1960s and 1970s with James Bond, *The Godfather*, and *Jaws*, and then exploded at the turn of the century with comic book characters, including *Spider-Man* and the *Avengers*. Through it all, *Toy Story* retained its impact and appeal. In a *Rotten Tomatoes* list of the one hundred computer animated sequels that earned the strongest reviews, the *Toy Story* entries finished first, second, fifth, and ninth.

Lots of people shared in *Toy Story*'s success, but the guiding force was Lasseter, whose ability to touch audiences with warm and uplifting stories recalled director Frank Capra and even Walt Disney himself. From the start, Lasseter and his team of writers and directors at Pixar had tried to relate what was happening to Andy and his toys to their own experiences with their children. The concept of *Toy Story 3* began innocently enough when Lasseter and his wife, Nancy, drove their son, Ben, from their home in Northern California to Los Angeles to start classes at Loyola Marymount University. After helping the youngster settle into his freshman dorm room, the Lasseters returned to the car where they gave their son a goodbye hug. They then got into the car and started discussing where to have dinner, assuming Ben had headed back to the dorm. As they looked into the rearview mirror, however, they saw him standing behind the car, still gently waving.

"That's when it hit us," Lasseter said. "It was like a big bang; I was a wreck. We started weeping, the memories raced back to this little blond-haired kid and taking him in the stroller to the park and the way he went down the slide in the cutest way, and all these other memories followed. It's such a profound moment in a family's life when your children go off to college."

In the film—directed by Lee Unkrich from a script by Michael Arndt and an original story by Lasseter, Unkrich, and Andrew Stanton—Andy's leaving home for college sets off a series of events, leading to the toys (except Woody) being donated to what everyone believes will be a haven, a daycare center where they will be surrounded by adorable children. When life at the center proves dangerous, Woody rushes to their aid.

Newman's songs attract the most attention of his film work, but the scores themselves represent the core of his contributions, and his emotional score for *Toy Story 3* was a prime example. Still, the songs add so much to the series' magic that the filmmakers reprised "You've Got a Friend in Me" once again, this time in a Spanish language version by the Gipsy Kings. The film was another spectacular success—scoring a 98 percent approval rating with critics, according to *Rotten Tomatoes*, and the first animated feature to sell more than $1 billion in tickets. It also earned four Academy Award nominations, including one for the jovial song "We Belong Together" that gave Newman his second Oscar.

To celebrate Newman's history with *Toy Story*, Pixar arranged for him to be saluted with the 2,411th star on the Hollywood Walk of Fame, a project designed in the 1950s by the Hollywood Chamber of Commerce to give tourists lots of photo opportunities. Unlike the Oscars, the Walk of Fame is a quasi-honor—a promotional opportunity with each star paid for, chiefly by film, recording, and broadcasting companies, which is why the list of stars range from legends such as Clark Gable and Marilyn Monroe to rows of long-forgotten names.

Newman took the June ceremony in good spirit; he'd be joining Uncle Alfred, who also had a star on the Walk. Randy also got a coveted location—in the 6600 block of Hollywood Boulevard in front of Musso & Frank Grill, a Hollywood institution for more than a hundred years, and he was also delighted to learn that Fats Domino had a star across the street and that Ray Charles was honored just a block or so away. In news photos of the ceremony, Newman posed with Lasseter, each holding a *Toy Story* doll. After the film's opening two weeks later, Newman headed to Europe for a short tour that included stops in Copenhagen and Barcelona, as well as a return to London's Royal Festival Hall.

~

In Los Angeles there was another attempt at transferring Randy's music to the stage, this time in the form of a show called *Harps and Angels* at the prestigious Mark Taper Forum in Los Angeles. While including some songs from the album, "A Few Words in Defense of Our Country" and "Potholes" among them, the show was more a look at Randy's body of work. The use of the *Harps and Angels* title was to make the show sound current.

The program itself was surprisingly conventional. Noted *Los Angeles Times* theater critic Charles McNulty, "This amalgam of songs, covered by an ensemble of six, is theatrical yet falls short as theater. . . . Nothing wrong with a homage, even an off-kilter one, but a cabaret act would have sufficed." Privately, members of the Newman camp didn't disagree, but there was good news. Jack Viertel, who conceived the show, also headed New York City Center's heralded Encores! musical theater series, which over the years showcased works by Stephen Sondheim and Cole Porter. Viertel wanted to someday feature Randy's music under the Encores! umbrella.

Though it seemed like Newman was missing in action again for those fans waiting for another studio album, he kept fairly busy in 2012, doing some three dozen concerts in North America, Europe, and Australia, and writing the score for the sequel to Pixar's *Monsters, Inc.* Actually, *Monsters University* was a prequel that traced the adventures of Mike (Billy Crystal) and Sulley (John Goodman) as they went to college to learn how to become Scarers, the term given to monsters who convert the screams of frightened children into energy to power the city of Monsteropolis. The film took in over $700 million, but it was the first Pixar feature that failed to get an Oscar nomination.

— IV —

While working on films, Newman kept watch on the nation's political scene, especially Barack Obama's historic rise to become the nation's first Black president. Displaying a charisma, oratory brilliance, and idealism reminiscent of John F. Kennedy, the second-term senator from Illinois upset Hillary Clinton, the former first lady and US senator from New York, in the Democratic primary. He then defeated veteran Arizona senator and war hero John McCain in the final election, gathering 52.93 percent of the vote.

From Inauguration Day in 2008, Newman had noticed a bitter opposition to anything Obama did, a stance that he felt was chiefly because of the color of Obama's skin. As the re-election campaign neared in 2012, Newman was so angry that he set aside his reluctance to avoid themes tied to the moment. The result employed an emotional musical strain that had held a special place in the American consciousness for decades.

Irving Berlin's "White Christmas" became a Christmas standard across the United States from the moment Bing Crosby's 1942 recording of it reached No. 1 on the nation's pop charts, where it stayed for almost three months. The song's sentimental theme took on added emotional significance because of World War II, making the tune's most famous passage about home and family an anthem of sorts.

In time, millions saw the song's innocence and devotion as a toast to the best of America, but Newman, assuming the voice of a racist narrator, twisted it into a salute to the worst instincts of the country. The song began:

George Washington was a white man
Adams and Jefferson, too
Abe Lincoln was a white man, probably
And William McKinley
The whitest of them all
Shot down by an immigrant in Buffalo
And a star fell out of Heaven

I'm dreaming of a white President
Just like the ones we've always had
A real live white man who knows the score
How to handle money
Or start a war
Wouldn't even have to tell me
What we were fighting for

Newman's most inspired—and outrageously funny—image was saved for the end:

He won't be the brightest, perhaps
But he'll be the whitest
And I'll vote for that

"I'm Dreaming" was released as a single before the November 2012 election, accompanied by a humorous and pointed video showing most of the country's white presidents. "Early on in Obama's term, there was heat generated by issues that you wouldn't think would cause such passion," he explained to *Slate* at the time. "Even the term 'Obamacare,' the way it's spit out, like he was some kind of witch doctor."

— **V** —

Nine years after his first Rock & Roll Hall of Fame nomination, Newman learned in October of 2012 that he was again going to be on the final ballot, and this time the more than 500 voters—record company employees, musicians, and critics—elected him and five others into the Hall. "I thought maybe I'd have to die before they let me in," he quipped to *Rolling Stone*. "I'm really glad it happened when I was still around to see it. . . . They're always a little doctrinaire about what's rock and roll and what isn't rock and roll. It's nice they opened up a little to let me in."

At the ceremony the following April in Los Angeles, Newman sat in the audience as Don Henley gave the induction speech. Henley had been a fan ever since he heard Cilla Black's impassioned recording of "I've Been Wrong Before" in the 1960s, though he didn't know Newman had written it until he met him at the Troubadour a decade later.

In his speech, he said: "Employing lyrics that are eloquent in their simplicity and set in a wide-ranging musical landscape, Randy has chronicled both the hypocritical and the honorable traits of our culture, often with dark and biting humor, but always with compassion and empathy for the human condition. No one has written more beautifully about love and loss. No one has written more bravely about racism, religion, politics, and war. No one has written more humorously about lust, greed, fame, and the family dynamic."

As Newman walked to the microphone in a dark suit and tie, he surely picked up on the irony of "Short People" being played in the background on a night he was being honored for creative excellence. At the microphone, he said "When I was a kid, I'd see my uncles conducting the orchestra at Twentieth Century–Fox and doing movies and things, and I always wanted to be respected by musicians. . . . And this night means a great deal to me. Don's speech means a great to me. . . . It's hard for me to express a genuine emotion, as you can tell by my writing. But I'm very happy to receive this award, and I hope the fact that I rushed my own song a little earlier doesn't mean I get kicked out on my first night in. Thank you. I appreciate it."

— **VI** —

Around this time, Newman learned that Encores! wanted to include a one-night concert version of *Faust* in its innovative summer Off-Center program. This was a big deal in New York theater circles because a single performance of artistic director

Jeanine Tesori and Brian Crawley's *Violet* in 2013 had led to a Broadway run, where the musical received four Tony nominations. Newman even agreed to take the stage in the role of the Devil. Michael Roth was brought in to handle orchestrations, vocal arrangements, and overall score supervision.

The audience response at City Center on July 1, 2014, was the strongest of any of the Newman-related stage efforts, likely due to Newman's presence on stage. The songs were divided among Newman and five other vocalists, including Vonda Shepard, who gained national attention as the bar singer in the television series *Ally McBeal*, and Michael Cerveris, whose Broadway career included several Sondheim musicals. The song list was shuffled once again, finally placing the showstopping "Happy Ending" in its rightful place at the end. The backing included an eleven-piece orchestra and the Broadway Inspirational Voices choir.

Early in the concert, Randy stepped out of character long enough to address the audience—again humorously. "This is my version of Goethe's *Faust*. . . . His *Faust,* of course is a masterpiece. I read the Classics comic book, and I concur." *Time* magazine critic Richard Corliss noted, "I think the crowd got a contact high from just being present at the only New York performance a Newman musical was ever likely to see." Randy also delighted the crowd by wearing red devil horns as he sat at the piano.

For all the excitement, the *New York Times*'s Charles Isherwood didn't see *Faust* following *Violet* to Broadway: "I do not foresee a similar fate for this shaggy but enjoyable take on *Faust,* although the evening provided a nice showcase for Mr. Newman, still in good form at seventy, drawling out his mordant observations on human folly." The *Hollywood Reporter* noted, "For all of the musical brilliance... the show never quite succeeds as cohesive musical theater."

Newman continued to hold out hope for *Faust*, another sign of how much he had changed from the early Warner days. He soon turned his attention to another album, one that would, in spirit and ambition, complete a sensational trilogy along with *Bad Love* and *Harps and Angels*. He was already in the early stages of writing what would be his most ambitious number ever, an eight-minute look at the national debate over religion and science.

CHAPTER TWENTY-SIX

Dark Matter
The Streak Continues

— I —

Lenny sensed something was different when Randy played a few new songs for him and Mitchell in the summer of 2014. Randy had tended to obsess over compositions, sometimes for weeks, to make sure every element was in place before sharing them in the studio. But the first song on this day was far from finished—a sprawling, gospel-flavored number.

Even in its early form, the song felt drawn from everything Randy had employed in his theater and film experiences of the last two decades; it was a tune designed more for the stage than the pop world. The structure was not concerned with verses and choruses, but scenes and acts. It even comes with a Greek chorus that offers some comic relief. When complete, it would be one of his crowning works—a funny, insightful, sharply constructed take on one of the most fundamental divisions in the country: science versus religion.

The song, which would ultimately be called "The Great Debate," brought together conflicting characters and viewpoints, running almost twice as long as any number in *Faust*. In the end,

Newman would still make the final decisions, but he was showing, by sharing material at this early point, a desire to have people he trusted help him sort through the various threads. Froom, especially, worked almost daily with Randy for weeks.

"Randy played an early version that was more focused on the idea of the song and where the narrative could go than the actual musical structure," Froom said. "He was just playing an up-tempo gospel feel and singing ideas over basically a one-chord groove. After he was confident about the direction of the lyrics, he started writing the music in sections, each designed to enhance the overall arc of the story. When it started taking shape, he was really excited. He liked the fact it felt so audacious. Nobody wants to get old and soft, particularly if you make music. You don't want to be the one where people go, 'Oh, he's a soft version of what he used to be.' So, Lenny and I encouraged him in that direction . . . [to] be as audacious as possible." The lyrics would eventually run nearly 150 lines.

"The Great Debate"—whose early titles included "Straw Man," "I'll Take Jesus," and "Someone Is Watching Me"—centers on a fictional public debate at a North Carolina arena that pits scientists against true believers. It doesn't matter to the celebrity narrator-moderator which side wins the debate because it was not a serious academic undertaking. In fact, stirring gospel choirs would represent the religion side, a statement about how faith can often be most effectively expressed through passion (those wonderful singers) rather than formal defense.

It begins:

NARRATOR:
Welcome
Welcome
Welcome

To this great arena
Durham, North Carolina
In the heart of the Research Triangle

We've come to this particular place tonight
Because we gotta look at things from every angle
We need some answers to some complicated questions
If we're going to get it right

To that end we have here gathered
Some of the most expensive scientists in the world
Eminent scientists, that is
We got biologists, biometricians
We got a quantum mechanic and an astrophysician
We got a cosmologist and a cosmetician
We've got an astronaut
We got Astroboy
We got he doctors, she doctors, knee doctors, tree doctors
We got a lumberjack
And a life coach

On the other side
We have the true believers

We got the Baptists, the Methodists, the Presbyterians
The Episcopalians are here
Pass the hat
We got the Shakers, the Quakers
The anti-innoculators
We got the Big Boss Line, it's Madison time
The Six Blind Boys, Five Tons of Joy
Give them room
Get out of the way

We got a Bible Belter from the Mississippi Delta
Have them all arrayed

Randy's narrator then moderates the first debate round.

Scientists!
Are you ready?

First question: dark matter
Oh, dark matter
Give me someone knows something about space
(Nice space music, Georgie)
Alright, what is it?
Where is it?
And can we get some?
Stand up, sir, would you?
You are standing, forgive me
Dark matter, go ahead

SCIENTIST:
Dark matter is out in space
It's 75 percent of everything

NARRATOR:
Just a moment, sir
Do yourself a favor
Use our music
People like it
And your music's making people sick
No? Alright. It's a free country, go ahead
Dark matter
What is it?

SCIENTIST:
We don't know what it is
But we think it's everywhere

NARRATOR:
I'd like to take a look at it
Can we get some down here?

SCIENTIST:
Ha ha ha ha ha ha ha ha ha ha ha
Of course not!

NARRATOR:
Let me get this straight
You don't know what it is
You don't know where it is
And we can't get any
Put that to the one side

Let's put the Lord, faith, eternity, whatever on the other side
A show of hands?

The narrator turns to the true believers to state their opinion.
The faithful rest their case in the shouts of a spirited, high-octane
gospel choir. There's no need, they believe, to prove their faith.

I'll take Jesus
I'll take Jesus
I'll take Jesus every time
I'll take Jesus
I'll take Jesus
I'll take Jesus every time
Yes I will, yes I will

Yes I will, yes I will
I'll take Jesus, I'll take Jesus
I'll take Jesus every time

The true believers win the round.

Next, the narrator turns to evolution, posing this question to a scientist:

The giraffe, to survive, must eat leaves high up on the yaba
*   yaba tree*
That's true, isn't it?
Of course it is
Everyone knows that
But Mr. Darwin's giraffe
A halfway giraffe with a halfway-giraffe neck
Could never have reached the highest branches of the yaba
*   yaba*
Therefore he could not have survived
It's only common sense
Unfortunately for you, Mr. Charles Darwin didn't have any
*   common sense*
Evolution is a theory and we have just now tonight
*   disproved it.*

Show of hands?

I'll take Jesus
I'll take Jesus every time
I'll take Jesus
I'll take Jesus
I'll take Jesus every time.
Yes I will, yes I will
I'll take Jesus every time.

The score is now two to nothing, and the debate goes on—until a true believer rises to call the whole thing a sham, rightly accusing Newman—"a self-described atheist and commonist" (*sic*)—of being behind it. Nervously, the narrator declares an intermission, which inadvertently confirms the event is simply a money-making scheme.

> *We're gonna take a little break, ladies and gentlemen*
> *Fifteen, twenty, twenty-five minutes*
> *Depending on how the merchandise is moving*
> *We'll be right back*

"The Great Debate" is a portrait of a country divided so deeply that neither side will consider the other's position. When Randy played it and a few other songs for Hurwitz in the fall of 2014, the executive wrote in his journal, "They are really sensational, a tour-de-force Jesus song with an encounter between a man of religion and a man of science. . . . They are deep, profound songs."

Dark Matter was such a long process that Randy took breaks to work on films, including a lively score for *Cars 3*, which also featured eight recordings, including cover versions by Andra Day of Bruce Springsteen's "Glory Days" and Jorge Blanco of Lennon-McCartney's "Drive My Car." More importantly, Newman wrote the music for another (mostly) serious live-action drama.

— II —

Despite everything the Pixar films meant to him, Newman had been longing for years to write the music for another drama, frustrated that Hollywood typecast him as a composer of comic or animated films after the success of *Toy Story* and *Meet the Parents*. "I would have never done another comedy if I had a choice because I don't write funny music, whatever that may be," Newman said. "Either the picture is funny or it's not. Music is not going to be much of a factor in changing that. But I had to deal with what I was offered, and serious dramas were rare." One observer recalled the time, deep into the Pixar run, that Newman joked to agent Gorfaine, "Please get me something besides another 'toon"—though the observer wasn't so sure later that it was really a joke.

When asked to name a film he wished he had done, Randy often cited *Out of Africa*. The 1985 romantic drama won seven Academy Awards, including best picture, best director (Sydney Pollack), best actress (Meryl Streep) and best score (John Barry)—even though numerous critics found its nearly three-hour length excessive and that the relationship between Streep and Robert Redford lacked any spark.

Director-writer Noah Baumbach's films were a long way from the widescreen grandeur of *Out of Africa*, but Newman was delighted when he learned his son Amos, who had taken over as his agent, told him that Baumbach wanted Randy to write the music for his next movie. Baumbach enjoyed wide respect in the industry for the intimacy and relentless sophistication of his films.

His next one, *The Meyerowitz Stories (New and Selected)*, sounded perfect for Newman—the story of a family that was smaller than the Newman clan, but no less rooted in competition, intensity, and affection. The plot centered on the final days of Harold Meyerowitz, a modestly successful New York sculptor and the extended family of wives and children who flocked to his side, trying to remember the good times, which wasn't particularly easy; everyone who entered his Manhattan apartment seemed to trigger some painful memory.

As it happened, Baumbach had long been hoping to work with Newman. He was born in New York City in 1969, and his parents, Jonathan Baumbach and Georgia Brown, wrote fiction as well as film reviews for *Partisan Review* and *Village Voice,* respectively. Baumbach was fifteen when his mother introduced him to Newman's music with a copy of *Sail Away.* But it wasn't until he was in his mid-thirties, after seeing *The Natural* and *Avalon,* that Baumbach went back and listened to the early Newman catalog.

"They're all untouchable, but *Sail Away* is perfect," he told *Pitchfork* about his musical tastes, which ranged from Bryan Ferry and Madonna to George Jones. "I still can't believe the title track is as beautiful and stark and upsetting as it is. His songs can work two ways: if you don't listen too closely, they can just be unbelievably great melodies. But when you really listen, he's taking on so much in the lyrics."

The film press was caught by surprise at the unlikely news that Baumbach, the indie auteur, was turning to the *Toy Story* composer. In *Variety,* longtime Newman watcher Chris Willman had fun with the move. "If you left off with the legendary singer-songwriter's composing work sometime in the early eighties, though, this is what you'd consider typecasting: Newman coming in to do something deeply bittersweet for serious drama, avoiding any of the trends of modern composing for something a little closer in classicism to what his uncle Alfred might've done in the fifties or sixties."

Baumbach's films had employed bits and pieces of pop music (one character performs Pink Floyd's "Hey You" in a talent show in *The Squid and the Whale,* and another dances along with David Bowie's "Modern Love" in *Frances Ha*), but music was going to be used sparingly in *Meyerowitz.* There was no new song or even an extended score. Baumbach's plan was for Newman to play the piano as he watched an early version of the movie. Newman wasn't sure about that; he preferred to have time to reflect on a scene rather than react in real time to what he was seeing. Baumbach had faith in Newman's instincts and pushed for the real-time approach. The results—sometimes just a few piano notes here and there—were stylish and warm.

In a talk at LACMA (the Los Angeles County Museum of Art), Baumbach paid Newman the ultimate compliment when he said the composer sent him a song the day after their first meeting that captured the feeling Baumbach had in mind so well that it was like "seeing my movie before I shot the movie."

Ultimately, the primary impact of Newman in the film was when Baumbach ended *Meyerowitz* with a song he heard on *Sail Away*. After all these years, "Old Man" remained a profoundly moving look at aging. Not a word was changed. As final credits began to roll, Newman fans likely got a lump in their throats when they heard the lyrics to the melancholy song, especially the memorable final verses in a son's farewell.

The sun has left the sky, old man
The birds have flown away
And no one came to cry, old man
Goodbye, old man, goodbye

You want to stay, I know you do
But it ain't no use to try
'Cause I'll be here and I'm just like you
Goodbye, old man, goodbye

Won't be no God to comfort you
You taught me not to believe that lie
You don't need anybody
Nobody needs you
Don't cry, old man, don't cry
Everybody dies

When *Meyerowitz* premiered at the Cannes Film Festival in May of 2017, it received a four-minute standing ovation, and critics praised the film when it was released that fall by Netflix, the nation's fast-growing streaming service. Academy Award voters, however, ignored it, the likely result of movie studios and major theater chain operators seeing Netflix and other streaming services as a threat to the old way of doing business. They wanted to avoid anything that would look like legitimizing them.

Though Netflix had won its first Emmy in 2013 (director David Fincher for *House of Cards*), the company's films wouldn't be a force in the Oscars until director Alfonso Cuarón Orozco's *Roma* broke the embargo six years later by receiving ten nominations, including best picture, and winning in three categories, including best director. *Meyerowitz* may have had no chance for an Oscar, but *Roma* meant the playing field would be more level.

~

On the *Toy Story 4* front, Disney, as usual, was slow to proceed. The studio didn't confirm the project until November of 2014, when it also announced that Lasseter would return as director. In fact, it would be four years before it arrived—and, to Newman's shock, Lasseter would no longer be involved.

~

Returning to *Dark Matter*, Randy continued to exhibit the energy and drive that he had shown during *Good Old Boys* and *Faust*. Waronker heard speculation in the industry about this possibly being Newman's last album, but he didn't buy it. Neither did Cathy Kerr. "In fact," she said. "I don't think I've ever heard Randy make a proclamation of this kind about albums, touring, or film scoring."

Two megalomaniacal figures loomed as major targets on the collection. Randy had long been fascinated by Vladimir Putin, the former KGB agent who had become president of Russia, and Donald J. Trump, the self-absorbed New York hotel businessman and TV celebrity who had long eyed the White House. He was first drawn to Putin as subject matter when the Russian leader turned up in a series of widely circulated shirtless photos that were taken during a vacation in the Siberian mountains in the summer of 2007. But it was nine years later, as Putin became more erratic, that Newman again put aside his rule against topical songs and wrote about him.

When the track was finished, there was enough enthusiasm at Nonesuch for the label to follow the game plan of "A Few Words in Defense of Our Country" and release a digital single of "Putin" and, at Cathy Kerr's urging, a video that showed Putin images with and without his shirt.

Looking back at the song in 2022, Newman wished he had made the Putin character reflect more of the evil that was unleashed that year by Russia's invasion of neighboring Ukraine. But it wasn't so much politics that struck the satirist in Newman; it was Putin's desire to be seen as some type of beefcake hero. "It's interesting to me that being president of his country wasn't enough for him," Newman said. "He also wanted to be Tom Cruise. He wanted women to know how beautiful he is. He wanted everyone's acclaim."

Part of the fun of the story is that in Putin's mind, his tale is too big for one person to tell, so Newman introduces the Putin Girls, a female choir, to help him. The story is a deft blend of historical, political, and psychological wordplay. Here's how the song introduces Putin:

He can drive his giant tractor
Across the Trans-Siberian plain
He can power a nuclear reactor
With the left side of his brain

And when he takes his shirt off
He drives the ladies crazy
When he takes his shirt off
Makes me wanna be a lady

The record drew an exuberant *Pitchfork* review from Greil Marcus. "Kurt Weill and Bertolt Brecht must be jumping up and down in their graves in happiness: this is so German, so 1920s, so after-hours-Berlin with everyone doped to the gills and shouting along. . . . In Randy Newman's best music, he leaves you wondering where you stand, what you think, what you believe, how the world works. This is a postcard that may take years to truly be delivered."

Newman toyed with a song about Trump, who didn't need to take off his shirt to reveal his naked exhibitionism. He felt no embarrassment bragging, without limits or concern for reality or how much people rolled their eyes. Like most Americans, Newman thought the idea of Trump becoming president was preposterous when the businessman announced his candidacy in the summer of 2015. By the time the primaries began a year later, however, Trump was dominating the debates and on his way to the GOP nomination. That's when Newman wrote these lines,

My dick's bigger than your dick,
It ain't braggin' if it's true.
My dick is bigger than your dick
I can prove it too.
There it is! There's my dick
Isn't that a wonderful sight.

Cooler heads prevailed. Newman thought the song was too vulgar—and too obvious. He stuck with Putin for *Dark Matter*.

~

Two other new compositions were far from the theatrical high-wire reach of "The Great Debate" and "Putin": short stories, beginning with "Brothers," a surreal account of the closeness of brothers, a theme rooted in Newman's own relationship with Alan.

In this fictional exercise, Randy places America's two most famous brothers, John and Robert Kennedy, in the White House where they are winding down at the end of a spring day in 1961. Sharing Irish whiskey and talking about sports, they are interrupted by an aide who wants to update them on a plan to help undercut the growing tensions between the United States and the Fidel Castro regime in Cuba. The president will have nothing to do with the Bay of Pigs invasion until he remembers there was a woman in Cuba he loves. All too aware of his brother's notorious flings, RFK declares, "Oh no, Jack!"

But the president assures his brother that he's not talking about another affair; he's in love with the woman's voice. He'll approve the Bay operation if it would rescue Celia Cruz and bring her to America. Part of the fun is imagining the delight Newman had in stitching the story together. The idea of rescuing Cruz was a likely jab at faulty government intelligence reports that contributed to the failure of the Bay of Pigs operation; Cruz had already left Cuba by the spring of 1961 and was living in Mexico, soon to tour the United States.

The other story, "Sonny Boy," was based on the unlikely history of two blues musicians who both called themselves Sonny Boy Williamson. One actually had that name—a top-flight harmonica player, singer, and songwriter who was widely known in the 1930s and 1940s. The other was an opportunist, variously known as Aleck or Alex Miller, who adopted the Sonny Boy name after Williamson's death in 1948 to piggyback on the late singer's popularity. The twist is that the second Sonny Boy enjoyed a distinguished career himself, causing blues historians to have to refer to them as Sonny Boy Williamson I and Sonny Boy Williamson II. In the song, Newman describes Sonny Boy I looking down from Heaven, angry that someone has stolen his name, but relieved that he's the only Sonny Boy beyond the pearly gates.

When an interviewer from *Pitchfork* mentioned that the song sounded like a tribute to a musician (Sonny Boy I) that Newman "really loved," Newman replied, "Yeah it is! Though I didn't really know who I loved. In retrospect, I fell for the stuff I heard [by Sonny Boy II] on the R & B station here in the late fifties, when I was thirteen—a couple of songs called "So Sad to Be Lonesome" and "The Goat." And one day not too long ago I went to look for a record of "The Goat" and there was the other guy! And his stuff was good too, like "Good Morning School Girl" and "Jackson Blues." I root for Sonny Boy I, of course, but the second guy was just as good, or better. I just think it's shitty that that guy would do that."

~

Not every song on *Dark Matter* was new. The ballad "She Chose Me" was written for *Cop Rock*. But that version was sung by a nondescript police detective who was thankful that his younger, prettier, and probably smarter wife would fall in love with someone as ordinary as him. The vocal and arrangement were too restrained to make much impression. Newman hadn't thought of the song in years but felt it would work in the new album if he could convince the listener that the man in the song meant every word. And Newman—with his ability to bring his characters to life—did exactly that; the lyrics are relatively plain, but his impassioned vocal made the track feel deeply heartfelt. Like so many of his ballads, the song, if watered down by mainstream pop gloss, could have been a pop hit.

Newman also reached back for "It's a Jungle Out There," the Emmy-winning song he wrote for *Monk*. Though the original version dealt humorously with Monk's various anxieties ("It's a jungle out there / Disorder and confusion everywhere"), Newman updated the song to comment on contemporary anxieties and phobias. One of the new verses:

> *It's a jungle out there*
> *Violence and danger everywhere*
> *It's brother against brother*
> *Pounding on each other*
> *Like they were millionaires*

Both songs were worthy additions to the album, but the remaining three songs gave the collection an endearing and soulful edge, balancing the theatrics of "The Great Debate" and "Putin" with a song with the supreme intimacy and heart of "Lost Without You."

∼

Randy was twenty-three when he wrote one of the songs that was considered by him and fans as one of his classics, "So Long Dad." A half century later, "Lost Without You" spoke of family, aging, and loss in even starker terms. The song reflected the raw, unflinching bite of prize-winning drama.

> *Even if I knew which way the wind was blowing*
> *Even if I knew this road would lead me home*
> *Even if I knew for once where I was going*
> *I'm lost out here without you*
>
> *Rocking the baby by that window there*
> *Planting tomatoes in the yard*
> *Naked by the mirror putting up your hair*
> *Baby, it's hard*

When the kids came to see you for the last time
I told them not to bring the children
The husbands, or the wife
I said, just the blood this time. Just the blood.
They asked to be alone with you
So I left them alone, but I didn't go far

They said, "Has he been drinking again?
He stumbled at the door.
He can't take care of himself, Mama
We can't do this anymore."

You said, "Hush up, children
Let me breathe.
I've been listening to you all your life.
Are they hungry, are they sick?
What is it they need?
Now it's your turn to listen to me.

"I was young when we met
And afraid of the world
Now it's he who's afraid
And I'm leaving.

"Make sure he sleeps in his bed at night.
Don't let him sleep in that chair.
If he holds out his hand to you, hold it tight.
If that makes you uncomfortable
Or if it embarrasses you
I don't care."

Even if I knew which way the wind was blowing
Even if I knew this road would lead me home

Even if I knew for once where I was going
I'm lost out here
Baby, I'm lost out here
I'm lost out here without you

"It's laid out more like a novel," Froom said. "It just keeps uncovering these uncomfortable moments . . . the mother telling the kids to shut up and listen to her—she wants them to take care of this guy when she's gone. It's so devastating. That's not normal fodder for a pop song. It's not easy for someone to listen to something so direct."

Talking about "Lost Without You" in *Pitchfork*, Newman said:

When you see people in your immediate family die, it's usually not just sudden. It's a longer process, and people behave in radically different ways, and some of that behavior has to be forgiven later. . . . When my mother was dying, my father was sort of taking care of her. But he was taking too much of this medicine, so he was falling around a little bit. He didn't seem like he was taking care of her right. So, my brother and I went to her and said, "Jeez, we're sorry that Dad's not doing the job for you." And she said, "Don't you say anything bad about him. From the very beginning of this, he couldn't have been better." And it really shocked my brother and I, because we never saw her express her love for him ever.

— III —

The album's remaining songs, "On the Beach" and "Wandering Boy," were also drawn, in part, from Newman's past. As a youngster, he spent a lot of time at the beach, relishing the freedom and adventure that the water and sand promised. But eventually he and the other kids grew up and went about their lives—except for the few who never left the beach. They encountered challenges, including drugs and sometimes dangerous living conditions, but they couldn't give up the vision of a carefree life of endless summers and surfboards to face the challenges and responsibilities of the adult world. With its youthful carousel backing, "On the Beach" feels like an ode to those who remained and for their safety—knowing the dreams are likely to run out at some point, and then what?

Waronker was particularly fond of the song. "I liked the way it described what we all went through as kids," he said. "There are a lot of people we were close to and they had a hard time. Randy was always interested in them. They were some smart guys who just didn't do the normal things just so they could be on the beach. Some of them just went over the edge."

"Wandering Boy" was written after hearing a song title— "Where is My Wandering Boy Tonight?"—whose key image struck a parental nerve in Randy. As was his wont, he first considered telling the story through the eyes of an unreliable narrator, perhaps a screwed-up father, but gradually he began thinking about how he'd feel if one of his sons ended up homeless or adrift on his own. "Wandering Boy" was set in one of the frequent Palisades parties where everyone was talking about the promise of their children, which makes the occasional downfalls all the more traumatizing.

> *Thank you for the party*
> *We're always glad we came*
> *I'm the only one from the family tonight*
> *But I know they'd say the same*
>
> *I came here with my father*
> *Then I brought my wife*
> *Three sons, a daughter*
> *Then the last baby boy*

The little caboose we called him
The light of her life
And that's who I'm waiting for

Where is my wandering boy tonight?
Where is my wandering boy?
If you see him, push him toward the light
Where is my wandering boy?

He went off of that high board there
When he was five years old
Laughing like a maniac
Shining in the sun like gold
He was afraid of nothin' then
He was loved by everyone
I see it clear as I see you
That day there in the sun

I hope he's warm, and I hope he's dry
And that a stranger's eye is a friendly eye
And I hope he has someone
Close by his side
And I hope that he'll come home

Where is my wandering boy tonight?
Where is my wandering boy?
If you see him, tell him everything's alright
Push him toward the light
Where is my wandering boy?

The song was so personal that Randy broke down when writing it and when he played it for people early on, especially when he got to the line, "Where is my wandering boy?"

It was equally emotional for Waronker and Froom, both fathers. After they finished the track, Froom tested "Wandering Boy" and "Lost Without You" on a few friends, something he did frequently with things he was working on, and he found a strong and immediate reaction to both. "The response to 'Wandering Boy' was especially strong," he said. "I had seen people be moved when I played them songs before, but I had never seen someone just outright cry, and all five or so of the people I played it for did cry."

Froom and Hurwitz both felt a connection between *Dark Matter* and Newman's debut album. "It's almost like a bookend to the debut album because they are both so different from everything else," Froom said. "*Dark Matter* is leaning heavily on music and not the big beat kind of thing. That's true of *Harps and Angels*, which some people find easier to take. *Dark Matter* for a lot of people is harder work, it requires more out of you. But I like that."

∿

Once again, the critical reaction to *Dark Matter* was affected by the cultural shift in pop criticism, with a large body of writers pretty much continuing to ignore artists associated with the classic rock era. The *Voice*'s critics poll placed it at No. 29, but that was a victory of sorts—the only album by an artist identified with pre-2000 rock to make the Top 30. Looking deeper, Newman's supporters found much to cheer. Robert Christgau, a critic who did continue to weigh pre-2000 artists, named *Dark Matter* the finest album of 2017. The collection was also widely praised in the *New York Times*, the *New Yorker*, *Rolling Stone*, the *Los Angeles Times*, *Pitchfork*, *Mojo*, and *Q*.

Dark Matter also led numerous pop and cultural observers to celebrate Newman's unique place in American pop. Conor Friedersdorf's essay in the *Atlantic* was especially eloquent. Titled

"The *Dark Matter* of America's Foremost Musical Satirist," the piece declared, "Newman is . . . a solo artist with a catalog as original as any in popular music. . . . In fact, there may be no one in the American songbook whose work did more to anticipate the tragicomic place the United States finds itself in today."

In *Paste*, Ryan J. Prado wrote, "Newman has enjoyed one of the more charmed careers of any composer or pop singer from the twentieth century. It's a rearview full of Grammys, Emmys, Oscars, and so much more. Yet it's Newman's drive to out-Newman himself that keeps audiences enraptured." *Pitchfork*'s Mike Powell ended a salute by calling Newman "the voice for characters nobody should have to listen to, curator of moments nobody wants to name. It is a painful, interesting way to be. And if it isn't love, then what does one call that feeling, and is there any more worth writing about?"

Waronker summarized, "I think people are catching up to who he is and what he has done."

PART SIX

There has never been anybody remotely like Randy New-man in the galaxy of popular singer-songwriters. Nobody with his depth of musical knowledge and ability; nobody with the range of compositional skills and the breadth of subject matter . . . the way he drops in on life and presents those simply-worded vignettes, those closeups that resolve into a panoramic view of the human condition. Each song is like a little play. There is no one more highly attuned to the compassion, the meanness, the absurdity of human behavior. He can be the protagonist or the antagonist, or both. He can be the reliable narrator or the unreliable nar-rator, but the truth, whether it's uplifting or ugly, always comes out, while he somehow remains guileless. And he does all this in a New Orleans accent. He is a unique amal-gam of American regional cultures: Southern California, the Deep South (New Orleans in particular), and Jewish culture, although not in any orthodox sense.

Above all, I admire his dogged dedication to writing songs that take a deep unflinching look into the issues of our time, whether they be personal or political, and he doesn't pull his punches. He pushes the boundaries. He can't help himself. I once asked him if he ever thought twice about being misunderstood or offending certain individuals or groups of people. His reply was, "I write what I write." That was inspirational, to me.

The bravery and beauty in Randy's work is unparal-leled and underappreciated.

DON HENLEY

Reluctant though I am to name names, I gotta, so ten seemed like a nice round number. Forgive me, and forgive me as well for camouflaging finer judgments in alphabetical order. Ahem: Bob Dylan, Eminem, Aretha Franklin, Jay-Z, Joni Mitchell, Prince, the Rolling Stones, Paul Simon, Kanye West, Stevie Wonder. All of these are acknowledged popular music titans who achieved preeminence by releasing long series of excellent albums, generally half a dozen or more, and over several decades to boot—which series were eventually interrupted by inferior albums. (To be clear, I don't believe the Beatles ever made a bad album. Their solo members, however, definitely did. Also, I agree that Eminem is a close call, and hereby postpone all arguments in re the Taylor Swift Exception until 2026, when she's put in her two decades.)

Why am I inserting this parlor game into a Randy Newman biography? you ask. Simple. Randy Newman has never made even a mediocre album. NEVER! He certainly had bad days because everybody does, and he probably had bad patches because that happens too. But he never truly faltered—sooner or later the new ideas always came. So listening back with tremendous pleasure to *Little Criminals* (1977), *Born Again* (1979), and *Land of Dreams* (1988), the only Newman albums I've graded a mere B plus, a benchmark almost all of my ten titans have slipped beneath, I concluded that most would probably now be As in any case, as would 1968's never-rated eponymous debut, which I gave a qualified rave back then while noting nervously that his singing voice, which sounds almost boyish in retrospect, combined a "grumpy mumble" with a "deliberate drawl." Equally important is that I'm a big admirer of 1995's unnecessarily controversial *Faust* as well as Newman's only solo albums of this millennium: 2008's *Harps and Angels*, where "A Few Words in Defense of Our Country" vies with James McMurtry's "We Can't Make It Here" as the greatest protest song of this dire century, and 2017's eccentric, playlet-loaded, surface mean, stealth compassionate *Dark Matter*, which with rock-crit demographics trending ever younger made few Top 10s or indeed 40s when it was released, but stands as my number one album of Trumpdom's inaugural year. Five more years have passed as I write. I'd love for Randy Newman to release another album, hopefully featuring his eternal "Venus in Sweatpants." And as his contemporary I believe he's got that album in him. But I know damn well he's not going to let us hear it until he's convinced he's got it exactly right.

**ROBERT CHRISTGAU, The acknowledged
"Dean of American Rock Critics"**

CHAPTER TWENTY-SEVEN

The Hollywood Bowl
An Historic Night

— I —

Randy had performed around a thousand concerts since the Lion's Share, where his brother brought along college friends to make sure he didn't walk out to an empty house, but the hometown Hollywood Bowl was always special—and it was once again on a summer night in 2018. In its grandest moments, the evening was a celebration—not just for Randy, but the Newman family musical tradition.

Ever since the Bowl's opening in 1922, the elegant outdoor venue's tranquil setting made it feel like a refuge from the hucksterism of Hollywood Boulevard just a mile away. Built by arts-minded community leaders as a nonprofit enterprise, the Bowl was designed to serve as the summer home of the Los Angeles Philharmonic, the site of annual Easter Sunrise services, and a world-class showcase to attract leading music figures from Broadway, classical music, and various pop genres. The stars have ranged from Jascha Heifetz and Frank Sinatra to Billie Holiday and the Beatles.

The Newman family ties went back to 1937 when Alfred's music for *Street Scene* was played during a salute to film composers. As a youngster, Randy attended Bowl events and loved listening to the orchestra, maybe even imagining being on that stage himself. He would prove to be such a valued Bowl artist—classy, gifted, and respected—that he would be named to the Hollywood Bowl Hall of Fame.

Don Heckman's review in the *Los Angeles Times* pointed out Newman's delight on stage during his Bowl debut in 1996. "Relaxed, amiable, cracking jokes with the musicians, occasionally pausing in one of his songs to offer an off-the-cuff comment ('Schubert wishes he could have written stuff like this!'), Newman was pleasant and outgoing, his congenial manner camouflaging the skill with which he commands a stage," Heckman wrote. "He played piano, sang, and conducted the orchestra, carefully identifying, by name, each of the soloists who performed at various times behind him."

The 2018 appearance offered even more—a toast to what once seemed impossible: the second generation of musical Newmans had extended the family's musical impact on American pop culture to a hundred years by matching—or even exceeding—the accomplishments of Alfred and the first generation. Randy was the chief force in the younger generation, but he didn't do it alone. Two of his cousins, Alfred's sons Thomas and David, also contributed greatly to continuing the legacy. Between them, the brothers composed more than 200 scores, earning Thomas fifteen Oscar nominations and David one (for *Anastasia*, a remake of the 1956 film for which his dad also received an Oscar nomination). Thomas's scores stretched from *The Shawshank Redemption* and *American Beauty* to *1917*. David's included *Heathers*, *War of the Roses*, and *Hoffa*.

The August 12 Bowl show would be the first time in America that the two wings of the second generation of the family came together as principals on the same stage when composer-conductor David Newman directed the orchestra for Randy. The only previous time the pair had been onstage together was in 2014 when David conducted a 110-piece orchestra in Vienna when Randy received the city's annual Max Steiner Film Music Achievement Award. There was no official honor this time, but for anyone aware of the Newman tradition, the night at the Bowl was a moving, historic moment.

Media attention has mostly been focused on Randy, but David and Thomas have their own noteworthy stories. As a teen, David longed to be the next Arturo Toscanini, a superstar conductor for much of the twentieth century, and Randy, who was ten years older, encouraged him, even introducing him to William Kettering, who had instructed Randy in conducting. But conducting would turn out to be David's third career. After studying violin at USC, he played in studio orchestras for years, including the sessions for John Williams's *E.T. the Extra-Terrestrial* and Jerry Goldsmith's *Star Trek*. He began composing in the mid-1980s and gained such respect as a conductor to be offered prestigious assignments around the country, including the annual movie celebration series launched by the Bowl in 2007. Film historian Jon Burlingame describes David as "the best conductor of film music of his generation, a genius conductor like his father." Randy, too, told the *Los Angeles Times*, "He's the best conductor in Hollywood now. He's kind of beautiful up there."

On this special night, David opened the program by conducting the orchestra in a six-minute suite from *The Natural*, including the music for the home run scene. Then Randy, in a bowling shirt, black pants, and sneakers, continued by singing "Birmingham," one of eight numbers from *Sail Away* and *Good Old Boys* that he'd perform that night. He closed the first half of the show with "You've Got a Friend in Me" and the second half with "Lonely at the Top."

Reviewing the concert for the *Times*, Mikael Wood—like Heckman—was charmed by Newman's asides to the orchestra. "I love musicians, and I always have," Newman said at one point, the review noted. "They're people who've accumulated tens of thousands of hours alone in a room getting good at what they do—much like snipers do."

The orchestra joined Newman on about half the songs and the result was usually magical, especially on "Louisiana 1927." Wood wrote, "Newman's account of a Southern city being washed away . . . sounded as beautiful at the Bowl as it ever has—pure American soul music, as deep and true as Ray Charles or Aretha Franklin. The place was so still when Newman finished the song that he seemed almost embarrassed."

Because of his age and recent farewell tour announcements by Paul Simon and Elton John, Newman's "I'm Dead (But I Don't Know It)" acknowledged the question of retirement and, at the same time, answered it.

"Why quit?" he joked. "No one taps you on the shoulder and says, 'You're really washed up—you ought to hang it up. And no one's applauding at home, so everybody keeps going. . . . I don't know what's gonna stop it . . . an elephant gun?"

In salute to the hometown setting, he opened the encore with "Feels Like Home" and followed with "I Think It's Going to Rain Today." Randy then walked to the podium where he and David embraced and took a joint bow.

"Besides writing those beautiful songs, Randy has a particularly unique, idiosyncratic way of orchestrating them," David said years later. "It was thrilling to be on stage with him. I just couldn't stop smiling. I felt like a spectator at times. It was just so wonderful conducting music that I had loved for so long. I'm very proud of my family and celebrate being part of it."

Maria Newman, a respected violinist and daughter of Alfred, was also at the Bowl that night, along with Lionel Newman's grandson Joey, a composer, orchestrator, and musician in films and television.

"Oh, no, not inevitable at all," she said when asked years later about careers in music.

I had a close relationship with my father, but I was only eight when he passed away, and I didn't learn until later that he didn't want us to go into music because he felt it was a risky business, all about being in the right place at the right time. He grew up poor and he wanted us to get a safer job. It was my mother who pushed us into music. She was determined to find the Alfred Newman gene in each of her children, so I took up piano at six and violin at eight. It was a requirement for us, like brushing your teeth. While other kids were out playing games, we had to practice.

No less excited was Thomas, who was also at the Bowl. "I just adore Randy," he said. "I'm in awe of what he's done, even before the film scores—those albums were brilliant. The songs were hysterical and deeply moving, right next to each other. He was always approachable when I was young, but it was scary because he cast a big shadow over any notion I had of being a creative person. Someone asked me once who I thought was the most important Newman and I replied, 'Randy," and they said, 'Not Alfred?' and I said, 'Randy.'"

When told years later about Thomas's comparison, Randy was touched. "It was hard hearing Al's music and thinking that I could ever do anything like that," he said. "Every once in a while, I would do something that I was really proud of, but I would never put myself ahead of Al or anybody in the family. I can always think of things that they can do that I can't do musically."

Like Randy, Thomas tends to be somewhat solitary and shy, which leads to an interesting dynamic between the two. Thomas only lives a few blocks away, but he rarely sees Randy even though he passes his cousin's house on his regular walks. He doesn't want to bother his cousin. At the same time, Randy often looks through the window and sees Thomas passing by, sometimes thinking Thomas must not like him because he never stops by. But Randy's admiration for his cousin is clear. "I think about

Tom sometimes when I'm writing," he said. "I think, 'Tom wouldn't do this' and I try to think of what he would do and pick between them."

Without a father or a Lenny pushing Thomas into music, it took him a while to find his direction. He had no concrete goal when he enrolled at USC.

> I ended up studying composition, I don't know why. It wasn't like this fierce need to make music. There were people in high school who were way better at piano than me. But I went to a two-week program sponsored by USC in Idyllwild the summer after ninth grade. I was in a cabin with a kid who wrote poetry, and it was the first time I was inspired to be a creative person. That's what got me started thinking seriously about music. But I was terrified. Because of people like Alfred and Randy, you realize that you can't just go through the same door. You have to find something musically that's your own.

Gradually, Thomas found his own voice. "In the early nineties, there was a film I did called *Flesh and Bone* where I was starting to sample 'found sounds,'" he said. "They were acoustically generated electronics, and when I combined them with lush strings that kind of changed everything for me."

— ‖ —

After the concert, the backstage area was filled with relatives and friends. Thinking back to that night at the Bowl, Gretchen and Elliot Abbott both spoke about the Randy they first knew and the one on stage that night.

"It was definitely thrilling to be at the Bowl, and I was beyond proud of him," Gretchen said. "I loved every minute and especially seeing him with a band, because I knew he was having fun and having David conduct was just a cherry on top. This may seem nutty, but as a person he has not changed in my eyes. Yes, his career has been a success, and we live well, but he is still the same kind, intelligent, generous, and funny guy I met all those years ago."

Abbott also spoke of the Randy he met in the 1970s and the Randy of the 2010s. "Randy isn't big on hugs, but we hadn't seen each other in years, and he gave me a big hug at the Bowl and he wouldn't let go," the former manager said. "We were both in tears. He was way, way happier than I had ever seen him.

"Back when I was working with him, he was so nervous about having to live up to the family tradition, and that night it felt like mission accomplished. But he was also overjoyed by having his family around him. He had lived up to the goal of being a good father. Thinking back, that may have been just as big a relief."

When Abbott's comments were relayed to Randy years later, he said:

Well, I hope I've always been a good father, so it makes me feel bad to think that it was really a second goal, after the music. I've thought about it plenty and it's complicated. Despite all my father's faults, he was there for me a lot, like Little League, and I tried to do that for Amos even though he wasn't really into baseball much because it was scary and he didn't feel comfortable at the plate. He wanted to quit when he was twelve, but I told him to give it a try, Pony League or whatever it was. In the first game, he goes up to the plate and the pitcher hits him in the head and he quit. I wasn't perfect, but I always tried. I wanted them to always feel loved.

Gretchen also stressed the role of the family.

"Like any wife and mother, I'd like to say having children would be the right answer, as parenting lasts a lifetime and he has five great kids," she said. "I would say that when we have all the children and grandkids here is when I see him at his happiest and most relaxed. All the other stuff is fun and great to celebrate, but it all fades away pretty quickly."

~

The Bowl night euphoria was short-lived.

Around three o'clock in the morning after the concert, Roswitha died in Los Angeles after a long illness. She was seventy-four. Though she married architect Donald Boss in 1992 and later moved to Sun Valley, Idaho, Roswitha remained a part of the children's lives. Randy, Gretchen, and all five children attended a memorial for her in Idaho. It was a loving sign of how well Randy, Gretchen, and Roswitha had done to make the five feel as one.

"My mom became comfortable with Gretchen, especially after watching her relationship with me and Amos and Johnny," Eric Newman said. "You go through my dad's house (now) and there are pictures of all of us. He didn't put them there, my dad's never put a picture anywhere. That's Gretchen. She and Roswitha both understood my dad had five children, not two, and they helped him make sure the children knew it."

Gretchen, too, emphasized Randy's and Roswitha's roles.

One of the biggest reasons I wanted to marry Randy was because he was such a good father to his sons. I wanted that for my future children. I had for many years witnessed the manner in which he communicated with them and realized that he didn't judge them or make negative comments when they were talking about something serious in their lives. He just listened, so they talked, and when it was the right time, he would advise them. He was the same with Patrick and Alice, and they all adore him and come to him for advice as adults. But none of this would have been possible without Roswitha.

CHAPTER TWENTY-EIGHT

The Family

— I —

Pop stars typically keep family members from talking to the media because they are nervous about the up-close-and-personal scrutiny; relatives aren't used to talking to reporters and they could say, well, anything, unwittingly damaging an artist's image. This wasn't the case with Randy. He welcomed his family's views.

"He wasn't like a soccer dad," Amos said in 2022.

> It was usually hard to get him out to shoot hoops or something, but part of that was because of work and he's got an introverted personality. When he wasn't writing music, he would read or watch television; it was his way of relaxing. We didn't take that as rejection. When we needed him, he was there—and he was a great listener.
>
> When we moved into a bigger house in Rustic Canyon after Eric was born, he built a studio, and we were able to spend time in there. When I started playing drums, we even set up a kit and we would sort of alternate times in the studio.

Even so, Amos realized most of the responsibilities for raising him and his brothers fell on his mother. Randy was devoted to the music—a career obsession shared by millions driven to succeed, not just musicians. In a time when nearly half of the nation's mothers were stay-at-home moms, it felt only natural that Roswitha took the lead in parenting.

"My father may have talked about things to my mom, but he had this kind of carte blanche thing to sort of do what he needed to do with his music and Mom would take care of the rest, including us," he said.

Early on, Amos became close to Lenny Waronker's son, Joey. "For the first ten or twelve years of our lives, we were inseparable, and music was a big thing with both of us," Amos said. Around age fourteen, he became intrigued by punk rock—Black Flag, the Circle Jerks, and some of the British bands. He even started a couple of punk-rock groups, Smashed Infant and Armed Response. But Amos, a drummer and sometimes singer, soon realized he wasn't committed to being a performer. He didn't think he could ever be good enough to have a career, and he also worried about the demands music made on Randy.

"When he saw I was interested in music, he told me what a struggle it was for him, but he didn't try to influence me either way," Amos said. "His message was, 'Do what you enjoy and don't do what you don't enjoy,' and he was totally supportive of our choice. I might mention one day that I would love to climb Mount Everest, and he'd go to Dutton's [bookstore] the next day and bring me a book on mountain climbing'."

Joey—who went on to become an all-star drummer, touring and/or recording with such leading acts as Beck and R.E.M.—recalled the good times around the Newmans. "The house was at the end of a dirt road on a creek, so Amos and Eric and I would play in the creek," he said. "We could follow it all the way to the beach. The house itself was perfect for hide-and-seek, making forts and things. We had great sleepovers. It felt comfortable and safe."

Following two years studying photography at the University of Colorado Boulder, Amos transferred to what is now known as the USC Thornton School of Music with the goal of becoming a record producer. Afterward, he went through a wide range of industry jobs working with such leading figures as Bob Krasnow and songwriter-producer Glen Ballard before spending four years with Gorfaine-Schwartz. He joined William Morris Endeavor in 2011 to start the company's new Music for Visual Media department, representing Hans Zimmer, the team of Trent Reznor and Atticus Ross and, eventually, his dad.

Before being named head of music at Endeavor Content, a film and television studio, Amos helped put Randy together on the Baumbach film. In the process, Amos got a sample of his dad's professional self-questioning. "He was tickled when I told him about working on a drama, but he went through this moment of uncertainty. 'I guess it's a good idea,' he said. 'I guess I'm good at that.' After all this time, he was asking himself if he could rise to the occasion."

~

Eric also attended boarding school briefly during his parents' separation, but he soon returned to Los Angeles and lived with his mom and younger brother Johnny (February 9, 1978) at the Rustic Canyon house. The boys typically spent one day a week and alternative weekends with Randy, and the rest of the time with Roswitha. "My dad lived at the Shangri-La Hotel [in Santa Monica] for a bit, then rented a house in Brentwood before buying one in Mandeville Canyon," Eric said. "The latter had a tennis court, and he was a surprisingly adept natural athlete. We had many good times there."

Ever since the Amsterdam concert where he became intrigued by his father's lyrics, Eric studied the words in Randy's songs, often asking his mom or dad about them if he was puzzled. Even though he knew Randy was writing about "ignorant Americans," he was terrified the first time he heard the N-word in "Rednecks."

"Early on, we knew never to say certain things," he said. "My father had a real conscience about bigotry. It was a really big issue with him. He wouldn't lecture us, but it was clear in what he said and how he acted. He'd also talk about the effects of the Reagan Administration on social programs, and I saw that bothered him. As I got older, I learned a lot about the world through his music. I'll tell you what he is, more than anything, is he's a humanist."

Eric attended Boston University for two years before enrolling at USC's prized film school. The list of notable alumni on the school's website is as long as the end credits of some movies— and Eric soon earned his place on it. He began working in development and production roles on numerous films, including a remake of George A. Romero's classic horror film *Dawn of the Dead*. His biggest success came when he formed his own TV production company, Grand Electric, and teamed with Netflix on *Narcos*, the hit series about Pablo Escobar and the drug war in Colombia. It was Eric's original idea and he also served at times as writer and showrunner during the show's six-year run. The success led to a continuing relationship with the streaming service, where he also produced *Bright*, starring Will Smith and Joel Edgerton, and *Spiderhead*, starring Chris Hemsworth and Miles Teller.

"I knew my dad was a star, but not someone who could sell out the Forum for five nights which, in retrospect, would have been overwhelming for all of us, like living in a movie or something," Eric said. "The cool thing was all the people I was impressed by were fans of his. I remember meeting Miles Davis with my dad in an airport and going to my dad's house for a barbecue and seeing George Harrison in the backyard."

But he also witnessed his father's difficult times.

There have certainly been times over the last fifty years where Dad has been melancholy. It's almost like he's been at war with a side of himself that goes back to childhood, trying to please his father and eventually going so far that he displeased him. But I have never thought of him as an unhappy person. I've thought of him more as a loving person. When I was a kid, he came back from some shows in Europe and he gave me a metal model of the Concord, which was this amazing new plane, but I told him what I really wanted was this giant plastic Godzilla, so he took me to a toy store and bought me one—even though he was so tired from the flight.

As the father of three himself, Eric has spent a lot of time in recent years thinking about his relationship with his dad. "I've always known he was a brilliant artist, but I've become increasingly proud of him as a father," he said. "After all these years, the thing I'd say to him is, 'I want you to know if you ask yourself if you did enough for us, which you sometimes do, the answer is, resoundingly, yes.'"

~

Johnny's memories of his dad go back to the studio at the family's Rustic Canyon house. "I remember Amos's drum set down there and this poster from *Born Again* that scared the hell out of me because my dad was wearing this clown makeup, and clowns were scary at that age," he said. "I didn't know who KISS was. There was also a big pinball machine. One of my favorite memories of him working in the room was when he composed the music for a film. He'd watch scenes from the movie on this VCR, and then he'd play something to go along with the footage. It was amazing."

Like his dad, Johnny started taking piano lessons early, some from one of the same teachers. But he didn't have a passion for music and, after studying literature for four years at Vassar College, he embraced film. "I've loved movies my whole life, but if I had to pinpoint a moment that made me want to be a screenwriter, it would probably be the first time I saw *Sunset Boulevard*, which is funny considering it starts with a screenwriter dead in a swimming pool, right?"

After working in various capacities for a few years, including writing for a while on *Narcos*, he became enamored with the idea of a film built around the campy, sideshow world of professional wrestling, basing a lead character after the swashbuckling, freewheeling Vince McMahon, the titan behind building the WWE wrestling empire. After five years, however, he gave up on the project.

In 2022, Johnny was torn between more screenwriting and returning to school to study a subject that also greatly intrigued his dad: psychology. He decided to stick with writing, but it wouldn't have been a big leap to psychology. He had spent much of his life hearing about and watching the labyrinthine twists and turns in the Newman family, and in the process he developed strong views about the delights and challenges of being a Newman.

"My dad is often misunderstood by people who think he's this cynical or jaded figure looking down on the people in his songs. He doesn't look down on anybody; he's not someone who thinks he's superior to these 'poor fools' or whatever," Johnny said, sitting at a table in the backyard of his father's home. "That doesn't mean he can't be mad in his songs."

"When people ask if he's happy, I think the better question is whether he's open to joy and the answer is an absolute yes. As hard as songwriting is for him, he can get great joy from his music, from being around musicians and, especially, from being around his children and grandchildren. He's an honest, loyal person, and I never questioned his love."

At the same time, Johnny was eventually at peace with the breakup of his first family.

Dad was a kid when he got married, and in some ways he's still a kid, but his parents didn't teach him how to be a parent. I think that my mom's relationship with my dad as caregiver was a little too one-way and not challenging enough. Both parents in second marriages wound up in better relationships, and largely because they found people that were complementary to their needs. He was a lot more involved as a dad in my little brother's and sister's lives. I don't know if he was confident enough to do it the first time around. In many ways, things have worked out for the best.

— || —

Patrick (born on February 11, 1992) was born in the glow of *The Natural*, and Alice (born on June 16, 1993) celebrated her second birthday amid the pending excitement of *Toy Story*. Randy was shedding the layers of stress. It was a time of much greater reassurance in his life.

"I once had to go to a recital for a kid that I babysat for and it was so boring, but Dad went with me," Alice said in 2022 at the family house, where she still had her old room though she lived in an apartment closer to Loyola Law School, about twenty minutes away. "He sat through it all and loved it."

Alice also remembered a dance class in the seventh grade that was for PE credit. "I got an A, and the teacher wrote something like 'Alice is a great dancer' on my card, and Dad to this day thinks I could have been a fabulous dancer, when the truth is everyone got an A in that class. Even as he got older and his eyesight problems prevented him from driving, he was around for everything. My mother would drive him to every recital, every basketball or soccer game."

Alice also credits her father with shaping her social values.

I'm attracted to doing criminal defense for indigent people who can't afford a lawyer. I'm similarly on the left politically and share his empathy for people who had less than we did. I think I learned a lot about various issues from his songs. I'd listen to the CDs in the car with my mom and she would explain the meanings of the songs to me at a pretty young age.

Some people listen to my dad's songs and think he's misanthropic, that he hates the world, but he is actually extremely sensitive. I remember the time at some school event when I was around ten or eleven and one of my brothers learned that Ray Charles had died. When my dad heard the news, he cried.

Patrick, who studied American history at Wesleyan, also mentions his parents' support. "I don't think my parents ever talked about their day when we'd get together . . . ever," he said. "They'd want to hear what we did. That meant a lot to us; it made us feel they cared about us, and it made it easier to talk to adults as we got older."

Like his siblings, Patrick didn't want to be a musician. "I think I always knew what I wanted to do," he said. "Not be a manager necessarily, but I wanted to work in entertainment some way, like on the production side. I just loved movies and TV. It was like my whole life." His first job was working for Broadway Video, the multimedia firm founded by Lorne Michaels.

In 2023, he was literary manager at Mosaic Media Group, a management and production company in Beverly Hills, where he represented a wide variety of writers, directors, animators, and producers working in the film, TV, and comic book industries.

I'm a manager for like writers and stuff, and even though in the back of my head I think, "Oh, I could write or do this or whatever," he said. I think the reason none of us went into music is that we watched our dad being creative and it was not fun— he was miserable. With so many artists, it was almost painful. Even Lenny . . . it was the bane of his existence to get my dad to write stuff in the early days, like pulling teeth.

When Dad started songwriting, he told me he didn't know if his uncles ever listened or cared about his songs. It's as if they thought pop songwriting was a lesser thing—and that's why I think one of the most amazing things about my dad is that he finally (took on the challenge) of film scores.

Patrick went to private schools with a lot of famous people's kids and felt a little different, more grounded. "I think my brothers were good examples on how to behave, and my mom had a lot to do with it," he said. "Even today, Johnny is my best friend. And I see Eric and Amos like every week. We're really close. We're one big family."

CHAPTER TWENTY-NINE

Toy Story 4
Marriage Story *and*
The Pandemic

— I —

As usual with *Toy Story* films, the birth of the fourth installment was a slow process. Disney didn't confirm the project until late in 2014, four years after *Toy Story 3*, when it also announced that Lasseter would return as director. "A lot of people said we shouldn't make another film because the arc between Woody and Andy ended so perfectly in *Toy Story 3*," said Lasseter, who had been working on a storyline with some of his regulars for two years. "But we eventually realized that we hadn't finished Woody's arc, and that the thing missing from his life was love." The awakening led to reuniting Woody with Bo Peep, who had been largely pushed aside after the original *Toy Story*. Though their love story remained the centerpiece, the story for the fourth film went through numerous revisions.

Still, everything seemed to be proceeding well when the shocking news came in November of 2017 that Lasseter was taking a six-month leave because of "missteps," which proved to be complaints by some female employees at Disney about alleged inappropriate behavior in the workplace. The studio announced seven months later that Lasseter would be severing all ties with the company at the end of 2018.

Lasseter, sixty-one, didn't leave the business, however. Nine days after the split with Disney, he was hired to run the animation division of Skydance Media, headed by David Ellison, son of Larry Ellison, the billionaire co-founder of Oracle Corporation. Skydance's live-action film output included numerous high-profile projects, including *True Grit* and *Jack Reacher*. The hiring drew criticism within the film community, including two-time Oscar winner Emma Thompson's decision to leave the cast of a Sundance animation movie in protest. In a statement at the time, Lasseter said, "I have spent the last year away from the industry in deep reflection, learning how my actions unintentionally made colleagues uncomfortable, which I deeply regret and apologize for. It has been humbling, but I believe it will make me a better leader."

~

Back at Disney, Josh Cooley, who Lasseter had brought in as co-director in 2015, took over as director on a final script credited to Andrew Stanton and Stephany Folsom. Lasseter was listed first among eight writers who contributed to the story. *Toy Story 4* proved to be another massive success, the second in the series to top $1 billion at the box office and the second to win an Academy Award for animated picture. Newman's "I Can't Let You Throw Yourself Away," a gospel-flavored expression of support for Forky, a chief new character in the series, was nominated for best song.

Despite no nomination for original score, Randy's presence in the film begins with him singing "You've Got a Friend in Me" over the opening credits and continues throughout, including "Throw Yourself Away," a new song in the comforting tradition of "Friend." If this was to be the final episode of the Newman / *Toy Story* relationship, it was a noteworthy one—touching on the maturity of the characters without violating the innocence of the series.

Throughout the project, Disney's Tom MacDougall asked himself if this would be Newman's last *Toy Story* score—or maybe even his last Disney score. If so, he didn't want the moment to pass without the team members expressing their affection and respect.

Knowing Randy's unease in the spotlight, MacDougall scheduled a modest gathering for March 29, 2019, the final day of recording, in a setting where Newman felt most comfortable: the scoring stage surrounded by musicians. No drinks, no food—just a gathering after work. The warmth of the event was captured in a home video that shows Newman shifting nervously as MacDougall saluted him. "This is my tenth movie with Randy and through those years . . . one question I get asked often is who is my favorite composer, and I think the greatest, best composer is Randy Newman." In the video, Newman expresses thanks as the musicians applaud vigorously.

— II —

Noah Baumbach felt a bit of déjà vu when he and Newman began work on *Marriage Story* in 2018. Just as Randy had written a moving theme for *Meyerowitz* overnight, he again quickly sent the director a piano melody that Baumbach felt was ideal for the new movie. Their relationship was so close that video footage of them working together was reminiscent of the warmth in the video of the *Toy Story 4* celebration.

In the DVD of the film, the footage shows Baumbach expressing his admiration for Newman's music. "Part of me feels like the grown-up director making sure this is . . . what I want for my movie . . . and then the other part of me is in some kind of fanta-syland, just watching someone he's admired for his whole life do something that he does as well as anybody on the planet."

For the new work, however, Baumbach envisioned music different from that of *Meyerowitz*. "With this one I wanted a kind of big, warm romantic score," he said. "So, I gave him the script and then he wrote back—and attached to . . . the email was a recording he'd done on his iPhone of him playing this melody on the piano. It was so beautiful that it made me cry, and I just kept this with me for the whole shoot, and I would play it for the actors sometimes. I would play it when I went home, and a year and a half later, we are on the Alfred Newman stage recording with an orchestra with this exact cue."

This film wasn't a narrow look at the death of a family patriarch, but a wider, more universal story of the breakup of a modern marriage. The most compelling element was how Baumbach mixed comedy and drama to keep the viewer uncertain about how things would turn out. Baumbach traces the ebbs and flows of the couple (played by Adam Driver and Scarlett Johansson) as they navigate their bicoastal relationship, step into the risky world of divorce lawyers, and try at every turn to comfort their young son. Whatever the outcome, Baumbach wants us to know these aren't bad people, and he wanted Newman's score to help make us care about them.

"I sort of thought of these characters as heroic in a way," the director told the *Los Angeles Times*. "And their love story—on one hand it's very human, the experience of the movie sort of mirrors qualities of real life. But I also saw it in the tradition of great movie love stories—like *Brief Encounter* or these stories of 'love that can't be' for whatever reason, but still love that is worthy of celebration."

To that end, Baumbach asked Newman to write a nearly eight-minute overture for the opening montage in which Driver's character tells Johansson's character what he likes best about her and vice versa. The director said:

> It's celebratory, it's compassionate, it's human. It's not romanticizing them, but it is loving, I think. The visuals that are accompanying it in the beginning are mostly images of domesticity, or coupledom, or individual characteristics that makes us unique. Ordinary moments. And I felt like the score could sort of celebrate it, make these ordinary moments extraordinary. Because they are, of course.
>
> But then the movie shifts. And suddenly that same music means something else. It both reflects back on what we've heard, so in a sense it becomes like the audience's memory, as well as the characters.' But it also now starts to mean something else.

The score was performed by a smaller, chamber-sized group of musicians rather than the usual massive studio orchestra.

As the DVD bonus footage showed, Baumbach was often in the studio while Newman was working on the score, sometimes sitting with him at the piano as scenes from the film are shown on a small monitor. "The thing we talked about a lot with this is that the music . . . is never about enhancing an emotion that was in the movie," Baumbach said. "What we wanted it to be was almost like, the movie's reaction to what was going on and often it was reacting with passion."

Baumbach spoke of making a documentary about Newman, but the pairing went to Alldayeveryday, a film production company that began work on the documentary, *Words & Music: Randy Newman*. This survey of Randy's life and career was directed by Brian E. Bennett and written by Matthew Broad. Coproduced by Warner Records, Fifth Season, and Alldayeveryday, the documentary was scheduled to be distributed by Sony Pictures Classics in 2025.

~

When Oscar nominations were announced in January of 2020, *Marriage Story* picked up six, including best picture, actor, actress, supporting actress (Laura Dern), original screenplay (Baumbach), and score. To make the night of February 7 at the Dolby Theater more special for the Newmans, Thomas Newman was also nominated for best score for *1917*. It was the third time that the cousins had both been nominated in the same year and the fifth time Randy had been nominated twice in the same year. His other 2020 nomination was for the song "I Can't Let You Throw Yourself Away" from *Toy Story 4*, pushing Newman's nomination total to twenty-two. The awards went elsewhere.

~

As Newman's songs for films continued to be saluted in the Oscar competition, it is absurd that none of the songs on his albums were acknowledged by the record industry's Grammy Awards—but not, in retrospect, surprising. Since the Grammys were started in 1959, the members of the National Academy of Recording Arts and Sciences were alarmingly out of step with the creative heartbeat of pop music, favoring mainstream bestsellers over cutting-edge innovators. Elvis Presley, whose landmark career began in 1954, didn't win a Grammy until 1967, and it was for a gospel performance, "How Great Thou Art," not for rock and roll. Dylan, whose first album was released in 1961, wasn't honored by the Grammys until eighteen years later, and it wasn't for any of his songs, but for best male rock vocal performance on the album *Gotta Serve Somebody*. Neil Young's first solo Grammy was for his role as art director of a retrospective boxed set in 2009, over forty years after his debut album was released. The Grammy voters were equally slow to recognize excellence in rap, which was largely relegated to its own category rather than nominated in the major Grammy fields.

Randy picked up enough support to be nominated in auxiliary categories seven times. But, ironically, the nominations were mostly for his film music, including best instrumental composition (*The Natural*) and best song for "When She Loved Me," "If I Didn't Have You," and "Our Town." None of his album songs were even nominated for best song or record.

As Randy and Gretchen left the Dolby, there was no talk of retirement. At age seventy-six, he was looking forward to more albums, film scores, and concerts; a series of shows in Europe was already set for the spring. But those sketchy news reports circulating at the time about a potentially deadly virus in China would change everything. With over 100,000 cases reported worldwide, the Covid-19 shutdown in the United States was only weeks away. The European dates were soon postponed. There was more bad news: a series of physical setbacks.

— III —

By Oscars night in February, Randy had already gone through two medical issues—for a hip replacement in November of 2019 and carpal tunnel syndrome in January of 2020—but there was lots more surgery ahead: for a knee in July of 2020, his neck in December of 2021, refractured neck surgery in January of 2022, additional neck surgery in August of 2022, and neck and back surgery in July of 2023.

Alan Newman traced his brother's body issues to a ruptured disc in his lower back when he was nineteen. "They wanted to hospitalize him for traction, but he refused and was put on bedrest at home," he said. "We became much closer during this time. I recall spending much of my time in his room listening to Dr. Demento and Firesign Theater into the night. He was very athletic, but he also had knee problems as a teenager, and there was unconfirmed talk of a mild case of polio as a baby, maybe in New Orleans. The rest is the result of degenerative arthritis, sleep disorders, and aging."

Randy would end up spending more time on hospital operating tables over the next three years than on concert stages or in recording studios, with some of the procedures lasting ten hours or more. The accompanying recovery periods, which meant limited mobility and weeks of physical therapy, left little time or energy for songwriting or performing. Between 2020 and 2023, he would only make four concert engagements—the Newport Folk Festival in July of 2021, the Argyros Performing Arts Center in Sun Valley, Idaho, in September of 2021, the New Orleans Jazz Heritage Festival in May of 2022, and the Jaqua Concert Hall in Eugene, Oregon, the same month. New dates were announced for the European tour in 2022 and again for 2023, but the shows would eventually be cancelled.

During that time, his fans would only hear one new song. In April of 2020, KPCC, a local public broadcasting radio station, asked Randy to make a public service announcement reminding people to be careful during the pandemic, but he went one step further and wrote "Stay Away," a love song to Gretchen and to the world to stay safe and keep your distance. It first aired on April 8, and a video was released of Randy performing it at home. Randy and Gretchen did an interview about the song for *CBS Sunday Morning*, and he performed it, remotely, on *The Late Show with Stephen Colbert*. Proceeds from the song were donated to the Ellis Marsalis Center for Music, a performance, education, and community base in New Orleans's Ninth Ward.

Venus in sweatpants
That's who you are
And when this mess is over

I'll buy you a car
We'll drive that car
So fast and so far
All your stupid friends
Will be left behind

Stay away from me
Baby, keep your distance, please
Stay away from me
Words of love in times like these
I'm gonna be with you twenty-four hours a day
A lot of people couldn't stand that
But you can
You'll be with me twenty-four hours a day
What a lucky man I am

Stay away from me
Wash your hands
Don't touch your face
How do you like that
Wash your hands
Don't touch your face
I saw you
Thirty years together
And we're still having fun
Once we were two,
Now we are one
Let's go out and get a burger
When you're done, you're done

Memories of the past
Be kind to one another
Tell her you love her every day

If you're angry about something, let it go
If the kids are frightened, tell them not to be afraid
But don't let them touch your face
Don't let them touch your face

Introducing the tune, Randy wisecracked that he had been asked to write the song because of his scientific background and followed the good-natured tune by saying, "Stay safe. It's hard for Americans who don't like being told what to do at all. But in this case, you know, let's do it. We'll be all right." Randy later contacted Covid-19 twice, but he was fully vaccinated, and the cases were mild.

— III —

The pandemic lockdown began loosening in the summer of 2020, but Randy continued to spend most of his time in the house that he and Gretchen built in the late 1990s, anchored there largely by his physical problems. Despite his medical issues, there was no sense of surrender. For someone known for a glass-half-empty outlook, Randy proved surprisingly resilient, even talking, in late 2023, about how one more knee operation could be the key to him returning to the concert trail. He still spent much of his time in his den, but he wasn't trying to isolate himself.

"I don't think he really likes to be alone the way it looks," said Gretchen, whose own cheerful instincts helped set a tone. "He makes anyone feel comfortable in the den with him, so it tells me he likes the company. What I think he does like about it is that he can watch as much TV as he wants, as well as listen to or play music when he wants. I don't think he is any different than others who have an office, kitchen, or bedroom where they go to be alone. And probably most importantly, it's comfortable for him. He can see the TV easily, and his chair is comfortable, too. Those are big things for him."

Randy's two-story home on a fashionable Pacific Palisades street boasted a backyard music studio, a pool, and lovely grounds, but the feature that struck most visitors was that the site was only 400 yards from his childhood home on D'Este Dr., where he and Lenny played ball and began talking about music almost seventy years earlier. Many guests assumed the location was a sentimental decision, but the proximity was largely coincidental. Gretchen said she and Randy looked in various neighborhoods before buying the property.

Still, there was something endearing about Randy and Lenny getting together regularly in the afternoon to watch sports or movies on television in a house so close to where they bonded as kids. During commercial breaks or lulls in the action, they would talk about a variety of things, from the news ("Trump is topping Biden in the polls!!!!???") to the various things that friends talk about.

Whatever the conversation, the elephant in the room was the question when Randy was going to start writing songs again.

CHAPTER THIRTY

Afternoon Visits
With Lenny and the
Hope for More Music

"What's that you're playing?" Lenny asked as Randy struck some unfamiliar notes on the piano during one of their afternoon get-togethers. "Is that new?"

"No," Randy said. "It's a song I wrote for some TV show that didn't make it. I've got a tape somewhere. I've got a lot of old songs around."

"Well, I'd love to hear some of them," Lenny said, longing for the day Randy would start writing or recording again. Aside from "Stay Away," the only song he had written since the pandemic was "Dinosaur," another humorous, even more adventurous look at the theme he introduced in "I'm Dead (But I Don't Know It)"—a veteran musician who worries that his time is up.

When I asked Randy if he thought he would ever make another album, he looked at Lenny in a nearby chair and said, "He wants me to."

"It's very doable," Lenny said, reassuringly, "especially when you say you've got all those songs you never had published, but there are other ways to go. We've talked about them before . . . we could make an album of you singing your favorite country and soul songs. Or maybe could put together an album of your movie music, tracks you've sung in films or others, like Sarah [McLachlan], have sung."

During these visits, Lenny had slowly fallen back into his role of motivator. It was easier now because Randy had shed enough memories to be able to speak about the early songs and recordings without the insecurity and struggles he long associated with them—a dramatic breakthrough that would have made another winning verse in "Potholes." He had moved even closer to glass-half-full hopefulness.

"I hadn't listened to some of those albums in forty years because I didn't want to be reminded of how hard it was," he said another afternoon, sitting in a large, comfortable white chair next to a piano. "But I listened to them again when Patrick did this podcast on the albums, and I thought they were pretty great."

"There were things about the songs and the early records that bothered me for years. It wasn't like I thought *Sail Away* was any better than the first album when I finished it. I still don't know why I was so tough on myself. I don't know if it did me any good. It certainly slowed me down. I wish I hadn't been that way."

Sitting a few feet away, Lenny offered his thoughts on the early trials. "I'm not sure there is any one answer," he said. "There's just the fact that Randy was never an 'up' person in those days, but I also think the Newman family had a lot to do with his thinking. As a group they were not what you would call a glass-half-full bunch; it was more a general hesitancy to show any kind of happy emotion, to always look for something wrong in what you've done—and as Randy got more confidence, he was able to move beyond it."

In turn, Randy picked up on the confidence issue. "It has come and gone over time, and I think that's true of most people," he said. "Johnny Williams may be the only film composer I've seen who seems to be confident all the time. Most people worry about what we do because it's so hard. I know Paul [Simon] knows he's good, and other people think I'm good, but sometimes I don't know it."

Lenny's positive attitude had been bolstered a few days earlier when Randy sang five songs—including "Love Story (You and Me)" and, surprisingly, "Short People"—at Patrick's wedding. "He sounded great!" Lenny said later. "His voice was so powerful and confident. He was ready to get back on stage—as long as he could get that knee taken care of to ease the pain. He has even done vocal exercises to get back in shape."

Though Randy, like most artists, doesn't like to rate his own work, he was relaxed enough to respond when I asked if he sided with hard-core fans who think *Sail Away* is his most consummate album from the 1970s or those who prefer *Good Old Boys*.

"I don't know, sometimes I think *Sail Away,* but other times I think *Good Old Boys*," he said. "I'll go with *Good Old Boys* today. What do you think, Lenny?"

"They're both great," Lenny said.

Randy then brought up his *Bad Love–Harps and Angels–Dark Matter* trilogy.

"I'm really proud of those albums; it was important to me that they be age responsive," he said. "I didn't want to be writing about someone who wanted to boogie all night or anything like that. In some ways, those three albums were harder than the others. There were two or three songs that came out real fast, but not many. I was a better arranger the more pictures I did and that made me want to reach for things like 'The Great Debate.' I don't think I could have done that when I was younger."

The conversation took a nostalgic turn when Randy started talking about some of the career moments that meant the most to him. Sidestepping the obvious spotlight ones, he mentioned more intimate, personal times. "One of the things that has always made me happy, musically, is solving a problem in a song, doing something that not a lot of people could have done. It also made me proud when I had dinner with some of the section heads of the studio orchestra and they stood up and made little speeches about me. It was touching. Another time was when I won a Grammy for arrangement of the year (for 'Putin' in 2018)."

Pausing a few seconds to think about something else, he brought up his musical.

"Someone might look at my life and works someday and think, 'What a mess,' when *Faust* the musical comes up, but I don't feel that way. It may be the best single thing I ever did, and it probably was the most fun I had."

Looking ahead, he mentioned the show that his son Eric and Lorne Michaels were urging him to do, a solo concert aimed at a special engagement on Broadway or maybe in Southern California. The idea would be to play some of his songs and speak to the audience about his life and music. It was all very sketchy. He was mainly looking forward to that knee operation and the chance to get back in front of audiences.

~

And so it went, afternoon after afternoon—these two old friends still together, talking about music, each hoping for the moment Randy makes another one of those early morning phone calls to Lenny. In the comfort and optimism of the den, both men seemed to believe it was going to happen. And why not? The prospect was no more unlikely than the journey that had brought them this far.

Before leaving them this late spring afternoon in 2024, I asked Randy for a few words about the state (and future) of the nation. But sharing was not in his nature. After all he had written about America, Randy was never comfortable in the role of public analyst or activist—and that hadn't changed. He preferred to let the songs express his thoughts. Just when I assumed the conversation was over, he looked up and did, briefly, waive his own reluctance.

The unshakeable dread of another Trump presidency led him to say, "For years, people talked about how the country was in trouble and falling apart, but I never quite believed it. But I now have some doubts." Those words echoed something he had said years earlier. After a pause he felt the need to give an update. "But I prefer to think people have enough good sense not to re-elect a man who has proven to be so dishonest."

ACKNOWLEDGMENTS

When talking to Randy Newman about his songs, our conversations went wonderfully well, but there came a point when I realized he was becoming uncomfortable. Randy has spent most of his career trying to keep himself out of his songs and interviews. He wanted the songs to be the story, not his life, and that goal made it difficult for him when I wanted to explore the connection between his art and his experiences. I thank him deeply for moving past his natural inclinations to help me better understand this essential part of his story.

I also want to express my profound gratitude to Randy's extended family—Lenny Waronker, his lifelong friend and career catalyst; his brother Alan, wife Gretchen and five adult children, Amos, Eric, Johnny, Patrick, and Alice. They each spoke about him with remarkable frankness and insight, traits that Randy encouraged and inspired in those close to him. Also invaluable: Randy's cousins who were generous with their time and insights—Carroll, David, Joey, Maria, Thomas, and Tim.

That same openness and affection was shown uniformly by others in Randy's inner circle, from his various managers (Elliot Abbott, Peter Asher, and Cathy Kerr), musicians and producers with whom he worked (Russ Titelman and Mitchell Froom to Van Dyke Parks and Ry Cooder to Mark Knopfler and Michael Roth). In addition, music industry figures (Robert Hurwitz and Michael Gorfaine) and key individuals in his film world (especially John Lasseter, Barry Levinson, Chris Montan, Tom MacDougall). I'm indebted to them all.

Thanks, too, to others who spoke to me about Randy or aided in other ways, including Rick Baptist, Georgia (Jo) Bergman, Pat Boone, Susan Brett, Larry Butler, Judy Collins, Jackie DeShannon, Barry Dickins, Scott Downie, Bill Flanagan, Guy Fletcher, Bruce Grimes, Lee Herschberg, Jim Keltner, Al Kooper, Michael Laughlin, Terry Licona, Steve Martin, Bob Merlis, Lorne Michaels, James Newton-Howard, Gary Norris, Peter J. Philbin, Jeannie Seely, Foster Sherwood, Danny Vuong, Joey Waronker, Dan Weiner, John Williams, and Frank Wolf. My heartfelt thanks, as well, to the superb artists and cultural commentators who contributed personal reflections on Randy's artistry and message.

~

Since leaving the *Los Angeles Times* in 2005 to write books, my respect for and gratitude to Luke Janklow, my agent, has deepened with each new project. He is equally sagacious in helping me choose book subjects, finding the right publishers and counseling when problems arose. This book was especially close to Luke's heart because Randy's son, Eric, has been one of his closest friends for over twenty years, and Luke spent many early Sunday dinners at The Ivy at the Shore with the Newman Clan. Luke's aide-de-camp, Claire Dippel, is gracious and tireless, always eager and able to follow through on my endless needs, inquiries, requests.

At Hachette, it was a joy to work with Ben Schafer, an editor who loves music as much as the printed page, someone whose passion for songs has led him to see nearly a hundred Bob Dylan concerts. He shares my belief in Randy as one of the greatest American songwriters ever and he brought a sharp mind and comforting manner to our time together. Also at Hachette, I'd like to salute the tremendous team of Carrie Napolitano, the ever-patient and gracious Fred Francis, Michael Barrs, Emma

Little-Jensen, Michael Giarratano, Abimael Ayala-Oquendo, Amanda Kain, and Terri Sirma.

In past books, I've thanked numerous editors, writers, copy-editors, and the marvelous pop music team held together by Richard Cromelin—each of whom made my thirty-five years at the *Los Angeles Times* such a wonderful time. Here I want to especially note the passing of the late Chuck Phillips, a Pulitzer-winning investigative reporter who died this year. Before Chuck, pop music reporting around the country was, in the main, timid and sporadic. He turned it into something relentless and uncompromising. I also value immensely Bret Israel, who was a gifted editor at the *Times* and continues to be a friend who was eager to advise on numerous editorial questions and knows just when to convey well-chosen words of reassurance.

Ultimately, everything begins with my own family, starting with my first wife, Ruthann Snijders, our daughter Kathy, son Rob, and grandchildren Chris, Lindsey, Genevieve, and Grant, and my wife of almost forty years, Kathi, and her children from a prior marriage, Kate Bond and Keith Bond, and granddaughter, Nicole Stetter.

Special thanks to Rob, Kathy, and Kathi. Rob, a huge Randy fan who also studied musical composition at UCLA, assisted in numerous ways, from transcribing all the interviews to (along with Michael Roth) helping me better understand the often complex nature of Randy's music and arrangements. Kathy, a design artist, was always ready with words of support and help gathering the book's photos. Above all, Kathi, whose support is reflected in reading and re-reading the drafts to find mistakes of all kinds and offering suggestions on how to help sharpen the text. Writing a book can often be a lonely journey, but she was a loving, indispensable partner on every step. Plus, she's a huge Randy Newman fan. What more could you ask?

APPENDIX

COVER VERSIONS OF SONGS FROM RANDY'S THIRTEEN STUDIO ALBUMS

More than 500 cover versions have been recorded of Randy's songs, mostly songs before he began focusing on the sociocultural commentary that defined him a writer. The following lists of select covers highlight the range of artists who have recorded his tunes—from Etta James to Barbra Streisand and Johnny Cash to Ray Charles. Gary Norris, Randy's long-time archivist, was invaluable in helping draft the cover lists, and he, too, contributed the discography, film, and television/documentary lists. Randy has often said, "Gary thinks he knows more about me than I do"—and he may be right. The covers are divided into two parts—songs that Randy recorded for the albums (the debut through *Dark Matter*) that represent the heart of his legacy, and a list of his other songs, mostly those from his pre-Warner Bros. and Reprise Records years—RH.

Song Title/Artist (Year, Label)
"The Beehive State"/Harry Nilsson (1970, RCA Records)
—The Doobie Brothers (1971, Warner Bros.)
"Bet No One Ever Hurt This Bad"/Linda Ronstadt (1969, Capitol)
"Cowboy"/Harry Nilsson (1970, RCA)
"Dayton, Ohio – 1903"/Harry Nilsson (1970, RCA)

—George Burns (1970, Pride)

"Feels Like Home"/Linda Ronstadt (1995, Elektra)

"God's Song"/Etta James (1973, Chess)

—Tracy Nelson (1978, Flying Fish)

"Guilty"/Bonnie Raitt (1973, Warner Bros.)

—Joe Cocker (1974, A&M)

"Have You Seen My Baby?"/Fats Domino (1970, Reprise)

—Peggy Lee (1970, Capitol)

—Ringo Starr (1971, Apple)

—The Flamin' Groovies (1972, Kama Sutra)

"I'll Be Home"/Barbra Streisand (1971, Columbia)

—Tim Hardin (1972, Columbia)

—Lorraine Ellison (1995, Ichiban)

"In Germany Before the War"/Marianne Faithfull (2008, Decca)

"I Think It's Going to Rain Today"/Julius La Rosa (1966, MGM)

—Judy Collins (1966, Elektra)

—Dusty Springfield (1968, Philips UK)

—Rick Nelson (1968, Decca)

—UB40 (1980, Graduate, UK)

—Bette Midler (1988, Atlantic)

—Irma Thomas (2008, Rounder)

—Peter Gabriel (2010, Virgin)

"Last Night I Had a Dream"/Fanny (1973, Reprise)

"Let's Burn Down the Cornfield"/Lou Rawls (1970, Capitol)

—Long John Baldry (1971, Warner Bros.)

"Living Without You"/Harry Nilsson (1970, RCA)

"Losing You"/Mavis Staples (2010, Anti-)

"Louisiana 1927"/Aaron Neville (1991, A&M)

—Sonny Landreth (2006, Sugar Hill)

"Love Story"/Rick Nelson (1968, Decca)

—Harry Nilsson (1970, RCA)

"Lucinda"/Joe Cocker (1975, A&M)

"Mama Told Me Not to Come"/Eric Burdon (1967, MGM)

—Three Dog Night (1970, Dunhill)

—Wilson Pickett (1972, Atlantic)

—Jackson 5 (2012, Motown)

"Marie"/Joe Cocker (1982, A&M)

—Allison Moorer (2006, Sugar Hill)

"Mr. President (Have Pity on the Working Man)"/Marshall
   Tucker Band (1982, Warner Bros.)

"Old Kentucky Home"/Beau Brummels (1967, Warner Bros.)

—Ry Cooder (1970, Reprise)

—Johnny Cash (1975, Columbia)

"Old Man"/Art Garfunkel (1973, Columbia)

"Rednecks"/Steve Earle (2006, Sugar Hill)

"Rider in the Rain"/Joe Ely (2006, Sugar Hill)

"Sail Away"/Bobby Darin (1972, Motown)

—Etta James (1973, Chess)

—Sonny Terry and Brownie McGee (1973, A&M)

—Ray Charles (1975, Crossover)

—Joe Cocker (1996, Sony)

"Simon Smith and the Amazing Dancing Bear"/Alan Price
   (1966, UK Decca)

"So Long Dad"/Liza Minnelli (1968, A&M)

—Kim Richey (2006, Sugar Hill)

"Yellow Man"/Ella Fitzgerald (1969, Reprise)

—Harry Nilsson (1970, RCA)

"You Can Leave Your Hat On"/Etta James (1973, Chess)

—Joe Cocker (1986, Capitol)

—Tom Jones (1998, RCA)

COVER VERSIONS OF RANDY SONGS NOT INCLUDED
IN THE THIRTEEN STUDIO ALBUMS

"Anyone Who Knows What Love Is (Will Understand)—
   co-written with others, including Jeannie Seely/Irma
   Thomas (1964, Imperial)
"Big Brother"/The Persuasions (1965, Columbia)
"The Debutante's Ball"/Harpers Bizarre (1967, Warner Bros.)
—Liza Minnelli (1968, A&M)
"Did He Call Today Mama?"/Jackie DeShannon (1963,
   Liberty)
"Friday Night"/The O'Jays (1966, Imperial)
"Happyland"/Harpers Bizarre (1967, Warner Bros.)
I Can't Remember Ever Loving You"/Petula Clark (1966,
   Warner Bros.)
"I Don't Want to Hear It Anymore"/Scott Walker (1968,
   Smash)
—Dusty Springfield (1969, Atlantic)
"Illinois"/Everly Brothers (1968, Warner Bros.)
"I've Been Wrong Before"/Cilla Black (1965, Capitol)
—Jerry Butler (1965, Vee-Jay)
—Dusty Springfield (1966, Phillips)
"I Wonder Why"/Ella Fitzgerald (1969, Reprise)
"Just One Smile"/Gene Pitney (1965, Musicor)
—Blood, Sweat & Tears (1968, Columbia)
—Dusty Springfield (1969, Atlantic)
"Let Me Go"/The Box Tops (1970, Bell)
—Barbra Streisand (1971, Columbia)
"Look at Me"/Bobby Darin (1964, Capitol)
"Love Is Blind"/Erma Franklin (1965, Epic)
—Lou Rawls (1965, Capitol)
"She Doesn't Understand Him Like I Do" written with
   Jackie DeShannon/Jackie DeShannon (1965, Imperial)
"Somebody's Waiting"/Gene McDaniels (1962/Liberty)

"Stoplight"/Spike Jones New Band (1964, Liberty)

"Take Her"/Frankie Laine (1963, Columbia)

"They Tell Me It's Summer"/The Fleetwoods (1962, Dolton)

"Vine Street"/Van Dyke Parks (1968, Reprise)

—Lulu (1970, Atco)

"Wait Till Next Year"/Lee Hazelwood (1969, LHI)

"While the City Sleeps"/Irma Thomas (1964, Imperial)

Discography

1968 *Randy Newman*

1970 *12 Songs*

1971 *Randy Newman Live*

1972 *Sail Away*

—A deluxe edition, released in 2002, featured five additional tracks from the same period.

1974 *Good Old Boys*

—A deluxe edition, also 2002, contained an extra CD of the demos for *Johnny Cutler's Birthday*, which evolved into *Good Old Boys*.

1977 *Little Criminals*

1979 *Born Again*

1983 *Trouble in Paradise*

1988 *Land of Dreams*

1995 *Randy Newman's Faust*

—A deluxe edition, in 2003, has the original working demos for *Randy Newman's Faust*.

1998 *Guilty: 30 Years of Randy Newman*

1999 *Bad Love*

2003 *The Randy Newman Songbook Vol. 1*

2008 *Harps and Angels*

2011 *The Randy Newman Songbook Vol. 2*

2011 *Live in London*

2016 *The Randy Newman Songbook Vol. 3*

2016 *The Randy Newman Songbook—The Complete Solo 2003–2010*

2017 *Dark Matter*

Major Film Work (including film score unless noted with *)

1971 *Cold Turkey*

1981 *Ragtime*

1984 *The Natural*

1987 *Three Amigos!* * (songs and co-screenplay)

1989 *Parenthood*

1990 *Avalon*

1991 *Awakenings*

1994 *The Paper*

1995 *Maverick*

1995 *Toy Story*

1996 *James and the Giant Peach*

1996 *Michael*

1997 *Cats Don't Dance* * (songs)

1998 *Pleasantville*

1998 *A Bug's Life*

1999 *Toy Story 2*

2000 *Meet the Parents*

2001 *Monsters Inc.*

2003 *Seabiscuit*

2004 *Meet the Fockers*

2005 *Cars*

2008 *Leatherheads*

2009 *The Princess and the Frog*

2010 *Toy Story 3*

2012 *Monsters University*

2017 *Cars 3*

2017 *The Meyerowitz Stories (New and Selected)*

2019 *Toy Story 4*

2019 *Marriage Story*

Notable Television Performances

Soundstage: The Music of Randy Newman, 1974. A retrospective of Randy's music taped with a 19-piece orchestra at WTTW in Chicago. Cool feature: Lenny joins in helping Randy pick his older songs off the top of his head.

Saturday Night Live: Oct. 18, 1975, NBC-TV. Randy performs "Sail Away" following Paul Simon's snippet of "Marie."

—Jan. 21, 1978, NBC-TV. Randy performs "Short People" and "Rider in the Rain" with the Dirt Band.

—Feb. 26, 1983, NBC-TV. Randy performs "I Love L.A." and "Real Emotional Girl."

Live at the Odeon: Dec. 8, 1983. London concert filmed for HBO and commercial home video. Ry Cooder and Linda Ronstadt perform with him. DVD.

Late Night with David Letterman: Oct. 11, 1985, NBC-TV. Performs "Stagger Lee" with the show's band.

Saturday Night Live: Dec. 6, 1986, NBC-TV. Performs "The Longest Night" and "Roll With the Punches."

Michelob Presents Sunday Night: Nov. 6, 1988, NBC-TV. Performs "I Want You to Hurt Like I Do," "Dixie Flyer," and Arthur Alexander's "You Better Move On" with Mark Knopfler and the house band.

Evening at Boston Pops: May 8, 1991. Performs "Davy the Fat Boy," "Sail Away," and "Political Science." Interviewed by John Williams.

Late Night with David Letterman: Nov. 12, 1992, NBC-TV. Performs "Dixie Flyer."

Documentaries and interviews

Land of Dreams—Randy Newman's America: 1994 on ITV England. Excellent.

The Hollywood Soundtrack Story: 1995. Randy hosted this outstanding hour look at the art of film scoring. The American Movie Channel.

Great Streets—Sunset Boulevard: 2001. No music, but Randy hosts this lively, one-hour PBS special that uses the classic Los Angeles street to tell a wider view of the city itself. Terrific.

...

Randy Newman in Conversation with Jon Burlingame: 2017. The production was co-produced by the Academy of Motion Picture Arts & Sciences Oral History Project and the Film Music Foundation.

ADDITIONAL NOTES

Unless attributed to another source, all quotes in the book come from interviews conducted by the author.

PROLOGUES

PRINCIPAL INTERVIEWS
Randy Newman, Alan Newman, Lenny Waronker.

PRINCIPAL ARTICLES NOT CITED IN THE TEXT
Enos, Morgan. "How Randy Newman's Family Built a Film Scoring Dynasty." *Fortune*, February 6, 2020.

Kamp, David. "How Randy Newman and His Family Have Shaped Movie Music for a Century." *Vanity Fair*, February 18, 2016.

Randy's mission statement, "I'm interested in this country...," from Timothy White's "Randy Newman's America—A Portrait of the Artist." *Billboard*, Dec. 9, 2000.

SIDELIGHT
One way to encourage someone to listen to the work of someone like Randy, who is not a blockbuster seller, is to get artists or commentators he or she admires to recommend him. With that in mind, I asked a dozen or so artists or commentators whom I knew to be admirers of Newman to write one- or two-hundred-word reflections about his music for the book. I was thrilled when the reclusive Bob Dylan was the first to respond. Within a couple of weeks, most of the others had also sent me their thoughts—a sign of the music world's respect for Randy.

CHAPTER ONE

PRINCIPAL INTERVIEWS
Randy Newman, Alan Newman, Lenny Waronker, Amos Newman, Eric Newman, John Newman, Carroll Newman.

FURTHER STUDY
White, Timothy. "Bet No One Ever Hurt This Bad." *Rolling
Stone*, November 1, 1979.

SIDELIGHT
Randy's family history is as complicated at times as it is culturally significant, and Randy's brother Alan and cousin Carroll
Newman (a television and film producer who is Lionel Newman's
daughter) have worked tirelessly on an invaluable family history,
which they shared with me.

CHAPTER TWO

INTERVIEWS
Randy Newman, Lenny Waronker, Alan Newman, Foster Sherwood, Jackie DeShannon, Jeanie Seely.

CHAPTER THREE

INTERVIEWS
Randy Newman, Lenny Waronker, Pat Boone, John Williams.

FURTHER STUDY
Michael Kelly's two-volume history of Liberty Records and its
stars (see bibliography).

Copies of the Fleetwoods' "They Tell Me It's Summer" and Randy's "Gridiron Golden Boy." Singles pop up occasionally on eBay

or at record collection conventions, but you can also find "Summer" on *On Vine Street: The Early Songs of Randy Newman*, a CD collection of cover versions of Randy's early songs (released by Ace Records in 2008). The original "Gridiron" recording is included in *Guilty: 30 Years of Randy Newman*, an outstanding four-disc CD set from Rhino Records that contains dozens of recordings from Randy's Warner Bros. albums as well as early demos and a generous number of his film music. *Bless You California: More Early Songs of Randy Newman* is a second collection of covers (released by Ace Records in 2010). Both recordings are also on YouTube.

CHAPTER FOUR

INTERVIEWS
Randy Newman, Lenny Waronker, Foster Sherwood, Al Kooper, Judy Collins.

FURTHER STUDY
Thanks to the success in England of Cilla Black's "I've Been Wrong Before" and Alan Price's "Simon Smith and the Amazing Dancing Bear," the British press began writing about Randy in the mid-1960s, and many of those articles are contained on the London-based *rock'sbackpages*, an excellent pay website that describes itself as "the archive of rock journalism." An early *Melody Maker* magazine article on Randy, found on the site, carried this headline, a sign of his self-deprecating nature, "The Man They All Dig Doesn't Dig Himself."

CHAPTER FIVE

INTERVIEWS
Randy Newman, Lenny Waronker, Van Dyke Parks, Ry Cooder, Mo Ostin, Eric Newman, Alan Newman, Foster Sherwood.

FURTHER STUDY

Constance Rourke's *American Humor: A Study of the National Companion,* a fiercely independent 1931 look at American culture, is an essential volume for anyone interested in learning more about the mix of humor and commentary that Newman embraces. Rourke was a historian, anthropologist, and critic who is deeply admired by a core of celebrated tastemakers, including Lewis Mumford, the noted critic who called *American Humor* "the most original piece of investigation and interpretation that has appeared in American cultural history. It is in every way a brilliant book." In writing the introduction to a 2004 reprint of the book, Greil Marcus added, "Rourke came armed with a style that matched her ambition: to define the American not as a Lockean philosopher or a Rousseauian natural man, a democrat or a plutocrat, but as a tall—tall story teller, a fabulist spinning yarn until "the final episode rose like a balloon with the string cut."

Long-time Warner Bros. Records executive Stan Cornyn's personal history of the label (written with Paul Scanlon) is a colorful, highly opinionated look at the company's place in the record business—as the title suggests, *Exploding: The Highs, Hits, Hype, Heroes, and Hustlers of the Warner Music Group* (see bibliography).

To understand the adventurous, idealistic nature of the Warner Bros. Records approach when Randy arrived, listen to Van Dyke Parks' free-wheeling *Song Cycle* collection.

SIDELIGHT

Mo Ostin, the hugely respected head of Warner Bros. Records for years, left the spotlight to the artists, turning down interviews even in moments of triumph for the label. But he sat down for nearly ten hours over two days with my Pulitzer Prize–winning *Los Angeles Times* colleague Chuck Phillips and me to "set the record straight" before leaving WB in 1994. In the interview, he explained the artist-oriented philosophy that made Warner Bros. Records the perfect home for Randy and other gifted, independent singer-songwriters such as Joni Mitchell, Neil Young, Van Morrison, James Taylor, Gordon Lightfoot, and the *Graceland*-period Paul Simon.

Through it all, he stressed the importance of creating a comfortable environment for the artists. "I don't know why, but corporate people have a tendency to think in terms of immediate gratification. Sure, you can squeeze another dollar out of anything, but that's not what makes a record company run profitably. This business is about (artistic) freedom and creative control."

CHAPTER SIX

INTERVIEWS
Randy Newman, Lenny Waronker, Lee Hershberg, John Boylan, Van Dyke Parks.

FURTHER STUDY
Wayne C. Booth's book *The Rhetoric of Fiction* addresses the unreliable narrator approach (see bibliography).

SIDELIGHT
One delight in writing the book was combing through back issues of *Billboard*, the industry's primary trade magazine, for articles on Randy and his work, including ads and chart positions for various singles and albums. You can buy individual issues of *Billboard* online, but there's a site that lets you browse every issue for free. Search the *World Radio History* site for a link.

Randy's lyrics are on various websites, but the easiest way to go through them is his home page. Once there (*RandyNewman.com*), click on the albums link.

Peggy Lee was a trailblazer in many ways, one of the first pop singers (male or female) to battle record labels for artistic control of their recordings. James Gavin's biography, *Is That All There Is? The Strange Life of Peggy Lee,* is a smart, fascinating account (see bibliography).

CHAPTER SEVEN

INTERVIEWS
Randy Newman, Lenny Waronker, Peter J. Philben, Alan Newman, Ry Cooder, Bruce Grimes, Russ Titelman, Maria Newman.

FURTHER STUDY
Robert Christgau's reviews of Randy's albums (and tons of other albums) are available for free on his website home page. Search *robertchristgau.com* and write Randy Newman in the CG search box on the left.

Bruce Grimes's *Rolling Stone* review ran April 16, 1970, and is available on Google by requesting *Rolling Stone*'s review of Randy Newman's *12 Songs* album.

SIDELIGHT
I was still a freelance pop critic when I reviewed Randy's opening night at the Troubadour in 1970, and I was feeling my way in terms of expressing my opinions—relatively guarded in my feelings. I didn't want to go overboard in terms of liking or disliking an artist (that came later, smile). But I found myself forgetting about the insecurity when it came to Randy. I pretty much raved. Here is part of that review:

> Randy Newman, who is appearing through Sunday at the Troubadour, is a singer-composer of immense talent and potential. He both sings and writes the blues with striking originality and

skill. In building his own contemporary style on a traditional music base, he is doing, in many ways, for the blues what others have done in recent years for other musical forms.

Bob Dylan's contemporary approach to folk music, for instance, has influenced a whole generation of singers and writers. . . . In time, Newman, a 26-year-old native of Los Angeles, may show blues-oriented singers and writers there is much more to be done with that rich musical field than merely trying to imitate the old masters. . . .

On each of (his) songs, Newman expressed a combination of wry humor, gentle insight, and human emotion. Perhaps "Love Story," an enchanting tale of love in various stages of development (from courtship to old age) incorporates these three elements best.

Looking back at the review all these years later, it seems odd to place him in the blues tradition, but I may have done it because the growl in his voice and the shuffle in the music suggested the blues more than a pop or rock sensibility at the time. There, too, is an element of suffering and complaint in much of his music that does draw from the blues. On record, with the orchestra, it was clearer just how revolutionary his music was going to be.

CHAPTER EIGHT

INTERVIEWS
Randy Newman, Lenny Waronker, Russ Titelman, Michael Laughlin.

FURTHER STUDY
David Felton's penetrating profile of Randy ran in *Rolling Stone*'s Aug. 31, 1972, issue and can be called up in a search. Titled "Randy Newman: You've Got to Let This Fat Boy in Your Life," the piece included this winning example of Randy's sharp wit: Felton tells of

the time Randy was approached early in his career by a Hollywood promoter who wanted to introduce him to Neil Diamond, possibly thinking Randy could benefit from the relationship because Neil was selling far more records. "Randy," the promoter said, "I think you and Neil here have something in common."

"Yeah," Randy wisecracked, "We're both Jewish." Actually, Felton noted, Randy told him he wasn't really that Jewish. "I played at some bar mitzvah once," he quoted Newman. "Wait a minute, no I didn't—just a regular wedding. Normal people."

SIDELIGHT

Bob Krasnow's idea of promoting Randy's live album as an underground bootleg was typical of the daring, off-the-wall thinking of a man who founded Blue Thumb Records (where he signed Captain Beefheart) before his Warner's days and resurrected a faltering Elektra Records (signing such thoughtful, passionate artists as Tracy Chapman) after the WB years. While at WB Krasnow, always searching for new acts, was so much part of the late-night Hollywood musicians' scene that he was the model for Randy's song "Uncle Bob's Midnight Blues," a good-natured tale of burning the candle at both ends in the hectic rock world.

CHAPTER NINE

INTERVIEWS

Randy Newman, Lenny Waronker, Russ Titelman, Jim Keltner, Marc Newfeld, Elliot Abbott, Gary Norris.

SIDELIGHT

One of the most influential early articles on Randy was written by Susan Lydon in the *New York Times* a few months after *Sail Away* was released. To demonstrate the excellence and range of Newman's music and ideas, a headline writer used several names to stress the range outlined in Lydon's feature on the budding pop sensation, "Randy Newman—Out of Cole Porter, Hoagy Carmichael, Bob Dylan, Groucho Marx, Mark Twain and Randy Newman." In time, the headline writer could have easily added Stephen Foster, Beethoven, William Faulkner, Alexis de Tocqueville, and *The Simpsons*. The article ran on Nov. 5, 1972. Can be found via search.

CHAPTER TEN

INTERVIEWS
Randy Newman, Elliot Abbott, Gary Norris, Russ Titelman, Nelson George, Bill Flanagan.

FURTHER STUDY
Good Old Boys is inspiring on its own, but Randy's accomplishment in the album is even more impressive when you read of the savage sociocultural forces unleashed by the nation's 1927 flood. John M. Barry's *Rising Tide: The Great Mississippi Flood of 1927 and How It Changed America* is an angry and detailed account of that aftermath. Capturing the complex emotions and reasons in a single album stands for Newman as one of his most remarkable accomplishments.

David Kastin's *Song of the South: Randy Newman's Good Old Boys* traces the path of Good Old Boys, from its *Johnny Cutler* roots to the album's final form (see bibliography).

The *Johnny Cutler* tape, included in the deluxe edition of *Good Old Boys*, provides a glimpse of Randy's thought process as a songwriter, a document so powerful that when combined with the *Good Old Boys* could serve as the foundation of a course in a forward-thinking college or music school.

Randall Kennedy's *Nigger: The Strange Career of a Troublesome Word* provides a detailed, scholarly look at when, if ever, it is appropriate to use the N-word in books, film, and music (see bibliography).

CHAPTER ELEVEN

INTERVIEWS
Randy Newman, Lorne Michaels, Amos Newman, Elliot Abbott, Alan Newman.

SIDELIGHT
If you find the *Ragtime* film even slightly interesting, check out E. L. Doctorow's far superior novel to see what might have been if the more imaginative Robert Altman had been left in control.

CHAPTER TWELVE

INTERVIEWS
Randy Newman, Elliot Abbott, Lenny Waronker, Russ Titelman, Eric Newman, Wouter Bulckaert, Larry Butler.

FURTHER STUDY
You can find the Gusto Records single "Tall People" by the group Short People on YouTube, but the novelty has garnered so little traction that Newman collectors could buy it in early 2024 for as little as eight dollars on eBay. Don't confuse it with "Tall People," a parody single by Wee Willie Small and the Little Band on Co-Star Records. That single, also on YouTube in 2024, was going for around five dollars on eBay.

CHAPTER THIRTEEN

INTERVIEWS
Randy Newman, Ry Cooder, Lenny Waronker, Russ Titelman.

FURTHER STUDY

In case you skipped the profile before, be sure to look up Timothy White's Nov. 1, 1979, *Rolling Stone* article titled "Randy Newman: Bet No One Hurt This Bad" via search.

SIDELIGHT

Record companies used giant billboards along Los Angeles's hip (and heavily traveled) Sunset Strip to advertise their album releases, and many were so colorful that it wasn't uncommon for drivers to slow down to take photos of the billboards, including such iconic images as the Beatles' *Abbey Road* cover or the Rolling Stones' outlandish *Exile on Main Street* cover. But few billboards captured the moment as strongly as the towering image of Randy's *Born Again* cover face. Some fans thought the billboard was advertising a new KISS album, but, upon closer inspection, the face in the make-up didn't look like any of the members of the colorful band. For confused Newman fans, the billboard resulted in a severe backlash.

CHAPTER FOURTEEN

INTERVIEWS

Randy Newman, Jon Burlingame, John Williams, Lenny Waronker, Michael Roth, Gary Norris, Alan Newman.

CHAPTER FIFTEEN

INTERVIEWS

Randy Newman, Lenny Waronker, Russ Titelman, Don Henley, Rob Tannenbaum, Michael Roth, Tim Newman, Elliot Abbott, Gretchen (Preece) Newman, Amos Newman, Eric Newman.

FURTHER STUDY

The breakthrough "I Love LA" video (and later "It's Money That Matters" video) are among numerous Tim Newman videos and clips on YouTube.

CHAPTER SIXTEEN

INTERVIEWS

Barry Levinson, Randy Newman, Michael Roth, Steve Martin, Lorne Michaels, Lenny Waronker, Elliot Abbott, Peter Asher.

FURTHER STUDY

In Bill Milkowski's conversation with Randy from the October 1984 issue of *Modern Recording & Music*, Randy was asked to name the masters of film score and he replied, "My uncle Alfred Newman was about the best." He went on to name several of Alfred's films to back up his view.

CHAPTER SEVENTEEN

INTERVIEWS

Randy Newman, Lenny Waronker, Russ Titelman, James Newton-Howard, Mark Knopfler, Frank Wolf, Guy Fletcher, Tim Newman, Cathy Kerr.

FURTHER STUDY

The DVD featuring the director's cut of *The Natural* (Tri Star) contains several worthy bonus features.

CHAPTER EIGHTEEN

INTERVIEWS

Michael Gorfaine, Randy Newman, Barry Levinson, Elliot Abbott, Gretchen Newman, Eric Newman, Lenny Waronker, Peter Asher, Frank Wolf.

FURTHER STUDY

Two more of Randy's most acclaimed scores are for *Avalon* (Tri-Star) and *Pleasantville* (New Line Home Video), and both DVD editions also offer numerous bonus features.

CHAPTER NINETEEN

INTERVIEWS

Michael Roth, Randy Newman, Peter Asher, Lenny Waronker, Cathy Kerr.

CHAPTER TWENTY

INTERVIEWS

John Lasseter, Chris Montan, Michael Gorfaine, Randy Newman, Lenny Waronker, Frank Wolf, Tom MacDougall, Gretchen Newman, Alice Newman, Patrick Newman.

FURTHER STUDY

John Lasseter writes (with Steve Daly) about *Toy Story* in marvelous detail in the book *Toy Story: The Art and Making of the Animated Film* (see biography).

A handy way to follow the *Toy Story* history is a five-disc box set, *Toy Story–4-movie Collection* (the fifth disc contains bonus features). It's on DVD from Disney-Pixar.

CHAPTER TWENTY-ONE

INTERVIEWS

John Lasseter, Jon Burlingame, Chris Montan, Randy Newman.

FURTHER STUDY

The beauty and emotion of "When She Loved Me" is captured in some Disney video clips on YouTube that contain both Sarah McLachlin's vocal and footage from *Toy Story 2*.

CHAPTER TWENTY-TWO

INTERVIEWS
Randy Newman, Lenny Waronker, Mitchell Froom, John Lasseter.

SIDELIGHT
It's easy to see why Randy was so upset after the commercial failure of *Bad Love* that he left DreamWorks (and Mo and Lenny). After years of hearing that *Sail Away* and *Good Old Boys* were his greatest albums, he delivered (while in his 50s, no less) an album, *Bad Love*, that rivaled by most measures those two albums. He wasn't being defensive when he called it the best he could do. The collection reflected growth in so many areas that it was in every way a creative rebirth. The problem was the way critics and the music industry changed in search of new voices, which DreamWorks, too, was showcasing at the time, including Rufus Wainwright and Elliott Smith. Randy was fortunate to find a new label that still served veteran artists and was excited about his future. It made him feel at home again.

CHAPTER TWENTY-THREE

INTERVIEWS
Robert Hurwitz, Michael Gorfaine, Cathy Kerr, Randy Newman, Mitchell Froom, John Lasseter.

SIDELIGHTS
Hurwitz's realization that an album of Randy revisiting his best songs would demonstrate how well his music fit into the Great American Songbook tradition. Ella Fitzgerald popularized the Songbook concept in a series of albums in the 1950s celebrating such leading Songbook era composers as the Gershwins, Cole Porter, Irving Berlin, and Harold Arlen. Hurwitz's idea was daring, but Newman and the songs stood up to the challenge. What

was remarkable is that the three volumes didn't sidestep Randy's most radical or controversial songs.

"Seabiscuit" wasn't the first time Randy walked off a film set early. In 1997, he was, in effect, fired because director Wolfgang Petersen didn't like the score Randy composed for the action film *Air Force One* and replaced him in the final weeks with composer Jerry Goldsmith (and added music by Joel McNeely). Still, Randy believed in his score so much that he bought the rights to it. Critics disagreed over the score. Some defended it vigorously, while others found it bordering on parody in places.

CHAPTER TWENTY-FOUR

INTERVIEWS
Robert Hurwitz, Cathy Kerr, Randy Newman, Lenny Waronker, Mitchell Froom.

CHAPTER TWENTY-FIVE

INTERVIEWS
Randy Newman, Alan Newman, Mitchell Froom, Lenny Waronker, John Lasseter.

CHAPTER TWENTY-SIX

INTERVIEWS
Lenny Waronker, Mitchell Froom, Robert Hurwitz, Randy Newman, Amos Newman.

CHAPTER TWENTY-SEVEN

INTERVIEWS
Jon Burlingame, Randy Newman, David Newman, Maria Newman, Thomas Newman, Gretchen Newman, Elliot Abbott, Eric Newman.

FURTHER STUDY

For more on the film music history of the Newman family, I'd suggest two sources: Jon Burlingame's 2000 book *Sound and Vision: Sixty Years of Motion Picture Soundtracks* offers a quick and valuable overview of film composers, including Alfred, David, Randy, and Thomas Newman (see bibliography), and David Kemp's profile, "How Randy Newman and His Family Have Shaped Movie Music for a Century" that ran in *Vanity Fair* on February 18, 2016.

CHAPTER TWENTY-EIGHT

INTERVIEWS
Amos Newman, Joey Waronker, Eric Newman, John Newman, Patrick Newman, Alice Newman.

CHAPTER TWENTY-NINE

INTERVIEWS
John Lasseter, Tom MacDougall, Randy Newman, Gretchen Newman, Alan Newman, Cathy Kerr.

CHAPTER THIRTY

INTERVIEWS
Randy Newman, Lenny Waronker.

SIDELIGHT
It was heartwarming to see the joy in Randy to finally get the opportunity to again write the score for another serious movie, and then pick up another Oscar nomination for his work on *Marriage Story*. He had so much to look forward to, including

the shows in Europe and then, quite possibly, writing and recording the fourth album in the series of triumphs that began with *Bad Love*. But the near constant health issues robbed him and his fans of seeing him regularly and welcoming that new album. Yet he and Lenny never spoke of their work together as finished.

BIBLIOGRAPHY

Aronowitz, Nona Willis, ed. *Out of the Vinyl Deeps; Ellen Willis on Rock Music*. Minneapolis: University of Minnesota Press, 2011.

Ball, Edward. *Life of a Klansman*. New York: Farrar, Straus and Giroux, 2020.

Barry, John M. *Rising Tide: The Great Mississippi Flood of 1927 and How It Changed America*. New York: Simon & Schuster, 1997.

Bartlett, Karen. *Dusty*. New York: Lesser Gods, 2017.

Berg, A. Scott. *Goldwyn: A Biography*. New York: Alfred A. Knopf, 1989.

Boerner, Peter. *Goethe*. London: Haus Publishing, 2013.

Booth, Wayne C. *The Rhetoric of Fiction*. Chicago: University of Chicago Press, 1983.

Brackett, Nathan, with Christian Hoard, eds. *The New Rolling Stone Album Guide*. New York: Fireside, 2004.

Burlingame, Jon. *Sound and Vision: Sixty Years of Motion Picture Soundtracks*. New York: Billboard Books, 2000.

Carlin, Peter Ames. *Sonic Boom*. New York: Henry Holt: 2021.

Castle, Alison. *Saturday Night Live: The Book*. New York: Taschen, 2015.

Cavalier, Stephen. *The World History of Animation*. Oakland: University of California Press, 2011.

Cavett, Dick. *Talk Show*. New York: St. Martin's Press, 2010.

Cavett, Dick, and Christopher Porterfield. *Cavett*. New York: Harcourt Brace Jovanovich, 1974.

Christgau, Robert. *Christgau's Record Guide: Rock Albums of the 1970s*. New Haven, CT: Ticknor & Fields, 1982.

———. *Christgau's Record Guide: The '80s*. New York: Pantheon, 1990.

———. *Christgau's Consumer Guide: Albums of the '90s.* New York: St. Martin's Griffin, 2000.

Collins, Judy. *Sweet Judy Blue Eyes: My Life in Music.* New York: Three Rivers Press, 2011.

Cornyn, Stan, with Paul Scanlon. *Exploding: The Highs, Hits, Hype, Heroes, and Hustlers of the Warner Music Group.* New York: Harper Collins, 2002.

Courrier, Kevin. *Randy Newman's American Dreams.* Toronto: ECW Press, 2005.

Davis, Philip. *Bernard Malamud: A Writer's Life.* New York: Oxford University Press, 2007.

Doctorow, E. L. *Ragtime.* New York: Random House, 1975.

Gavin, James. *Is That All There Is? The Strange Life of Peggy Lee.* New York: Atria, 2015.

George-Warren, Holly. *Janis: Her Life and Music.* New York: Simon & Schuster, 2019.

Hill, Doug, and Jeff Weingrad. *Saturday Night: A Backstage History of Saturday Night Live.* San Francisco: Untreed Reads, 2014.

Horowitz, Mark Eden. *Sondheim on Music.* Lanham, MD: Rowman & Littlefield, 2019.

Hoskyns, Barney. *Hotel California.* Hoboken, NJ: John Wiley & Sons, 2006.

———. *Waiting for the Sun: A Rock 'n' Roll History of Los Angeles.* Milwaukee, WI: Backbeat Books, 2009.

Jones, Rickie Lee. *Last Chance Texaco.* New York: Grove Press, 2021.

Kastin, David: *Song of the South: David Newman's Good Old Boys.* New York: Turntable Publishing, 2014.

Kelly, Michael. *Liberty Records: A History of the Recording Company and Its Stars, Volume One.* Jefferson, NC: McFarland & Company, 1993.

———. *Liberty Records: A History of the Recording Company and Its Stars, Volume Two.* Jefferson, NC: McFarland & Company, 1993.

Kennedy, Randall. *Nigger: The Strange Career of a Troublesome Word.* New York: Pantheon, 2002.

———. *Say It Loud! On Race, Law, History and Culture.* New York: Pantheon, 2021.

Kezich, Tullio, and Alessandra Levantesti. *The Life and Films of Dino De Laurentiis.* New York: Hyperion, 2004.

King, Carole. *A Natural Woman*. New York: Grand Central, 2012.

Kooper, Al. *Backstage Passes & Backstabbing Bastards*. New York: Backbeat Books, 2008.

Kort, Michelle. *Soul Picnic: The Music and Passion of Laura Nyro*. New York: Thomas Dunne, 2002.

Lasseter, John, and Steve Daly. *Toy Story: The Art and Making of the Animated Film*. New York: Hyperion, 1995.

Leiber, Jerry, and Mike Stoller, with David Ritz. *Hound Dog: The Leiber & Stoller Autobiography*. New York: Simon & Schuster, 2009.

Long, Huey Pierce. *My First Days in the White House*. Harrisburg, PA: The Telegraph Press, 1935.

Malamud, Bernard. *The Natural*. New York: Farrar, Straus and Giroux, 1952.

Marcus, Greil. *Mystery Train*. New York: Plume, 2015.

Martin, Steve. *Born Standing Up*. New York: Scribner, 2007.

Martyn, Beverley. *Sweet Honesty*. Guildford, UK: Grosvenor House, 2011.

McBride, Joseph. *Steven Spielberg: A Biography*. New York: Simon and Schuster, 1997.

Neupert, Richard. *John Lasseter*. Urbana: University of Illinois Press, 2016.

O'Brien, Lucy. *Dusty*. London: Michael O'Mara, 2019.

Palmer, Christopher. *The Composer in Hollywood*. London: Marion Boyars, 1960.

Passman, Donald S. *All You Need to Know about the Music Business*. New York: Simon & Schuster, 2015.

Ronstadt, Linda. *Linda Ronstadt: Simple Dreams*. New York: Simon & Schuster, 2013.

Rourke, Constance. *American Humor: A Study of the National Character*. New York: Review Press, 2004.

Sanneh, Kelefa. *Major Labels*. New York: Penguin Press, 2021.

Secrest, Meryle. *Stephen Sondheim: A Life*. New York: Alfred A. Knopf, 1998.

Shipton, Alyn. *Nilsson: The Life of a Singer-Songwriter*. New York: Oxford University Press, 2013.

Smith, Joe. *Off the Record: An Oral History of Popular Music*. New York: Warner Books, 1988.

Smith, Susan, Noel Brown, and Sam Summers, eds. *Toy Story: How Pixar Reinvented the Animated Feature.* New York: Bloombury Academic, 2019.

Stafford, David, and Caroline Stafford. *The Life & Music of Randy Newman.* London: Omnibus Press. 2016.

Streisand, Barbra. *My Name Is Barbra.* New York, Viking. 2023.

Templeman, Ted (as told to Greg Renoff). *Ted Templeman: A Platinum Producer's Life in Music.* Toronto: ECW Press, 2020.

Thompson, David, ed. *Altman on Altman.* New York: Faber and Faber, 2006.

Whitburn, Joel. Album Cuts 1955–2001. Menomonee Falls, WI: Record Research, 2002.

———. *Billboard Pop Charts 1955–1959.* Menomonee Falls, WI: Record Research, 1991.

———. *Hot 100 Charts: The Sixties.* Menomonee Falls, WI: Record Research, 1990.

———. *Hot 100 Charts: The Seventies.* Menomonee Falls, WI: Record Research, 1990.

———. *Hot 100 Charts: The Eighties.* Menomonee Falls, WI: Record Research, 1991.

———. *Pop Memories, 1890–1954.* Menomonee Falls, WI: Record Research, 1990.

———. *Top Pop Albums 1955–2016.* Menomonee Falls, WI: Record Research, 2018.

———. *Top R&B Singles 1942–2016.* Menomonee Falls, WI: Record Research, 2017.

———. *Top Pop Singles 1955–2018.* Menomonee Falls, WI: Record Research, 2019.

White, Timothy. *The Nearest Far Away Place (Brian Wilson, the Beach Boys and the Southern California Experience).* New York: Henry Holt, 1994.

Williams, Paul, ed. *The Crawdaddy Book.* Milwaukee, WI: Hal Leonard, 2002.

Williams, T. Harry. *Huey Long.* New York: Bantam Books, 1970.

Zollo, Paul. More *Songwriters on Songwriting.* Cambridge, MA: Da Capo Press. 2016.

———. *Songwriters on Songwriting.* Cambridge, MA: Da Capo Press. 2003.

LYRICS PERMISSIONS

The author is grateful to be able to quote lyrics from the following songs.

"BALTIMORE." Words and Music by RANDY NEWMAN. Copyright © 1977 SIX PICTURES MUSIC. All Rights Reserved. Used By Permission of ALFRED MUSIC.

"THE BEEHIVE STATE." Words and Music by RANDY NEWMAN. Copyright © 1968 (Renewed) UNICHAPPELL MUSIC, INC. All Rights Reserved. Used by Permission of ALFRED MUSIC.

"BEST LITTLE GIRL" (*From Randy Newman's Faust*). Words and Music by RANDY NEWMAN. Copyright © 1995. RANDY NEWMAN MUSIC. All Rights Reserved. Used by Permission of ALFRED MUSIC.

"BET NO ONE EVER HURT THIS BAD." Words and Music by RANDY NEWMAN. Copyright © 1965 UNICHAPPELL MUSIC, INC. All Rights Reserved. Used by Permission of ALFRED MUSIC.

"BIRMINGHAM." Words and Music by RANDY NEWMAN. Copyright © 1974 (Renewed) WC MUSIC CORP. All Rights Reserved. Used by Permission of ALFRED MUSIC.

"THE BLUES." Words and Music by RANDY NEWMAN. Copyright © 1983 SIX PICTURES MUSIC. All Rights Reserved. Used by Permission of ALFRED MUSIC.

"BURN ON." Words and Music by RANDY NEWMAN. Copyright 1970 © UNICHAPPEL MUSIC, INC. All Rights Reserved. Used by Permission of ALFRED MUSIC.

"CHRISTMAS IN CAPETOWN." Words and Music by RANDY MUSIC. Copyright ©1983 SIX PICTURES MUSIC. All Rights Reserved. Used by Permission of ALFRED MUSIC.

"DAVY THE FAT BOY." Words and Music by RANDY NEWMAN. Copyright © 1968 (Renewed) UNICHAPPELL MUSIC INC. All Rights Reserved. Used by Permission of ALFRED MUSIC.

"THE DEBUTANTE'S BALL." Words and Music by RANDY NEW-MAN. Copyright © 1967 (Renewed) UNICHAPPELL MUSIC, INC. All Rights Reserved. Used by Permission of ALFRED MUSIC.

"DIXIE FLYER." Words and Music by RANDY NEWMAN. Copyright © 1988 TWICE AS NICE MUSIC. All Rights Reserved. Used by Permission of ALFRED MUSIC.

"A FEW WORDS IN DEFENSE OF OUR COUNTRY." Words and Music by RANDY NEWMAN. Copyright © 2006 RANDY NEWMAN MUSIC. All Rights Outside the U.S. and Canada Administrated by WC MUSIC CORP. All Rights Reserved. Used by permission of ALFRED MUSIC.

"FOLLOW THE FLAG." Words and Music by RANDY NEWMAN. Copyright © 1988 TWICE AS NICE MUSIC. All Rights Reserved. Used by Permission of ALFRED MUSIC.

"GHOSTS." Words and Music by RANDY NEWMAN. Copyright © 1979 SIX PICTURES MUSIC. All Rights Reserved. Used by Permission of ALFRED MUSIC.

"GLORY TRAIN" (From *Randy Newman's Faust*). Words and Music by RANDY NEWMAN. Copyright © 1995 RANDY NEWMAN MUSIC. All Rights Reserved. Used by Permission of ALFRED MUSIC.

"GOD'S SONG (THAT'S WHY I LOVE MANKIND)." Words and Music By RANDY NEWMAN. Copyright © 1970, 1975 (Copyrights Renewed) WC MUSIC CORP. and RANDY NEWMAN MUSIC. All rights administered by WC MUSIC CORP. All Rights Reserved. Used by Permission of ALFRED MUSIC.

"THE GREAT DEBATE." Words and Music by RANDY NEWMAN. Copyright © 2017 DARKMATTER MUSIC. All Rights Reserved. Used by Permission of ALFRED MUSIC.

"THE GREAT NATIONS OF EUROPE." Words and Music by RANDY NEWMAN. Copyright © 1999 RANDY NEWMAN MUSIC. All Rights Reserved. Used by Permission of ALFRED MUSIC.

"GUILTY." Words and Music by RANDY NEWMAN. Copyright © 1973, 1975 WC MUSIC CORP. and RANDY NEWMAN MUSIC. All Rights Administrated by WC MUSIC CORP. GROUP All Rights Reserved. Used by Permission of ALFRED MUSIC.

"HALF A MAN." Words and Music by RANDY NEWMAN. Copyright © 1979 SIX PICTURES MUSIC. All Rights Reserved. Used by Permission of ALFRED MUSIC.

"HAPPY ENDING" (From *Randy Newman's Faust*). Words and Music by RANDY NEWMAN. Copyright © 1995 RANDY NEWMAN MUSIC. All Rights Reserved. Used by Permission of ALFRED MUSIC.

"HARPS AND ANGELS." Words and Music by RANDY NEWMAN. Copyright © 2008 RANDY NEWMAN MUSIC. All Rights Reserved. Used by Permission of ALFRED MUSIC.

"HAVE YOU SEEN MY BABY." Words and Music by RANDY NEWMAN. Copyright © 1970 (Renewed) UNICHAPPELL MUSIC, INC. All Rights Reserved. Used by Permission of ALFRED MUSIC.

"I LOVE TO SEE YOU SMILE" (From *Parenthood*). Words and Music by RANDY NEWMAN. Copyright © 1989 TWICE AS NICE MUSIC and UNIVERSAL-MCA MUSIC PUBLISHING, a division of UNIVERSAL STUDIOS, INC. All Rights Reserved. Used by Permission of ALFRED MUSIC.

"I'M DEAD (BUT I DON'T KNOW IT)." Words and Music by RANDY NEWMAN. Copyright 1999 RANDY NEWMAN MUSIC. All Rights Reserved. Used by Permission of ALFRED MUSIC.

"I'M DREAMING." Words and Music by RANDY NEWMAN. Copyright © 2003 DARKMATTER MUSIC. All Rights Reserved. Used by Permission of ALFRED MUSIC.

"I MISS YOU." Words and Music by RANDY NEWMAN. Copyright © 1998 RANDY NEWMAN MUSIC. All Rights Reserved. Used by Permission of ALFRED MUSIC.

"IN GERMANY BEFORE THE WAR." Words and Music by RANDY NEWMAN. Copyright © 1977 SIX PICTURES MUSIC. All Rights Reserved. Used by Permission of ALFRED MUSIC.

"I LOVE L.A." Words and Music by RANDY NEWMAN. Copyright © 1983, 1990 SIX PICTURES MUSIC. All Rights Reserved. Used by Permission of ALFRED MUSIC.

"IT'S A JUNGLE OUT THERE" (From *Monk*). Words and Music by RANDY NEWMAN. Copyright © 2002 RANDY NEWMAN MUSIC. All Rights Reserved. Used by Permission of ALFRED MUSIC.

"IT'S MONEY THAT I LOVE." Words and Music by RANDY NEWMAN. Copyright © 1979 SIX PICTURES MUSIC. All Rights Reserved. Used by Permission of ALFRED MUSIC.

"IT'S MONEY THAT MATTERS." Words and Music by RANDY NEWMAN. Copyright © 1988 TWICE AS NICE MUSIC. All Rights Reserved. Used by Permission of ALFRED MUSIC.

"I THINK IT'S GOING TO RAIN TODAY." Words and Music by RANDY NEWMAN. Copyright © 1966 (Renewed) UNICHAPPELL MUSIC, INC. All Rights Reserved. Used by Permission of ALFRED MUSIC.

"I WANT EVERYONE TO LIKE ME." Words and Music by RANDY NEWMAN. Copyright © 1999 RANDY NEWMAN MUSIC. All Rights Reserved. Used by Permission of ALFRED MUSIC.

"I WANT YOU TO HURT LIKE I DO." Words and Music by RANDY NEWMAN. Copyright © 1988 TWICE AS NICE MUSIC. All Rights Reserved. Used by Permission of ALFRED MUSIC.

"LAUGH AND BE HAPPY" (From *Cats Don't Dance*). Words and Music by RANDY NEWMAN. Copyright © 1999 RANDY NEWMAN MUSIC and TURNER PICTURES, INC. All Rights Reserved. Used by Permission of ALFRED MUSIC.

"LIVING WITHOUT YOU." Words and Music by RANDY NEWMAN. Copyright © 1968, 1973 (Renewed) UNICHAPPELL MUSIC, INC. All Rights Reserved. Used by Permission of ALFRED MUSIC.

"LONELY AT THE TOP." Words and Music by RANDY NEWMAN. Copyright © 1970 (Renewed) UNICHAPPELL MUSIC, INC. All Rights Reserved. Used by Permission of ALFRED MUSIC.

"LOSING YOU." Words and Music by RANDY NEWMAN. Copyright © 2008 RANDY NEWMAN MUSIC. All Rights Reserved. Used by Permission of ALFRED MUSIC.

"LOST WITHOUT YOU." Words and Music by RANDY NEWMAN. Copyright © 2017 DARKMATTER MUSIC. All Rights Reserved. Used by Permission of ALFRED MUSIC.

"LOUISIANA 1927." Words and Music by RANDY NEWMAN.
Copyright © 1974 (Renewed) WC MUSIC GROUP and RANDY
NEWMAN MUSIC. All Rights Administrated by WC MUSIC
CORP. All Rights Reserved. Used by Permission of ALFRED
MUSIC.

"LOVER'S PRAYER." Words and Music by RANDY NEWMAN.
Copyright © 1970 (Renewed) UNICHAPPELL MUSIC, INC. All
Rights Reserved. Used by Permission of ALFRED MUSIC.

"LOVE STORY (YOU AND ME)." Words and Music by RANDY NEW-
MAN. Copyright © 1967 (Renewed) WARNER-TAMERLANE
PUBLISHING CORP. All Rights Reserved. Used by Permission of
ALFRED MUSIC.

"MAMA TOLD ME NOT TO COME." Words and Music by RANDY
NEWMAN. Copyright © 1966, 1970 (Renewed). UNICHAP-
PELL MUSIC, INC. All Rights Reserved. Used by Permission of
ALFRED MUSIC.

"MARIE." Words and Music by RANDY NEWMAN. Copyright ©
1974, 1975 (Copyrights Renewed) WC MUSIC CORP. and RANDY
NEWMAN MUSIC. All Rights Administered by WC MUSIC CORP.
All Rights Reserved. Used by Permission of ALFRED MUSIC.

"MEMO TO MY SON." Words and Music by RANDY NEWMAN.
Copyright © 1972 WC MUSIC CORP. and RANDY NEWMAN
MUSIC. All Rights Administered by WC MUSIC CORP. All
Rights Reserved. Used by Permission of ALFRED MUSIC.

"MR PRESIDENT (HAVE PITY ON THE WORKING MAN)."
Words and Music by RANDY NEWMAN. Copyright 1974
(Renewed) WC MUSIC CORP. and RANDY NEWMAN MUSIC.
Administered by WC MUSIC CORP. All Rights Reserved. Used by
Permission of ALFRED MUSIC.

"MR. SHEEP." Words and Music by RANDY NEWMAN. Copyright
© 1979 SIX PICTURES MUSIC. All Rights Reserved. Used by
Permission of ALFRED MUSIC.

"MY COUNTRY." Words and Music by RANDY NEWMAN. Copyright © 1999 RANDY NEWMAN MUSIC. All Rights Reserved.
Used by Permission of ALFRED MUSIC.

"MY LIFE IS GOOD" (From the music/theater piece *The Education of
Randy Newman*). Words and Music by RANDY NEWMAN.

Copyright © 1983 SIX PICTURES MUSIC. All Rights Reserved. Used by Permission of ALFRED MUSIC.

"NEW ORLEANS WINS THE WARS." Words and Music by RANDY NEWMAN. Copyright © 1988 TWICE AS NICE MUSIC. All Rights Reserved. Used by Permission of ALFRED MUSIC.

"OLD KENTUCKY HOME." Words and Music by RANDY NEWMAN. Copyright © 1970 (Renewed) UNICHAPPELL MUSIC, INC. All Rights Reserved. Used by Permission of ALFRED MUSIC.

"OLD MAN." Words and Music by RANDY NEWMAN. Copyright © 1972 (Renewed) WC MUSIC CORP. and RANDY NEWMAN MUSIC. All rights administered by WC MUSIC CORP. All Rights Reserved. Used by Permission of ALFRED MUSIC.

"POLITICAL SCIENCE." Words and Music by RANDY NEWMAN. Copyright © 1972 (Renewed) UNICHAPPELL MUSIC. INC. All Rights Reserved. Used by Permission of ALFRED MUSIC.

"POTHOLES." Words and Music by RANDY NEWMAN. Copyright © 2008 RANDY NEWMAN MUSIC. All Rights Reserved. Used by Permission of ALFRED MUSIC.

"PUTIN." Words and Music by RANDY NEWMAN. Copyright © 2017 DARKMATTER MUSIC. All Rights Reserved. Used by Permission of ALFRED MUSIC.

"REAL EMOTIONAL GIRL." Words and Music by RANDY NEWMAN. Copyright © 1983 SIX PICTURES MUSIC. All Rights Reserved. Used by Permission of ALFRED MUSIC.

"REDNECKS." Words and Music by RANDY NEWMAN. Copyright © 1974, 1975 (Renewed) WC MUSIC CORP. All Rights Reserved. Used by Permission of ALFRED MUSIC.

"RIDER IN THE RAIN." Words and Music by RANDY NEWMAN. Copyright © 1977 (Renewed) SIX PICTURES MUSIC. All Rights Reserved. Used by Permission of ALFRED MUSIC.

"ROLL WITH THE PUNCHES." Words and Music by RANDY NEWMAN. Copyright © 1988 TWICE AS NICE MUSIC. All Rights Reserved. Used by Permission of ALFRED MUSIC.

"SAIL AWAY." Words and Music by RANDY NEWMAN. Copyright 1972 (Renewed) WC MUSIC CORP. and RANDY NEWMAN MUSIC. All right administered by WC MUSIC CORP. All Rights Reserved. Used by Permission of ALFRED MUSIC.

"SAME GIRL." Words and Music by RANDY NEWMAN. Copyright © 1983 SIX PICTURES MUSIC. All Rights Reserved. Used by Permission of ALFRED MUSIC.

"SANDMAN'S COMING" (From *Randy Newman's Faust*). Words and Music by RANDY NEWMAN. Copyright © 1995 RANDY NEWMAN MUSIC. All Rights Reserved. Used by Permission of ALFRED MUSIC.

"SHAME." Words and Music by RANDY NEWMAN. Copyright © 1995 RANDY NEWMAN MUSIC. All Rights Reserved. Used by Permission of ALFRED MUSIC.

"SHORT PEOPLE." Words and Music by RANDY NEWMAN. Copyright © 1977 SIX PICTURES MUSIC. All Rights Reserved. Used by Permission of ALFRED MUSIC.

"SIGMUND FREUD'S IMPERSONATION OF ALBERT EINSTEIN IN AMERICA." Words and Music by RANDY NEWMAN. Copyright © 1977 SIX PICTURES MUSIC. All Rights Reserved. Used by Permission of ALFRED MUSIC.

"SIMON SMITH AND THE AMAZING DANCING BEAR." Words and Music by RANDY NEWMAN. Copyright © 1966 (Renewed) UNICHAPPELL MUSIC INC. All Rights Reserved. Used by Permission of ALFRED MUSIC.

"SO LONG DAD." Words and Music by RANDY NEWMAN. Copyright © 1967 (Renewed) UNICHAPPELL MUSIC INC. All Rights Reserved. Used by Permission of ALFRED MUSIC.

"SONG FOR THE DEAD." Words and Music by RANDY NEWMAN. Copyright © 1983 SIX PICTURES MUSIC. All Rights Reserved. Used by Permission of ALFRED MUSIC.

"STAY AWAY." Words and Music by RANDY NEWMAN. Copyright © 2020 DARKMATTER MUSIC. All Rights Reserved. Used by Permission of ALFRED MUSIC.

"SUZANNE." Words and Music by RANDY NEWMAN. Copyright © 1970 (Renewed) UNICHAPPELL MUSIC, INC. All Rights Reserved. Used by Permission of ALFRED MUSIC.

"THE WORLD ISN'T FAIR." Words and Music by RANDY NEWMAN. Copyright © 1999 RANDY NEWMAN MUSIC. All Rights Reserved. Used by Permission of ALFRED MUSIC.

"THEY TELL ME IT'S SUMMER." Words and Music by RANDY NEWMAN. Copyright © 1962 (Renewed) EMI UNART

CATALOG, INC. All rights controlled and administered by SONY MUSIC PUBLISHING (Publishing) and ALFRED MUSIC (Print). All Rights Reserved. Used by Permission of ALFRED MUSIC.

"TRUMP SONG." Words and Music by RANDY NEWMAN. Copyright © 2017 RANDY NEWMAN MUSIC. All Rights Reserved. Used by Permission of ALFRED MUSIC.

"WANDERING BOY." Words and Music by RANDY NEWMAN. Copyright © 2003 DARKMATTER MUSIC. All Rights Reserved. Used by Permission of ALFRED MUSIC.

"YELLOW MAN." Words and Music by RANDY NEWMAN. Copyright © 1970 (Renewed) UNICHAPPELL MUSIC INC. All Rights Reserved. Used by Permission of ALFRED MUSIC.

———

Permission to reprint the following two Randy Newman compositions courtesy of Walt Disney Music Company.

"WHEN SHE LOVED ME." Words and Music by Randy Newman. Copyright © 1999 Walt Disney Music Company (ASCAP). All Rights Reserved. Used with Permission.

"YOU'VE GOT A FRIEND IN ME." Words and Music by Randy Newman. Copyright © 1995 Walt Disney Music Company (ASCAP). All Rights Reserved. Used with Permission.

INDEX